MERLIN'S MAN

Merlin's Man at Harlech Castle

MERLIN'S MAN
Love, War and Adventure in the Life of
a Welsh Seafarer

by
LANSDALE HUMPHREYS

P.M. Heaton Publishing
Abergavenny, Gwent
Great Britain
1995

All rights reserved. Except for normal review purposes, no part of this book may be reproduced or utilised in any form or by any means, electrical or mechanical, including photocopying, recording or by any information storage or retrieval system, without written consent of the publishers and author.

ISBN 1 872006 06 X

© First Edition May, 1995: L. Humphreys

Printed in Great Britain

Anything fictional about persons living or dead is unintentional on the part of the author.

Published by P.M. Heaton Publishing, Abergavenny, Gwent, NP7 9UH
Printed by The Amadeus Press Ltd., Huddersfield, West Yorkshire, HD2 1YJ
Typesetting by Highlight Type Bureau Ltd., Bradford, West Yorkshire, BD8 7BY

AUTHOR

Lansdale Humphreys, born in Philadelphia, Pennsylvania, U.S.A., is the daughter of the late Amy Oakley, author of best-selling travel books, and of Thornton Oakley, internationally known artist and illustrator. She attended college and music schools in Philadelphia and New York. Early career as pianist and composer, later switched to writing, mainly music criticism and articles on travel and the environment for various magazines and newspapers, including the National Geographic and the New York Times.

Married 1) George Podbereski, Polish lawyer and aviator with highest Polish military honours, who was Major in RAF during World War II. Two children from this marriage. m 2) Captain Richard Humphreys, British Merchant Navy. She is duel citizen of Britain and the U.S. Permanent home is on the Isle of Man.

To the memory of my husband,
Captain Richard Humphreys, British Merchant Navy
Born 11 May, 1909, Harlech, North Wales
Died 1 May, 1988, Ramsey, Isle of Man
and for his family, and any others
interested in the life of an adventurous seafarer.

Richard Humphreys, gallant and courageous Welsh officer, lover of the sea, of nature and of his fellow men, born in the wild mountain area of North Wales, held a firm belief that his life was under the protection of "Old Merlin", he of magical powers, who, in Welsh legend, did not die, but, like King Arthur, lies sleeping, ready to awaken when needed by his countrymen.

CONTENTS

Author		5
List of Illustrations		8
Preface and Acknowledgements		11
Part I. Master Mariner		
	Youth	
1.	Growing up in Wales	15
2.	Grammar School Days	30
3.	Apprentice Seaman	41
4.	Symi	48
	The Young Officer	
5.	Working towards his Masters	52
6.	Spanish Civil War	59
	An Encompassing War	
7.	Sinkings: The Ionian	68
	The Mardinian	73
	The Estrellano	81
8.	The Royal Navy: A Secret Mission	89
	Background to Sabotage	95
	The Danube Expedition – 1940	97
9.	The RAF	116
10.	Anzio Beachhead and a Russian Convoy	119
	The Long Voyages	
11.	Pacific Interlude	140
12.	Balik Papen	148
13.	The Booth Line	153
14.	Commandanté Jacaré	160
	Part II. The Amazon Mermaid	
	Her Story	
	Preface	174
15.	An American at Sea	177
16.	The River Weaves its Spell	222
17.	Jungle Fever	254
18.	The Headwaters	296
19.	The Andes and Beyond	313
	Into the Maelstrom	
20.	Love Letters	320
21.	Honeymoon Ship	328
22.	Merlin's Heritage	357
	Notes	377
	Bibliography	383

LIST OF ILLUSTRATIONS

1. "Merlin's Man" at Harlech Castle (Frontispiece).
2. "Pant Mawr", Harlech, Richard's birthplace.
3. Richard's parents, Captain Owen Humphreys and his wife, Jane.
4. Captain Owen Humphreys in uniform.
5. Richard as a child, in his sailor suit.
6. Harlech Castle, from print circa 1840.
7. Richard and his sisters, Jen, Pomi and Cass.
8. Richard when an Ellerman Line Cadet.
9. The Ellerman Line's *Estrellano*, on which he was Third Mate, and also Chief Officer when she was torpedoed and sunk on 9th February, 1941. (Laurence Dunn Collection).
10. Richard as Third Officer.
11. Richard and Chrissie on their wedding day.
12. Richard, then Second Officer, and other crew members following the sinking of the *Ionian*. (Newcastle Journal and North Mail).
13. The Ellerman Line steamship *Mardinian* in which Richard was serving as Chief Officer when she was torpedoed and sunk, on 9th September, 1940. (World Ship Photo Library).
14. The Liberty Ship *Samboston* was built in the United States in 1943 and bareboat-chartered to the Ministry of War Transport. She is shown here under her later name of *City of Rochester*. (Carl Andersen Collection).
15. Richard's aunt and uncle, Clar and Meurig Griffith, photographed with son William.
16. Richard served on the Liberty Ship *Samdonard* and after her sale to the Claymore Shipping Co., Cardiff, for whom she traded as their *Daybeam*. She was his "happiest" ship. (Welsh Industrial and Maritime Museum, Cardiff).
17. Richard as Chief Officer.
18. Richard's first ship with the Booth Line was the *Dominic*. She had been built in the U.S. in 1945 as the *Hickory Stream*. (FotoFlite).
19. The Booth Line steamship *Dunstan* was briefly owned by Lamport & Holt (1956-57) and then sailed as the *Sallust*. Richard was her Chief Officer, later becoming her Master when she was resold to Booth. (FotoFlite).
20. Booth Line's *S.S. Denis* normally traded from Liverpool up the Amazon to Manaus, taking more passengers than the company's smaller ships. (Tom Rayner).
21. Built in 1956 in Holland the *Crispin* was designed to trade up the Amazon from New York. (FotoFlite).
22. Norwegian-built in 1954, the *Vamos* was bareboat-chartered to Booth for 14 years. She was Richard's first command. (A. Duncan).
23. The *Bede* was briefly in the Booth fleet, from 1961-63. (A. Duncan).
24. The *M.V. Clement* went to logging ports along the coast of Brazil and as far North as Montreal. (A. Duncan).
25. *M.V. Veloz*, the first of the small motorships built for the Booth Line's service from New York to the West Indies, North Brazil and the Amazon. It was on this vessel that the Author met and fell in love with Captain Richard Humphreys. (A. Duncan).
26. *M.V. Venimos*, sister-ship to the *Veloz*, also specially built to go 2,300 miles up the

27. The Captain cuts hair on the Bridge of the *Veloz*.
28. The *Veloz* enters the Amazon with a load of American cars for Belém.
29. Floating islets of bric-a-brac drifting downstream can be a hazard to shipping.
30. Typical bamboo house on stilts as seen near the "Narrows" from the *Veloz*.
31. Our ship enters the "Narrows".
32. Dale pictured on the deck of the *Veloz* on the Amazon.
33. A mushroom-shaped rain cloud threatens the *Veloz*.
34. Small house and clearing on riverbank near Leticia.
35. People live and trade on small boats such as this one photographed from the *Veloz*.
36. The heart of Amazonas impenetrable jungle, viewed as we sailed close to shore.
37. Iquitos – the Floating Dock, with Pat Nicholls, the Booth Line agent in the foreground looking up at our ship.
38. At Iquitos, "The Headwaters of the Amazon", the river is still wide.
39. A heavy load, particularly when the river is low.
40. Eva Podbereski, the author's daughter, on canoe trip near Iquitos.
41. George Podbereski with son Jerzy at bus stop on the Trans-Andean Highway.
42. Richard sighting the little island, Sombrero, from the *Venimos*.
43. Although the Captain had warned that there would be a big bump when crossing the Equator, Rus, a passenger, was startled when his deck-chair collapsed
44. Good service on board from a Steward on the *Venimos*.
45. Richard and Dale relax on the deck of the *Venimos*.
46. Richard standing under bow of his ship at Belém dock.
47. Rickety pier to which we tied up at logging camp near the Narrows.
48. At Pifuelle on the Solimões – an immense tree to which we tied up
49. Pifuelle – an Indian woman with baby comes aboard.
50. "Mrs Captain" helps Richard keep a watch.
51. The Sawmill of the Astoria Importing & Manufacturing Company, on the Nanaye River.
52. The *Venimos* docked at the Sawmill.
53. The Sawmill's Manager and Richard consult ashore.
54. Tugs and barges delivering mahogany from Pucallpa.
55. Loading the hold with plywood.
56. The ship loading plywood.
57. Deck cargo on the *Venimos* for New York.
58. Marcy Elden, Proprietor of the Hotel Victoria Regia, Leticia, with her friend Johnny.
59. Richard with enthusiastic British passenger, Arnold W. Monks.
60. After the long flight home from Brazil, Richard smiles happily as he reaches the border of Merionnydd.
61. Richard's younger daughter, Janet, with whom we celebrated with an evening at a Tremadog hotel.
62. Jerzy in Reno, Nevada, where his mother and Richard were married.
63. Richard and Dale, before their wedding.

Maps

Drawn by Duncan Haws
1. Location of wartime sinkings.
2. The Danube from estuary to the Iron Gates.
3. The Amazon.

PREFACE AND ACKNOWLEDGEMENTS

In the first pages of this book I have tried to record the main facts Richard told me about his early life. When my own life became interlaced with his, a personal slant became unavoidable. Here my Amazon journal is included without cuts, to show what these voyages were like that formed such an important part of Richard's seafaring life. He read and approved it.

I have been fortunate in receiving help and encouragement in writing this book, not only from family and friends, but from total strangers. Without the kindly advice of military and nautical experts, whose suggestions have proved invaluable, my book would have been blatantly inaccurate. A big obstacle in writing an authentic biography several years after my husband's death became apparent when I could not verify items such as dates of his voyages and names of his ships; and piecing together the full story of the "Danube Expedition" proved to be a major challenge.

First, I must mention Bryn Parry, County Archivist and Museums Officer, Caernarfon, whose interest in Richard's sea stories gave me the idea to write this biography.

For help in researching Richard's war assignments, I am particularly grateful to John Keegan, Military Editor of the "Daily Telegraph"; Ivor Porter, author of "Operation Autonomous"; M. McAloon and R. M. Coppock, both of the M.O.D.; Professor Sir Harry Hinsley of St. John's College, Cambridge; Mark Seaman, Imperial War Museum; Gervase Cowell, S.O.E. Adviser, Foreign and Commonwealth Office; Neil Sommerville, BBC Written Archives Centre; Robert C. de Bruin, Research Consultant; and Gilbert Dowdell-Brown, WW2 Research, who encouraged me by writing: ". . . this research is I think, the most intriguing that has ever been offered me."

Thanks go to the Rt. Hon. Lord Amery, who contacted Sir Alexander Glen about my book. To Sir Alexander, a prime organiser of the Danube Expedition, goes special gratitude for his careful reading of my chapter concerning this, verifying facts and writing in some suggested changes. Help about this little known top-secret operation also came from Tim Martin in Australia, who had served in the RAN during the war; and from Mrs Melissa Kaye Van Prooyan, a Petty Officer in the RAN, whose father-in-law, Leading Seaman Terry Van Prooyan, was a volunteer to the Expedition. Information about Liberty Ships and convoys was sent me by another Australian, Ian J. Stewart. Not to be forgotten is Miss Christiane Sherwen, Curator of the former residence (Paris) of the Duke and Duchess of Windsor, who confirmed the dates when they might have had a Danube cruise.

I must thank the staff of the Philadelphia Maritime Museum, who sent documentation about the Anzio convoys, and on my behalf contacted Bernard F. Cavalcante, Head of the U.S. Naval Historical Center, Washington, D.C., who sent me copies of the official records of the Anzio convoys in which Richard took part.

Being able to work at nautical research in the Library of the Merseyside Maritime Museum, Liverpool, was of tremendous assistance, thanks to cheerful help from Miss Margaret Evans and other efficient staff members. In this connection, thanks should also go to the Department of Transport's General Register and Record Office of Shipping and Seamen, Cardiff, which supplied me with ships' logs and crew lists; to the Cardiff Maritime Museum for the history of the Claymore Shipping Company; and to D. Peate of the

Booth Steamship Company Ltd., Liverpool, who sent useful information concerning Richard's service with them. Lively letters were much appreciated from Chief Engineer P. Ronald Duckworth, and Captain A. W. Kinghorn, both of whom had served as young officers under Richard.

The following have revealed many facts about Richard's wartime voyages, or tried, unsuccessfully, sad to say, to contact fellow crew members from this period: Capt. Wm. C. Dawson, M.N. (Rtd.), Hon. Sec. of the U558 Association; Barrie Osborne, Midland Sec. and President of the Merchant Navy Association; Bill Hudson, their National Secretary; John Overett; Colin Knight; Duncan Haws (of TCL Publications); also the members of Liverpool's Anchorage Club, including its helpful Secretary, Captain R. G. Morrison. Mrs Susan Emmons and Dr Margaret Mann have given moral support and helpful suggestions in my endeavour, as has James S. Kane, of Northern Ireland.

Finally, but not least among those who have helped me is George V. Monk, a retired Marine Radio officer, whose knowledge of the history of the war at sea is encyclopaedic.

Equally important as everything mentioned above has been the patient support of my project by Richard's family, all of whom have added a great deal to my image of Richard in the years before I met him. Thanks goes especially to Mrs Clarice Griffith and to the late Miss Frances Williams for their delightful reminiscences; to my step-daughter, Janet, and her husband Dr Donald Shirley, who were among the first to read through an early draft; to my other stepdaughter, Christine Govier, for her moral support; to Richard's nephew, Mr J. Owain Jones, who with great care checked the manuscript for slip-shod errors; to my brother-in-law, Richard Francis Williams, who also checked for errors; to Richard's cousin, Richard H. Williams, who sent from Australia a detailed letter describing his wartime memories of Richard; and to Mr Ronald Owen, of Borth-y-Gest, North Wales, another cousin, who helped with the Owen-Humphreys genealogy, as did the Gwynedd Family History Society, Pen-y-Sarn, Anglesey; and the Area Record Office, Gwynedd County Council, Dolgellau. Help also arrived from my own cousin, James Brooke, Bureau Chief of the "New York Times" in Rio de Janeiro, who checked on an item I needed verified from Brazilian political history.

Good friends in Pennsylvania, Miss Hebe Bulley, Mrs Phyllis Bulley, and Mrs Boudinot Sheppard, read an early version of my manuscript with enthusiasm. Warm expressions of enjoyment in reading it also arrived from California, from Count Zachary and Countess Marisha Tchernicheff-Besobrazoff, and from Joy Shirley in Seattle. With American liberality, they encouraged me, in the face of some British criticism of the frankness of my writing, to stick to my chosen form of telling this true story in a direct and uncensored fashion. In an era when freedom of the press is valued, authors owe readers candid, vivid, and full accounts, otherwise a biography cannot come to life. One man's truth is, of course, another's fiction, but each has a right to his own version. naturally, this story is told from the point of view of the author.

It is important to add that this book would never have been completed if it had not been for tireless hours spent by my son, Jerzy Podbereski, in editing it on his computer, particularly difficult as innumerable changes were necessary due to my constant revisions.

Lansdale Humphreys
Isle of Man, 1995

Part I.
MASTER MARINER

Youth

"Pant Mawr", Harlech, Richard's birthplace

1. GROWING UP IN WALES

Richard was born in "Pant Mawr", Harlech, Meirionnydd, in Snowdonia, overlooking Cardigan Bay in the Celtic Sea. He was the son of Captain Owen Humphreys and his wife Jane (née Williams). "Pant Mawr" was a farm on the Ffordd Uchaf road. The old farm house still stands. It was rented by Richard's parents. Many members of the Williams family were farmers.

Richard's father was in the British Merchant Navy, with the Ellerman Line. At the time of his son's birth, he was Master of steam ships, taking cargoes of phosphate up from the Caribbean, slate from the Welsh quarries to the Mediterranean, then North to Labrador and Newfoundland for salt fish (a staple food at that time.) Previously, he had been co-owner with his uncle, William Humphreys Owen, of the 3-masted schooner *Venedocian*, which was "probably the first Porthmadog vessel to sail regularly in the Newfoundland trade".[1] He held a 32/64 share in this vessel (the shares of ships in those days curiously being divided in 64ths, each share representing part of a ship!) He sailed many times in her. Besides the *Venedocian*, his family owned another Porthmadog schooner, the *R. J. Owen*, built especially for them, and of which William's son, Capt. Owen Humphreys Owen of Borth-y-Gest, was Master.

Richard's grandfather, was also named Owen Humphreys and was a Master Mariner. His brother, the above mentioned William Humphreys Owen,[2] was a Trinity Pilot. He was largely responsible for developing Porthmadog as an important harbour. At one period, there were 18 sea Captains in the family. An early sea-faring ancestor was right-hand man to the notorious Welsh buccaneer, Henry Morgan. Richard enjoyed boasting about this! However, this ancestor was not a lucky man. He was caught (before Sir Henry had become respectable with his Knighthood), and hanged. Richard's father retired at 59, due to high blood pressure, brought on, no doubt, by his constant diet at sea of salt fish and hard tack – no fresh meat, green vegetables or fruit in those days. Richard, himself, as an Apprentice Seaman, had a very meagre diet, but nothing as bad as what the older generation had to put up with.

Richard had a closely knit family, with three sisters: Catherine ("Cass"), Jenny ("Jen"), and Eleanor ("Lena"), nicknamed "Pomi" by immediate family. Pomi was the youngest, with Richard a year older. Being an only brother, the girls persuaded him to spend a lot of time with them in the kitchen. He became their official "taster", and wash-up boy. Watching them, he learnt the secrets of good cooking. They all grew up to be fine cooks. In later years, Richard won First Prize at a W.I. (Women's Institute) Bazaar for his Victoria Sandwich Cake. Traditionally, seamen have a reputation for being

Richard's parents, Captain Owen Humphreys and his wife, Jane.

good cooks. Being away from their families for long periods probably forces them to be able to take over in the galley if the grub gets too unappetizing.

Richard's mother got good fresh produce from the local farms (no artificial fertilizers in those days), plus homegrown beef; and lamb – the best in the world, due to aromatic plants on the hillsides, pastures that remain green all winter, and the salt licks by the sea. Of course, fish was plentiful. Summer fruits were quickly converted by all the housewives into jars of home-made preserves, to line the larder shelves. Richard's grandmother

Captain Owen Humphreys in uniform

Williams had the greatest variety. He would often stop by her house for a "snack" on his way home from school. He said she made the best macaroni and cheese that he ever tasted. In fact, he thought she was the best cook in the world! The expression "Fill your boots, you're at your Granny's now!" was very applicable.

He loved his grandmother very much, and often talked about her. She used the Welsh spelling for Richard, "Rhisiart"- using the soft sh sound, as in French, or the Scots Gaelic. Everyone else called him "Rich" except me, his second wife, who always called him Richard, because to me he seemed like Richard "The Lion-Hearted".

His grandmother was an expert in the medicinal uses of wild herbs and plants, and she was very much in demand as a consultant, doctors being few and far between in the country. She cured his sister, Jen, of St. Vitus Dance with a sedative known from Roman times, made from the dried root of Valerian.

Richard's family moved several times when he was a child. First, to a small house opposite the Elementary School (which now houses Harlech Public Library); then, to the building on the main street that is now "Gwalia Stores", the Ironmonger. At that time, his Granny lived on the neighbouring corner, in "Clogwyn House". Across the street from her was the bakery, now a potter's (the old ovens are still there.) The housewives all mixed their bread at home – Richard, as a child, enjoyed pounding the dough – and took it to the bakery to be baked. A delicious aroma of baking bread permeated that street. The bread had real body to it, with a crispy dark brown crust. Nothing was tastier, when still warm. After growing up on this, Richard could never stand super-market "cotton-wool" bread. Water from a spring supplied the nearby houses, no chlorine added. Richard credited his strong teeth to the minerals in the pure mountain water. The spring has long since been plugged up, and covered with tarmac. To drink from a spring anywhere in the countryside today, even on the mountains, is considered to be dangerous, due to various pollutants, particularly "Sheep Dip".

It was a lively, happy neighbourhood. Across from the bakery was the Village Blacksmith, a gathering place for locals. Richard spent many an hour there watching the horses being shod, and listening to old men's tales. One tradition was that if one had a wart on one's finger. and stuck it in the water used for cooling the molten iron, the wart would fall off.

Once upon a time, Harlech had briefly been the County Town, but over the years it had not expanded much. It had more the feeling of a village. Imagine a small place high on a hill, grey stone houses lining each side of the one main street. In those days, there were no sidewalks, and the road could get gooey with mud. Tourists were scarce, and cars still a curiosity. Very few houses had bathtubs. The town had a public bath-house. When the Humphreys moved into a bigger house that had a tub with running water, they let neighbours come in to take their weekly baths.

Any long trip was taken by train. One could get all the way to London by train, with fast service. More than can be said today! When the family went for a day's outing to visit Humphreys cousins, who had a farm about 10 miles up in the mountains near Trawsfynydd, they went by horse-drawn carriage.

Richard's mother's youngest sister Clar (Clarice), was more like a sister to the children than an aunt, being only 10 years older than Richard. Before she married, she spent a lot of time with them, and took part in their games. Richard said she could run faster than any of them!

Richard's mother went to Liverpool to meet her husband when his ships came into port. The ship would not always stay long enough for him to get home. Then she would stay in Bootle with a man and his wife who rented rooms to seamen who had shore leave. The husband was a retired stevedore. Richard's father's ships came in nearby. She would go alone, often at night, and walk up and down the usually cold, windy, isolated pier waiting for the ship to arrive. It would often anchor in the river waiting for a berth, and she would have to go out in a dinghy, and climb up the ship's side on a rope ladder. Rather daring in those days for a proper married woman in long skirts!

Usually, the children would be left at home with their grandmother. Clar would look forward to this as much as they did as they all had such fun together. A large attic room had been converted into a playroom. It contained an old bed with a lumpy mattress, on which they used to jump up and down. Years later, when they got together they'd laugh about it.

Of a winter evening they would sit over a coal fire roasting chestnuts, and telling ghost stories. Wales abounds with ghosts. The Celts are particularly psychic, as are the Cornish. Richard's first wife is half Cornish, so my step-children inherit a sensitivity to the supernatural on both sides of the family. They claim that "Eryl-y-Don", the Humphreys' last home, is haunted by the ghost of a strange woman. Both my step-daughters feel this presence strongly in the house, and it makes them not want to stay there too long. Janet (my younger step-daughter) actually saw the ghost. When she was a teenager visiting her Aunt Pomi, who then lived alone in the house, she was asleep in one of the big, high-ceilinged upstairs bedrooms when she woke up to see a woman carrying a lamp coming in the door. She was dressed in a long old-fashioned dress, and had dark hair hanging down her back. Janet thought that she must be a friend of her aunt's who had come unexpectedly for the night. The woman did not appear to be unfriendly, although she did not speak. She seemed to know her way around the room, and was looking for something. She walked to the far side of the room, where there was a fireplace with a mantle piece. There she looked carefully at a clock that stood on the shelf. She then turned, and walked quietly out of the room.

The next morning Janet asked her aunt about the woman. Her aunt replied that no one had come to the house, and that the doors were locked at night. She knew nobody who looked like Janet's description of the woman. Then, Janet decided that she must have been a ghost.

The next time Janet stayed at "Eryl-y-Don", she asked for a different bedroom, and did not see the woman, but she still felt her presence. Christine (my older step-daughter) has felt this presence independently of Janet. She said her husband, Robin, has also felt it. There is no explanation about whose ghost it may be, or what the woman was looking for. Sceptics may well ask why a lady in Victorian dress should haunt a house built in 1925, but ghosts, no doubt, move by their own rules.

Another ghost story involving Richard himself concerns "Cae Nest", a 15th Century mansion, now a "Country House Hotel", in Llanbedr, 3 miles from Harlech. This was originally part of a large farm. Richard and his sisters when teenagers used to go there when the owner at that time was an old lady who loved music. She gathered friends around her piano to have a sing-song. The house was dark and gloomy on a winter evening, with only a small fire spluttering at the back of the large fireplace in the main hall. A handsome wooden staircase goes up from this room. Here, a long time ago, a man and his wife fought bitterly, one murdering the other, which left a blood-stain on the stairs. No amount of scrubbing could ever remove it. More recent owners have tried cutting out and removing the wood, but the stain always returns! It has now been a hotel for sometime under various owners, who have all kept a heavy carpet firmly tacked over the stairs.

The locals all know the story. It is good for business. American tourists love haunted houses! The murdered wife – or was it the husband? – has been seen on the stairs. Shrieks are heard in the night, and the sound of galloping horses. This was once a smugglers' rendezvous, like Daphne du Maurier's "Jamaica Inn". Ships sailed up the uninhabited coast, and unloaded illegal tax-free liquor, which was brought at night upriver, and hidden in "Cae Nest", which lies concealed in a hollow back of hills.

When Richard was young, the old lady living there told him that it was his ancestor who was murdered, and that he was the rightful owner. If he bought the property the bloodstain would disappear.

Today the house appears cheerful (by day!), and has central heating, and all modern conveniences. Palmettos and fuchsias grow in the spacious garden, where peacocks walk. But Richard never bought the property. It has 16 bedrooms. He was never tempted to buy a hotel just to lay a ghost!

Everyone knew everyone else in Harlech and the surrounding countryside, and were probably related. They all helped each other when the need arose. Richard's mother was particularly respected for her untiring care of the old and the ill. She would walk miles over rough farmland in all sorts of weather, even when quite elderly, carrying a basket of provisions and medicine, if she heard that someone in an isolated cottage was bedridden.

Men with education had to leave Wales to find work, so it left a lot of responsibility on the women. The remaining men were mostly farmers, fishermen, or quarry workers, all earning a pittance. Chapels or pubs were the only places where they could let off steam, by soul-raising singing of Welsh hymns. But the pubs were off-bounds to respectable women. The loving community could become immediately hostile to a non-conformist.

The Humphreys were strong Welsh Baptists, of the strict Scottish sect. On Sundays they went to Chapel three times, and the children were not allowed to play games. Richard's mother told him he'd go straight to Hell if he went swimming on a Sunday, but he had already started out as a young rebel, as he'd go tearing down the hill to the beach, with his mother shouting after him. With 7 miles of flat sandy beach, with no undertow to disturb its crystal clear water, what more could a boy want? His own reasoning told him that nothing bad would happen.

The highlight of Sunday to the children was the big mid-day dinner, to which the Preacher, a severe-looking gentleman in a stiff black suit, came. He loved his food, and often appeared for "High Tea" also. Dinner would be a feast, with a big roast, lots of vegetables, and several desserts: trifle, fruit jelly, or apple tart with custard. "Tea" was equally filling, with cold meats, cheese, and salads, lashings of homemade bread, farm butter, jam and honey, ending up with varieties of cakes – all washed down with endless cups of tea. This was not the end! The family would, before going to bed, consume "Supper": meat pies, chops, eggs, or something like that. And perhaps stewed fruit with cream.

It was apt to be freezing cold in the Chapel, which was, and still is, high on a wind-swept hill, so I guess to keep warm a lot of nourishment was needed. Richard showed me the pew right up front where his family always sat, and where he had secretly carved his initials. They are still there! The children were allowed hard candy to help them through the long sermons. In this sect, "Sunday School" is not only for children, but for adults, too. Richard, when he became a teenager well-versed in the Bible, taught the class the Bible stories in Welsh.

The family, of course, spoke Welsh at home, although they were bilingual. Richard never forgot his beautiful Welsh, and spoke it fluently even after years of being away at sea. He spoke the old classical Welsh, often commented upon later, as since the war the language has become less pure.

About a mile up a steep hill from the Chapel was an icy pool, which was used for baptism by total immersion. The whole congregation would march up for these ceremonies, even in freezing wintry gales. Richard was never baptized. When he was about 16, the age when he would have been, he decided to no longer attend Chapel, for the following reason:

A local girl, who always attended Chapel with her parents, who were leading supporters of it, became pregnant, and gave birth to an illegitimate child. The father of the baby offered to marry her, but, as she did not love him, nor find him congenial, she did not think it would be a happy marriage, so she refused. The Elders then held a meeting, and decided to throw her out of Chapel.

As this was extremely cruel, and not in the Christian spirit, particularly at a time when she needed moral support, Richard was very upset. It was not his idea of religion. To him, real religion was expressed by one's attitude to people and to life, not by attending church. His family were personally hurt by his attitude, and for some time did not want to speak to him, including his own mother. It was a difficult time for him, but he courageously stuck by what he considered to be right, and in doing so, was beginning to shape his own life and destiny.

To return to the girl, herself. Later on, she was married, (but not to the father of her child) and so again became "respectable" in the eyes of the Elders, who allowed her back. She always attended Chapel after that. I'm sure that if it had been me, I never would have returned.

Richard's sisters continued to attend Chapel for the rest of their lives. Pomi was a mainstay of it after the war, when the congregation became very small, as it was too stern and bleak a religion to appeal to most modern youth.

Richard's grandfather was the biggest influence in his developing an interest in going to sea. He was retired, a widower living alone in "Yskoldy" ("The School"), a small cottage in the hamlet of Ynys ("The Island"). "The name suggests that this portion of rising ground was at one time cut off from the mainland."[3] He lived near "Traeth Bach" ("The Small Estuary"), where the joined waters of the Rivers Glaslyn and Dwyryd flow into Tremadog Bay.

The area has great atmosphere. At low tide one can walk way out on the sands of the estuary to where, at high tide, there is an island (inhabited only by sheep). One must watch out for the rising tide, and also beware of quicksands. Past Ynys on the shore is "Môr Edrin", the former residence of Richard Hughes, the late eminent novelist ("A High Wind in Jamaica"). Further on is a house originally an inn called "The Ferry Arms", dating from the days when there was no bridge across the estuary. One can continue walking around the point, where there is now a National Bird Sanctuary, and join the beginning of Harlech Beach.

In the churchyard of Ynys' church, "Llanfihangel-y-Traethau" ("St. Michael-of-the-Beaches"), stands an ancient stone with this inscription:
"Here is the tomb of Wleder, mother of Odelau, who
first built this Church in the time of King Owain."

It is dated "at about 1150. . . unique as being the Only Dated Stone in Meirioneth." (See Note 3)

As a child, Richard loved to visit his grandfather. Behind the cottage was a field in which lived a large white Shire horse. The horse was extremely docile, and his grandfather would lift Richard onto his back, and often, his sisters, too. The horse's back was big enough for all of them! They would ride around and around the field. Richard became an expert rider as the time went on, and when he was older, he used to ride bare-back in the mountains helping the farmers round up wild horses.

When we lived for a while on a ranch in Nevada, and went riding (on Western saddles), I did not know this. I laughed when he got on his horse, as I was sure a sailor would not be able to ride, and that he'd fall off. However, when the horses went galloping over the prairie, rushing down dried gullies, then leaping wildly up the other sides, Richard had no trouble at all. Whereas, although I had ridden a good deal as a school-girl, and had taken riding lessons, it was all I could do to stay on. The next day I was so stiff that I could hardly walk, while Richard was fine, and laughing at me!

Richard's grandfather had a small sail-boat, which he taught Richard how to sail. They would often go fishing together, to catch their supper. They usually caught dabs or plaice. Sometimes his grandfather would wake Richard up early to go out to catch their breakfast!

They often sailed across Tremadog Bay to Porthmadog. There were treacherous currents in the estuary, as well as sudden squalls, or fog. The child, at first sea-sick, would shrink down in the bottom of the boat, cold, wet and miserable. But he soon became used to it.

His happiest recollections from early childhood were of his grandfather grilling freshly-caught fish over a coal fire in the cottage (the cottage remains, but stiffly modernized, so the charm has gone.) After supper, Richard would climb up to the loft (which was like a sail-loft) to sleep, while his grandfather entertained his cronies, two or three retired Captains like himself, who lived nearby. They would tell enthralling tales of their adventures at sea.

"Strong talk, and not for children", his grandfather would say.

But Richard would quietly open the door and listen, sometimes even creeping down to sit, wide-eyed, in a corner.

These stories were to inspire him with a longing to go to sea himself, not only to become a sailor, but to see the world. This is what he early decided to do, and the desire grew with the years.

Sometimes the whole family would spend the day with his grandfather. Then, they would walk home after dark, a good 4 miles down the road. Richard, half asleep, half carried between his mother and "Tada", as the children called their father.

Richard was very fond of animals, particularly cats, who recognized this and always came to him. The family had a series of them, usually named "Ginger Nuts". One large one learnt to jump up and push down the latch of the kitchen door, so he could open it. There was also a robin who adopted the house, and who used to fly into the kitchen, demanding to be fed. Fortunately, the cat never caught the bird.

Richard's father brought home a large Amazon parrot, which soon became Richard's special pet. He would let the bird go out in warm weather, and it would ride on the handlebar of his bike. He also had a tame jackdaw.

The parrot and "Ginger Nuts", strangely, were the best of friends. But the parrot (who was simply called "Polly"), used to tease the cat. When "Ginger Nuts" was napping before the fire, Polly would waddle up and give his tail a nip, then run (as fast as his awkward feet would take him) to the long curtains, up which he would climb, chuckling. In spite of this, Ginger Nuts slept at night in Polly's cage, without bothering him.

When Richard grew up and went to sea, his mother looked after Polly. Although well cared for, he died of a broken heart. Parrots form a strong attachment to one person, and if this person goes away, often sicken and die.

As a special treat, Richard would be taken by his mother on board one of his father's ships. As a very small boy, he remembered his father showing him the *Vendocian*. She had been sold to Irish owners, but still sailed into Porthmadog. Richard said she was beautiful.

He already loved everything nautical, except for his sailor suit, which his mother had made for very special occasions. He hated it!

Richard as a child, in his sailor suit

The family had a dressmaker come to the house to make their clothes from the very best materials, as was the custom in those days, when store-bought clothes were hard to find, and of poor quality. The girls always wore fashionable outfits, and Jane (their mother) was extremely elegant. They would all be very dressy for Chapel, especially on "Palm Sunday" (which Richard always called "Flower Sunday"), when people in Wales then wore their new spring outfits, rather than at Easter.

Richard did not enjoy wearing uniforms, generally speaking. I never saw a photograph of him in his Captain's uniform. On board a cargo ship, then without air-conditioning even in the tropics, it was too hot to wear. He only put it on when the Marine Superintendent, or another company "big wig", came on board. When he left the Booth Line at the end of his final command, he promised he'd have a photo taken for me, but his trunk containing his uniform, which the company was sending him from Brazil, disappeared in Trinidad, where it had been left for trans-shipment. It must have been put in the Booth Line's warehouse, but it was never found. Many things have disappeared from the docks in Port of Spain.

Every member of the Humphreys family had their own special chores. One of Richard's was cleaning boots. He even had to clean the maid's! He thought this was unfair.

They had a maid who lived in, and helped around the house. She was a young local girl who wanted training in housekeeping, usually the daughter of someone the family knew. When she got married, she would quickly be replaced. She would be treated like a member of the family, and always ate with them.

Another of Richard's jobs was to polish the brass. They had plenty of it. It was useful, rather than ornamental, so especially important to keep clean. Candlesticks, warming pans, huge cauldrons in which they made jam, and, most tedious, brass stair-rods to hold down the carpet. Richard would try to get out of doing this, but his Auntie Clar told him that they all wanted *him* especially to do it, as he was the best brass cleaner in all the world. He said he was a real sucker, and believed her!

Another person who came in to work was a laundry woman. She scrubbed clothes by hand on a scrubbing board, then hung them out to dry; and, I presume, did the ironing, too.

Richard was terrified of her. She was a huge woman, like a giant, in the eyes of a child, and was very ugly. She had just one tooth in the middle of her mouth, which looked like a fang. When she smiled, she appeared extremely sinister. He thought that she was a witch, and might have an evil eye.

When Richard got a little older, he delivered newspapers for his mother's brother, "Uncle Will". He had to get up early to do it before school. It would still be dark in the winter months. Delivering papers to the neighbourhood, he heard all the local gossip, as everyone enjoyed a chat.

Richard was a mischievous boy. The expression in his eyes in early photographs reveals a twinkling sense of humour. He was often involved in boyish pranks, such as snitching apples and pears, particularly from Colonel Lloyd, a crusty retired gentleman who owned a big orchard in the middle of town. He always seemed to be peering out of his window, and would rush out and chase Richard when he saw him. If Richard saw the local "Bobby" approaching, he would hide behind a hedgerow.

Once Clar was walking along and saw Richard climbing a tree. At that point, the "Bobby" appeared. Richard saw him, and hung upside down in the foliage of the tree, which hid him from view. The "Bobby" said to Clar:

"Now, Clarice, you know, and I know, that he is here, so you might as well tell me."

Clar replied: "I may know, but I'm not telling anything!"

Richard even snitched apples from Lord Harlech's trees. Lord Harlech was the only "Lord" permanently residing in the area. He owned most of the nearby farms, which had been rented out to the same families by the Harlechs for generations (they were "Tenant Farmers"), besides running a model farm himself. It would be a serious offence to be caught taking his apples. Years later, Richard happened to meet his son, David, who had inherited the property, along with the title. He was at that time the British Ambassador to the United States. They were fellow passengers on the *Queen Mary*, and the Captain seated Richard next to Lord and Lady Harlech at dinner, telling them that Richard was also "a Man of Harlech". When Richard told them about his boyish escapade, Lord Harlech had a good laugh.

The Harlechs, whose family name was Ormsby-Gore, (coming originally from Anglesey), did not mingle much socially with the locals, as having many English interests, they spent more time in London, and at their additional property in Shropshire. I lived many years in Harlech, but never met, or even saw them. The second Lady Harlech, being American, and an editor of "Vogue Magazine", was a good deal in the news, but kept a low profile locally.

"Glyn Cywarch", their mansion near Harlech, is of great architectural interest. It dates from 1616, and is considered to be the finest country house in that part of Wales. Sadly, one can only see the roof and chimney pots from the road, and the house is never open to the public. Since the tragic death of Lord Harlech in a car crash, his son has taken over running the property. Hopefully, he will be environmentally conscious, and keep the farmland for the farmers. Richard believed that the older Lord Harlech had made a sad mistake when he sold a big strip of land below Harlech Castle (from the area called "The Morfa") to the District "for the benefit of the community". Instead of doing something to enhance the environment, as had been hoped, the land was used to build a conspicuous sprawl of "holiday flats", most of which were not rented by local people. In an area of outstanding scenic beauty, such a density of building seemed a pity. Town and Country planning, as well as Architecture, of course, are matters of personal taste!

The Welsh are democratic, and are not impressed with titles or ancestry, unless it is Welsh! Their nobility goes so far back before the English invasion that the lines of heredity become lost in the "Dark Ages". Very poor records were kept in those days, and many lost.

When Edward I. built the ring of castles around Wales in the 13th Century, he proclaimed his son "Prince of Wales", thereby disinheriting any Welsh successor to the true Prince, Llywelyn ap Gruffyd. Prince Llywelyn, killed in battle fighting for Welsh freedom, on the King's orders had his head cut off and transported to London, where it was put on a stake outside the Tower. His Coronet was stolen by Edward. All this, in spite of Llywelyn's wife being the King's own cousin. The King, himself, had attended their wedding.

The dividing line between the English and the Welsh is still very strong. How many know that "WALES", as the country is now known, comes from the Saxon word for "Foreigner", whereas "CYMRU", its Welsh name, means "Our People"?

Richard was truly horrified when he discovered that I, his own wife, am a direct descendant of blood-thirsty Edward I. Americans are impressed by noble ancestors, and I had always been proud of mine, not for snobbish reasons, but because it made me feel personally closer to great events in British history. Perhaps one psychically feels a connection with one's bloodline. Only when Richard first took me to Wales did I think of mentioning it.

In English history, Edward was known as "The Law Giver", and was considered to be one of the greatest kings. Being descended from him means nothing special in England. In the 30's, it was published that there were more than 13,000 living direct descendants of King Edward – and without a doubt, many more today!

In Wales, it means less than nothing – it almost makes one a criminal! As King Edward wanted to subdue Wales, and Richard was a pure Welsh patriot, we certainly should have been enemies. Richard took the mystic view that we might have met in a former life (or sooner in this one), but that it had taken centuries to exorcise this curse.

Compensation for their bad treatment by the English was finally given the residents of Harlech, who now, officially, are allowed to personally use the coats of arms, found in Harlech Castle, of Owen Glyndwr, the last native Prince of Wales. He managed to seize, and hold, the castle, in 1400, for 8 years, fighting for Welsh freedom against the English Prince (son of Henry IV.)

His coats of arms had "four lions rampant quarterly counterchanged or and gules".[4]

Well, never mind all that! When Queen Elizabeth II. visited Harlech on her Silver Jubilee Tour, the whole population turned out to celebrate, and cheer like mad – including ourselves! A small group of demonstrating Welsh Nationalists were booed, hissed, and pushed aside.

Harlech Castle, on its rocky promontory above the sea, is surely like a dream of an enchanted fairy-story castle, from the Golden Age of Chivalry. In the distance, like a backdrop, rises mighty Snowdon with its cloud-capped range. It must, indeed, have stimulated imagination, and feeling for history, in children growing up nearby, and playing there. Richard used to climb all over its then crumbling, ivy covered walls and towers, long before too many tourists, guards, and entrance fees paid to the "Ministry of Public Works" limited its access.

Returning home from the north, Richard and I would rival each other in who would first see the castle, visible from miles away. Suddenly it would appear, looming mysteriously in a mist, or glittering in sunlight, banners flying, romantically beckoning.

"Oh look! There is *our* castle!" Richard would exclaim with joy.

Harlech Castle, from print circa 1840

2. GRAMMAR SCHOOL DAYS

Richard attended Harlech Elementary School, then went on to Barmouth Grammar School, from which he graduated at 16 with highest honours.

He and his school-days' "sweetheart", Elen, were great rivals, and were usually running neck and neck for top marks. I was jealous when he told me stories about Elen, as evidently they liked each other very much. One story was that on a Saturday he'd play soccer all afternoon, then take Elen to the movies. He would then have to walk all the way home, about 10 miles, as it would be too late for the train.

He was a great walker in those days. As he grew older, he usually had sore feet, so it was hard to get him to take a long walk. Sea Captains don't walk much, anyway. They are used to sitting and giving the orders!

He told me that he had broken some toes while playing soccer as a young man. Instead of waiting for them to set properly, which the doctor said he should do, he continued playing the same day.

His daughters, Janet and Christine, said they'd never heard of that! They claimed that all the Humphreys, including their grandfather, had "bad feet", and "hammer toes". Knowing looks were exchanged, as though this was some minor genetic defect, or, "Just our old Dad!"– not my Welsh knight!

Everyone in the family remembered that Captain Owen Humphreys had always had trouble with his feet. He walked with a limp, and had one shoe a different size from the other. His nephew, Richard Williams, who as a child lived with Richard's parents for 7 years, told me the real reason for this disability. Owen told him that when he was 14, one day he was crossing the then narrow main road on Harlech's "Morfa" when a horse and cart, going very fast, swerved, knocking him down, and running over his foot. It was badly crushed, but the boy managed to hobble home, and did not complain too much about it. One had to be stoic in those days. Doctors were few and often far away, so were rarely called upon; instead, home remedies were commonly used. However, the bones in Owen's foot must have been too badly broken to set properly without expert aid.

In Richard's case, most likely the main cause of his sore feet was corns, a chronic problem due to muscular imbalance. He too had suffered a serious accident, sometime before I met him, with broken bones that did not set properly. He ended up having one leg slightly shorter than the other; they weren't evenly aligned, so he walked with an exaggerated "seaman's roll", just right for a sailor anyway!

Richard kept up with Elen after leaving school. As her family lived near Clar, who had married and lived in Barmouth, they heard news about each other. Down the years, they always exchanged Christmas and Birthday cards.

I asked Richard if he had ever considered marrying her, but he said no, as he never thought it would work. He said she might have been willing, but he thought she had a roving eye! They were really school pals, not lovers.

When we lived in Harlech, she and her second husband came to see us. They were both pleasant. We had a permanent invitation to stay with them where they lived in London.

I am sure Richard, quite unknowingly, broke many of the local girls' hearts, being certainly the most "eligible" boy around, coming from a leading family in the community, and, in addition, being most attractive, talented and ambitious, with a cheery nature.

Richard was a top-notch all-round athlete. Cass and Pomi were also good at sports. Pomi was Captain of the girl's hockey team at school, and Cass was a fine swimmer. Richard himself was a powerful swimmer. His grandfather

Richard and his sisters, Jen, Pomi and Cass

had taught him to swim by throwing him in the water from his boat. (I think this would have put a lot of people off swimming for life!)

Jen was the only one who just paddled around the edge of the water. One must remember that the water is very cold in Harlech. Although heated by the Gulf Stream, it is not like the Caribbean! Only at high tide, when the water comes up over sand heated by warm summer sun does it get to be a pleasant temperature. It can get really hot sitting in the sand-dunes on Harlech Beach in summer, so even a cold swim feels good. Sometimes one gets so paralysed by cold water that one no longer feels it!

The Welsh are rugged, however, like their mountains and weather, and have great endurance. As a boy, swimming was Richard's greatest pleasure. From April (BRRR!) through September he could hardly wait to get home from school so he could get in the water.

Richard believed that the years of swimming in cold water may have saved his life later during the war, when his ship was sunk in the North Atlantic, and he was in water of 35°F for almost 5 hours before being rescued.

He used to swim far out, where the water is really icy, although he never swam across the straits, with its treacherous currents, to Porthmadog, which he used to think he'd like to do.

When he started school in Barmouth, he had to take the train, on a scenic route along the shore. Called "The Cambrian Coast Line" today, it was a few years ago saved by public support. The Highway people would have preferred pulling out the tracks and building a vast North-South Motorway, which would have ravaged the coast-line.

Today, the train trip is a leading tourist attraction. However, it still delivers pupils to school, but in the opposite direction, as the Grammar School has now been transferred to Harlech, where it is now a "Comprehensive".

When warm spring weather arrived, temptation was often too much for Richard, and he'd play hooky. He'd leave the train a mile down the line at Llandanwg, where it stopped at the boat haven, to have a swim off the bridge. Then he'd continue to school on a later train.

At Barmouth Grammar School, he found the teachers inspiring. He also liked them as people, and kept up with them long after leaving school.

He excelled in his studies. English Literature was his favourite subject. He especially loved the Romantic poets. Later, when he went to sea, he always had a copy of the "Oxford Book of Verse" with him. He, himself, wrote poetry. I have a lot of very moving poems he wrote to me.

He also won top marks in Maths and Geometry. On top of this, he had unusual artistic talent, and became winner of the John Ruskin Award in Art for all of Britain.

His fellow-students were a congenial, happy bunch. Among them he made many lasting friends. They did not have the disciplinary problems existing in schools today.

The teachers were dedicated to, and well-qualified in their subjects, and so could hold the interest of the classes. This, in spite of being very poorly paid. One cannot imagine such teachers walking out on strike and abandoning their students. The teachers were firm, and expected the students to take their work seriously, which they did. They respected and admired their teachers, so wanted to do their best. Good results naturally followed. Classes were small enough so that a teacher could take a personal interest in each member of his class.

Of course, sometimes things got out of hand, no boy being perfect. Once they broke the rules by growing their hair too long, and wearing baggy trousers ("Oxford Bags") to school, copying the style set by the Prince of Wales (the later King Edward VIII.) and his Jazz Age circle. The Head Master wisely did not reprimand anyone, but quietly called Richard into his office. He told Richard that if he would cut his hair, as an example to the others, he would give him ten shillings (a big sum in those days). As Richard was top boy in his class, and leader in sports, the other boys looked up to him, and copied whatever he did.

This strategy worked! The next day all the boys appeared with haircuts.

The worst thing the boys did was to one of the teachers, and it might have had tragic consequences. This teacher was the only unpopular one in school. Evidently, he was difficult to please, did not get along with people, and was rather "namby-pamby".

One day when they were all on the beach after school, he appeared for a walk, although he never took part in their games, or went near the water. They decided to gang up on him. They grabbed him and pulled him down to the water, pushing him in and holding him under, half drowning him, and, no doubt, badly frightening him.

In this case, the Head Master gave all of them a "caning", but not hard enough to injure them. It did not seem to leave any bad psychological after affects. They knew that they had deserved it. It was the accepted punishment, and there were no complaints from parents.

Something everyone looked forward to during school was a good meal. Barmouth Grammar was superior to a lot of other schools in this respect. The girls in the Home Economics and Cooking classes, under the supervision of their teachers, cooked and served several big dinners a week for the whole crowd, and it was delicious home cooking. It had to be, as this practical work was part of their cooking course.

Richard was not only head boy in his studies, but was Captain of the Soccer Team; and School-boy Welter Weight Boxing Champion of Wales. He suffered a badly broken nose boxing, but this did not dampen his enthusiasm for the sport. No wonder he was looked up to.

A first-class soccer player, he was invited to join the Harlech Soccer Team, an honour for anyone so young, as this was a well-known adult amateur team.

He had to make room in his schedule for their practice sessions and games on Saturdays. Sometimes he played 2 games in one day, one for them, and one for the school. He also travelled with the Harlech team, playing against the teams of neighbouring towns, usually in miserable winter weather.

If anyone has seen the football fields of North Wales' mountain towns, such as Blaenau-Festinog or Corris, they will know that they were usually wet, muddy, with an icy wind blowing, and gloomy under a low grey blanket of cloud. The nearby houses, also grey, built from heavy local stone and slate, had dirty smoke from coal fires puffing out of each chimney. One had to be strong, resilient, and very keen about football to retain one's enthusiasm under such conditions.

Richard was all of this. He was 6 feet tall, with broad shoulders, and, although quite thin, he was extremely muscular. This good health, which he claimed came from "natural" country food, water full of the proper minerals for strong bones, and clean sea and mountain air, remained with him all his life. It saw him through dangerous situations which would have killed a weaker man. He added that the Welsh are fighters by nature, and the will not to give up was all important to survival.

At this period, (soccer and boxing not being enough activity!) he developed an abiding interest in motor bikes.

An older friend rode in Reliability Trials. Through him, Richard learnt to do the same. The motor bike manufacturers lent these young men their latest models, and paid them to try them out over some of the roughest territory– unpaved roads and trails all over Wales, England, and even Scotland. In this way, Richard saw places in Britain he otherwise could never have visited. He became better travelled than the most enthusiastic tourist. He was the first person up Snowdon on a motor bike!

His friend was also a recognised racing driver. Richard was often his "passenger", evening up the weight and balance of his side-car quite an art in itself. They went to the Isle of Man for one of the early T.T. Trials. This visit to the lovely island remained a fond memory in years to come.

Richard's mother did not approve of his riding motor bikes. She considered them to be too dangerous. He would be gone for days, when she did not know where he was. So she would periodically hide his driving licence.

All Richard did then was to walk to Harlech Police Station, where the local policeman, who knew all the residents (and their problems!) would say:

"Well, Rich, has your Mother hidden your licence again?" He would immediately fix up a duplicate!

When his father found out about all this, he put a stop to it.

Richard was so adventurous that he caused his mother a lot of anxiety, particularly when his father was away, as she could not share her worries.

One summer day, he and two friends took his grandfather's sailboat out to fish in Cardigan Bay. It was such lovely weather that they decided to sail on to Ireland!

Evening came, and no boys returned home. His friends' families became alarmed, fearing an accident at sea. But Richard's mother, in this case, did not worry. She knew that he could handle a boat, and had perfect confidence about that.

The next day, she had a phone call from the "Guarda" (Irish police) in Wicklow. They told her they had picked the boys up selling their catch on shore, without any permits! They asked what they should do with them?

"Just give them a good feed, and let them sail home," Jane calmly replied.

Richard played soccer with the Graves boys, who lived in "Erinfa", just north of town. Their father, Alfred Percival Graves, or "Daddy Graves", as everyone called him, was a "minor" Irish poet; he was also Superintendent of Schools. Their mother was German.

Richard often went to see this large, hospitable family. Robert Graves (who would become world-renowned as a poet) was a good deal older than Richard. One of his brothers was nearer Richard's age. Their sister, Clarissa, was friendly with Richard's sisters. In later life, she lived in Jen's house in an upstairs apartment. She was rather eccentric, and would not eat with the family, preferring to eat alone in the dining room when everyone else had finished.

Harlech had, even in those days, a group of "foreign" intellectuals– writers, musicians, artists– (all with private incomes, no doubt!) living there attracted by the beautiful environment.

Mr. George Davison, Co-founder of Kodak's Kodachrome film process, was one of these. He bought land in 1908, and built a mansion, "Y Wern Fawr". It took 3 years to build, out of hand-dressed stone, and had a huge Music Room with an organ. This room was later incorporated into the newer wing of Harlech College.

Although Mr. Davison's stay was short (he sold the property in 1925) he is still remembered. His circle included many celebrities, and his musicales became famous. Eugene Goosens, the Conductor of the Rochester (New York) Symphony Orchestra, plus his family, all brilliant British musicians, gathered there during the summer to play chamber music.

Strange to say, I was already familiar with this "entourage" long before I ever met Richard, or went to Harlech. My friend Lucille Harrison, former Harpist of the Rochester Symphony, used to give me lively, detailed accounts of the gatherings, and the temperamental personalities involved. She was intimate with Eugene Goosens' sisters, who were First Harpists, for a record number of years, with the BBC and the London Symphony Orchestras.

Richard's family knew the Davisons, and attended the musicales. His grandmother had been very helpful in looking after Mr. Davison's daughter, who was an invalid. She used to go there and stay with the girl when these big gatherings were taking place.. Mr. Davison was especially grateful for her giving his daughter such loving care. Richard remembered going to the musicales himself, although he was only 16 when the place was sold.

Among famous "summer residents" were "Bertie" (Lord Bertram) Russell, and George Bernard Shaw, with his "parlour pink " friends, who shocked the locals by walking through the town with bare legs and sandals!

One of North Wales' own intellectuals was Sir Clough William-Ellis, architect and builder of the popular tourist resort, "Port Meirion", an Italianate fantasy across the estuary from Ynys.

David Lloyd George, from the Lleyn Peninsula, was the outstanding Welshman of the period in the public eye. Pomi knew his sister, and first went to work, after she had completed a secretarial course, for Lloyd George's brother, a lawyer who had an office in Porthmadog.

Pomi later worked in Penrhyndeudraeth, for the Deudraeth District Council. She remained there for the rest of her working life, as their respected Deputy Clerk. My brother-in-law, Richard Francis Williams, ("Dick"), Jen's husband, worked in the same office.

The Council had great influence in local affairs. They were all strong Labourites, working hard to improve the generally low living conditions caused by unemployment.

An interest in civic affairs must run in the family, as Dick and Jen's son, Eryl, became County lawyer for Merionnydd, and is now Deputy Head of the County. My other brother-in-law, Cass's husband, James Idwal Jones, was Labour MP for Wrexham, as was his brother Tom, the late Lord Maelor. They were both self-educated coal miner's sons. Richard, the rebel as usual, never took much interest in politics, being away so much at sea, but was Conservative by nature, and voted for Mrs. Thatcher!

Beginning about 1921, a series of "Musical Festivals" were held in the courtyard of Harlech Castle. Oratorios were given – Mendelssohn's "St. Paul", "Mount of Olives" by Beethoven, "Stabat Mater", Rossini – with massive choruses of up to 1,500 voices, soloists, and full orchestral accompaniment, all singers and players being Welsh.[1]

Welsh plays and concerts were also given, including "The Harlech Historical Pageant" (Authors: Ernest Rhys and Alfred Percival Graves). Opera companies and orchestras also came from London.

Richard would sit on a hill above the Castle, where he could hear the music, but did not have to pay admission!

Before leaving school, Richard added to his outdoor activities by caddying at the Royal St. Davids Golf Club. The 18-hole course held tournaments in which international golf champions competed. Richard would get big tips for caddying for these players. Sometimes he went around the course twice in one day. He always kept his interest in golf, and became a good player himself, when he had the time to do it.

Scouting was another interest. He became an Eagle Scout, and attended a huge Boy Scout Jamboree in London, which was sponsored by HRH The Prince of Wales. He was chosen to guard the Prince's tent all night, a very special honour and responsibility.

Remnants of a glorious past enchant the traveller in the Welsh countryside, where folklore mixes with truth. Standing stones, cromlech, hillforts, round houses, St. Patrick's Causeway. Bardsey Island ("Island of 20,000 Saints") connect one like electrical currents to mythological eras.

On special days when the bay is calm and clear, looking down from Harlech one can see St. Patrick's Causeway through the water. On it, St. Patrick was said to have walked to Ireland. The huge stones forming it are very real, and must be avoided by fishing boats and yachts at low tide. Like the legend of "Ys" (Debussy's "Sunken Cathedral"), or "The Bells of Aberdovey", perhaps under the water a village still exists that once a year will rise up at midnight, with its church bells ringing.

Bardsey Island (Ynys Enlli) "became the Rome of Britain" (Cymry) from the 6th Century on. Every pilgrim who made the dangerous crossing by small boat to the island was regarded as a "Saint"; this is how it came to be known as "the Island of 20,000 Saints".

"For many centuries the island was to Welshmen what Westminster Abbey is to Englishmen – the consecrated place of entombment of all the best and bravest in the land. . . So great was the estimate of the sanctity of the place, that three pilgrimages to Enlli were regarded as equal to one pilgrimage to Rome." [2]

Recent research by that extraordinary scholar, Dr. Norma Goodrich, has revealed that there was an historical Merlin, none other than St. Dubricius, Archbishop of Wales, who, on perilous journeys through Britain, adopted the disguise of "Merlin".[3] He truly was King Arthur's right hand man. As Archbishop, he crowned Arthur King, casting off his disguise to do so. The exploits of "Merlin" have become legendary throughout Wales, and the entire world, whereas Dubricius is forgotten.

Dubricius-Merlin did, indeed, die in a cave, near Whithorn Abbey, Galloway, in 538 A.D. His body was taken for burial on Bardsey, designated by Welsh bards "as the land of Indulgences, Absolution and Pardon, the road to heaven and the gate to Paradise".(See footnote 2)

In the 12th Century his bones were reburied in Llandaff Cathedral (Cardiff), where he still lies today. But Merlin's spirit did not die, and is alive in Wales.

Richard had the particularly Celtic sensitivity to things of the spirit, with strong, intangible feelings relating to past and future. Periodically, over the years when he was growing up, he had a recurring dream. He dreamt of a small bleak island in the sea. It was an extinct volcano. Inside what was once the crater was a deep and sheltered harbour. At the back of the harbour was a little port, with houses built in tiers on the hillside.

He would be walking (in his dream) along the waterfront, passing a café and a few small stores. People sitting at the open-air café, or standing around the harbour, smiled and nodded as though they knew him. From the waterfront, he could climb a steep narrow road towards a church. This had a domed roof with a strange cross.

Walking down from the church towards him would be a bearded priest, dressed in a long black robe.

As they passed each other, the priest would say, in a familiar and friendly way: "Good evening, my son."

Richard knew this is what he said. Perhaps he said it in a foreign language, and Richard translated it by some kind of telepathy.

The dream never continued farther than that, and it was always the same. Richard had no idea where the place was. Later, when he sailed to Greece, he realized that the cross was an Orthodox one, and the priest Greek Orthodox.

As a schoolboy, Richard did not know much about modern Greece, nor had he seen pictures of the Greek islands. Neither his father, his grandfather, nor their seafaring friends had ever described anything like the island he dreamt about. Every detail was so vivid in his dream that if it had been described to him when awake he would have recognized it at once.

Richard felt that the dream had some hidden meaning for him, which would be revealed.

Richard's artistic talent, combined with being good in Geometry and Trigonometry, made his father think that he should study architecture. His father was anxious for him to become an architect, and not go to sea.

He knew of Richard's continuing interest and love for the sea and ships, but he thought, from his own experience, that life at sea was much too hard. It is true that it was extremely arduous. The Merchant Navy had poor pay, very little home leave, and dangerous working conditions.

Before he left school, Richard's parents had bought a beautiful site overlooking the sea. They asked him to design a house for them. He became excited about the project. It was an artistic and technical challenge, and he did it well. It was a large house, which became their permanent home. They named it "Eryl-y-Don", ("Ruler of the Waves").

However, as Richard was an unqualified schoolboy, a professional architect had to be called in, by law, to draw the final plans, and to supervise its construction.

The architect in charge, although conceding that the boy had talent, did not hesitate to change important features of Richard's original plan, making some parts of the house awkward, such as having the staircase too steep and narrow. When Richard complained, the architect paid no attention to him, as he was just a boy. Perhaps the architect wanted to take all the credit for himself.

When the house was finished, Richard was disappointed in it. He never really liked the house, as it had not turned out as he had visualized it.

When Richard left school with many subject passes in his school certificate, he was accepted as a student of Architecture at Bangor University.

All he remembered with any pleasure about his stay in Bangor was taking a little ferry from the Victorian pier, and going across the Menai Straits to a nice old pub on the other side. A good escape from Architecture!

He only stuck out the University for 3 months! He had wanted to please his father by going, but it had never been what he, himself, wanted to do. Now, at Bangor, he fully realised this, and there was no point in his continuing there. He had come to the firm decision that no more time should be wasted, as his real calling was the Sea.

When his father knew how strongly his son felt, he had to finally accept it. When he became reconciled to the idea, he told Richard that he must do it properly, and train as an Officer. He said he would help as much as he could by sponsoring his training as Apprentice with his own company, the Ellerman Line of Liverpool.

Richard sailed as a Cadet on his first ship in September, 1926, one day after his Aunt Clar's marriage to Meurig Griffith of Barmouth. Unable to attend the wedding, he sent them a telegram, showing that although he was himself starting a new life, they were also very much in his thoughts.

Richard when an Ellerman Line Cadet

3. APPRENTICE SEAMAN

An "Ordinary Apprentice's Indenture" was signed with Richard's father as Surety, on December 14, 1926, for a 4- year apprenticeship. It is strict, and worded in quaintly old-fashioned legal language.

"Richard Humphreys hereby voluntarily binds himself Apprentice unto the Ellerman Line. . . and will faithfully serve his said Master, his Executors, Administrators and Assigns, and obey his and their lawful commands, and keep his and their secrets, and will, when required, give him and them true accounts of his or their goods and money which may be committed to the charge, or come into the hands, of the said Apprentice; and that the said Apprentice will not, during the said term, do any damage to his said Master, his Executors, Administrators, or Assigns; nor will he consent to any damage being done by others, but will, if possible, prevent the same, and give warning thereof; and will not embezzle or waste the goods of his Master, his Executors" (etc.). . . "nor give or lend the same, and to others without his or their license; nor frequent Taverns or Alehouses, unless upon his or their business; nor play at unlawful games. In Consideration Whereof, the said Master hereby covenants with the said Apprentice, that during the said term, he . . . will and shall use all proper means to teach the said Apprentice. . . the business of a Seaman, and of a Ship Officer as applying to Steamships in the Merchant Service.

"Sufficient Meat, Drink, Lodging, Medicine and Medical and Surgical Assistance" to be provided by the Company.

Also, £100. pay to the Apprentice over 4 years: £10. the 1st year; £20. the 2nd year; £30. the 3rd year; and £40. the 4th year.

"All sea-bedding, wearing apparel, and necessities" to be provided by the Apprentice himself." (In this case, by his father.)

On 22 September, 1930, the Company wrote:

"We hereby certify that the Indenture has been completed to our entire satisfaction. The various Masters under whom Mr. Richard Humphreys served his Apprenticeship have reported most favourably as to his character, conduct, sobriety and ability.

"Mr. Humphreys served the last twelve months and twelve days of his Apprenticeship as acting 3rd Mate on one of our small steamers."

"ACTUAL TIME ON ARTICLES 40 MONTHS 4 DAYS"
Signed by Manager and Marine Superintendent

Richard's first letter of recommendation by a Master:

S.S.*City of Lancaster* 3/9/1929
Reg. Liverpool'
Ellerman Line Ltd.

"To certify that the bearer R. Humphreys has served in the above vessel as apprentice from 5th May 1929 to present date. During this period I have found him to be very efficient and trust-worthy, and at all times sober and attending to his duties.

"I can recommend him to all who require his services."

H. Stone,
Master

First entries appear for voyages in his "Continuous Certificate of Discharge" book (issued by the Board of Trade), when he was still Apprentice, but Acting 3rd Mate.

The Ellerman Line's *Estrellano,* on which he was 3rd Mate, and also Chief Officer when she was torpedoed and sunk on 9th February, 1941

(Laurence Dunn Collection)

The ships listed below, unless otherwise noted, were the Ellerman and Papayanni Line. In 1902, when "Ellerman Lines Ltd. was incorporated and one of the greatest shipping lines in the world was officially born", Ellerman had bought out Papayanni, but operated it as a separate unit.[1]

SHIP	ENGAGEMENT	DISCHARGE	RATING
1) S.S. *Estrellano* (Registered Liverpool) Gross Tonnage: 1,963	12/9/29 Hull	22/1/30 Hull	3rd Mate

DESCRIPTION OF VOYAGE; R.A. Oporto
For Ability: Very Good
For General Conduct: Very Good

2) S.S. *Estrellano*	23/1/30 Hull	13/7/30 Hull	3rd Mate

DESCRIPTION OF VOYAGE; R.A. Oporto
For Ability: Very Good
For General Conduct: Very Good

3) S.S. "*Estrellano*	14/7/30 Hull	18/9/30 Hull	3rd Mate

DESCRIPTION OF VOYAGE: R.A. Oporto
For Ability: Very Good
For General Conduct: Very Good

A "Continuation Book" issued Jan. 1939, contains stamp of "Certificate of Efficiency as Lifeboatman, 17 Oct. 1930, Liverpool."

Three more letters of recommendation, from 3 different Masters he served under on the above voyages, follow:

1st Voyage) "During this time he was in charge of a Watch. He is honest and strictly sober, and attentive to his duties, and can be confidently recommended."

2nd Voyage) "He was in charge of the 8-12 Watch AM and PM. During that time I found him strictly sober and at all times a competent officer."

3rd Voyage) "He has been in charge of the 8 to 12 AM and 8 to 12 PM Watches from Port to Port. He has proved a good bridge Officer, and his Navigation and Chart Work has been satisfactory. He is strictly sober, and at all times attentive to his duties. He now leaves on his own accord to pass for 2nd Mate, and I can, with confidence, recommend him to anyone requiring his services."

This ended his Apprenticeship, and began his long-term engagement as an Officer of the Ellerman Line.

I note a strange coincidence: the *Estrellano*, the first ship on which he officially served as an Officer, was also the last ship, of three, on which he was sunk during the war – on February 9th, 1941.

Unfortunately, I can find no record of what ships Richard served on before he became "Acting 3rd Mate" on the S.S. *Lancaster*. I do know they all sailed to the Mediterranean, on the "Wine Trade". He told me that he spent 18 years altogether coming and going between the "Med." and the U.K. from the beginning of his apprenticeship until after the war. Outward bound, Oporto was a regular call, then on to Marseilles, Italian ports, (he especially liked Palermo), Malta, the Greek islands, the Levant, Turkey, Black Sea, Constanţa and Danube ports; returning came Istanbul, Cyprus, Lebanon, Syria, Alexandria, Israel, Algeria, Morocco, Gibraltar and Spain – usually to Barcelona, Malaga, Cadiz and San Sebastian.

The life of an apprentice in 1926 meant hard work. He learnt seamanship from the ground up: scrubbing decks, polishing brass (he couldn't escape this by going to sea!), learning the many nautical knots, splicing ropes (Richard excelled in this, today, somewhat forgotten art), becoming fluent in the Morse Code and signalling with flags. Everything connected with the operation of a ship, and its safety was studied, from the cargo hold, the engine room, the galley, up to the bridge. Most important was "Navigation"- taking "Sights", and chart work.

Four hours on and four hours off was the steady routine. No fussing about "Overtime", or Union Rules, in those days. There was always a "Chippy" (ship's carpenter) on board, but sailors were expected to give a hand with scraping, painting, cleaning, and any necessary repairs whenever they had free time. A vessel was kept "Ship Shape" at sea, if possible. This meant time saved in port, and money saved for the owners.

The trading business itself was leisurely. Sometimes a ship would spend days, or even weeks, in port, part of the time anchored waiting for a berth, part time unloading, part time waiting for cargo.

Richard then would have lots of shore leave. He was eager to see foreign sights, curious about the history of new places, and anxious to get to know the people. Having grown up bi-lingual, he picked up languages easily (a knowledge of Welsh helps a lot in learning new languages.) He soon became fluent in Portuguese, which he never forgot. He used this much later in Brazil, mixed with Indian dialects on the Amazon. He learnt Spanish, a little French, and, at a later period, some German and Dutch. He even had a smattering of Arabic.

Many sailors Richard knew went haywire ashore, their only interests being drink and girls. They could get into serious trouble this way with the port authorities and with their superior officers, as their shore leave often ended up in drunken brawls.

It was fortunate that Richard had other more intellectual interests. His father had warned him about the dangers of catching diseases from the waterfront girls. Although he liked a pretty face, and a good time ashore as well as the next guy, he was not tempted to get into trouble with prostitutes. No doubt there were flirtations and brief affairs with a few better class girls along the way, but, a romantic at heart, he often said that he thought "one-night stands" were a dead end.

Enjoyable moments of leisure came when, unexpectedly, he met his father, as sometimes their ships happened to come in to a port at the same time. They met several times this way in Alexandria, and could explore the then fascinating city together.

At that time, a strict rule in the Merchant Navy was that father and son were not allowed to serve on the same ship, so it was exciting when they did meet, and could compare notes about their voyages.

Richard's father did not smoke or drink – not on account of religious belief, but because he did not care for the taste and smell of either. However, he always brought home good wine for family and friends, as well as cigars especially for his father, who enjoyed them.

Richard's mother always kept some wine in the house to offer guests, but she did not know one vintage from another. Once, during the war, when there was a shortage of everything, a special guest arrived. Jane wanted to offer some refreshment, but feared the wine cellar was empty. As luck would have it, when she looked, she found one bottle on a shelf, and gave her guest a glass of this, believing it to be wine. The guest, a formal and proper old lady, drank it without a comment. Only after she had gone, Jane tasted it, and discovered that she had served her vinegar!

At the age of 7, Richard secretly took one of his grandfather's cigars, and smoked it back of a barn. It made him very sick! Unfortunately, he persevered, pretending to be "grown up", and gradually got used to them. His mother later supplied him with cigarettes. No one in those days realized that smoking was harmful. He was a heavy smoker for the rest of his life, a real addict, and without a doubt, it shortened his life.

At the age of 8, Richard was trusted by his mother with a demijohn of "scrumpy" (hard cider) to take over the fields to a neighbouring farmer. It was a hot summer day, and Richard decided, when he had walked about half way, that he'd better have some, as he was thirsty. He drank a lot.

Much later, he was found asleep under a hedgerow. When Richard was a young Apprentice, he had another adventure with local brew. He had a friend in Harlech who made his own Mead. This drink, made from fermented honey, was favoured by the Early Celts and Vikings, and was equally popular in

Medieval times.

One evening when Richard was home on leave, he stopped by to see his friend. "I've always heard stories about your Mead," he said. "How about letting me have some?" Richard had never tasted it.

His friend, rather reluctantly, brought out a bottle. He poured two drinks in thimble-sized glasses. Richard tasted it, and found it good.

"But why such small glasses?" he asked.

"You just wait and see!" teased his friend.

After they had talked for a while, Richard asked for a refill. "I still don't feel any affect," he said.

When he finished his drink, he got up to go. Although his head felt perfectly clear, he discovered to his surprise, that his legs were like rubber, and his feet so heavy that he could hardly walk.

"I told you so!" his friend laughed. "That's the affect of Mead."

Richard had to walk home, zigzagging all the way. He thought he'd never make it! Fortunately, it was dark (no street lights in those days), and nobody saw him. His parents let him use a shed back of the house, which was fixed up with a bed, for the summer, so he could be independent and not disturb anyone if he arrived home late at night. This was fortunate!

Commercially made Mead, put out in Wales today for the Tourist Industry, is not the real stuff. It tastes like a sweet bodiless wine, and leaves no after affect.

One of the most terrifying experiences Richard ever had at sea occurred in the notorious Bay of Biscay. Crossing this every 6 weeks regularly in a small, heavily laden freighter (or, even worse, in an empty boat without ballast) was no joke. It lives up to its reputation as being a graveyard for ships of all sorts, some disappearing without a trace. That is why the women of Ouessant and Ile de Sein, whose men were all fishermen, always dressed in black.

Here there was no escaping frequent severe storms. Mountainous waves would break over a ship, which would be rolling and pitching at the same time ("bucking and hawing", in yachting parlance). Its stern would give terrible wobbles each time it slammed down hard on the water. Every time the ship heeled over it would seem as though it would never right itself. If a ship's rudder broke in the force of the storm, and its movements could not be controlled, it could become swamped, or turn turtle. Sometimes the cargo in the hold would break loose, which was one of the most dreaded things to happen. Many small coasters around the Greek islands have been lost in this way.

Richard was never seasick, and was always courageous, but he said that only a fool would lack respect for the power of sea and wind. The sign of a good seaman was whether he conquered his own fear, and acted calmly in a crisis.

On one of Richard's ships, in the Bay of Biscay at the height of one of the worst storms, a lifting boom for the forward cargo hatch broke its retaining halyard, and started slamming back and forth in the gale force winds. The Captain ordered Richard, then an Apprentice, to climb up the mast to try to secure a mooring line.

However, the halyard was broken, and there was no way of holding the boom without it.

Grabbing a new rope, Richard climbed out onto the swinging boom, edging his way along to where he might be able to attach a line with which to pull it back. When he had finally wormed his way right to the end, and was trying to attach the line, the boom was suddenly flung out over the water, as the ship heeled way over. Richard was submerged under a big roller.

He hung on with all his strength, fighting against the enormous weight of the water. He knew that if he was torn loose that he would be lost in less than a minute, engulfed by huge waves, and swept away with no hope of rescue. He said he was really scared. Fortunately, he was young and very strong, and managed to hang on like a leech, in spite of being half-drowned.

Miraculously, the ship, after what seemed like an eternity, finally righted herself, as she climbed slowly to the top of a swell. The boom swung back over the deck, with Richard still clinging to it.

He instantly lashed the rope, which, somehow, he was still holding, around the mast, and then tied the boom firmly in place.

This storm was so bad that the bridge was smashed. One sailor was swept away.

The ship was in such difficulties that there was real danger of sinking. Labouring low in the water, it was all she could do to wallow through the heaving swell into the protection of the nearest harbour. People ashore were amazed that she had survived under such conditions.

4. SYMI

Now comes one of the most extraordinary episodes in Richard's life, which was to leave an abiding influence.

Richard, on his voyages as Apprentice, had already been in Greece, and to the Aegean. He knew Crete, Rhodes, Cyprus. Then, his ship sailed to the Dodecanese, north of Rhodes, and put in at a small island called Symi. It lies close to KardBr off the East coast of Turkey.

This was not a regular port of call, and none of his ships ever stopped there again. On the maps of the Greek isles it is just a dot. At that time, it was completely isolated, and unvisited. (Today, alas, it is sometimes mentioned in travel articles as being one of the islands favoured by the "more discerning" type of tourist – but still, a "tourist"!) To young sailors in those days, it was an off-beat, adventurous place to stop.

Late one afternoon, the ship sailed into the deep, circular harbour, surrounded by volcanic outcrops, at the back of which was a small port. The ship anchored, but it was not staying long.

Richard was frightened when he looked ashore. He knew the place. This was the island about which he had often dreamt!

Leave was given to some of the crew to take a boat and go ashore. Several of Richard's pals called to him:

"Come on with us. Lets take a walk and see what this place is like."

Richard hesitated. He had a very strange feeling of foreboding. However, he tossed it off. Perhaps it would be better to explore the town, and see if it really was like his dream in all details. It might just remind him of it, but not really be the same.

As soon as Richard put his feet down on the dock, he knew where he was.

"Lets walk along the waterfront in this direction", he pointed, "and we'll see a café, and further on, two or three small shops", he told his mates.

"How do you know? You've never been here before!" they laughed.

They walked along, and there was the café, with locals sitting outside, who smiled and greeted him like an old friend.

"But, you are known here!" exclaimed his friends, puzzled. "How come?"

"Because I've often dreamt about this place," he answered.

"Oh, go on! that can't be true!" they exclaimed, unbelievingly. "And how would they know you?" They gave him a startled look.

"I don't know! But they do! Now," Richard went on, "we'll turn here, and walk up a steep hill. Here it is. Now, look up, and you'll see a white church. It has a domed roof, with an Orthodox cross on the top."

There it was!

Richard then knew that it was exactly like his dream.

"And now," he continued to his baffled, now rather worried friends, "we'll meet a Greek Orthodox priest, wearing a long black robe, walking down the hill."

Right after he said that, the bearded priest appeared, walking from the church. He slowed as he approached them, then half-turned, smiling at Richard.

"Good evening, my son," he said, and then went on his way.

"We're scared!" Richard's mates cried. They turned, and started to run down the hill.

"And what do you think I am?" Richard shouted back, running after them. They ran, faster and faster, until they reached their boat. Almost falling into it, they rowed back to their ship as fast as they could.

When Richard told me this story, I asked: "Why didn't you stop and tell the priest your dream, and ask for his explanation?"

"I was too scared," Richard replied. "Remember, I was very young. It all seemed supernatural. I just wanted to leave."

"And did he speak English?" I asked. "He must have," Richard said, puzzled. "Maybe not! I just understood him."

When Richard got over being scared at the time, he did a lot of quiet thinking. He came to the conclusion that there would have been no reason for a prolongation of the dream, or for him to stay longer and to converse with the priest. What he saw ashore exactly matched his dream, and that was all that was necessary. The meaning of the whole experience slowly clarified.

He saw that the purpose of it was to reveal to him that he had once lived on Symi, in a past life. This had been his home. He had been a Greek!

He was sure of it. Maybe it was vitally important for him to know this.

To him, this proved, without a doubt, that there is life after death, in the form of reincarnation on earth.

When I told the story to Richard's son, thinking it might reassure him after his father's death, he just said:

"Oh, phooey! Its just a case of 'Déjà vu'. Often people arrive in a strange place, and think it looks familiar. Maybe it reminds them of some other place, or they once saw a picture of it, and have forgotten that they did. Or maybe its transference of an image into the brain, something like a radio wave, or telepathy."

He had not had the experience himself, so could not feel the deep meaning behind it.

Richard, after this, did not just "believe" in life after death, He always said: "I know."

Perhaps the loss of fear in this respect helped him to survive many perilous situations later. This might have been the true meaning and importance to him of this unusual experience.

But why should *he* survive? Why was he not washed overboard in the storm, rather than the sailor who had perished? This was a riddle still to be explained.

Richard as Third Officer

The Young Officer

5. WORKING TOWARDS HIS MASTER'S

Richard left the service for a year to study at Liverpool Polytechnic for his 2nd Mate's ticket.

He returned to sea September 23, 1931. Captain Gustaf Erikson, of Mariehamn, Åland, owned the last fleet of commercial deep-sea sailing vessels on the Australian wheat run, and was successfully trading with them during the 20's and 30's. When Richard was beginning his career as a young officer, one of these famous Baltic ships came into port. Richard was lured by the siren song of sails. He thought it would be great to be a Master of Sail as well as steam. He went on board and asked for a job-although he was due to sail on an Ellerman Line ship the next day! Capt. Erikson had started sea-schools on three of his vessels. "Youths from all over the world were flocking to the Erikson ships, and paying anything up to £100. for the privilege of working."[1] He told Richard that, due to his fine nautical training, he would take him on as an officer (with salary!) if he could get out of his next assignment. However, the Ellerman contract had been signed, and they would not let him go.

The Cape Horn ships were authentic square riggers, with no auxiliary motors. Most had been built in the 1890's, but were beautifully maintained. I, myself, when travelling as a passenger on the old S.S. *Scanpenn* in the Baltic in 1936, had been thrilled by the sight of Erikson's ships under full sail. Capt. Erikson died in 1947. After the war, only two of his ships remained.

The below listed voyages which Richard then made, all but one on the S.S. *Flaminian*, were again to the Mediterranean, on the "Wine Trade". His "Ability" and "Conduct" were always marked "Very Good". He was 3rd Mate on these ships.

SHIP	ENGAGEMENT	DISCHARGE
4) S.S. *Flaminian* G.T. 3,227 From: Liverpool Discharge: Hull	21/Sept./1931	7/Dec./1931
5) S.S. *Flaminian* From: Hull Discharge: Dock St. E.H. (Hull)	8/Dec./1931	29/Jan./1932
6) *Flaminian* From: Poplar (London) Discharge: London	22/Feb./1932	14/May/1932
7) *Flaminian* From: Liverpool	11/June/1932	30/June/1932

Discharge: Alexandria		
8) S.S. *Assyrian"*	1/July/1932	16/July/1932
G.T. 2,962		
From: Alexandria		
Discharge: Liverpool		
9) *Flaminian*	24/Aug./1932	2/Nov./1932
From: Liverpool		
Discharge: "		
10) *Flaminian*	19/Nov./1932	5/Jan./1933
From: Liverpool		
Discharge: "		
11) *Flaminian*	24/Jan./1933	27/Mar./1933
From: Liverpool		
Discharge: "		
12) *Flaminian*	5/April/1933	7/June/1933
From: Liverpool		
Discharge: "		
13) *Flaminian*	28/June/1933	29/Sept./1933
From: Liverpool		
Discharge: Liverpool		

Richard said that during these voyages he got so hungry that sometimes at night, when off duty, if everything was quiet, he and one or two other young seamen would creep into the galley, which was officially out of bounds! They would fry eggs (which they only got once or twice a week), or perhaps fry a fish that one of them had caught, and make mugs of hot chocolate.

Even as an officer, his first thought when going ashore was to get a good feed, even before catching the train home. He'd go into a café and fill up with bacon, eggs, and fried bread, his favourite meal at that time.

Richard met some interesting people on these trips. Once, his ship stayed for several weeks in Alexandria. He and some of the crew rigged up a dinghy with a sail, and went sailing. They had noticed a very fancy yacht anchored out in the harbour, so they sailed around her to get a close look. A young man came out on deck to watch them, and chatted with them over the side. He turned out to be King Farouk!

Richard said he was pleasant, and quite good looking. It was a pity he later got so fat, and unhealthy looking (by Western standards, that is).

On one visit to Istanbul, he and some other officers went ashore to a well-known nightclub. There they met Kemal Ataturk. They spent the night drinking and talking with him. Richard said he was extremely interesting. In Richard's own words, "He was a great fellow."

As Ataturk died in 1938, Richard must have met him on one of his early voyages. Although Richard admired Ataturk, and thought he did a lot for his country, many people thought that he had tried to modernize the country too fast (the same criticism brought against the Shah of Iran).

There was much prejudice against the Turks, no doubt because the majority were Muslims. To Western eyes, they appeared to be unattractive. Moreover, politically at that time, Westerners were apt to side with Greece. As for me, I always thought that it was a pity that Ataturk would not allow the Fez to be worn, which was a cruel infringement on age-old customs.

Richard sailed many times along the coast of Turkey. He liked the people he met there very much. He thought the coastline, then completely undeveloped, was fantastically beautiful. What a tragedy that the recent influx of tourism has now encouraged much tacky building.

Once, he was anchored in a bay near a Turkish seaport when an earthquake occurred. As he stood on the deck idly looking at the town, suddenly all the buildings shook, and then collapsed in just a few seconds. As many people as could swam or took boats out to his ship, which became crowded with refugees until the tremors subsided.

Another time, in the Bosphorous, a crew member came down with Bubonic plague. The ship was put into Quarantine, and no one was allowed to leave it until the danger of contamination was over, and the "Yellow Flag" was taken down.

Every one on board was frightened. Of course, some of the men had to look after the sick man. He did survive, and luckily no one else became ill.

Richard was extremely lucky that he never caught any virulent diseases on his voyages. He did once have a bout of malaria, but managed, with the help of quinine, to throw it off. It never recurred.

One of Richard's greatest pleasures at sea was to study the night sky. In startling comparison to the usually dull, overcast British sky, in the Med. the stars gleamed brilliant and crystal clear, making conditions perfect for their study. An old Welsh Captain, affectionately called "Pop" by his crew, under whom Richard served at this time, was a keen astronomer. Through him, Richard gained knowledge of the constellations and their movements.

Inspired by "Pop", he developed an abiding interest in Astronomy. He passed his enthusiasm on to many others, both on sea and land.

I remember his pointing out the Southern Cross to an American friend in St. Lucia, who had lived there for years, but who had never seen the Cross, not knowing where or when to look. In this latitude, it is quite low in the sky. If one lives in a hilly area, it is apt to be hidden.

She said the first time she saw the Southern Cross was a big moment in her life, and she mentioned this to Richard many times afterwards.

"Pop" taught Richard Star Navigation. Richard became a top-notch navigator, not only by the stars, but with the sextant. His dead-reckoning was near perfect, and it used to amaze his crews. Perhaps to be a good navigator one has to have not only enthusiasm and knowledge, but also inborn talent.

Now that navigation is done via satellites and computer, there is no need for painstaking working out of "tables". However, Richard always commented that if something went wrong with the computer, how many seamen today would be able to quickly calculate their position? He felt the same about "Auto-Navigation", a boon to single-handed yachtsmen who need to get some sleep. But, if relied upon too much by big ships, with no senior officer on watch, it can have disastrous results. If something goes wrong with the electronics, this can result in total wrecks, and loss of life. A recent (1989) example of this is the pollution of the environment in Prince William Sound, Alaska, caused by America's most serious oil spill, plus the loss of a valuable tanker, when the Captain of the *Exxon Valdez* was in his cabin, not looking after his ship in dangerous waters. He faced criminal charges.

A frequent port of call for Richard's ships was Oporto (called "Porto" in most atlases), where they stopped to load wine, and, especially, of course, Port.

This was one of Richard's favourite stops. He became friendly with a family who owned one of the leading vineyards on the Rio Douro. When his ship stayed long enough, he would go up river to see them. They always gave him a great welcome, giving him a delicious meal, and treating him like a member of the family.

They had several lively daughters, and I used to tease him by saying maybe thats why he went there so often!

Richard loved Portugal particularly because the people were so outgoing, and the country beautiful and unspoiled. He often talked about it.

Pasajes, the port of San Sebastian, was another favourite place. He used to go ashore for a meal in a small "bodega" (tavern), on the waterfront, much frequented by fishermen. Here they would serve a huge platter of fresh fried sardines, a homegrown mixed salad, and crusty French (I should say, "Spanish!") bread, accompanied by full-bodied local wine. A feast, indeed.

When Richard left the *Flaminian* in Liverpool, in September, '33, he took 6 months' leave to study for Chief Officer.

In his Discharge book, his next voyages are still marked "R.A. Foreign".

SHIP	ENGAGEMENT	DISCHARGE
14) S.S.*Maronian* G.T. 3,385 From: Liverpool Discharge: "	12/Mar./'34	31/May/'34
15) S.S. *Lisbon* G.T. 1,964 From: Hull Discharge: "	3/July/'34	13/Jan./'35

16) *Lisbon* 14/Jan./'35 14/May/'35
    From Hull
    Discharge: Liverpool
17) *Lisbon* 30/May/'35 25/July/'35
    From: Liverpool
    Discharge: Dock St. E (Hull)

Two days after this last discharge, he was married, on July 27, 1935, in Moreton Parish Church, Cheshire, to Chrissie Hughes.

Richard and Chrissie on their wedding day

On August 2, he was back on board the *Lisbon*, for a voyage of 7 months. Then, after a stopover for 1 night in Liverpool (whether he was allowed to see his wife I do not know), he sailed again with the ship for another 5 months.

This would be a disastrous start to any marriage. Studying the records of these continuous voyages, one is immediately struck by how little time seamen had at home. It would have been very difficult for the closest, most understanding couple. In many cases, couples would have drifted steadily apart, with scarcely any life together to share. Most companies at this period would not allow wives to travel with their husbands. Children, also, hardly knew their fathers.

Richard, as an example, said he saw so little of his family that when he went home he did not discuss his life at sea. He thought nobody – and that included his sisters – would be able to understand it. Perhaps they could not understand it because he did not tell them enough about it. The sea was his real life, life ashore but an interlude.

Many people show no interest in hearing about a way of life they cannot visualize. Clar, for instance, much as she loved Richard, said, after I had given her a copy of this biography, that she only wanted to read about his youth, in which she had a part. She skipped over the accounts of his life at sea, which was outside her realm of experience.

Chrissie, the girl Richard married, was a daughter of the family Richard lived with when he was a student at Liverpool Polytechnic. Her parents were old friends of, and possibly related to, the couple with whom Richard's mother always stayed in Bootle. The Hughes were half Cornish, half Welsh, but had lived in the Liverpool area for so long that they felt that was their home.

Marriage to a seafarer in those days was surely a gamble. Wives left alone for such long periods, having to cope with the full responsibility of looking after children, making ends meet on small allotments, not to mention constant tiring housework without benefit of modern electrical aids, were often left exhausted and discouraged. Having little in common with their husbands, when these came home on leave, bickering could easily break out. It would not have been surprising if many such marraiges failed, had it not been that divorce in Britain was still regarded as a disgrace. Instead, a stoic attitude was usually adopted.

One of Richard's attractions was that he faced life with happy optimism. He could not understand these problems. Had not his mother and father, and indeed, most of the couples whom he knew, faced the same? Chrissie, however, may have felt the need of extra sympathetic support, as she often felt ill and depressed. In such a case, it was nobody's fault that circumstances, plus the differing nature and genetic make-up of each worked against them.

Faithful and forbearing, Richard did not admit , as time went by, that he was not completely happy, and Chrissie, herself, never complained about her marriage. This explains why, years later, when the couple split up, it came as a bad shock to all concerned.

After his marriage, Richard would make four more voyages in the *Lisbon*, again as 3rd Mate.

SHIP	ENGAGEMENT	DISCHARGE
18) S.S. *Lisbon*	2/Aug./'35	4/Mar.'36
From: Dock St., E 1, Hull		
Discharge: Liverpool		
19) *Lisbon*	5/Mar./'36	1/July/'36
From: Hull		
Discharge: Liverpool		
20) *Lisbon*	11/July/'36	29/July/'36
From: Liverpool		
Discharge: "		
21) *Lisbon*	8/Aug./'36	28/Nov./'36
From: Liverpool		
Discharge: London		

6. SPANISH CIVIL WAR

Shortly before the outbreak of civil war, I myself was a witness to the distressing conditions in Spain.

One evening in June, 1935, I was standing on the boat deck of *the* American Export Line S.S, *Excambion*, a freighter that also took passengers. As she ploughed through heavy cross-currents entering the Straits of Gibraltar, the pitching bow tossed exhilarating spray high in the air. A balmy breeze blew off the coast of hidden Africa. Stars sparkled above Gibraltar, which loomed ahead, darkly beckoning.

I was 19, just out of college, and looking for adventure. For landing in "Gib.", I was hopefully dressed in a glamorous pale grey skirt, and cape trimmed with soft, fluffy fur. My mother had teased me, and my friend of the same age, who was on board with her parents. She said maybe we'd have "ship – board romances!" Alas, there were no young men travelling with us, only a dull, middle-aged doctor came to the lounge to play bridge, or listen to "the fights" on the radio.

Spain had been in turmoil since 1931, when King Alfonso XIII had been deposed. We saw bullet holes in the thick walls of the Royal Palace in Madrid, a grim warning of more troubles to come. Outsiders felt uneasy. Indeed, the year following our visit, the Civil War broke out.

In Gibraltar's famous "Rock Hotel", much favoured by the British, my mother, to her disgust, found a bedbug in her room. The Manager, very embarrassed, said that it must have fallen off a local maid. Down the hill to the town centre, Spanish women wrapped in heavy black like Arabs, with ragged, underfed children, sat listlessly on the ground, with closed, hopeless faces. Surly, belligerent men hissed, and made contemptuous remarks as we passed, an unpleasant, disturbing introduction to "Sunny Spain". Prosperous-looking American girls in revealing summer dresses were deeply resented. In cities all over Spain the atmosphere was the same.

My mother, a successful travel writer, had been asked by her New York publisher to look the situation over, with the idea of her writing a book on Spain for tourists.

The time was not right. Only in Madrid did she meet a group of moderately liberal intellectuals, teachers in the University, who still had hope for peaceful settlement of Spain's many problems.

My father, an artist, who illustrated my mother's books, was occupied in sketching. He captured the startling beauty of the landscape, the fantastic variety of its walled towns and castles, and, overall, the brilliance of sizzling southern heat. A series of large paintings, which he later did at home from these sketches, won the Philadelphia Water Colour Club Award.

Shocked and frightened by the dismally dissatisfied population, yet I, too, was fascinated by the country, about which I had read many romantic tales. Just to be in Cadiz, where we went after Gibraltar, was exciting. We lunched there in an elegant waterfront restaurant. It was like a dream come true. Cadiz, close by the famous vineyards; Cadiz, of song and story!

My father, more prosaic, considered it just a good place to get some fresh seafood.

In the meantime, Richard was also in the "Med.", on the S.S. *Lisbon*. This ship often stopped at Cadiz, to take on Sherry. He had eaten in the same restaurant!

Was he there that day? He might have been, but, looking back years later, he did not think that he went in to Cadiz that voyage.

What if we had met before his marriage? He said he would have known that I was the right person for him. I was 7 years younger than Richard, an unworldly romantic, and from an entirely different background. He said none of this would have mattered – nor did it, later.

Many times that year our paths would cross: San Sebastian, Pasajes, Seville, Malaga, even Gibraltar. Again, the following year, when, on a Baltimore Mail Line steamer, I arrived in the Port of London.

And yet we did not meet. A feeling of anticipation lurking in these places, unexplained forewarning of something important for us waiting "just around the corner", was all "Old Merlin" would allow.

July 17, 1936, had marked the beginning of the Spanish Civil War, when "Spanish Army units in Morocco proclaimed a revolution against the Madrid Government." On August 6th, Franco fled from Madrid, going to Seville. On November 6th, the siege of Madrid by Franco's forces began, and on the 18th Germany and Italy recognized the Government of Franco.

At Franco's request, "Hitler had supplied transport aircraft to carry 1,500 men of the Army of Africa to Seville . . .and Italian fighter planes covered merchant ships ferrying 2,500 men with equipment from Morocco to Spain. Foreign involvement in the Civil War is extensive. Germany and Italy send volunteers and equipment to support rebel forces. . ."

"Meanwhile, Britain and France press for non-intervention by European powers. . . Germany, Italy, and the USSR continue to provide . . . assistance."[1]

Having left Liverpool on August 8, on what was to be his last voyage on the *Lisbon*, Richard had sailed again to the Mediterranean, on the "Wine Trade". This was a voyage of over 3 months. Turning West on her homeward run, the ship reached Spain early in November. By October. this had become a dangerous area for merchant shipping. Franco's navy "had asserted control of the Straits of Gibraltar, and was stopping neutral flag ships and in many cases ordering them into Ceuta" (Morocco) "for inspection. If they were found to be trading with the Republic their cargoes were confiscated, and a number of ships were seized. . ."[2] However, the presence of British Naval vessels based at the "Rock" gave British ships some protection.

With some time off duty as they sailed down the coast, Richard was standing alone on the boat deck, enjoying watching the shoreline drift past. Suddenly, as he looked up, he saw groups of German planes flying in the direction of Madrid.

Richard had always been keenly interested in aviation, so immediately knew that these were German fighter planes – Stukas – the single engine dive bombers that Hitler used as a mobile substitute for army artillery. Hitler was using the Spanish Civil War as a testing ground for his air strategy.[3] These planes were based in Spanish Morocco.[4]

Luckily, Richard had his camera with him, and he photographed the planes.

As soon as his ship arrived in Gibraltar, he hurried to the Royal Navy Headquarters to report what he had seen.

The information he gave them was extremely important for Britain and her Allies. So far, it had been suspected that Hitler was helping Franco, but there had been no real confirmation of the fact. Hitler had denied involvement (as he was, the following year, to deny the bombing of Guernica.)

Richard was the first eye-witness to actually see and record the planes on their way to bomb Madrid. The ranking officers to whom Richard talked confiscated his film, and would not let him have a copy. They made him promise not to mention the episode to anyone. His information was very sensitive, and had to be kept secret until the highest authorities in Whitehall decided what action to take.

The officers added that they greatly appreciated his coming to them with such vital information. However, he could expect no official recognition of his action, since Britain was not at war with Germany, and was trying to remain neutral.

Returning to London on this eventful trip, the *Lisbon* carried a cargo of Vintage Port and Sherry for the Coronation of King Edward VIII. As Edward abdicated on December 10, it was actually used for George VI. whose Coronation Day was May 12, 1937.

These wines were kept in barrels in the hold, under temperature-controlled conditions. They had to periodically be tapped and sampled for quality by Richard and his men during the voyage. A pleasant job!

Richard, before leaving the ship, managed to siphon off a few bottles to take home. He said to himself:

"What's good enough for King George the VIth is good enough for me!"

When in London, he was taken by one of the Port officials on a tour of their underground storage of impounded wine and liquor. These cellars covered a huge area under the docks, a vast cavern containing thousands of bottles. Very few people who visited the docks knew over what they were walking. Richard said it made him thirsty!

Between November, 1936, and June 24, 1937, Richard was again on shore, back studying at Liverpool Polytechnic, this time for his Master's "ticket".

He passed the difficult exams, which lasted 2 days, and were both written and oral, with flying colours.

These exams were an ordeal, covering everything connected not only with handling a ship, but with the business end of it. He had to thoroughly know the basics of marine architecture and engineering, and was asked questions about a ship's stability. He had had to take a medical course, in case of illness on board, as freighters carried no doctors. Also, he was tested psychologically to see whether he would be capable of being in charge of a crew.

The examining officers were older men who knew his father, and this made it even more nerve-wracking.

He told me that he was, at 28, the youngest person to have passed these exams, on June 7, 1937.

His certificate reads as follows:

Certificate of Competency

as

MASTER

of a Foreign-going Steamship   No. 40186

To Richard Humphreys

Whereas it has been reported to us that you have been found duly qualified to fulfil the duties of a Master of a foreign-going Steamship in the Merchant Service, we do hereby, in pursuance of the Merchant Shipping Act, grant you this Certificate of Competency.

By Order of the Board of Trade, this 10th day of June, 1937
J.B. Harrold Registrar General   S.V. Foley,
                                                    One of the Assistant
                                                    Secretaries to the
                                                    Board of Trade

Richard and Chrissie had set up house-keeping in Saughall Massey, Cheshire, renting a small "semi-detached" house with garden.

Saughall Massey is a village, with a "pub", and several half-timbered, thatched roofed cottages (although theirs was a modern house.) One would think it was in the heart of the country, although just on the other side of the Mersey from Liverpool, not far from developed areas. Richard used to take the bus to the ferry, on which he commuted back and forth.

Richard became quite attached to the place, although he found the English locals hard to get to know, unlike the outgoing Welsh, or even the warm-hearted, jolly "Liverpudlians". He said that when he first went to the pub, the regulars were stand-offish, sticking together as a group. If spoken to, they would say "Good evening", but did not have a drink with him.

It took about 5 years before the barrier was broken down. One day, one of them came up, and invited him to have a drink. From then on, he was one of them.

Years later, he took me to see Saughall Massey, and we visited the pub. He had not been there since the war, but many remembered him, and greeted him like a returned native. Joe Brewster, a local market gardener, long since retired, and then a man of 80 or so, when informed that we were there, walked from his home especially to see us.

He had been very kind to Richard and his family during the war, when fresh fruit and vegetables were scarce. He kept them well supplied from his garden, even adding eggs, and lovely flowers as a bonus.

We admired his cottage, which was right next to the pub, and surely must have been Elizabethan.

Richard, always an animal lover, acquired a large Bull Terrier named "Peter". The dog was very gentle and intelligent. When his first two children, Richard and Christine, became big enough, they would ride on his back.

Richard would give Peter a penny to go to the store. He would carry it in his mouth, then drop it by the counter. The store-keeper would say:

"Oh, Peter! Come for a cone again, eh?" and would give him an ice-cream cone.

When Chrissie, much later, again became pregnant, she was afraid the dog might knock her down. Without Richard's consent (he was at sea at the time), she had him "put down", for which Richard never forgave her. He felt that animals became members of a family, and should be treated as such.

The cat he had in Saughall Massey was also memorable. He would cross a field and wait on a wall until Richard's bus appeared. When Richard got off, he'd give a flying leap, and land on his shoulder.

Later, the family moved to Wallasey, not far from Moreton, where Richard and Chrissie had been married.

This was a much bigger house, at No. 90, Breck Road. It stood on a hill overlooking a busy thoroughfare (which today is a motorway leading to the Mersey Tunnel), and the docks and quays along "West Float".

After getting his Master's Certificate, Richard returned to sea, as 2nd

Mate of S.S. *Dido* again going to the "Med".

SHIP	ENGAGEMENT	DISCHARGE
22) S.S. *Dido* G.T. 3,554 From: Liverpool Discharge: "	24/June/1937	21/Aug./1937
23) *Dido* From: Liverpool Discharge "	2/Sept./'37	28/Oct./'37

Richard was at sea on the next voyage, when his first child, a son, also to be named Richard, was born, on November 11, 1937.

24) *Dido* From: Liverpool Discharge: "	31/Oct./'37	16/Jan./'38
25) *Dido* From: Liverpool Discharge: Dock St. E 1	5/Feb./'38	27/Mar.'38
26) *Dido* From: Poplar Discharge: Liverpool	14/Apr./'38	6/June/'38

The next voyages were on the Company's fine new ship, the S.S. *Ionian* G.T. 3,114, which was being put through trial runs. Richard was again 2nd Mate.

27) S.S. *Ionian* From: Liverpool Discharge: Hull	26/June/'38	28/Aug./'38
28) *Ionian* From: Liverpool Discharge: Hull	7/Sept./'38	31/Oct./'38
29) *Ionian* From: Hull Discharge: Dock St. E 1	17/Nov./'38	5/Jan./'39
30) *Ionian* From: Dock St. E 1 Discharge: Hull	6/Jan./'39	17/Mar./'39

The *Dido*, during these voyages, sailed to Gib., then continued on to Malta, Cyprus, Alexandria and Tunisia.

The *Ionian* kept a similar itinerary, with the addition of Patras, Constanta, and Izmir. On a return voyage, it is interesting to note that she delivered goods to Antwerp.

Between November 28, 1937, to February 27, 1939, Franco had declared "a naval blockade of the Spanish coastline. . . to prevent resupplying of

Loyalist forces."[5]

Laurens Van Der Post, in his book "A Walk With a White Bushman",[6] makes this interesting comment:

"The Franco blockade of the Basque port of Bilbao was being broken by an ad hoc fleet of British cargo ships commanded by some formidable Welsh skippers who all belonged to the great and distinguished clan of Jones."

The Welsh, of course, were special friends of the Basque, due to their common Celtic blood.

Their feats were reported daily by George Steer in "The Times", and on the radio both in Britain and the U.S. My parents and I listened with excitement, as did everyone with Republican sympathies, as the dramatic saga of intrepid Welsh seamen unfolded. The leading captains were nicknamed by the popular press for their cargoes: "Potato" Jones, of the *Marie Llewellyn*; "Corn Cob" Jones, of the *Macgregor*; and "Ham and Egg" Jones, of the *Sarastone*.[7]

Ellerman Line ships did not run the blockade into any Spanish ports. Officially, the British Government was against such attempts, as they did not want Britain involved in the war.

On April 1, 1939, the Spanish Civil War officially ended. The Franco Government was recognized by Great Britain, France, and the United States. Following this, Richard made two more voyages on the *Ionian*:

31) *Ionian*   3/Apr./'39   26/May/'39
    From: Hull
    Discharge: "

32) *Ionian*   3/June/'39   14/Aug./'39
    From: Hull
    Discharge: "

LOCATION OF WARTIME SINKINGS

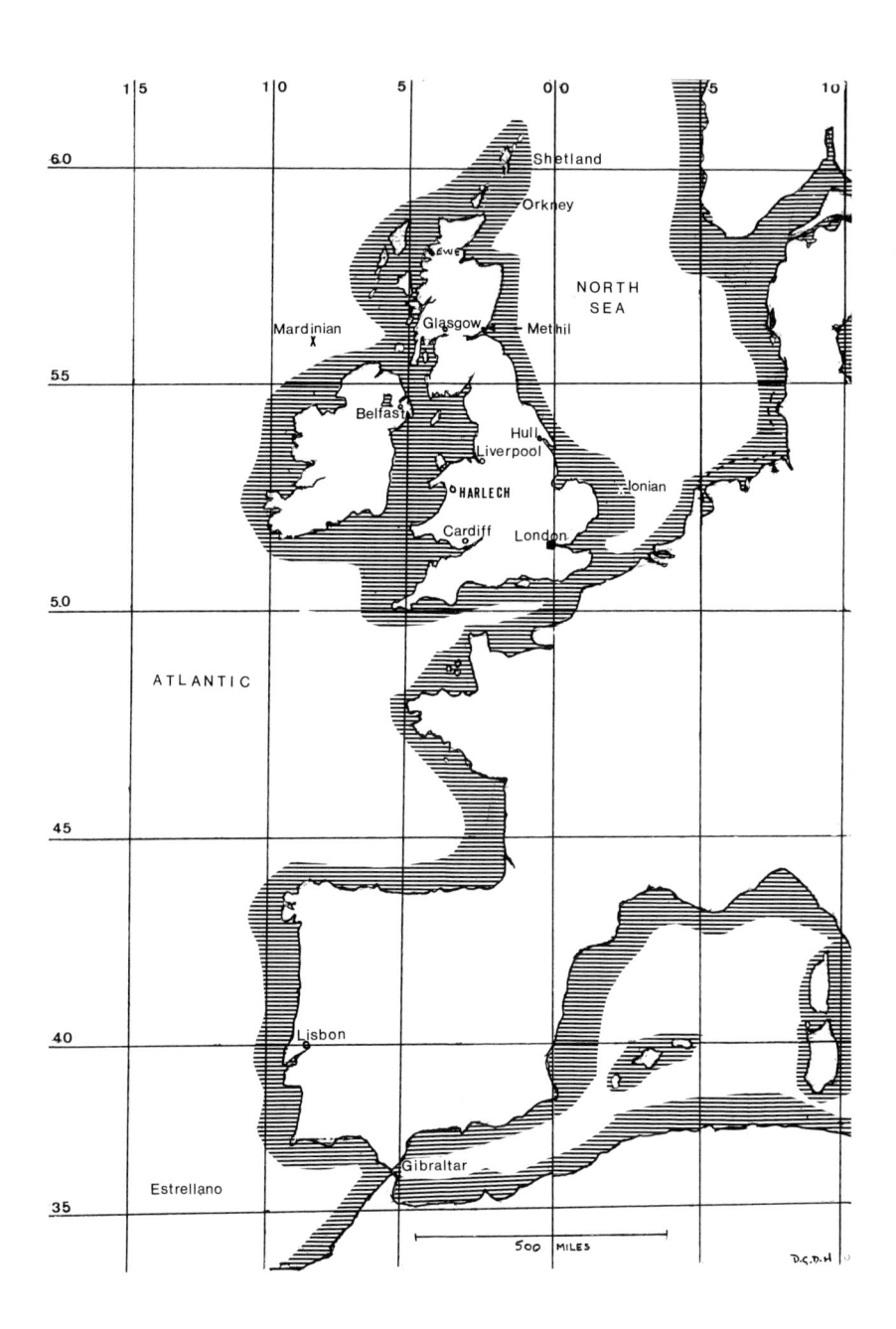

An Encompassing War

7. SINKINGS

The IONIAN

When Poland was attacked by Hitler's forces (Sept. 1, 1939), Britain declared war on Germany two days later.

Richard was again on the *Ionian* (voyage No. 33 on his Discharge book). They had sailed to the Med. on August 24.

On the return voyage sailing from London to Hull, on November 29, the ship was "sunk by enemy action", in the North Sea. The ship was hit by a German magnetic mine, at 132°, 1½ miles S.E. of Newarp Light Vessel. (Position of L.V., 52.48N., 01.55E.) She was then abandoned. After drifting on a tide of probably 4½ knots for approximately 1 hour, 20 minutes, she sank 4 miles N.W. of the light vessel.

Broadcast on the BBC 8AM News, Richard's cousin William was first in his family to hear about it.

The *Ionian* had unloaded most of her cargo in London. Her remaining cargo consisted of currants and mohair, but she was largely in ballast. Being a new ship, she was still undergoing sea trials. She joined Convoy FN43 ("Fast North") at Southend-on-Sea, at the mouth of the Thames. Late that night she was hit by the mine.

G.V. Monk, a retired Marine Radio officer, writes from personal experience about the area in which she was sunk: [1]

"During the war this particular area was known as `E-boat Alley'. E-boats used to lay in wait to attack the daily convoys, aircraft dropped mines, and other aircraft attacked and bombed ships. It was a perpetual `front line', and the Merchant Navy was in it throughout the war. I do not think the people ashore had any idea of the convoy battles which took place just a few miles off the East Anglian coast."

The Admiralty chart shows the area peppered with wrecks, many caused by sandbanks and treacherously strong tides.

Not mentioning the cause of the sinking, nor the ship's exact position, in case such information might be of aid to the enemy, "The Newcastle Journal and North Mail" for Thursday, November 30, 1939, gave the following account:

"Crew of 38 Land in North-East
Rescued by Warship after Vessel was Sunk
Cat only Casualty

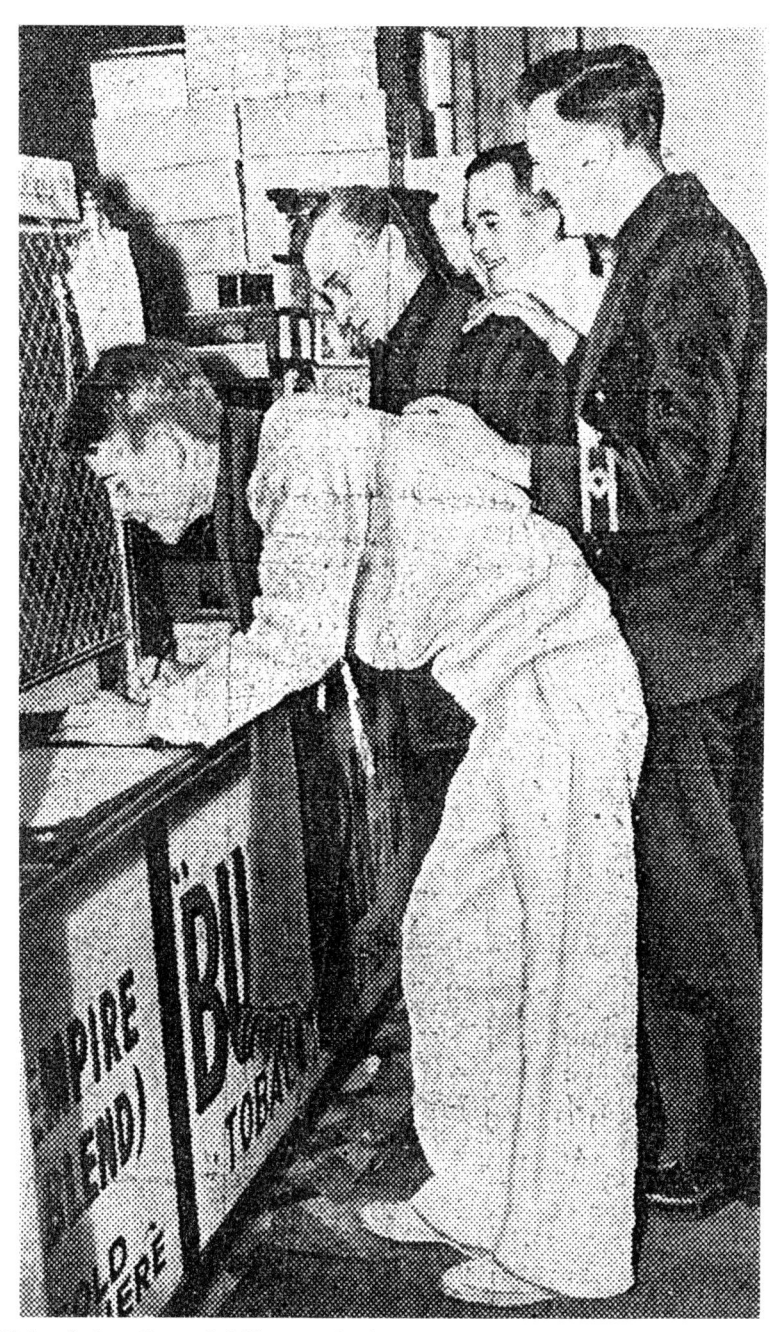

Richard, then Second Officer, and other crew members following the sinking of the *Ionian*. *(Newcastle Journal and North Mail)*

"Thirty-eight survivors [2] of the Liverpool steamer *Ionian* (3,114 tons), sunk in the North Sea early yesterday, were landed at a N.E. Coast port last night from a British warship.

"All the crew, most of whom belong to Liverpool and Hull, were saved and only two suffered slight injuries.

"The only North-East member of the crew was Kenneth Hill, a 19-year old apprentice of Whitley Bay.

"The only casualty was the ship's cat, which, though searched for was not found, and it is feared, was drowned." (This cat did survive, Richard told me. He was later found floating ashore on a plank of wood!)

"After being landed, the survivors were taken to a Mission for Seamen institute, where they were provided with a hot meal and accommodation for the night."

In the Admiralty report, the Captain is quoted as saying: "We were steaming at 9 knots, 3 ships ahead of us all passed (safely) over (the) mine."

The Newcastle newspaper continued:

"The master of the *Ionian*, Captain W. Smith, of Wallasey, told a 'Journal and North Mail' representative that the explosion occurred at about 12.40 AM yesterday. 'There was a terrific explosion and all the lights went out, he said.

'The explosion occurred right under the bridge. I was lying on a settee in the chart room when it happened. The force of the explosion threw me to the floor, and fittings collapsed on top of me.'

"Anchors Jammed"

'Second Officer, Mr. R. Humphreys, who was on watch when the explosion occurred, hauled me out of the chart room. Some of the boats were lowered and we got clear of the ship. Afterwards I went back with three of the crew in a naval boat. We tried to anchor the ship but both anchors and cables had jammed and we had to give up the attempt. We were all picked up by a warship.'"

This was the HMS *Hastings*, from whose deck they watched the *Ionian* going down. "A dismal sight", Richard recalled.

The Newcastle newspaper continued:

"Hendrikus McIntyre, 20, ordinary seaman, of Ceylon Street, Hull, who was landed with an injured wrist, said: 'I was at the wheel when the explosion occurred. I found myself on the floor of the bridge with the second mate lying on top of me. Broken glass and ventilators were flying all over the place. The chart room partition behind us collapsed. We managed to pick ourselves up and scramble on deck.'

'When the explosion occurred I must have kept hold of the wheel and my wrist was sprained. . .'"

"One of the trimmers, Charles Frederick Young, 27, of Hull, said he was in the stoke hold when the ship was rocked from stem to stern by a terrific explosion. He suffered a dislocated ankle."

Another newspaper account reads: "The *Ionian*, owned by the Ellerman Lines Ltd., of Liverpool, was one of their fastest ships, having been completed last year at West Hartlepool."

The Captain told the Reporter:

"There was a terrific explosion, and the vessel seemed to crumple amidships.

"Debris fell on top of me. I remembered nothing more until I found that the Second Officer Humphreys had got me on to the boat deck.

"I ordered all the boats to be got away. . . She" (the ship) "afterwards went down by the stern."

"The Liverpool Echo" had a picture of the *Ionian* with a caption saying: "She is the fourth ship which Ellerman Associated Lines have lost since the outbreak of the war."

Richard told me that when the mine exploded, ripping up the engine room ventilators, toxic fumes were released, which he inhaled. This left him with mucus in his lungs, resulting in often recurring coughing fits. It affected his digestion, leaving him with a delicate stomach. He said he permanently retained these after effects the rest of his life. He later consulted his doctor, who said that nothing could be done to get rid of the condition.

Richard was more seriously injured than the other two seamen, but he did not mention his injuries, as he feared it would delay his getting home. His hearing had been deadened by the noise of the explosion, but he thought that would go away. His hearing did come back to normal in his right ear, but his left one had a burst eardrum. He never regained the hearing in that. Eresipilis, a streptococal infection of the skin, developed, becoming chronic in his inner ear. In those days, the operation to repair it was considered to be very dangerous. He got so used to not hearing with his left ear that later on it did not bother him. He said that he heard more with one ear than most people did with two!

Besides this, he felt as though both feet were broken. When he was thrown down by the explosion, some falling debris hit them. When he got home, he had his feet strapped up. The doctor thought he had sprained ankles, and said he should stay home for a while, and not walk. But he went back to sea in spite of this, hobbling on a cane.

Although place names were never mentioned in wartime newspapers, Richard told me that the men had been put ashore in Robin Hood's Bay, a windswept, lonely place just south of Whitby, N. Yorkshire. This was considered by the officers of the *Hastings* to be safer than taking them by sea to a large port.

When we visited Whitby in 1987, he said he had no desire to see that bay again!

The Admiralty report gives their landing place as South Shields, on the River Tyne, a good 55 miles as the crow flies up the coast. They must have been driven there by military transport for shelter, debriefing, and to catch a train back to Liverpool.

For bravery in rescuing him, Captain Smith wanted to recommend Richard for the OBE. But this would have meant that he would have had to take the time to fill out a lot of papers upon landing, plus getting witnesses to do the same.

He said he was in too much of a hurry to get home to bother. That was a pity. His family would have been very proud if he had received this recognition.

A newspaper picture shows him with other officers eagerly lined up at the Post Office to send their families telegrams saying that they were safe.

One reason why Richard was so anxious to get home was that his second child was about to be born. His discharge was signed December 4. On December 7, a daughter, Christine, was born. On December 9th he was back at sea. Richard explained why most of the Merchant Navy fellows who qualified for awards felt the same way he did. They said "OBE" stood for "Other Buggers' Efforts".

The Merchant Navy men felt bitterly towards the Government during the war, as they were not given the same credit as the Armed Forces.

For readers unfamiliar with this period of the war at sea, here are a few notes of interest:

Cargo ships were all armed during the war. They were Defensively Equipped Merchant ships, although one or two guns on deck could not have stopped a torpedo!

Richard received a Certificate of Proficiency in the Merchant Navy A/A Gunnery Course and became "qualified in the firing and maintenance of a machine gun". This was signed by a Lt. Commander of the Royal Navy, June 24, 1941. He completed a defence Refresher Course in Oct. 1942. The certificate reads:

"This Officer has completed Part 2 of the Merchant Navy Defence Course and is considered capable of taking charge of the Armament of a Defensively Equipped Merchant Ship."

Richard was also trained during the war in single-handed unarmed combat, as used by the Commandos and the S.A.S., which saved his life when he was landed on Anzio Beachhead.

Full credit is given to the Merchant Navy by Mark Arnold-Forster, in his book "The World at War":[3]

"The Battle of the Atlantic" (1939-45)

"One main reason why it" (the Germans' submarine warfare) "failed was the extraordinary tenacity of British merchant seamen."

The official book written about the Merchant Navy [4] gives this estimate of the staggering losses:

"At the outbreak of the Second World War Britain's merchant fleet was still by far the largest in the world. . . at 18 million tons gross. . ." With a total of approximately 145,000 British seamen then serving, "40,000 of these valiant men lost their lives, and British losses of merchant shipping exceeded 11 million tons." On the German side, a total of 1,162 U-boats were involved in the war, and 785 of them sank.[5]

Mark Arnold-Forster continues:[6] "The overall casualty rate in the British Merchant Navy during World War II was higher than that in any of the armed services. . . British merchant seamen were never actually compelled to sign on for another voyage. Nor did they do it for money. In 1939 the pay for an able seaman was £9.00 (then $36.00) per month, plus 12½p per day danger money. These civilians went back to sea again time after time simply because they were sailors and thought they should."

Cargo ships were vital to Britain's survival, bringing in necessary supplies under the most dangerous conditions. However, they were sitting ducks for Hitler's "Wolf Pack", subs which picked them off one by one.

When war broke out, Richard realised this would happen. He wanted to be in a position to fight, not be a helpless target. He immediately volunteered for the Royal Air Force. However, he was one year too old to train as a pilot, and was not accepted.

The MARDINIAN

Richard was promoted to First Mate on his next ship, the S.S. *Mardinian*. The first two voyages again took him to Middle Eastern ports: Jaffa, Haifa, "Alex", then on to Greece and Turkey.

SHIP	ENGAGEMENT	DISCHARGE
34) S.S. *Mardinian* From: Liverpool Discharge: Manchester	9/Dec./'39	19/Feb./'40
35) *Mardinian* From: Liverpool Discharge: "	3 Mar./'40	21/May/'40

Voyage 35 was of military importance, but only Richard and the Captain knew this.

On March 7 the *Mardinian* sailed for Constanţa, stopping first at Milford Haven. Leaving there March 12, she arrived in Gibraltar March 14. In Liverpool the ship had taken on cargo marked "Oil equipment on route for Budapest", and later at sea they had picked up 67 "merchant seamen", actually Naval ratings in disguise. Men and cargo were left off in Sulina, at the mouth of the Danube. The crates actually contained explosives and ammunition.[7]

The Ellerman Line steamship *Mardinian* in which Richard was serving as Chief Officer when she was torpedoed and sunk, on 9th September, 1940. (*World Ship Photo Library*)

From 1939, an extended series of unsuccessful Allied undercover operations had taken place to try to demolish the Romanian oil fields, and also to block the river to German shipping. This latest attempt was under joint sponsorship of the Foreign Office and the S.O.E.[8]

It combined British, French, Egyptian, Australian, and Romanian forces, coordinated under Commander Watson of the Royal Navy. Called the "Danube Plot" by "Deutschland Radio"[9], this was uncovered by the Germans before the mission was accomplished.

Before describing this operation in detail, I shall continue with the final voyage of the *Mardinian*.

36) *Mardinian*   3/June/'40
    From: Liverpool
    "Sunk by enemy action", 9/Sept./1940
    Position 56° 37 N /0900 W (which is N of Ireland and W of Stanton Banks)

The ship had sailed to Trinidad. She was, for this voyage, on charter to T.& J. Harrison, as Ellerman Line ships did not go to Trinidad. The Harrison Line today can find no record of this, but it is confirmed in the survivors' intelligence report (Admiralty file 199/141, pages 229/239). This presents an interesting example of the difficulties encountered when searching for lost wartime records. Harrison suggests that the ship was on a Ministry of War Transport charter from Ellerman's, as all ships during the war were controlled by this Ministry. Harrison would have acted as their agents on the docks in Trinidad.

In Trinidad they loaded on a cargo for London of 3,500 tons of asphalt from the "Pitch Lake". Before leaving Port of Spain, the rats (which were plentiful on Trinidad docks) all left the ship. This alarmed the crew, who believed in this old seafarers' evil omen. They almost refused to sail. Richard tried to calm them by saying that this was just a superstition.

Leaving Trinidad August 6, they made an uneventful voyage north, arriving safely to Sydney, on Cape Breton Island, Nova Scotia, to await an Atlantic convoy. The ship's orders were for Methil, on the Firth of Forth, where they would join an East Coast convoy, then on to London.

They waited for 6 days in Sydney until, on August 25, they could join a convoy of merchant ships headed for Britain, Convoy SC2. This was large, consisting of 53 vessels, sailing in 9 columns. The *Mardinian* was assigned No.11 in the convoy, which was on the front line, in the port corner, a dangerous and disliked position.

"Manned by some 2,000 men, these ships, many old and slow, the majority dirty coalburners, virtually set out for the unknown."[10]

What SC2 did not realise was that submarines had been trailing them from the start. This was "the first successful U-boat Wolf Pack operation" of the war. Before, it had been difficult for the Germans to pin-point the exact location of a convoy, as the planes could not carry enough fuel to fly far in their search over water. SC2 was unfortunate, as on August 30th German Naval Intelligence had cracked the secret Allied code. This told them "the route instructions, and escort meeting point on 6 September." [11] The U-boats went in for the kill. These were under Germany's ace commanders, listed by the historian, Prof. Dr. Jurgen Rohwer, as: U99, Korvetten-Kapitan Otto Kretschmer, the outstanding U-boat commander, responsible for the sinking of a quarter of a million tons of shipping; U47, "the notorious Leutnant Kapitan Prien", who sank the *Royal Oak* in Scapa Flow; and U28, Kapitan Leutnant Günter Kuhnke, Knight's Cross, who later became Commander of the 10th U-boat flotilla at Lorient. Also taking part was U65, under Lt.Cmdr. von Stockhausen.

I should mention here that World War II convoys consisted of "large formations of up to 60 ships escorted by anti- submarine warship escorts."[12] The escort line had not been completed across the N. Atlantic until 1941. "In the early part of the Battle of Britain the commanding officer of a single sloop or corvette could find himself responsible for the safety of 40 or 50 precious merchantmen. . . by Sept. '41 . . . subs were plentiful and the escorts still too sparse. The tonnage of imports into Britain had been halved."[13]

Evasive alteration of course (called "zig-zagging") was often taken in case of attack, the ships doing this together in a block. The width of Convoy SC2 was around 3 miles; the distance between each column around 3 cables (a third of a mile). In "The World at War", pp.91-2, Mark Arnold-Forster states that "keeping station in a formation of 50 assorted merchant ships in bad weather is not an easy piece of seamanship. . . a practice which ran counter to the basic instinct of an ocean-going master which is to keep well clear of other ships." If one ship (particularly with a leading outside position) failed to follow instructions, or lagged behind due to engine trouble, she would become "a straggler", and would be open to attack. She might also disappear from sight of the others. This was to happen to the *Mardinian*.

"This convoy", wrote Duncan Haws, ". . . revealed a weakness in that no one was responsible for recording ships lost". [14]

After this, the convoy system was changed, and ships were required to communicate with each other with rockets and flares.

On September 7, three of SC2's ships were sunk. As listed in "Lloyd's War Losses", these were:

    1) *Neptunian*, British. She had sailed from Santiago with a cargo of sugar. 35 crew lost, & 1 Naval Gunner.

    2) *Jose de Larrinaga,* British. Had sailed from New York, cargo of steel and linseed. All crew of 40 lost.

    3) *Gro,* Norwegian

When the *Neptunian*, sank, the convoy made emergency zig-zags, in an effort to shake off the enemy, but seventy-five minutes later, the *Jose de Larrinaga* was torpedoed by Prien, and "virtually disappeared into the night". [15]

At 23.30 the night of the 8th, the *Possidon* (Greek) was sunk. "She broke in two and sank in a few minutes. Survivors were rescued from a raft by a British Warship after 45 hours."

The attack on the *Mardinian* came 4 hours later, at approximately 03.46 (Central European Time) on the 9th. She was sunk by U28. Lt. Commander Kuhnke had been steadily following them.

After piecing together various, sometimes conflicting, reports, a vivid overall picture emerges, of which I am sure men on the individual ships knew little.

After *Possidon* was sunk, the convoy changed course to 40° to starboard, in evasive action. The escort vessel, HMS *Lowestoft*, then made loops around the convoy, searching for any sign of subs.

She was "about 1½ miles on the port bow, keeping listening watch, when she heard an explosion... *Lowestoft* turned to port and ran out about 3 miles. No signals were observed and as there was still no visible evidence, she deemed it inadvisable to fire star shell... It was not until daybreak that she was aware that *Mardinian* had been sunk." [16] In the meantime, subs had continued with attacks, although unsuccessfully.

"*Asiatic* and *Shaftesbury* reported that torpedoes were seen to pass down their starboard sides, travelling slowly, some ten minutes after the *Mardinian* was sunk." S/S *Ingerfire*, next ship astern the *Mardinian*, noticed that "her engines had stopped at 04.36" (Greenwich Mean Time), "causing her to drop astern. She also sighted a torpedo track soon after."

Reports differ. One states that 10 minutes before this, she was seen to turn inexplicably to port, then disappeared from view. But the Master of the *Mardinian* claimed that there had been no problems, she was going steadily at 6 knots (the speed of the convoy) and not zig-zagging.

A Naval chart issued by the A/S Warfare Division, October,1940, shows the position of the ships during the attack on *Possidon* and *Mardinian*, and of U28. Unfortunately, although in scale, the chart gives no indication of latitude and longitude The distance shown that the convoy would have covered in 4 hours 23 minutes (between the two sinkings) is 26½ miles. However, writes my expert, Mr. Monk, "the official Admiralty records shown state that the convoy passed through 16 minutes of longitude (09.16W to 09.00W) in the time which equates to around 9 miles. Therefore, the Admiralty and HMS *Lowestoft* records/logs are incorrect.

He goes on to explain that "in cases like this it is better to look at the German U-boat records, which are generally immaculate. The system used is the German Grid Square one."

With this reckoning, the distance between the 2 positions does work out at around 26½ miles. This makes the alignment of the course somewhat different than shown on the Admiralty chart, with the position where the *Mardinian* was hit being 56.33N, 09.11W, rather than 56.37N, 09.00W. This may be of interest mainly to nautical students, but it does show the difficulties in reconstructing the attack.

The old saying that there are as many versions of what happened at the scene of an accident as there are witnesses might apply here. One thing that can be certain is that the *Mardinian* lost contact with the other ships, and was seemingly alone on the sea when she sank.

Richard told me that there is nothing more desolate than to watch one's ship disappear beneath the waves, and to be left alone floating in sub-Arctic waters. They did not fear the sub, which had gone away searching for other prey, but they were fearful that they might not be found. They were but tiny dots on a vast expanse of ocean. There was the rolling North Atlantic swell to contend with, with plenty of icy spray drenching the men. The water temperature was 35°F, only 3 degrees above freezing- and no survival suits in those days.

There had been time to launch two life-boats, but not to dress. As it was 4.40AM, the men, except for the night watch, were asleep in their cabins. Richard said he threw a heavy bathrobe on top of his pyjamas, and a greatcoat over that. This statement has been queried by veteran seamen I have told it to, who said that in a convoy under attack, such as SC2, the men would never have undressed – particularly the Chief Officer!

My policy has been to check Richard's reminiscences with all possible records. By doing this, much light might be thrown on his character. I knew that he was straight forward and honest in personal relationships, and strong and courageous at sea. But how had he reacted under the pressures of war? Had he sometimes boasted, or exaggerated his exploits, as many have done? Even so, these are very human weaknesses.

When telling this story, Richard revealed that the Captain was a heavy drinker. Richard had sailed with him before, and had no confidence in him. However, the Company said it was probably his last engagement, and hinted that if Richard went on this voyage he might inherit the command. Richard knew that this man was quarrelsome, argumentative, and vacillating, so disliked the idea of again sailing under him. But if he would stick the voyage, the Company told Richard that in an emergency he should take charge.

For most of the voyage, the Captain had been too befuddled to take much notice of his surroundings, so Richard had more or less taken over. Now that a real emergency had arisen, Richard did not want to take any chances or waste time in conflicts of opinion.

The Captain had immediately proclaimed that he and Richard should take charge of one boat, with the other officers in the second one. Richard did not fancy being in the same small boat with a drunkard in the open sea. He firmly told the Captain that he would take charge of one of the boats, as he had a better knowledge of navigation than either the 2nd or 3rd Mates, so the Captain should take charge of the boat they were in.

Before any argument could start, Richard got two of the crew to help the drunken man into one boat, then quickly, with the men assigned to accompany him, launched the other. As the Captain later reported to Naval Control, from a crew of 37, there were 19 in his boat, and 12 in the other. What had happened to the other 6 men?

When telling the story, which I have heard him do many times, Richard always said that there was no loss of life. It was quite a shock when I found out differently. To give Richard credit, perhaps in the crisis of the sinking, he did not really know that there were men missing.

In the report made by the Master when the survivors reached Belfast, he stated that when the torpedo struck, the Bo'sun and 5 others had panicked. Without waiting for the ship to stop, and without orders, they threw two rafts in, and jumped in after them. They were never seen again. Their names are listed on the Merchant Navy War Memorial in London.

The following information about the sinking was sent by the Flag officer, Belfast, to Commander in Chief, Western Approaches: [17]

"The *Mardinian* was seen to fall astern at 03.35. The explosion was not violent, and failed to awaken some hands."

"03.50 Torpedo struck vessel on port side, after end of No.2 hold, almost under bridge, wrecking same.

"Two boats were lowered and lay off. The 1st boat got away at 04.10, the 2nd at 04.20. The ship sank at approximately 04.40."

The Captain, in interviews with shipping authorities, also stated that she took 50-55 minutes to sink.

Lt. Kuhnke, Commander of the U28 which sank the ship, wrote in his War Diary that he watched her sink "within half an hour". This is probably correct. However, the "Secret" Monthly Anti-Submarine Warfare Division of the Naval Staff (M.O.D.) in their journal for Sept.-Oct.,'40, stated that "the ship sank in 15 minutes"!

Weather: these reports also differ. When interviewed by the Shipping and Casualties Section, Trade Division, on September 13, the Captain stated that there was a moderate westerly wind, moderate sea, and visibility fairly good. The Naval report, on the other hand, says: "overcast, no moon, wind N.W. Force 5, heavy swell. This quickly freshening Force 5 N. Westerly had increased to Gale Force later in the morning, when another convoy in the area experienced it.

To continue with Richard's account, the two boats floated for awhile side by side. As dawn came early, the depressed men silently watched their ship go down. After waiting to see if any help was coming, the Captain decided to hoist a sail, and make for the coast of Scotland, which he believed was about 90 miles away. Richard likewise rigged a sail, but quietly decided that he would sail to Wales, as he was anxious to get home fast. He knew his men felt the same way. As Richard could navigate by sun and stars, and moreover, knew these waters well, he was certain of his direction.

They sailed the rest of the night without incident, the two boats going along near each other, then gradually drifting apart, due to wind and currents.

At about 8 in the morning, a British merchant ship spotted them, and signalled that the survivors should come aboard. But this vessel was outward bound for Canada, going into the worst area for submarines. The men agreed that they did not want to turn back, to run the risk of being sunk again. They trusted Richard, and knew he would get them safely to Ireland or Wales. The weather as yet was not too bad, and they had survival rations and water. So they signalled that they would prefer to go on by themselves.

"Good-bye, and good luck!" came the response. A little later, another ship found them. This was going North, in the right direction. By now, the men were getting tired, so, reluctantly, Richard agreed they should board her. He had to give up his vision of landing with his men on Harlech beach, like an Early Celtic Warrior.

Richard always said this was "a trawler", but never mentioned that she was a Royal Navy anti-submarine trawler, the HM *Apollo*, which had been patrolling the area on the look-out for subs. She was actually one of the escort vessels for SC2, but miraculously spotted the survivors by accident, for, as I have said, at that time there was no communication between ships when one of them disappeared from sight.

"Old Merlin was again looking after his own!" thought Richard.

As he stepped from the ladder onto the deck, he pulled out of each pocket a bottle of brandy. Several of his men did the same, The liquor cabinet of the *Mardinian* had been well raided!

"Well," exclaimed the *Apollo's* Commanding Officer, "I'm glad we rescued you! We're short on rations, and have been out of drinks for a long time."

Richard gave the Captain 2 bottles, and asked his own men to give several to the crew, so everyone could have a celebration. It was a happy ship that night, in spite of Hitler!

The Captain and his boatload had not gone far, and were also picked up safely by the same ship. The *Apollo* then returned to the sinking position and a search was made for the raft. The raft was later sighted but no one was on it." The 2nd raft was never found.

They sailed for Northern Ireland, all in good shape, except for Richard's lifeboat, which had been tied to the stern of the trawler. It was a strong boat, well worth saving, but, as it was being towed, it soon filled with water, the line parted, and it was lost.

Arriving in Belfast, the survivors were outfitted with new, warm clothes, by a fine wartime charity for ship-wrecked mariners. Here he was lucky in meeting an aviator whom he knew, so got a fast lift across the Irish Sea. He arrived home for a happy family reunion,

The ESTRELLANO

On May 16, 1940, the Admiralty had closed the Mediterranean to British merchant shipping, due to the fierce battles taking place there. However, in spite of the danger involved, Richard wanted to get back to sea. After his last sinking, he had been given 3 months' leave, so was now anxious to return to work.

On December 3, 1940, he again sailed out of Liverpool (Voyage No. 37), as Chief Officer of the *Estrellano*.

This was his old ship, on which he had served as Acting 3rd Officer while still an Apprentice 10 years previously. On this voyage, they went to Portugal.

His Discharge book for this voyage reads:
"Sunk by enemy action", 9/Feb./1941

Returning from Oporto, the *Estrellano* had sailed for home, joining Convoy HG 53 (Home Gibraltar).

In order to avoid German U-boats, convoys leaving Gibraltar first headed west to around longitude 15W/20W, then northwards, and finally eastward to reach the coastal waters of the northern channel between N. Ireland and Scotland.

Far out in the North Atlantic they were found by U37, commanded by Lt. Comdr. N. Clausen. The *Estrellano* was torpedoed at 35° 53 N/13° W, 160 miles SW of Cape St. Vincent. "Over a two hour period the *Estrellano, Courland'*(Currie Line), and *Brandenburg* (also Currie) were all sunk."[18]

This sinking also occurred early in the morning, at 4.30AM. Before telling the story of what happened, I should say that Richard, generally speaking, used great discretion in talking about his life. Not because he was secretive by nature, but because he thought no one would be interested. Most of what he did tell was easily proved true. He did, however, dislike talking about the war, and omitted many details of his war experiences. For instance, he never mentioned the dreadful attacks on his later convoys to Anzio. Research filled in most of that, and brought to my attention one of the most dreadful sea battles of the war.

The same can be said of the vicious attack on Convoy HG 53. Richard always began when telling about it by saying that of his 3 sinkings, this was the most frightening. Over the years, I have heard him tell this dramatic story many times, not only to family, but to seafaring friends alike. However, when doing research, I have recently found that he had switched a lot of what had happened on the *Estrellano* to the *Mardinian*, and vice-versa. This could not have been caused by lapses of memory, as over the years, he never varied any details of his stories. This would have been very difficult to do, if what he told was untrue. I wondered why he took the chance, as it would have been so easy to check up on at the time. He must have had good reason for doing so.

One thing that comes to mind is that seafarers sunk during the war were asked to say very little when they went ashore. It was bad for morale, and also "A thoughtless word may help the enemy!" many posters warned. In this case, Richard being a sociable person, might have wanted to share a little of what he had been through, and thought it safe to do so if he changed the order of some things around.

Vivid accounts of the attacks on the *Estrellano*'s convoy follow:

1) From "Convoy", by J.Winton.[19] This concerns the proximity of a German heavy cruiser – the *Admiral Hipper*.

"*Admiral Hipper* sailed again on 1/1/41. One very unfortunate convoy, the homeward bound Gibraltar HG53, was sighted by U37 (Korvetten-Kapitan Clausen) S.W. of (Cape) St. Vincent on the evening of 8 February. U37 closed and sank two ships, maintained contact and homed five Kondors (bombers) of 2/KG40 group in to the attack on the 10th, and the following day, by which time the survivors of the convoy had scattered, *Admiral Hipper* caught and sank one straggler." (the *Iceland*)

A total of nine ships were sunk from the original 16 in the convoy.

2) In "The Red Duster at War". John Slader says that the U37 had fired 2 torpedoes simultaneously, one hitting the *Courland*, and the other the *Estrellano*. The *Brandenburg* (Currie Line) lagged behind to pick up the *Courland's* 30 survivors from the water. Moreover, right after the air attack at noon the next day, the *Brandenburg* was sunk by Clausen, who again fired two torpedoes. Heavily loaded with a cargo of iron ore, she went down like a stone, with all hands, including her Captain and 23 crew members, and the men from the *Courland*.

3) "Periscope Depth", by Kenneth Poolman [20] is more detailed:

On the evening of the 8th, "Nicolei Clausen in U37 intercepted the Convoy HG53 halfway between Portugal and the Azores, en route from Gibraltar to Britain. He sent a sighting report, which was forwarded to KG40 (the German bomber headquarters), via Flag Officer, Submarines, at Lorient. .
. In the early hours of the 9th U37 attacked . . . Clausen then continued shadowing the convoy, reporting the position, course and speed."

"At 6am five 4-engine Condors took off from Bordeaux- Merignac, led by

Hauptmann Fritz Fleigel. CO of 2 Staffel. They found the convoy at noon some 400 miles SW of Lisbon. 14 ships steamed along in ragged lines, protected by nine escort vessels. Clausen watched the Luftwaffe in action, and when they had done their worst he torpedoed the 1,473 Ton *Brandenburg*." Between them, aircraft and U-boat had sunk 8 ships, half the convoy's strength.

4) The ADMIRALTY reported in their "List of Merchant Ships Lost or Damaged":

HG53) Ships sunk by enemy action (Folke-Wolff Condors flying at masthead height):

Varna (Danish) *Britannic* (Norwegian) *Jura* (British)   *Dagmar* (Danish) *Tejo* (Norwegian)

5) The sinking of the *Estrellano* –

From an Admiralty file [21]

This starts with the time. "At 05.38". Here I note that Clausen's log says 04.40, other reports 04.35. The difference of 8 minutes would be that between the time of attack, and when the torpedo struck. A difference of one hour between some reports is due to their being given in C.E.T (Central European Time), whereas ships' time is always G.M.T. However, in winter, D.S.T. was used. one hour ahead of G.M.T.

To continue with the report: "At 05.48 the *Estrellano* torpedoed on port side of the hold, abaft the engine room; the Confidential papers and code books were thrown overboard. The only boat to get away capsized, and the crew left swimming about in sardine oil; or clinging to upturned boat. Of the 5 men missing the Radio officer (D.J.Mahaon) was probably trapped in his wireless room which was seen to collapse under weight of concrete covering it. The remainder were probably caught in the suction of the ship sinking." (Or, possibly the 3rd Engineer and the Donkeyman were trapped in the engine-room.) "Good weather and calmness and fortitude of officers and men of sunk ships were largely responsible for so many survivors picked up."

The report adds that from a crew of 27, there were 21 survivors.

Particularly heartbreaking was the loss of the young Galley Boy, only 16, who was pulled from the sea onto the *Deptford*, but died the same day of fatal injuries received in the explosion.

6) Richard's account:

He said that the ship sank within minutes, and there was no time to properly launch the lifeboats. Hearing the Radio officer screaming from his cabin, Richard rushed to his aid. Heavy debris had fallen over the cabin, and the door was jammed. He tried to force it open, but could not budge it. The man was trapped. The crew were all abandoning ship. No one was nearby to help.

Richard ran out on deck, and found it flooded, the ship already sinking into the sea. Jamming his officer's cap down over his ears, he stepped from the deck into the icy water. He was the last man to leave the ship. For the rest of his life he would be haunted by the screams of this officer.

Luckily Richard and a few other men swimming nearby spotted an overturned lifeboat that had floated away from the sinking ship. They managed to grab hold of it and hang on. More men swam up and joined them. Most of them managed to climb onto the overturned boat. Richard followed suit, but said straddling it was too uncomfortable. He had to grip it tightly with his legs to keep from falling off when it rolled. His legs became very chaffed and sore due to the salt in the water. So he got back in the water, which he said felt warmer that the air.

"But it was mighty cold!" he added.

I have checked the surface water temperature for the general area north of the Azores in winter. The "Times" Atlas gives this as 5°-10°, not as cold as where the *Mardinian* went down. However, lower temperatures prevail off the West African and Portuguese coasts, due to currents coming down from the north, along with big swells.

TV interviews with survivors from similar sinkings during the war have revealed the horrific condition of men fished out of the stormy Atlantic in mid-winter. Even if not in Arctic regions, after long exposure they were half frozen, and scarcely able to walk, so what Richard said about this sounds correct.

When the torpedoes struck the 2 ships together, there must have been a scene of total desolation, Around the *Estrellano* the water was not only full of debris from the sinking vessels, but was covered with fish oil, from her cargo of 1,110 tons of canned sardines, which broke open in the explosion.

As in a nightmare, Richard saw men thrashing around in the water, too far away to help, They simply disappeared, either too weak to stay afloat, or were sucked beneath the sinking ship.

Terrible as it was, Richard, supported by some inner courage, remained calm, and did not panic. This, combined with years of strenuous athletic training, and his naturally strong physique, without a doubt saved him.

"I firmly believed I would survive, but I did not know why."

It is not said in the official accounts how long it took before the men were rescued. Richard said it was 4½ hours. They were then rescued by the sloop HMS *Deptford*, one of the escort vessels.

Leaving Richard in the water for a minute, I shall quote from a first hand description of the attack sent to me by Mr. Bill Bowen-Davies, who was Radio Officer on the *Empire Lough*, a coal and iron carrier. This paints a vivid picture of what happened.

"You are quite right in saying that your husband's ship *Estrellano* was one of the first two ships torpedoed. She was torpedoed three minutes after the

Courland was hit and sunk. It was not until the next day the rest of the convoy was attacked by 5 or 6 Folke Wolffs. We picked up crew from one of the ships, but which it was I cannot say, most of us were in a pretty dazed state – I was anyway! It all happened so quickly" (they were not allowed to keep diaries). "Your husband's ship was at the head of our column. We were the 4th ship in line. It was my first trip and quite an introduction to the Battle of the Atlantic!"

He goes on to say that "The U-boat attack was by night so we did not see anything of that, but immediately after the attack by air I went out on deck to see just the two masts showing of one ship, which had sunk very rapidly, possibly an iron ore carrier like us. The scene was indescribable, with men floating and shouting in the water – I think one of them was blind. It is certainly a scene I shall never forget. The convoy carried on for a while until we met very bad weather and then we seemed to disperse with only a handful of ships reaching port at the same time. With a double crew aboard we kept double watches, shared the sparse amount of food and had to keep washing in the same water. But it could have been worse. One of the rescued officers had left his false teeth behind and asked for all his food to be put through a mincer! Good humour prevailed all around, and when off watch we swapped yarns and jokes to keep our spirits up. We were very glad to see the local escort come out to meet us, as we only had two destroyers.

Here he explains why the men from the *Estrellano* were not picked up right away, and might easily have been over 4 hours in the water.

"I think the trouble about rescuing men from the sea is that the escort's job is to locate and destroy the submarine before it can sink more ships. Later in the war they had special rescue ships. properly equipped for the job, which enabled the escorts to concentrate on locating the U-boats by asdic, and blowing them out of the water. We were so desperately short of escorts at the beginning of the war. So many of the few we had were being used for other purposes, invasion of Norway, Dunkirk, anti-invasion patrol, apart from the Mediterranean, out East and Russian convoys."

When the *Deptford* returned to find the survivors of the *Estrellano* , she signalled that she would sail slowly by close to them, and would throw them a line, but that the ship could not stop, due to the danger from the sub, which might reappear at any time. The men had to catch the line, otherwise. they'd had it. In their weakened condition, this was a difficult thing to do, but they managed to get hold of it. A rope ladder was lowered over the side, and one by one, they laboriously climbed it.

Richard was the last man up. With the dragging of the line, caused by the ship's continuous forward movement, it was all he could do to grab hold of the lowest rung, and hang on.

His life depended on his hands gripping firmly, in order to support his weight. In the cold air, they literally froze shut. To make matters worse, with each roll of the heavy hull above him, he was totally submerged back into the water. It seemed impossible to pull himself up.

The Naval officer in charge of the operation sent two men down with a rope, which they tied around his waist, and so could drag him up. When they reached the deck, they had to pry his hands open.

As he was heaved onto the deck he heard a Cockney voice exclaiming: "Blimey! This bastard's got his hat on!"

The men were given hot drinks, laced with rum, stripped of their icy wet clothes, and put into hot baths. The ship had no extra berths, so they were given blankets and bedded down on the deck. Richard was so happy to be alive and safe that he slept well.

In the morning, he was so stiff that he could hardly move, and his chaffed legs were like raw meat, but he managed to dress in his clothes, which had been dried in the engine room. He heaved himself up, and staggered into the dining room. He did not feel ill, or depressed.

"I ate a big breakfast," Richard laughed.

None of the others got up. They were too exhausted to move, and were suffering from shock.

Later, Richard was asked to make out a list of the survivors to give to the company, so that their families might be notified. He was so concerned in getting down their names that he forgot to include his own!

When they stepped ashore onto the Liverpool dock, an Ellerman Line representative sent there to meet them had a shock when he saw Richard.

"Well," he joked, "I might have known we wouldn't get rid of you!"

Before returning home, the survivors were again outfitted with new clothes, this time by a big department store. Then, they held a "Survivors' Dinner", in Reece's downstairs restaurant, one of Liverpool's most elegant (now sadly, this has been closed down.) The first time I visited Liverpool with Richard, he took me to Reece's for dinner, where he pointed out just where they had sat.

There had been 13 of them, the remainder perhaps not feeling up to it. Some of the men did not like the idea of 13 sitting down to the table, so they asked one of the waitresses from the upstairs dining room to come and sit with them.

Then they all went home on leave, everyone seemingly alright. No one had any injuries. However, once home, Richard was later told, these men all sickened and died, for no visible reason. This, if true, must have been the result of exposure, followed by severe shock. It is quite possible this might have happened, for if they died at home sometime later, their names would not have been on the War Memorial. Many survivors from the Battle of the Atlantic told how they had an incomplete idea of what happened during the attacks, and many wild rumours circulated about the fate of those who took part.

To be honest, I must admit that I have found among Richard's papers a memo from the Ellerman Line telling which officers went back to sea after sinkings, and which remained on shore. Drink or no drink, the Masters of both the *Mardinian* and the *Estrellano* did return to sea. There went Richard's promised command! It is perfectly possible that several years after the sinking, Richard might have been left as the sole survivor, as he always claimed.

Another survivor whom Richard did know had returned to sea was a cadet, nick-named "Tizer", because he drank a lot of this popular soft drink. (I never knew his real name.) He had sailed under Richard before, and Richard had more or less taken him under his wing. He said that "Tizer" was almost like a son. After the sinking, the young man took the first ship out again he could get. This was immediately torpedoed, and "Tizer" drowned.

Tears came to Richard's eyes whenever he spoke of "Tizer", who he thought the finest type of young man, and who for him became the most poignant example of a promising life lost in the horrors of war.

I cannot verify this story, but as Richard felt his loss so keenly, it must be based on fact. There were no Cadets listed as such among crew members of the *Estrellano* and the *Mardinian*. There may be a few men still alive who had served on these ships who might remember, but it has been impossible to trace them.

By good luck, however, I did find one, H. Taggart, who came from the Isle of Man, His sister, Mrs. Cain, who still lives here, has been most helpful. She told me that her brother, although listed as "Deck Hand", was actually the Gunner on both the *Mardinian* and the *Estrellano*.

Her account parallels what Richard had told me about "Tizer", for after the sinking of the *Mardinian*, Taggart went back to sea, taking the first berth he could get. Again his ship was torpedoed, and this time, sadly, he was drowned.

His sister describes him as an attractive, energetic man, popular on the island. He had worked as a seaman before the war on some of the Isle of Man Steamship Company's ferries. Musically gifted, when not at sea he played in the Douglas Band.

Was he "Tizer?" Richard pictured "Tizer" as a young apprentice, but the gunner was an experienced seaman, 7 years older than Richard, who was then 31.

Obviously, Richard switched some of the details of his stories around, perhaps because seamen returning ashore during the war had been asked for security reasons not to say much about their experiences. However, the basic facts of his sinkings as he described them were true, and Richard himself remained a patriot.

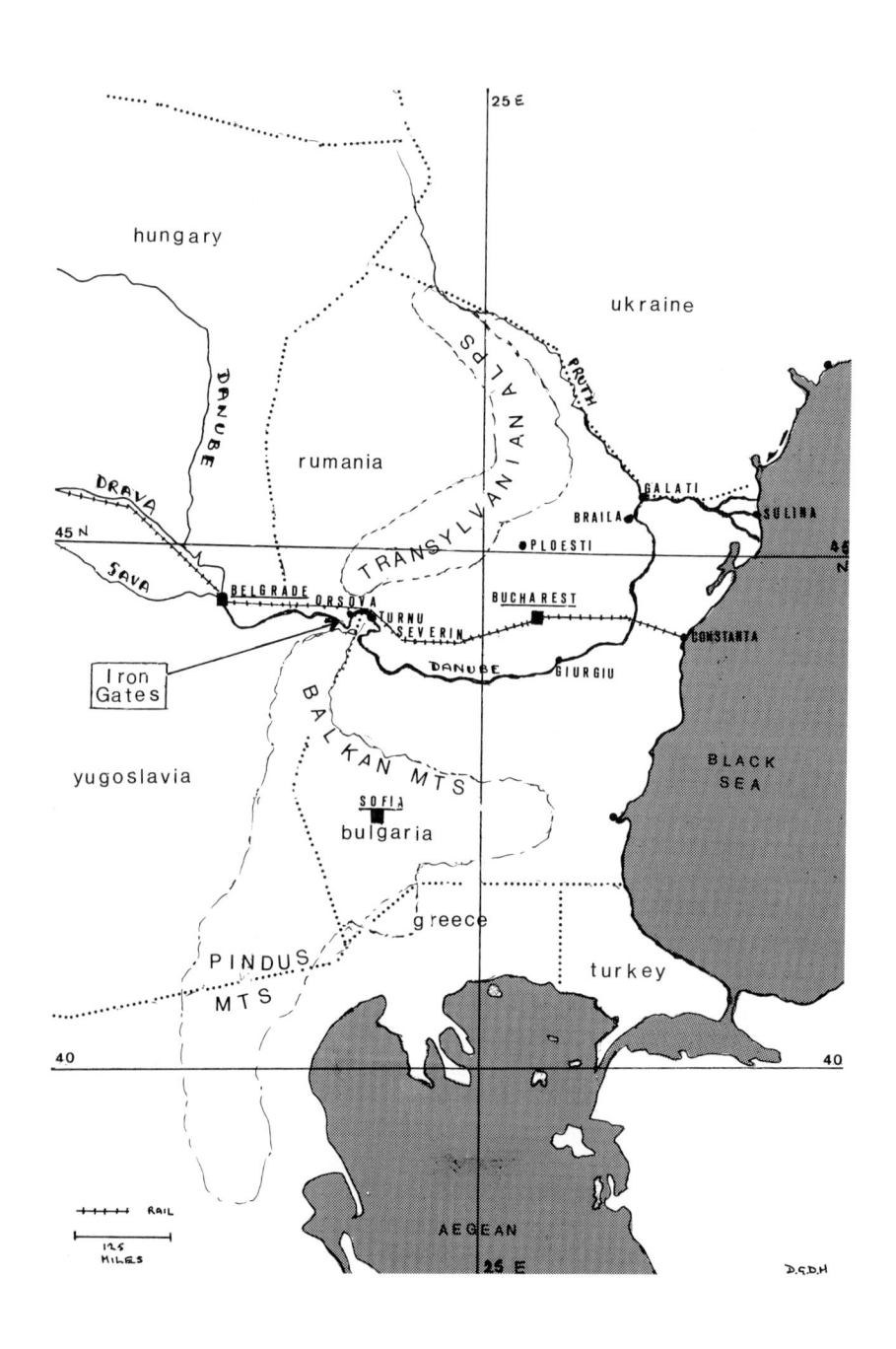

THE DANUBE FROM ESTUARY TO THE IRON GATES

8. THE ROYAL NAVY

Part 1.- A Secret Mission

Here is a full account of Voyage 35, of the *Mardinian*.

After his first sinking, Richard felt depressed, as it clearly confirmed his fears that merchant ships would be easy targets for the Germans during the war.

Walking along the street between voyages, he was gloomily reviewing his rejection by the RAF, when he was accosted by an old acquaintance, now a high-ranking officer in the Royal Navy.

"What are you doing wasting your time here?" he asked. "I have better work for a man of your calibre."

The Navy, he explained, was looking for a volunteer, who would be put in charge of a top secret mission. It would be extremely dangerous work, possibly fatal. It required a daring, courageous man, with Richard's knowledge of seamanship, who must be in top physical condition, and have already been trained in self-defence. He must be a proven patriot, and be absolutely calm and reliable in a crisis.

This description surely fitted Richard! He immediately jumped at the chance.

Richard was called in for an interview at the Admiralty in Whitehall. Here, after quite a wait, he was ushered into a boardroom. Behind a big table sat some of the top-ranking Naval "Brass", men he had never met, but whom he had read about as being leaders in Britain's war effort, probably including the Director of Naval Intelligence, Admiral J.H. Godfrey; the Director of Plans, who at that time was either Ralph Edwards or Tom Brownrigg; also likely was Lt.Commander Ian Fleming, then working in the Naval Intelligence Division of the Admiralty, and possibly Dillon, a member of the Danube Comission. [1]

They questioned him thoroughly.

"Are you Richard Humphreys, son of Captain Owen Humphreys, of Harlech, North Wales, whose father was also a Captain in the Merchant Navy?

"You, too, hold a Master's Certificate, and are at present Chief Officer of the S.S. *Mardinian*, of the Ellerman Line? You were sunk on your last ship, the *Ionian*? You have served with the Ellerman Line since your apprenticeship?

"You live in Saughall Massey; and you have a wife, and a son and a daughter?" etc., etc., the questioning went on.

They knew everything about him, and about his family, in detail, and only needed his confirmation of the facts, and, no doubt, an opportunity to look him over.

If he accepted the commission, they warned him, he would get no public recognition if it succeeded; and he might very well lose his life. In this case, he would still get no posthumous recognition. The Navy would keep it completely under cover. However, if he were killed, he would have given his life for his country, and the Navy would guarantee to look after his family.

Richard, in spite of the danger, agreed to do it. He felt that if the Navy needed him, it was his patriotic duty to accept. Also, he was somewhat of a dare-devil. This would be better than sitting behind a desk; and much better than living with the expectation of being sunk at sea. It was cloak-and-dagger stuff, which appealed to his active nature.

So the Navy "commandeered" him. Officially, he was still to remain Chief Officer of the *Mardinian*, and would return to his ship in that capacity, as a cover-up on the mission.

The mission was so secret that he had to swear never to tell anyone about it, not even his closest family. They were to think that he had gone back to sea, which, in truth, he would be doing. As he never talked much at home about his voyages, anyway, they would not expect to hear anything about this one, either.

Richard was then immediately commissioned as Lieutenant.[2]

A thorough briefing on his assignment followed. The purpose of the project was to send a group of men, hand-picked from the various Services, up the Danube. They were "sappers", all highly trained in the use of explosives.

The objective was to blow up the "Iron Gates" of the Danube-"Portillo de Fier" ("Iron Gate Gorge"). One side of the gorge was in Romania, with the Yugoslavian border across the river. The river, itself, being "International Waters".

At Turnu Severin, last port upriver before the "Iron Gates", the river makes a sharp U-turn, leading into a section of turbulent rapids, the worst in Europe. Navigation was only possible through a canal, whose strong current also presented a hazard for shipping. (Later the Germans built a barrage to make navigation easier.) Above the rapids, the river narrows, winding for 8 miles between the high cliffs of the Carpathian mountains. Shallow water poured over rocky ledges, with a channel in the middle. "Locally, this defile is called the Gorge of Kazan or the Kissura. . . The Iron Gates are the rapids at the bottom end."[3] On most maps, the whole area is loosely called "The Iron Gates". (Recently, a huge controversial dam has been started nearby.) If the gorge could be blown up in order to block the river, and the pipe-lines, which were on the Romanian side, broken up so the oil would be absorbed into the ground, Hitler would be unable to use it to transport oil, said the

Admiralty.

Although the productive Romanian oil fields had American, Dutch, French, and British shareholders, Hitler, as early as March, 1939, had reached an agreement with Romania that he would be allowed to get oil, at very cheap rates, from the Ploiesti oil fields. (A pipe-line still runs from these fields to the Iron Gates today.)

In spite of these oil-fields being well over 100 miles from the Iron Gates, the pipe-lines had been run there, as transportation at that time was extremely difficult. By 1940, the Royal Navy had successfully blockaded the Mediterranean, including the Aegean and the Black Sea, to German shipping. The only other means of getting out the oil was over the Carpathian mountains, on a narrow-gauge railroad, which could be sabotaged. Indeed, in 1941, Hitler told his generals that "the life of the Axis depends on those oil fields."[4] If the river were blocked, his invasion plans would be seriously hampered.

It is interesting to note that a similar operation to block the Germans taking Romanian oil took place during World War I. The Germans remembered that Colonel Tom Masterson had then won a D.S.O. "for helping to destroy Romanian oil installations, including those at the Iron Gates, before the German occupation of 1916."[5] Indeed, this same officer, Col. Masterson, was appointed to Belgrade in November, 1940, to take over control of the S.O.E. operations in Yugoslavia.

In World War II, Admiral Canaris, Head of Abwehr (the German Secret Service), had therefore correctly assumed that the British Secret Service "would initiate sabotage acts against the production centres of oil and against its means of transportation."[6] Hitler had alerted his spies about this danger.

Sir Alexander Glen, who in 1940 was Assistant Naval Attaché in Belgrade, has stressed the historical significance of the Danube as a major artery to Germany. He writes: [7]

"Certainly recognition of the Danube's importance was clear already in World War I with the British flotilla of shallow- draft gunboats under Admiral Troubridge, with whom Despard (Captain Despard, active in the 1940 operation) served, incidentally bringing Empress Zita to safety from Budapest in 1918. The oil section of M E W (Military Economic Warfare) under Maurice Bridgerian and Mark Turner were especially conscious of this already in 1938, as was the new DNI, Admiral Godfrey, who sent me to Belgrade in 1940 for this purpose."

Early attempts in 1939 and 1940 had failed, due to explosives that did not go off, men poorly disguised, and information leaked to the police. Geoffrey Household, in his autobiography, "Against the Wind", tells of a failed plan in which he took part to destroy the Ploiesti oil fields, this only shortly before Richard's "Danube Expedition". A mis-carried effort to block the Iron Gates was also made by a group including Merlin Minshall, who claimed "to have been one of the originals of Ian Fleming's James Bond, certainly he shared Bond's susceptibility for blondes."[8]

A British businessman, Julius Hanau, code-named "Caesar", had tried "to block the Iron Gates by blowing up the cliffs which tower over the Danube from the Yugoslavian side. This, it was hoped, would make the river unsafe for navigation for sometime, and so impede the flow of Romanian oil to Germany, but their preparatory tunnelling had been discovered by the Yugoslavian police during the winter (of 1940) and the plan had been abandoned.[9]

Following the expulsion in succession of Julius Hanau and Bill Bailey, Sir Alexander had taken over the responsibility for control of SOE activities. He has sent me this account:

"The Iron Gates were an obvious bottleneck and indeed there were two separate attempts. The first organised from Belgrade involved late in 1939 the purchase of a small holding on the Yugoslav side of the Kazan Gorge including a convenient small cave which was to be filled with high explosives and when exploded would bring down enough of the cliff to block the Gorge. Explosives were to be brought up by mule, in full view, by the way, of both the Romanian and Yugoslav frontier patrols, and the outcome was predictable, involving the expulsion from Belgrade of several SOE ("Special Operations Executive") members."

"The second attempt was more ambitious and more organised, involving the overall direction of Captain (later Admiral) Darell Watson RN, who was involved with Ploiesti itself."

Sir Alexander comments that "organisations such as SOE newly set up for clandestine work were new and in retrospect very amateur."

Now, financed by the the Ministry of Economic Warfare, an "Anglo-Danube Shipping Company" was set up, the Goeland Transport and Trading Co., which proceeded to buy or rent available river boats, so the Germans could not use them. They would also bribe the Danube pilots not to work for the Germans. Purchasing by MEW of Danube tugs and barges by these companies culminated, writes Sir Alexander, "in that of the Simon Schultz fleet based in Pancevo" (on the river near Belgrade) "to interdict their use to Germany. The attack on Yugoslavia in April 1941 brought all this to an end, the owners in Pancevo were executed, and an expensive investment terminated."

Speed in carrying out this mission was all important. Austria and Czechoslovakia were already occupied by Hitler; Hungary was collaborating with him, as was Bulgaria. Yugoslavia was being infiltrated, in order to neutralise Romania. So Romania, although fundamentally pro-Ally, was under heavy German pressure, and, although not invaded by Hitler, many high-ranking Nazis were coming into the country in civilian clothes, "smuggling in their weapons in empty tank cars." [10]

The plan of action, Richard was told, was for him and the saboteurs to land at Sulina, at the mouth of the Danube on the Black Sea, south of Odessa (Ukraine). (Here, in June, the Romanian border provinces of Besarabia and Northern Bukevina would be handed over to the Soviet Union, thanks to a secret pact made between Ribbentrop and Molotov in August, 1939.)

From Sulina, the men would have to undertake, by barge, the long and hazardous trip of over 500 miles up the river, especially dangerous due to the state of turmoil of the surrounding areas, with Nazi sympathisers, and Hitler's spies, everywhere.

Richard's special assignment was to command the barge on which the saboteurs would be transported. His was a key role, as he had to see that the barge was handled skilfully, and that it arrived safely at its destination, without arousing suspicion. He was an experienced river pilot already, exceptionally allowed by the pilots to keep the wheel himself when taking ships up the Thames. They had even told him that they would offer him a job as Thames River Pilot if he ever wanted it. He had, of course, sailed many times into the Black Sea, going to the port of Sulina and other Danube ports.

Before continuing with Richard's journey, an explanation may be of interest showing how in writing about the "Danube Plot" (as the Germans called it) I have had to work against smoke screens of "Disinformation",[11] particularly in confirmation of dates. In transcripts of German news broadcasts it is not surprising to find facts distorted. More difficult, there is no official confirmation of Richard's brief service with the Royal Navy. As they had warned him, there was no written record kept of this clandestine assignment. Not to be daunted, I had written to the Royal Navy Headquarters in London. A courteous secretary at the Admiralty checked the files, and could find no record of this, nor Richard's name in lists of officers. It was indeed, "Top Secret", and as far as the Navy is concerned, Richard a "non-person".

Richard told no one about it until about 30 years after it had taken place, when the "Official Secrets Act" would have expired. He then told me the story, in a purposefully vague way, with few explicit details, throwing a smoke screen over dates, what ship he was on, and names of people with whom he was involved. The story was told late at night, after a few drinks, as though it was still top secret. He later repeated the story to a few intimate friends, in a similar manner.

I was led to believe that the mission had occurred in 1941, after his three sinkings, as when he repeated the account of his interview at the Admiralty he would have the interviewer say: "You have three children?" Of course, in 1940, his third child had not been born. And, "You have been sunk three times?" For early 1940, this would have been incorrect.

Later, after his death, when I decided to write about his adventure, I could find nothing about such a mission to Romania for 1941. He had said: "I got on a merchant ship", but gave no name for the ship. I knew he had been without a berth and had had a shore job in March and April of '41. A further search showed no mention in his discharge papers that he had served on any ship at all during this period. This again, might have been "disinformation". Although the Med. by 1941 had been closed to merchant shipping, Richard might have been assigned to a Ministry of War transport. However, he always said: "I got back on my old ship." The *Mardinian*, of course, had been sunk by 1941.

To confuse the issue, I had been personally told by an eminent British historian that there had indeed been a joint Allied mission up the Danube, April 3 - June 21, 1941, under Wing Commander Gibson, of "Dam-Buster" fame, who had written a 50-page account of this. The connection here seemed to be two men in the team with Richard, explosives experts who later actually did take part in the "Dam Buster" mission with the famous RAF Squadron 617.

The longer I thought about this, however, the more suspicious I became that these facts were incorrect. Surely Commander Gibson of the RAF would not have been in charge of a Naval operation. The confusion arose, I later discovered, because a man named Gibson was the Senior Naval officer on the spot, in charge of the operation – he was Commander Gibson of the Royal Navy! It was he who wrote the report.

Thanks to help from Ivor Porter,[12] who was lecturer for the British Council at Bucharest University at the time; excerpts from the journal of Denis Wright, then British Vice-Consul at Constanța [13] (as quoted in Mr. Porter's book, "Operation Autonomous"); and records from the BBC Written Archives Centre, I felt that I was getting closer to the truth.

After this, came an especially helpful letter from the Foreign and Commonwealth Office, which included copies of reports of the mission made at the time by the Anglo-Danube Shipping Co.

Mr. Gervase Cowell, SOE Advisor to the FO, wrote: "What I can say with some certainty is that the operation in which your husband took part was the 1940 one. There was not a similar operation in 1941."

"Unfortunately there is no SOE record of the names of the naval personnel who took part, so the best that I can say is that the description of your husband's movements is convincing evidence that he was part of the operation in the attached papers."[14]

Note that I have since learnt that the SOE never kept written notes on their undercover operations, and their operators were not even allowed to keep diaries.

The reports from the Anglo-Danube Shipping Co. were originally sent to the Legation, which unfortunately employed some Germans on their staff; and might also have been read by pro-German Romanians at the company's offices. Therefore, these reports only dealt with the official explanation about the purpose of the expedition, and the movements of tugs, lighters, and barges on the river.

Following this, at Mr. Cowell's suggestion, I wrote to the Ministry of Defence, Naval Historical Branch, from whom I got the best response of all, telling me that "the `Report of Proceedings for the Expedition' has been preserved and is in the custody of the Public Record Office." Evidently, it had only recently been deposited there – after 50 years!

This kind officer, M. Aloon, from Naval Staff Duties (Historical Section), wrote: "I am sorry I cannot be more helpful, especially as your letter is extremely well laid out and argued and, more noticeably, shows ample evidence of personal research – a rarity in the 2,000 or more letters we receive each year." [15]

I now possess a copy of these Proceedings of the "Danube Expedition, 1940", as it was called, which was written by Commander Gibson, the officer in charge, and submitted to the Commander in Chief, Mediterranean, on August 20, 1940, the day he successfully delivered the flotilla of Danube River boats to the British in Alexandria. (Three days later, Commander Gibson was killed when HMS *Hostile*, the ship to which he had been transferred, hit a mine.)[16]

Commander Gibson's report, which is in detail, also takes the "official" line. The arrival of over 100 Naval officers disguised as seamen, with false passports, and fully armed, was bad enough in a neutral country, but the Romanian officials were willing to go along with this as long as it was not discovered by the Germans. The more important secret part of the mission was never put in writing, even in this confidential report. But much can be read between the lines.

So now I have fully verified that in March and April, 1940, an important naval operation did take place in Romania, under the joint sponsorship of the MEW and Section "R" (fore-runner of the SOE, which was not officially organised until July.) The S.S. *Mardinian* did disembark 68 "Naval Ratings and Officers" in Sulina. Richard was one of these.

But, before continuing with his story, here is even more that I have learnt about the organisation of the mission.

Part 2.- Background to Sabotage

As far back as 1938, three embryo organisations, which would in July, 1940, merge into the SOE, were studying "black propaganda" – "Electra House", under Sir Campbell Stuart; MIR ("Military Intelligence Research") headed by

Col. J.C.F. Holland and Major Colin Gubbins under the War office; and "Section D", under Col. Lawrence Grand. When the War Cabinet was set up, SOE also comprised Sections SO1 and SO2 from MI5. (In Cairo, the SOE was camouflaged as the "MO4".) Additionally, each branch of the Military Services had its own intelligence service.

"M.I.(R.) also had an affiliated organisation in the Middle East called `G'(R), which had distinguished itself early in the autumn of '39 by detailing a party of sappers in the Canal Zone for duty in Romania, issuing them with civilian clothes and passports and sending them to Romania, where it was hoped they would escape and succeed in blowing up a large quantity of oil consigned to Germany. The plan was wrecked because someone talked, and the party had to be sent back to the Middle East."[17]

Even before the war, Col. Gubbins had looked over the Iron Gates, with sabotage in mind. By 1940, disruptive operations began to be planned by the above mentioned groups, with the use of high explosives. Small scale paramilitary and para-naval operations were started. The under-cover groups often had to act independently on the spot and not consult the FO, who might say no to the project.

Geoffrey Household writes [18] that "Four trains left Dieppe in August, 1939, full of naval ratings for the Mediterranean Fleet, of officers of Wavell's army recalled from leave, of essential civilians staffing harbours, depots and cables; of everyone in fact who had to be at his post before Germany could close the overland routes to the east, and Italy delay the passage of the Med. Warsaw and Bucharest might be cut off at any moment, so the Polish and Romanian military missions were dispatched to Egypt from where, by rail or air, they could go to their stations on declaration of war." Two military missions claimed "to be so secret that they were not allowed to mix with their fellows during passage to Alexandria."

The Romanian mission "could only enter Romania secretly and as civilians, for the object of our mission was wholly destructive . . . to concert plans with picked engineers of the oil companies and our opposite numbers from the French Army for the damage of the fields and destruction of the refineries . . . When the plans, responsibilities and the methods had been worked out" (on the sites of the oil fields) "we were all taken on to the staff of the Legation, following the German practice of giving minor diplomatic status to the professional toughs."

"The Military Attaché, Geoffrey Macnab, was a master of his art, not allowing his right hand to know what his left hand was about. . . Our real operational command, oddly enough, was naval. All detailed planning was directed by Commander (later Admiral) Darell Watson, with the assistance of such local business men as Gardyne de Chastelain, sales manager of the British Unirea Oil Company, and W. Harris-Burland, head of the Anglo-

Danube Shipping Co."

Bickham Sweet-Escott, for 5 years in the SOE, reveals how, from their London Headquarters in St. Ermin's Hotel, "supplies of detonators, explosives, specially constructed time-fuses, weapons, and above all money" were collected and sent by train to the Balkans.

"The methods of keeping our people in the Balkan capitals supplied . . . seemed simple. . . There was a storeroom on the fourth floor full of such things . . . and it was one of my duties to assemble and pack them in large bags. . . The bags were then given to dispose of as they knew best to a number of young gentlemen complete with Wagon-Lits reservations to Bucharest; taxis, sometimes 2 or 3 if there were a heavy load, were summoned, the bags loaded, and off the party went to Victoria Station."[19]

Sir Alexander continues: "A new Naval Attaché in Belgrade, Captain Despard, brought detailed knowledge of the river, having served on one of HM gunboats on the Danube in 1917/18." (See Part 1) "He made a major contribution to the planning in Bucharest, especially with Lieutenant David Field (in real life Michael Mason, who had combined years in Arctic Canada with world class professional boxing and a large estate in Oxfordshire). Field played a major role both in Giurgiu and Bucharest, a John Buchan character of enterprise and competence", Sir Alexander recalls.

"These two men were essentially professional, hard bitten men who might have succeeded in the impossible. Their objective was to close the Danube, no petty harrassing or Boys' Own Paper Games, but the inexperience and folly of colleagues frustrated what might have been a 1000-1 chance."

According to the "FO report on the 1940 Operation", written by W. Harris Burland of the Anglo Danube Shipping Co.,[20] towards the end of 1939 sub-rosa plans were commenced to "draw up and plan for military operations on the Danube, involving the arming and manning by naval officers and ratings of several of the Goeland Company's vessels."

"The object of the scheme was never closely revealed" (my italics) "but it was understood to be partly to destroy Danube shipping in the event of emergency, and partly to attack any German armed vessels which might come down the river."

This would be the cover for the operation in which Richard would take part.

The stage had been well-set for the Danube Expedition.

Part 3.- "The Danube Expedition 1940"

Continuing Richard's story: so he set sail again, as Chief Officer of the *Mardinian*. None of the crew, bar the Captain, suspected that he was not just rejoining them as their regular First Mate, or that he would soon be leaving them.

The ship sailed from Liverpool March 7 for Constanţa, after having loaded on board a cargo of ammunition and explosives, "in 95 sealed crates disguised as and invoiced as CHRYSLER spares, destined for the CHRYSLER agent in Budapest, and to be transported in bond from Sulina via the Danube."[21]

"List of Arms shipped SS *Mardinian*:" [22]

4	.303" VICKERS machine guns with spare parts
12	LEWIS guns
20	Rifles
50	Revolvers
14,000	Rounds of .303" ammunition
10,000	Rounds Incendiary "
1,000	Rounds Revolver "
600-lbs.	H.E.
49	Limpets
5 Boxes of	Cannisters

Stopping at Milford Haven, the *Mardinian* left there on March 12, arriving at Gibraltar March 14. Milford Haven was an important Naval base during the war. It is quite possible that secret instructions were given there to the *Mardinian's* master, Captain J. Every.

Arriving in the Med. the ship rendez-voused with a Naval vessel, far out at sea, in the middle of the night. It would seem strange if Richard, as Chief Officer, did not know the exact location, but he never revealed it. I now have reason to believe that this was off the coast of Egypt, where specially trained sappers had been waiting to join the mission, along with a group from Malta. At a given signal, the *Mardinian* stopped and waited. In darkness a boat came alongside, and a British voice called:

"Permission to sword you?"

Those hearing this thought that "board you" was what was meant. Possibly it was an identification code. Permission granted, a motley crowd of darkly-clad, tough-looking men, carrying guns and heavy equipment, climbed onto the deck.

"The toughest looking bunch you've ever seen!" Richard would say. "They looked like pirates."

To the surprise of the merchantman's crew, they silently arranged their belongings, some in already prepared cabins, some on deck, while the Navy boat disappeared into the night.

There were 67 men. Richard, who had been told he would have a hand-picked group of a dozen or so, said he was amazed. But, it being wartime, no questions were asked. (The smaller group would identify themselves to Richard upon arrival to Sulina.)

Through help from Australia, I have learnt the identity of the ship which delivered the men. [23] This was the HMAS *Stuart*, flagship of an Australian Destroyer flotilla based in Malta. Called on German radio "the Scrap Iron Flotilla", this amusing title was unofficially adapted by the Australians.

These five old but sturdy vessels of World War I vintage had been giving good service transferring armaments to the coast of Africa.

The men who climbed aboard the *Mardinian* at midnight were especially chosen Naval volunteers for the Danube Expedition, among them 12 Australians. The majority of men had been stationed in Egypt. They assembled in Malta to undergo a 2-week training course in the use of explosives and weapons.

Before leaving, they were addressed by a top-ranking Royal Navy officer, believed to be the Commander-in-Chief of the Eastern Mediterranean Fleet himself, Admiral Andrew B. Cunningham. He told them that if anyone wanted to back out from this extremely dangerous operation, they would be allowed to do so without it being used against them. No one did.

The Admiral promised that if they got out alive, they would be "Mentioned in Dispatches", and sent home on leave.

"But we did not get either", later complained Zach Lardner, an Australian volunteer, in a memoir, "War Experience". Terry van Prooyen, another Australian chosen for this special service brigade, in an interview in the "Australian Post", (Nov. 19, 1987), noted that "we were given four shillings a day danger money (I think the Poms only got sixpence), and £10 each to buy civilian clothes." Additionally, each had to buy a suitcase, in which he was to lock his Naval uniform and cap.

I had often wondered how 67 men could be accomodated on a small freighter. Only recently, when reading Van Prooyen's memoirs, I discovered that a secret compartment had been made, hidden between 2 decks of cargo, and here the men stayed concealed until they reached the Danube. As no search was ever made of the ship when sailing through the Dardenelles, and along the coast of neutral Turkey, he suspected that this might have been discretely arranged ahead of time. Indeed, as Chief Officer, Richard himself must have supervised the construction of this compartment. It also would have been necessary for him to know the exact location of the rendez-vous, the identity of the ship, and how many men to expect. In any case, he continued to treat these details as "Top Secret" over the years, succeeding in covering them up very well when telling the story. When I finally found out about the secret compartment, I believed this gave me ample cause to be suspicious of the *Mardinian* on her next voyage!

They sailed past Greece, still unoccupied by the Axis. (The first U-boats would not be into the Med. until September, although much earlier the Italians had planted mines.) Then they went through the Bosphorus, and along the coast of Bulgaria. This was uncertain territory. German aid in rearming the country was well underway, leading to a take-over by the Germans. When the *Mardinian's* men would sail up the Danube, the left bank in Bulgaria would be a danger spot for them.

On they went to Romania, and north along the coast to Sulina, where they were to disembark, arriving there on March 29.

Commander Gibson, with a flotilla of tugs, tankers and assorted barges, had in the meantime been waiting since March 15, upriver at Braila. These vessels were the two powerful sea-going tugs, *Princess Elisabeth* and *Britannia*; four motor tankers, *Danube Shell II., King George, Lord Byron*, and *Scotland*, plus the large English *Schleppe* (lighter) *Termonde*, and, additionally, many other barges. The tugs and tankers had been "fitted out to accommodate a party of about 100 Naval officers and ratings. This work was carried out at Braila under the supervision of the Naval Attaché's assistants, who also arranged to put on board the two tugs (unknown, of course, to the port authorities), "a quantity of stores and equipment, including firearms, ammunition, detonators and 6 wireless transmitters for distribution at a later date." [24]

In these ships already were 17 more RN officers and "ratings", who had arrived in Constanţa the day before from Egypt on the "Transilvania" (of the Romanian State Maritime Service). There were also 4 Frenchmen, who had also come from Egypt. Additionally, 12 more men had arrived from England overland. These men were all in "civies", disguised as "merchant seamen" to man the Danube river boats.

It is possible that Richard had not been told that his own mission would be part of a much bigger operation. If he knew, he kept it to himself. In telling the story of what happened on the river, he only mentioned the small group with whom he was assigned. Upon landing, they must have separated from the others, and gone their own way. True to secret service methods, for security reasons one group would not be informed what the others were doing.

On March 28, Commander Gibson took the two tugs and the *Termonde* down to Sulina. Accompanying him was Captain Constantinescu, a Romanian Reserve officer who was employed by Goeland, and was helpful with the port authorities. G.B. Marshall, who was also employed by Goeland, was with them. Marshall was largely responsible for the local organisation of the expedition. He "was temporarily attached to the Naval Attaché's staff to act as liaison with the Romanian authorities."[25] He would remain on the *Princess Elisabeth*, flagship of the flotilla, during the whole operation.

Upon arrival of the *Mardinian* the following day, they went out into the roads to meet the ship, "accompanied", wrote Commander Gibson,[26] "by *Bayard*, a small semi-seagoing tug, which I wanted for communication with *Mardinian* before she entered the river. *Bayard* flies the Greek flag."

Incidentally, the party were forced by local law to employ some native seamen and cooks, the majority of whom "were Greeks of a very low order, dishonest and unreliable . . . who caused our agencies at Braila and Sulina untold trouble by making exaggerated demands for remuneration and generally using obstructive tactics to obtain better terms", reported Marshall. The *Princess Elisabeth,* which played a key role in the flotilla, had a Greek Captain of this order, about whom more is written later.

Commander Gibson hoped to save time by transferring the men and cargo from the *Mardinian* onto his ships in the roads, but the weather, which was blowing a gale, defeated them, and they had to bring the ship into port.

Gibson reported [27] that "At this time there was still a considerable amount of ice coming down the river and the basin at Braila was just thawing." Even upriver in Giurgiu, recollected Terry van Prooyen, "it was bitterly cold – the Danube was flowing fast, with ice everywhere."

"We were all expecting some decisive move on the part of the Germans as soon as navigation was restarted", continued Gibson, "and I was therefore most anxious that, as soon as the rest of the party and arms arrived in the country, the ships should go upriver and arm with the least possible delay." The plan was to go to Giurgiu, where the International Waters began, and there to redistribute the cargo of arms among the other boats.

In Sulina, the principal officer was the Commandant of the Garrison, Commander Dimitriu of the Romanian Navy. He was apparently friendly to the Allies. However, "the Government was only prepared to look the other way so long as there was no Franco-British activities so open and outrageous that the German legation would be justified in protesting."[28] "Romanians knew about the armaments. What was not known to the British was that the Ministry of War and Marine was being subsidised by the Germans and accordingly set out to wreck the undertaking." Only a few days later, a German report said: [29]

"6 tons of gelignite, three pounders, grenades, etc." had been unloaded from the *Mardinian* alone. "The military stores were loaded on to the lighter *Termonde* and declared as oil equipment en route for Budapest."

But the Germans had this wrong! It was much more than they had estimated. G.B. Marshall wrote in his report that the *Mardinian* had unloaded a cargo of 30 tons.

Not only the cargo seemed suspicious, but the large number of men disembarking, plus the fact that they all had bogus passports issued in Malta, where the forgers did not know how to fabricate old stamps and visas. "Similarly," wrote Admiral Cunningham, Commander-in-Chief, Mediterranean, "when forged bills of lading were required for S.S. *Mardinian*, these had to be produced in a very amateur way by two officials of my staff who had, I believe and hope, no previous experience in the art."[30]

As an example, Commander Gibson's visa for Romania read: "A.P. Gibson, Tugmaster (Uncertified)"! In spite of the obviously phoney passports, transhipment of the men was allowed. However, it was not until the following evening, March 30, that they could leave for Braila, as it took time to tranship the cargo to the *Termonde*, which then had to be sealed until they reached International Waters. A Customs guard was assigned to accompany them as far as Giurgiu on the tug which towed the "arms lighter". They were also shadowed by a "Monitor" (a Romanian Gunboat). Their orders, not revealed until they reached Braila, said Terry van Prooyen, were to sail to Orsova (upriver from the Iron Gates) and there block the Danube by blowing up the lighters.

Additional comment and speculation about the real nature of their cargo had been aroused before leaving Sulina when they had been forced to pay duty of £900. This was considered noticeably too high for crates of machine parts, and bribery was much more likely.

Worse problems were to follow:

". . . on arrival at Braila it was learnt that one of the Naval Attaché's assistants had been involved in a brawl and had threatened a well-known doctor with a revolver. . . This point is mentioned as it is considered the origin of the trouble subsequently encountered." [31] Two British Navy Lieutenants were actually involved in this episode, one being Minshall, the "James Bond" character who liked blondes.

When the men from *Mardinian* arrived in Braila they found the 2 men had been in jail. Only with the help of the British Legation was the incident smoothed over, the men transferred to Bucharest, and soon sent out of the country.

It was bad publicity for the start of a secret expedition, which was no longer very secret. Not known then to Commander Gibson, people on the street were already talking about the men having weapons. Perhaps, when given shore leave, some of the party had talked too openly. Geoffrey Household, whose own attempt to blow up the Ploiesti oil wells had been uncovered just before the Danube Expedition took place, remarked that "some of the bluffer British, while they could be trusted to blow up anything, including if necessary, themselves, were incapable of not talking loudly in cafés." [32]

Another development that boded no good was that the men had been visiting prostitutes in Sulina, with upsetting results. Enclosure No. 2 of the "Danube Expedition" file concerns "Health of the Romanian Special Service Party":

"During the five months from April to August, 1940, the health of the party was good. The only problem was a high incidence of venereal disease. There were eleven new cases. This is due to the extremely high local incidence, which is estimated at between 80-95% of the local population over the age of 15. . ."

Becoming frightened that they might have caught syphilis, upon arrival in Giurgiu some of the men consulted the port doctor, who turned out to be German, and an informer.

In Braila, nearly 36 hours were wasted smoothing over such problems, and redistributing the units among the tugs and lighters, "with a number of empty lighters in tow, to give the operation the appearance of a purely commercial character." [33] These barges were, Sir Alexander informed me, later loaded with scrap and concrete and were to be sunk in the Iron Gates Canal to impede navigation. "I am of the opinion", wrote Sir Alexander, "that the operation was well enough known to the Romanian authorities and the Germans and the likelihood of its purpose being achieved was small."

Nevertheless, at 23.59 the night of April 1st, the unwieldy and conspicuous party proceeded upriver, arriving in Giurgiu on April 3rd. Van Prooyen noticed along the way that "Romania was full of Germans, every second ship tied up along the river bank carried the Swastika."

Returning now to Richard's part of the story, and the way he always told it: (The facts I have now learnt about the expedition bear out that there is overwhelming evidence to show that this is what really happened.)

He said that upon arrival in Sulina, after Immigration had cleared all their passports, he and his group, consisting of eleven sappers and dynamiting experts, were quickly whisked away by a Legation official, and taken to where a barge lay concealed from public view. It had been well-prepared ahead of time, and was only waiting for them to come on board. This was the barge, Richard was told, on which the Duke and Duchess of Windsor had spent part of their honeymoon! Still regally fitted out, it had a large locker full of vintage wines and liquor. The safe contained quantities of money in assorted currencies. They were not to worry how the money was spent. They had been given instructions to entertain people lavishly along the way. The barge must have been self-propelled, which would have made it easy to handle; and they found a cook, and a few trust-worthy (it was hoped!) native crew members already on board.

I have tried to find the name of this barge, as it might have been mentioned in one of the dozens of books written about the Windsors, but have had no success. There is no reason to suspect that such a barge did not exist, as HRH the Duke had particularly asked the press to leave them alone, as they wanted a strictly private honeymoon. Little has been written about these 3 months in their lives. It is known, however, that they travelled from Vienna to Budapest during this period, on their way to stay at an Hungarian hunting lodge, "Borsodivanka". So, it is perfectly possible that they enjoyed a trip on the Danube by barge.[34]

However, always suspicious about "disinformation", I tried, in my mind, to turn the arms lighter *Termonde* into Richard's barge, but too many known facts worked against this. The *Termonde* was a working barge, with no accommodation, and the men lived on the tug that towed it, usually the *Princess Elisabeth*, but sometimes *Britannia*. Richard never mentioned a tug, or being with any other men except his own small group. When the *Termonde* was searched in Giurgiu, only beer cans were found – no mention of any bottles of better drinks! Richard's barge, he said, was never searched, nor his cases opened. He did not know of the difficulties the rest of the party were having in Giurgiu, nor what had caused the difficulties. The fact that he finally had to turn back came as a complete surprise. Richard's barge had no radio, whereas the 2 tugs and the 4 tankers had, so the men on these could have known when the Germans broadcast about the expedition.

Richard and his men were disguised as traders, albeit wealthy ones. It is to be hoped they did not have their Navy uniforms with them on board. The men on the bigger boats had been ordered to have them in locked suitcases – a stupid order, as naturally the Germans found them, and all was up! As the barge had been lying unused, there was nothing surprising in their having taken it over as a trading vessel. At first, going independently, there seemed to be nothing to connect them with the larger group of suspicious "traders". In reality, Richard's barge also contained many sealed crates similar to those on the *Termonde*, marked "IN TRANSIT", containing not merchandise, but explosives, guns and ammunition. This had been collected from quantities of arms already brought clandestinely into Romania. The "IN TRANSIT" seals were no doubt forged.

All the men, including Richard, were well armed, "bristling with weapons", as Richard put it, concealed under their clothing. With German troops moving into surrounding countries, many of whose populations were pro-Nazi, they could take no chances. These countries, however, did contain strongly independent groups remaining friendly to the Allies, particularly in Yugoslavia. The Romanian population was about 100% pro-Ally, but the officials were mortally afraid of irritating the Germans. Friendly Romanians in high positions had been forewarned of the mission, but could only be helpful as long as it remained undercover. Gafencu, the Foreign Minister, was pro-Ally, but had little power against German officials already in the country, nor the powerful pro-Nazi "Iron Guard", set up by King Carol.

Sadly, the size of the operation made it too conspicuous to insure success. With so many unusual river craft moving upstream, manned by strange crews, it looked immediately questionable.

Richard, trained to command, had wasted no time in getting going, nor in worrying about unknown obstacles. They slipped quietly upriver, having made a start of nearly 12 hours ahead of the main group. They had gained another 48 hours, at least, before this unwieldy flotilla behind them had even left Braila.

Along the river on the Romanian side an underground network had been prepared for their approach, although their sympathizers had not been told any details about the mission, as this might have endangered them. So, in each place they stopped for their "trading", they were contacted by people who expected them, and who were helpful. They brought anything needed on board, pretended to trade, and told the men what the situation was locally.

Other people came on board who were not friendly, who posed as government officials, or local businessmen, but who were actually secret informers to the Nazis. They would insist upon inspecting the barge and its contents, after showing that they thought there was something suspicious about it.

In such cases, Richard would postpone showing them "samples" of the merchandise, Acting the part of a genial host, he would insist that first they must have some refreshment. A heavy meal would be served, with plentiful drinks. When the guests had gotten into a mellow mood, presents of money were passed around, with the explanation:

"We would be happy if you would accept a little gift to help your community, as we know that living conditions here are at present very difficult."

The presents were quickly accepted. If, after further drinks, they still seemed uncertain about the use of the barge, Richard would give a secret signal, and some of his men (all trained assassins) would ask the visitors to accompany them ashore for an after lunch stroll, as "a walk in the countryside would be beneficial"; or, perhaps they would ask to be taken for a tour of a village.

Once ashore, they would wander around until they found an uninhabited area, where the "visitors" were quietly "liquidated". This was a gruesome enterprise, but a necessary ingredient of the "fortunes of war".

Richard, himself, did not take part in these James Bond tactics, although he knew what was going on. His job was to look after the barge, upon which their safety depended. He had to remain on board, constantly alert, and always, himself, prepared for sudden ambush.

Making good progress upriver, they successfully passed Giurgiu, about half way to the Iron Gates. Here the flotilla following them was to be held up. They did not stop at this port, but remaining in mid-stream to avoid Customs, they sailed undetected (or so they thought), into International Waters. Such manoeuvres, when uncovered by the Germans would give them good cause for complaint. G.B. Marshall, when summarizing the expedition, said that during the course of the expedition "almost every rule governing navigation on the Danube had been broken." [35]

Continuing onwards for about a day and a half, the barge was fast approaching the Iron Gates, and the men were becoming hopeful that they might reach their objective. Nearing Yugoslavia, however, and Turnu Severin, the last Romanian port before the Iron Gates, news was rushed to them by their contact, who had anxiously been looking out for them. He told them that the Fascist traitor, William Joyce, who broadcast as "Lord Haw Haw", had somehow discovered the true purpose of their mission, and had just given out information about it on his daily radio program "Germany Calling", and had even mentioned Richard by name!

They were now sitting ducks, and to continue would be useless. The mission would have to be scrapped. They were strongly advised to try immediately to leave Romania. An overland escape through Yugoslavia would be too long, difficult, and dangerous. They did not have a guide, and did not know the language. Their only chance was to return down river very fast (the current would help them along), relying on their underground friends for any needed help. This is what they did. The Germans must have been too occupied elsewhere to bother about them. They successfully managed the trip back as far as Giurgiu. There, their courageous voyage came to an abrupt end.

I have been unable to locate a transcript of "Lord Haw Haw's" broadcast, which must have been picked up on short-wave, but I have the following excerpts from the daily "Deutschland" newscasts, transmitted in German for Germany. [36]

11.30 BST   8.4.40   Long Wave
DANUBE PLOT. "Radio News Service has just received the following message: An English attempt at military sabotage by military means on the Danube was the preface to critical action against the Danube states. As D.N.B. learns, the Foreign Office is in possession of precise evidence of a monstrous attempt at sabotage planned on a large scale by the English Secret Service with the support of British military on the Danube."

13.00 BST   8.4.40
DANUBE PLOT; FURTHER DETAILS. "As already reported, the criminal terrorists of the English Secret Service have carried out a monstrous outrage against the peace of South-East Europe in an attempt to dislocate Danube shipping. . ."

"We learn the following details of the attempt of the British Secret Service to dislocate the Danube, by means of the British military and dynamite, as the trade route of the South-Eastern States.

"Last Friday, 5th April, it became known that, accompanied by the English speed boats, the tugs *Britannia, Elizabeth, Danubia Shell* (?), *King George, Cobbler* (?) and *Lord Byron*, further a Greek tug with four trailer barges chartered by England, and *Albion* with five trailer barges, were sailing up the Danube. Through an indiscretion of the members of the English crew, the following became known about the tasks, cargoes, and crews of these ships. On board the English ships were quantities of revolvers, signal pistols, hand grenades, machine guns, depth charges, mines, empty shell cases, and several thousand boxes of dynamite. The crews consisted of over 100 special English soldiers with special passports, disguised as sailors, further five English officers, several flying officers, technical personnel of an English dynamiting detachment, and sappers. The cargo was described as transit goods. The leader of the British action is an English Secret Service chief in Romania, disguised as a British vice-consul. The aim of this enterprise, drawn up on military lines, was the dislocating of trade between the South-Eastern countries and Germany. . . By abusing diplomatic rights, falsifying the rules of international trade traffic, and breaking the neutrality of the South Eastern countries, England makes herself guilty of a monstrous violation of neutrality with this attempt which she prepared on neutral soil as a military action against Germany. In the Romanian port of Giurgiu, Romanian control units detained the suspicious ships."

21.00 BST   8.4.40
DANUBE PLOT; B.S.S. CHOOSES "IRON GATES". "Concerning the incredible act of sabotage of the British Secret Service, it is reported from Bucharest that for days the movements of British ships have been known in the Romanian capital. . . Romanian competent quarters consider that the act of destruction was to be aimed at the Iron Gates. It had been intended to block the Danube by blowing up portions of the banks and to cause them to collapse into the Danube."

ROME (ITALY)   SHORT WAVE;   IN ITALIAN FOR ITALY
13.20 BST   9.4.40
BRITISH EXPLOSIVES ON DANUBE. "Much prominence is given to the planned action of *British naval units disguised as a commercial convoy*" (my italics) "which was aimed at severing the Danube trade with Germany. A Bucharest message reveals that 61 members of the British Royal Navy were arrested in Giurgiu. The arrests took place on the denunciation of a Romanian sailor."

My note: the "Romanian Sailor" was, no doubt, the Greek captain of the *Princess Elisabeth*. The "61" men arrested were detained onboard their ships, but were later released with the understanding that they would not continue upriver. Richard's group, by the way, were never arrested, nor was the cargo on his barge opened for the whole time he was on it.

While Richard and his men were still upriver, here is what had happened to the rest of the party:

> April 3) The flotilla had arrived in Giurgiu, where they anchored in two groups amidstream, thinking, I believe, that they were in International waters, and could start reorganizing. It was from here that they had planned to get a group of the men ashore with their equipment, who should continue undercover to Ploiesti to try to blow up the oil wells. If they were questioned by Port Authorities at their anchorage, their official reason for stopping there was to take on oil.

The *Princess Elisabeth* and the *Termonde*, first to arrive, were immediately boarded by the Customs, Port Police, and Harbourmaster's officials, and were given a very thorough search. On the *Princess Elisabeth* British Naval uniforms were discovered (proving that the men were not just simple sailors), arms, and money – £500. in cash, which seemed to upset them more than anything.

Without a doubt, it had been Tsimaris, the Greek Captain, who had forewarned the Port Captain about the arms. This man later disappeared ashore.

"Unfortunately," wrote Commander Gibson,[37] "in Romania the authority who conducts a search is the Captain of the Ports department and the Captain of the Port in Giurgiu is a Pro German and a scoundrel. . . This officer, I understand, started life in the Romanian Navy. He was, however, convicted of stealing a small sum of money and was removed from the service. Fortunately for himself he was related to Admiral Pais (at present the Secretary of State in the Ministry of Air and Marine) and so obtained employment in the Harbour Master's department. During our stay at Giurgiu he was frequently seen in conversation with an Official from the Office of the German Naval Attaché who was in Giurgiu at the time.

"Drencianu (the Captain of the Port) does not come onboard himself on these occasions; the proceedings are conducted by his second in command, who is I am told a Transylvanian German and behaves as such."

Things, however, were smoothed over by the British consul on this occasion, and later in the day, some of the men were allowed shore leave. Serious trouble was to follow. These men, as I have previously written, went to the doctor, who they did not know was German, and did too much talking. Van Prooyen has written that a curfew was ordered, but later relaxed enough to allow the men about 2 hours leave off the ships every day. "We drank ashore with the Jerries. It was a really strange affair."

Sir Alexander, who was in Giurgiu at the time, has verified that working on shore with Commander Field "were others who lacked security or even discretion, resulting in the operation being finally blown in a fracas in a nightclub, if I recall in Giurgiu itself."

The man whose stupidity and irrational behaviour was specifically responsible for the disaster was a British colleague. He was knocked out flat by the former boxer, Mason (alias Field), but it was too late to salvage the operation.

This explains why the mission failed. Richard, himself, never knew how they were betrayed.

> April 4) The whole group of ships put in to the port at Giurgiu, where they anchored, waiting to take on oil. Delaying tactics were used by the Port Authorities before permission to get the oil was granted.
>
> April 5) The *Princess Elisabeth* and the tanker *King George* proceeded to the oiling berth, 4 miles below the town, leaving the *Termonde* and the remaining ships and barges at anchor.

Commander Gibson, that same day, went to Bucharest by car to consult people at the British Legation about their problems. With the spotlight on them, the Ploiesti sabotage idea would have to be scrapped, especially as it had become known that the region of the oil fields was now well-guarded and swarming with Germans.

Before leaving the *Princess Elisabeth,* he had sent Commander Field to the *Termonde*, as there was no officer on board, to see that it was not interfered with. However, the same afternoon, under pressure from German officials, the Customs again searched this lighter. Mr. Embury, the British Consul in Giurgiu, as well as Commander Field, was onboard when the authorities came, but could not stop them. They went into the hold, where they broke the IN TRANSIT seals, and opened up the crates. The cargo was immediately confiscated, although it was not unloaded ashore until the following day, as the British, playing for time, said it was very dangerous to handle without expert supervision, and might explode!

"On one ship alone more than 400 sealed boxes were found to contain large quantities of high explosives", reported Deutschlander radio (11.30 BST 8.4.40).[38] It was later said that it required 19 trucks to contain the cargo.

"British circles, while admitting that the explosive material was on the boats, protest against the seizure, saying the material was destined for destruction of Allied vessels in case of sudden German invasion. The British Chargé d'Affaires made representations requesting the release of the seized goods." (ROME 13.20 BST 9.4.40)

Commander Gibson writes that it was agreed in a deal "made between Hankey" (British Chargé d'Affaires) "and Gafencu that the Romanians should take over the whole lot giving us the right of periodical examination."[39] Needless to say, the British never got their armaments back.

German radio continued: (8.4.40   13.00   BST)[40]

"Detailed evidence concerning this attempt at sabotage planned on a large scale by the English Secret Service, with the help of English military on the Danube, is in the possession of the Foreign Office.

"With machine guns and quick-firing guns, the ships could be turned into warships. From orders found on the ship it is evident that, in case the dynamiting scheme was disturbed by frontier guards or Government troops of some of the South Eastern countries, landing manoeuvres were to have been carried out and sabotage was to be conducted from that base. Certain points of the Danube banks and waterfalls were to have been blown up, and freight barges were to be sunk in the navigable channel of the river. Certain parts of the Danube were to have been jammed with mines, and the navigable channel blocked by the use of depth charges. Swift action by the Romanian police authorities frustrated this monstrous outrage against the peace and order of South-Eastern Europe."

19.00 BST
"From the instructions found it was clear that these were Government troops who intended to carry out a landing manoeuvre on the South-Eastern States and from this base to perpetrate acts of sabotage. They were to blow up certain parts of the Danube cataracts and to sink barges in the shipping channels. Further, they were to lay mines and depth charges in certain parts of the Danube."

19.00 BST   9.4.40   DEUTSCHLANDSENDER (Germany)
BRITISH SABOTAGE IN ROMANIA; NEW PLANS. "New English sabotage plans in Romania are now reported from Bucharest. In Constanta a fortnight ago, various cases containing so-called bomb grenades of English origin were confiscated. These shells are particularly suitable for destroying the subterranean pipe lines of oil shafts, and thus allowing the oil to trickle back into the earth."

> April 6) Gafencu informed the British Legation that he insisted that some of the men involved be sent out of the country. Gibson, in his report, writes:[41]
> "I finally left for Giurgiu . . . .with orders to send eleven men and one officer to Constanţa by train for passage to the Mediterranean."

Without a doubt, this carefully specific number, "11 men and one officer", referred to Richard and his saboteurs – proving that both German and Romanian authorities knew about them right away!

By then, Richard and his group had safely arrived in Giurgiu, and had boarded the *Princess Elisabeth*. Presumably, their arms and crates had been jettisoned along the way. No doubt the barge, itself, had also mysteriously disappeared.

When Commander Gibson arrived back that evening, a full gale was blowing and embarkation was difficult.

"As soon as I did get off to the ships I ordered the departure of one A.B. from each unit and one officer (other than a Commanding Officer). The men were to be drawn for."

This story, of course, was fabricated so he would not have to admit or put in writing that Richard and his men formed a special unit that the Germans wanted to get rid of.

Gibson continues: "I had arrived onboard about 19.30 so it was not possible to send the men ashore until the following morning. . . Embury had arrived at midnight previously but had been unable to get aboard. He finally got onboard at 07.30 bringing me news from Hankey (the Legation's Minister of Foreign Affairs) that I was to send the men ashore as soon as possible and that a Romanian Officer would accompany them to Constanța."[42]

They were considered to be very dangerous men, indeed!

"Yet our naval personnel were not interned; they were expelled and allowed to return to their bases in Malta and Egypt unscathed", Ivor Porter comments.[43] Apparently, the Romanian authorities still, underneath, had pro-Ally sympathies.

> April 7) Cmdr. Gibson wrote:[44] "We tried to land the men using *Britannia* as a Picket Boat but she broke down as she shoved off from alongside the remainder and had to anchor. Later, *Princess Elisabeth* got underway and landed the men, who proceeded to Bucharest by taxi. Hankey's instructions to me stated that the incident was finally settled. . . in the meantime our release was obtained on condition that we went down river."

After the searches, Cmdr. Gibson burnt all his records and crew lists, and told the officers in charge of the other boats to do the same. Perhaps that is one reason why there are no lists of names in his report, nor mention of their assignments. In the "List of Enclosures to Letter of Proceedings Concerning Work of the Danube Expedition, 1940", "Enclosure No. 5 – Movements of Personnel", has been crossed out in ink and is missing.

> April 8) Denis Wright, the Vice-Consul in Constanța, "noted that as a gesture to the Germans, the Romanians had expelled 12 seamen whom he had escorted on board a British tanker bound for Istanbul." [45]

> This corresponds to Richard's own account. Although he did not mention Wright by name, he said that "thanks to skilful management by our British friends" they found a tanker waiting in Constanța to pick them up.

On the same day, Gafenco decided that it was not enough to deport this group. The ships were overmanned, he said, and asked for 30 more, including the 12 RAN, to be sent away. This Gibson did, getting them off the ships, then overland to Braila, not out of the country. Arriving there with the ships, he found the port authorities would not allow the men back onboard; however, he smuggled them back, and set sail. There was a sea-chase, but he succeeded in out-sailing the river patrols and getting down to Sulina.

By April 23, Gafencu was asking for Gibson and all his men to leave the country! But Gibson, with a considerable number of men, managed to stay on. After many vicissitudes, he succeeded in getting most of the fleet of river boats, including their voluntary crews, out of Romania, and delivered safely to the British in Egypt by August – but that is another story in itself.

"On 14 April Manfred von Killinger, a `diplomat' with high Nazi connections, who had been sent to Eastern Europe to impede `the enemy's secret operations', reported to Berlin the successful defeat of the Iron Gates operation." [46]

Summing it up, G.B. Marshall wrote:[47] "It must be admitted that the expedition was ill-conceived, badly organised and proved a dismal and costly failure."

I am no military expert myself, but it does seem obvious that a smaller, less conspicuous group might have had greater chance of success.

Commander Gibson, however, was less pessimistic about the outcome, writing after the failure of the Iron Gates project:

"The Romanians also started ejecting foreigners from the country, including Germans. . . At the same time the International Commission of the Danube produced a large number of new regulations concerning river craft and navigation on the Danube generally. I think our activities must have been responsible for the spate of legislation which WAS very hampering to the German trade on the river. So the expedition had been of definite value although our teeth had been drawn." [48]

Arriving back in Istanbul, Richard had met his "contact", in order to arrange the trip home. This man turned out to be Welsh, a "Mr. Jones"! Amazingly, they met again by chance in Llanfair, near Harlech, after the war.

The *Mardinian*, which had gone to Thessaloniki, sailed back to Istanbul, where she picked up the men on April 15. Then, stopping at the Turkish ports of Rodesto (today called "Tekirdag") on the Sea of Marmara, Burghaz and Izmir (Smyrna), after leaving off some of the men who would return to their outfits in Egypt and Malta. she continued on to Gibraltar, arriving to her home port of Liverpool on May 20.

Before leaving the Mediterranean, the men had a rendez-vous, "somewhere at sea", with the Admiral of the Fleet, Andrew Cunningham. They were invited on board his flag-ship, HMS *Warspite*, as he was most anxious to hear their story firsthand.

Richard always said that this was Lord Mountbatten. No doubt this was a bit of disinformation to confuse his listeners, as he felt he should not be too specific when telling the story, but this would have been easily seen through for those familiar with the Naval history of the war. Mountbatten was at that time the Captain of the destroyer *Kelly*, then engaged in battle off the coast of Norway, and guarding the "North Western Approaches". He did not become Admiral of the Mediterranean Fleet until after the war.

The Admiral then on *Warspite* was Sir Andrew B. Cunningham, and it was he who later received Commander Gibson's written report on the Danube Expedition. Cunningham, who in 1942 would become Allied Naval Commander-in-Chief under Eisenhower, has been described by Walter Monckton (Acting Minister of State in Cairo, 1942) as an officer embodying the same gallant and courageous Naval tradition as Mountbatten himself. "A sea-dog if ever there was one, there was no creek in the Mediterranean he did not know, no battle which was fought there he did not understand, and could not have fought again, and there was not an Italian ship which put to sea which was not as afraid of his name as the Spaniards used to be of Drake's." [49]

Richard said that the Admiral interviewed him personally and listened carefully to his detailed account of the escapade. He thanked Richard warmly for his help. He also talked to the eleven others, telling them that he thought they had carried out the mission as well as possible under the circumstances. It was not their fault that they had been betrayed. Although it had not succeeded he regretted that the effort could not be publicly recognised, and those involved rewarded.

It was, indeed, "The Magnificent Failure". Shortly after the war, Richard heard that a book about the mission, with this title, had been written by a newspaper man, who had somehow unearthed the story. Perhaps this book was censored before it ever appeared. Richard himself had kept his vow of secrecy. Even today, it has been difficult to piece the full story together from the incomplete fragments published. Some Australians, hearing rumours about it, thought it was a tall story someone had made up.

Sir Alexander Glen has written to me describing the follow-up of the operation, which I do not believe Richard ever knew.

"This all sounds a tragic and ill thought out piece of history but the Danube was not forgotten, and in 1943, only two years later, three causes combined to make possible earlier operational objectives: the development of long range aircraft together with that by HMS *Vernon* of more mines capable of being dropped in shallow water, and Italian bases.

"Early 1943: Major Greenwood and Rootham with Cetnik [50] forces from Homoye made an attack on shipping in the Iron Gates with success.

"Autumn 1944: Start of the aerial mines laying by RAF, continuing through spring, 1944. Some 2000 mines were dropped into the Danube, mostly upriver from Vidin, and down river from Pancevo. The cost was, I believe, one aircraft, the outcome paralysis of upriver traffic but with the unexpected bonus of unflinching desperate impact on the Wehrmacht's supply to their forces in the Caucasus and even more on their later withdrawal from the Crimea.

"Credit for this must largely go to Admiral of the Fleet Sir John Cunningham, (not to be confused with Sir Andrew B.), who in his own words was `a convinced Danubian', with equal credit to Marshall of the Air Force Sir John Slessor.

Sir Alexander concludes:

"Your husband's earlier efforts were in no sense in vain."

It is a pity that Richard and all the others involved could never see the letter to the Secretary of the Admiralty which accompanied Commander Gibson's report, written by Admiral Sir Andrew B. Cunningham on August 20, 1940, and marked: "Secret".[51] Summing up the expedition, he wrote:

"This interesting report tells its own story of the resource, determination and cheerfulness which animated the officers and men selected for this difficult and disappointing enterprise.

"All the officers and men who were selected from the Fleet for this enterprise carried out their duties in a most able manner and their loyalty and cheerfulness under the most adverse conditions was beyond praise."

AUSTRALIANS
A Special Note

So long afterwards, all this is now a part of history. Much as I love Great Britain, my American heritage is not so secretive as the British. Like the Australians, I believe there comes a time when the public has a right to know what actually went on "Behind the Scenes" in Government, the Armed Forces, and yes, also in the Secret Service.

Terry van Prooyen believed that the Australians who took part in the operation should have received some recognition. His daughter-in-law, Melissa van Prooyen, herself a Petty Officer in the RAN, believes the same. She has herself written a short outline of the operation, used as a "Brief" for her management training course.

Admiral Cunningham did not live up to his promise of "Mention in Dispatches" for the men. Perhaps this had been wishful thinking on his part. Naval Intelligence and the FO would surely have been opposed to any publicity. It would have been impossible to give the Australians any specal mention over the others, as the Australian Armed Forces were under British Operational Control of the Admiralty during the war. All the men involved had been told at the start that none would ever receive recognition, and no records would be kept of what they had done. If it had not been kept quiet at the time, and for a great many years afterwards, Britain might have found herself in a badly compromised position.

I would like to end this account by mentioning the names now known of RAN men who valiantly took part. Sad to say, most of these have died.

RANVR	Lt. Scott	Commanded motor tanker *King George IV* on the Danube
RANR	Sub. Lt. Milne	Commanded motor tanker *Scotland*
RAN		
AB	Frank Barry	From H.M.A.S. *Stuart*
"	Arthur Collins	
"	Joe Dix	
"	Dominic Owens	
"	Parkhurst	
"	Terry van Prooyen	Served on *King George IV*
"	J. Sherwood	
Officer's Steward	Harry Craven	From H.M.A.S. *Stuart*
Stoker	R. "Zach" Lardner	
"	F. Peale	
"	"Curly" Sutton	

3 others, either from *Voyager* or *Vampire*,
Baumgarten, Mahoney and Scardon (positions unknown).

9. THE RAF

After "The Magnificent Failure", Richard resumed his job with Ellerman. His family, as he had thought, upon his return showed no curiosity about where he had been.

Richard did not realise it, but his long service with the Ellerman Line was now coming to an end. After his three sinkings, he would never again put to sea as one of their regular contract officers. Fearing that on another voyage he might be lost, the Company told him:

"You will be of more use to us as a Marine Superintendent than returning to sea. We do not want to risk losing one of our best men."

When ashore in Liverpool, besides his work for Ellerman, he continued his association with the Navy, and was attached to officers of the First Sea Lord of the Admiralty – Admiral Sir John Pound – Pound being succeeded upon his death in Oct. '42, by Admiral Cunningham. During the war, Headquarters of the Western Approaches Command had been transferred from Plymouth to Liverpool. This office, under Sir Max Horton, was responsible for the safety of all shipping going in and out of Britain's North Atlantic ports. In this mammoth project, the RN had the collaboration of RAF No.15 Group Coastal Command.

Under an eye-catching headline, "Darkest Hour – How Britain won the Battle of the Atlantic 50 years ago – A place in history for Atlantic HQ", the "Daily Post" of February 6, 1991, recalls that this was "the nerve centre of the Western Approaches Command, from which the Admiralty defied the nightly air raids and waged war on Admiral Doenitz."

"The Liverpool bunker in the strengthened basement of Derby House in city centre, from which Admiral Max Horton waged war on Hitler's U-boat packs, could soon be a museum of international standing." Which it now is.

Richard was working on the docks during the worst of the "Blitz" of Liverpool (May, 1941).

He witnessed terrible scenes of death and destruction, which were a living nightmare, a nightmare that retained its horror when he described it to me years later. His office had somehow escaped being blown up, but walking from the docks to the ferry he had seen rows of houses with their fronts blown off. Inside were men sitting in chairs, or at tables, who, from a distance, looked normal, but upon closer inspection he saw that they had parts of their bodies blasted away, and they were dead.

Half of Liverpool was demolished. It is something that no one who lived through will ever forget.

When I first went there in the late 60's, there were still vast empty spaces which had been bombed out, and this alone was upsetting to see.

No words can ever describe the horrors of the war, nor the undaunted courage of the British people. For visual drama and emotional impact, Noel Coward's magnificent salute to the men of the Royal Navy, "In Which We Serve" (a 1942 film), comes as close to real experience as one can get.

Richard's fate would not allow him to long remain secure in a shore job (if one can call working on a dock that is being "blitzed" secure!) He had again met a friend on the street, this time an officer in the Air Force, who immediately arranged for him to serve with the RAF, although not as a pilot.

He was attached to the RAF in a civilian capacity, and became one of their leading teachers of Navigation, based at the Sealand training camp in Deeside, Clwyd. This job would, at least partially, fulfil his ambition to fly. He had to go up in the planes with his pupils, and he, himself, soon learnt to fly. Perhaps his pupils thought it would be safer if their Navigation teacher could handle the plane in case of emergencies. A Tiger Moth, a small training plane such as he flew, is still displayed on the grounds of RAF Sealand.

Richard flew over his house one day, where Christine, now at the talking stage, was watching out for him, and waving as he swooped down low. She asked her mother:

"Will Daddy come down by parachute?"

Christine was an imaginative child. At this period, when her father showed her the stars, she said:

"That's where I came from."

Richard taught with the RAF for several years. It was an intermittant job. He returned to sea whenever he could, then went back to teaching Navigation in between voyages. Good navigation was extremely important for hitting the targets. Without navigational aids, night raids were impossible, and during the early years of the war, when radar had not yet been developed for planes, many targets were missed, as it was suicidal to fly them low enough to get a good sighting.

Richard flew with his crew on several bombing missions over Germany. As a civilian, he was definitely not meant to be doing this. It was never officially recorded. However, he was set on going. As a keen observer, his technical knowledge may have been very useful to them. These men, whom he had taught, and who liked and admired him, therefore let him come, although strictly undercover. They flew from a Bomber Command station in Eastern England.

"I wanted to get my own back," he told me, grimly. In 1943, he went on bombing raids over the Ruhr. These first British night raids were to Essen. Before that, the bombers had been too small to carry enough fuel to reach Germany and get safely back. The new longer range planes, quickly built for this purpose, were the Lancasters. Richard told me the sight from these of the exploding factories at night was spectacular.

"The Twentieth Century, An Almanac"[1] describes these raids:

"March 5-6 (1943): British Bomber Command sends 443 aircraft to bomb Essen, Germany, the first attack in what Air Marshall Harris calls "The Battle of the Ruhr". By the time it ends on July 12 there will be 43 major raids to destroy the Germans' industrial heartland. 1,000 Allied aircraft are lost, and the Germans continue producing.

"July 24 – August 2: RAF and U.S. planes make a series of bombing raids on Hamburg. . . that result in some 50,000 civilian deaths and 800,000 homeless. Most of the casualties result from the fire storm created by incendiary bombs."

Air Chief Marshall Arthur Harris, known as "Bomber Harris", Commander-in-Chief of Bomber Command, was the most controversial of the British commanding officers. With Churchill's approval, he organised the extensive bombing of Germany. Although first concentrating on the industrial areas, his later bombing of cities, resulting in heavy civilian casualties, was criticised, particularly Dresden and Berlin. What people did not realise was that he had been ordered, with the U.S.A.A.F. to bomb Dresden. Afterwards he was sad that anyone would think that he decided what to bomb. All he could decide, he said, was which of the appointed targets could be attacked in the prevailing weather conditions and what force he should use. He did feel, however, that these swift air attacks would save more lives in the long run, as the war would be won faster.

Richard thought that this strategy was correct. However, the Government turned against "Bomber Harris" at the end of the war. He was the only commander not to be made a Peer of the Realm, and, very unfairly to the brave veterans of the RAF, Bomber Command was not awarded its own campaign medal.[2]

In commemoration of the 50th year since the start of the war, a fine BBC film about him was shown on British TV.

Richard kept his own participation in bombing missions as secret as his stint with the Royal Navy, although I do not believe he was under any obligation to do so. Well balanced and stable during his whole life, here under extreme stress Richard proved himself to be unusually strong. Many people would have fallen apart psychologically after undergoing such emotionally draining experiences, and would have had an uncontrollable urge to talk to someone about them. Richard just put all this behind him, and got on with his own life.

10. ANZIO BEACHHEAD AND A RUSSIAN CONVOY

Ever since Ellerman put him ashore, Richard had been looking for another ship. He was now freelancing looking for jobs.

His cousin William told me that Richard had been very bitter at that time about how the Ellerman Line was treating its officers. The men who had been sunk, but then returned to sea, lost their seniority in the line-up for promotion. Was this because they were allowed a long leave after each sinking? Richard believed much intriguing was going on by "Company Servants" who had shore jobs. Whatever the reason, it was unfair to the brave officers who had been risking their lives at sea. They should have come first for promotion.

Shortly after achieving the rank of "Commanding Officer", he had joined the "Navigators and Engineer Officers' Union". He found them helpful. His name was put down as a fill-in for whenever an officer was needed, although he remained firm that he would accept no post lower than "Relief" Chief Officer. Otherwise, the knowledge he had painstakingly acquired would be wasted.

At that time, Richard thought the seamen's unions were good protection against overbearing employers. However, after the war, he disapproved of all the unions' increasingly dictatorial policies, with the bitter strikes that would break the back of the Merchant Navy, and ruin Britain's ship-building industry.

At last, he again found a berth as "Chief Officer", but only for 8 days- March 8, 1942, to March 16, 1942. This was on the *Spero*, Ellerman Wilson Ltd.

During the war, this ship was operating regularly between Algeciras, Gibraltar, and Liverpool. She miraculously escaped German subs. However, the week Richard was on board she remained in the port of Liverpool, and never put to sea!

After this, he was back on the ship on which he had first served as "Acting 3rd Mate":

SHIP	ENGAGEMENT	DISCHARGE
39) S.S. *City of Lancaster* (Ellerman Lines Ltd.) From: Glasgow Discharge: " Description of Voyage: "Intended Foreign"	28/Mar./'42	7/Apr./'42

As the Mediterranean and most Continental ports were now closed to merchant shipping, the small ships on which he served at this time operated as "coasters", although continuing the then dangerous passage to Portugal and Gib.

Another short, hard-won engagement followed:

40) S.S. *Harrogate* (G.T. 1,029)
    Wilsons & N.E. Line
    From: Liverpool   6/May/'42   19/May/'42
    Discharge: "

Five months of unemployment again went by before he found other vacancies, all again with his old company, Ellerman & Papayanni.

41) S.S. *Algerian* (G.T. 2,305)
    From: Liverpool   2/Oct./'42   7/Nov./'42
    Discharge: Hull
42) S.S. *Oporto* (G.T. 2,352)
    From: Liverpool   1/Dec./'42   18/Dec./'42
    Discharge: "
43) S.S. *Oporto*
    From: Liverpool   18/Feb./'43   2/Mar./'43
    Discharge: "

Ten days after Richard had left her, the *Oporto*, which had joined a convoy on a voyage to Gib., was torpedoed and sunk, along with 3 other ships.

Of Ellerman's fleet of 105 ships, 58 were sunk during the war; E. & P. owned an additional 25, of which 19 were sunk.

When Richard was serving on the *Oporto*, his father had died, on December (the Welsh "Racfyr") 10, 1942, at the age of 63. Although not discharged until Dec. 18, he was given leave to be present at his father's funeral.

After his retirement, Owen Humphreys had spent most of his time gardening. "Eryl-y-Don" had a large, mostly undeveloped garden. Two close neighbours, also retired Captains, were similarly occupied. The three old cronies spent long hours together, comparing their gardens, and reminiscing about their lives at sea.

Owen had suffered a fatal stroke when in the garden, and died shortly afterwards. Richard believed that his father had killed himself doing too much work there. With chronic high blood pressure, he certainly should not have done such a lot of digging. The earth was heavy, and filled with endless stones and rocks that had to be excavated and lugged away before anything could be planted. No doubt this put too much strain on his physique.

For this reason, Richard hated gardening himself. However, whenever, after his father's death, he had a long leave and went home to Harlech, his mother would ask him to work in the garden. He had to take over where his father had left off, laying out a big vegetable garden, and new flower beds.

He was young, and in good physical condition, but he would rather have been doing something else. He loved flowers, and enjoyed watching vegetables grow, and being able to eat them freshly picked, if he didn't have to have all the work of looking after them.

Pomi and Jen did not have the time nor the enthusiasm for gardening, but Cass had a "green thumb", as the saying goes. Like her father, she was happiest spending hours every day in the garden, but she did have the sense not to exhaust herself. Her garden in Ponciau (near Wrexham), where she lived after her marriage, was a showcase.

Her son, Owain, inherited a love of plants, and the gift of making them grow. He shows an unusually artistic eye when it comes to the lay-out of a garden.

Richard's next two voyages were again on the *City of Lancaster*:

44) *City of Lancaster*   22/July/'43   29/July/'43
    From: Barrow
    Discharge: Glasgow

45) *City of Lancaster*   30/July/'43   14/Aug./'43

He remembered these trips in and out of Glasgow with displeasure. They were dreary trips, along a bleak, unfriendly coast, cold and wet even in July. They would anchor in uninhabited Loch Ewe, south of Ullapool, in north-western Scotland, to be concealed from enemy shipping while waiting for cargo, and a Naval escort.

However, he thought the Scottish seamen with whom he sailed were excellent. He sailed with men of all different nationalities during his long career, and got along with all of them. He said he did not care what race they were, or what part of the world they came from, as long as they did their work well.

He did, personally, prefer the Celts (naturally!), including the Breton and the Basques. He also found sailors from Barbados particularly reliable, and he had a good word for the East Indians. But Greeks and Italians came way down on his list, as being too careless and excitable.

One of the small ships on which he sailed out of Scotland at this period turned out to be a whaler. He said although the experience was interesting, he soon discovered that whaling was awful, brutal and cruel, and the smell at all times was nauseating. He had an offer to join one of the big factory ships on a permanent basis, but declined. Although the pay was good, he had too much love for the majestic mammals to want to spend his life killing them.

Following these, came a ship from South Wales, the last Ellerman Line ship on which he ever sailed (discounting the *Samboston*, a Ministry of War charter).

46) S.S. *Pandorian* (G.T. 3,146)
    From: Newport   27/Aug./'43   10/Sept./'43
    Discharge: "

Richard's next voyage lasted ten months, and was memorable:

The Liberty Ship *Samboston* was built in the United States in 1943 and bareboat-chartered to the Ministry of War Transport. She is shown here under her later name of *City of Rochester*. *(Carl Andersen Collection)*

47) S.S. *Samboston* (G.T. 7,265)
    From: Liverpool   1/Nov./'43   14/Aug./'44
    Discharge: London

The *Samboston*, a "Liberty Ship", had been built in the United States in 1943, at Bethlehem-Fairfield Shipyard, a wartime emergency yard in Baltimore, Maryland. Newly launched as the *Willis J. Abbott*, she had been taken to England to be used by the Ministry of War Transport, with Ellerman and Papayanni as Managers. She was to serve as a supply ship to the British armed forces in the Med. When Richard joined her, she was still uncompleted, and was taken back to America to the same shipyard, to have the final work done, which Richard supervised.

In 1943, Roosevelt had proclaimed that the U.S. shipyards, besides building ships, would repair and refuel British naval vessels to help the war effort. This offer included the American-built "Liberty Ships". So many British merchant ships had been sunk and shipyards bombed, that it was vital to keep the existing vessels operational, and to have a safe place in which to do the work.

The *Samboston* arrived in Baltimore on Nov.13th, where she stayed until Dec.9th, then transferring to a shipyard in New York City, and, later, back again to Baltimore.

As the shipyards were very busy, particularly with orders for the American Navy, which had priority, Richard knew it would take nearly two months for the job to be completed. Instead of idly waiting, which he thought would be boring, he decided to go to New York and get a job. The Company agreed to this, and paid his expenses. He was put up in the "Times Square Hotel". From there, he could easily go to Baltimore by train when needed.

His stay in New York would be lively, productive, and pleasurable, a welcome change from the high tension under which he had been living.

First, he had to apply for a "Green Card", which gave him unlimited entry to the U,S., and included a work permit. This was immediately given to him. He always kept this unlimited entry visa, which came in very handy when he visited the United States after that. No doubt the U.S. then welcomed British men of his calibre.

When he got a job, he also got a Social Security card. He applied to Macy's Department Store for a job. The personnel manager said that anyone from Britain should know all about fine English china! She took him to see their line of china. Keeping a straight face, he rattled off a few famous names: Wedgewood, Royal Doulton, Spode, Crown Derby, etc. He had heard his sisters discussing various kinds of china, but, actually, knew little about it himself.

He was immediately hired, as Supervisor in the China Department! I think the charming Welsh voice did the trick.

Richard took the opportunity of being in New York to look up his cousins, who lived on Long island. The forebears of this branch of the family had come over from Wales in the 19th Century to work with Linus Yale (inventor of the lock). They were expert craftsmen themselves. Their descendants had remained, and prospered through the years.

He enjoyed meeting the family, and seeing their beautiful estate right on the waterfront, at an exclusive end of the island. When he visited them, their little girl sat on his lap, and stared with big eyes as he talked.

"My, you talk cute!" the child exclaimed.

A member of this American branch of the family, Mrs. Anne Wheaton, became General Eisenhower's Secretary when he was President. She settled permanently in Washington, D.C. After she retired, she visited North Wales, and stayed with Pomi. Richard was home at the time, and had to take her around the old churchyards, and wait while she read the inscriptions on many family tombstones. She was interested in tracking down her roots, and this, plus old church records, was a good way to do it.

In his free time, Richard appeared in full uniform, selling War Bonds. Most Americans did not know one British uniform from another. He was given the V.I.P. treatment. People thought that his Merchant Navy uniform was Royal Navy! He, himself, was just as proud of it as though it had been Royal.

Society girls in flashy convertibles used to stop and offer him lifts (in reality, just "pick-ups"!) They believed it was their patriotic duty to be nice to servicemen, particularly officers, and even to invite them home. Richard did not fall for this trap. However, he had a lively time, and met a lot of people.

He even went to the fashionable night spots, such as "The Stork Club", and "21", then at the height of their popularity. These were frequented by "Café Society", and people in the news. Famous film stars, such as Ginger Rogers, Loretta Young and Irene Dunne, went there, doing their patriotic duty by being seen being nice to servicemen. Richard met these actresses at the "Stork Club", and talked to them. He had always enjoyed their movies, but he said the girls weren't nearly as pretty in real life, and looked rather hard-boiled.

I was studying music in New York at the time, and being young, was dying to go to these glamorous night spots. However, I and my student friends all lived on shoe-strings, and we could not afford such flashy places. It is strange, however, that I may have actually seen Richard selling War Bonds on Times Square.

Richard became friendly (in a platonic way, he said!) with a girl named Joanne Dru, who later became a "Starlet" in Hollywood. She and her two sisters had a singing and dancing act. They performed nightly at one of the big East Side hotels. Their show was in good taste, and he said they were very pleasant, well-behaved girls. Their mother was a strict chaperon. They all happened to be on the same train as Richard, giving him a glamorous and cheery send-off when he went to Baltimore for the final time to rejoin his ship.

The refitting now completed, the *Samboston* sailed for "N. Africa", as reported in Lloyd's Shipping Index. She had joined an American convoy, No. NGS 28, at Lynnhaven Roads on Christmas Day – the men must have felt depressed about that! Stopping first at Hampton Roads near Norfolk, Virginia, to pick up more merchant ships and Naval escorts, the flotilla safely made the dangerous Atlantic crossing, arriving in Gibraltar on January 10.

When Richard was a crew member, the *Samboston* made two such long voyages between New York and the Mediterranean, taking supplies to Anzio Beachhead, where some of the worst fighting of the war was then taking place. Richard said the ship was used for this purpose as she was especially designed so that she could sail close to shore for unloading.

For those too young to remember, the battle there lasted from January 22, 1944, to the end of May. Anzio is on the Italian coast, near Rome. On this long, open beach some 50,000 Allied troops, mostly British and American, were landed, to try to break the German "Gustav Line" that stretched across Italy.

It was thought that by surprising the Germans, this operation would be easy, and that they would be able to get through to help the main Allied armies, particularly the hard-pressed Poles at Monte Cassino.

The American General Lucas was in command of this joint operation, with the 3rd American Division, and the British 1st.[1] However, the General made a serious tactical error. He thought that there was no hurry, and delayed giving the order to advance. But, with a good Intelligence Corps, the German General Kesselring was not surprised. He quickly attacked, and succeeded in isolating the Allied troops from the mainland, by putting them under siege on the beachhead.

The Allied garrison was powerless, and was bottled up for several months. Many thousands of lives were lost. (For a full account of this calamitous operation, read the book on Anzio by the famous Welsh war correspondent, Wynford Vaughan Thomas.)

Unable to move, and constantly raided, the troops on the beachhead became totally dependent on supplies delivered by sea.

On her first voyage to the Med., the *Samboston* arrived at Augusta (Sicily) on January 15, immediately continuing on to Naples, which the U.S. Army had taken in October, and now made the base for their operations. Therefore, although in Allied hands, Naples was still considered to be an extremely dangerous area. It was constantly overflown by German planes, which tried to disrupt aid to Anzio.

On January 22nd & 23rd, massive Allied forces would be transported by sea from Naples to Anzio Beachhead. In preparation for this, the "Samboston" found the bay and harbour in turmoil. After the Royal Navy had supplied her with extra guns and gunners, the *Samboston* followed the troopships. For three weeks, she would shuttle back and forth between Naples and Anzio, the distance between these being approximately 95 miles.

Richard always intimated that he had a tough time at Anzio. This, indeed, was the case. Fighting on this long beach with its huge bay was extremely heavy. "In the four months of the engagement the British, Americans and Germans each lost more than 22,000 men."[2]

". . . Anzio had the reputation of being the most dangerous anchorage to which Allied warships or merchantmen could be dispatched. As a rule, therefore, supplies were transferred to military vessels in Naples." Although Nazi resistance at the time of Allied landing was slight, fierce attacks by German forces followed before the *Samboston* left the area. Upon Richard's return with his ship in April, the beachhead would still be in a state of siege. One report reads:

> "20—21 April Mediterranean One-man torpedoes (`Neger')
> are used against Allied ships off Anzio. Of 37 which enter the
> water, 14 get stuck on sandbanks and 23 attack. They obtain no
> success. Only 13 `Neger' return." [3]

There were quiet periods when supplies could be landed, but Richard and his men were warned to be wary of sudden German skirmishes.

After supervising a delivery on shore, Richard was slowly walking back along the beach towards the lighter, which would take him out to where his ship was anchored. He was curiously observing the scars of battle visible on the ground all around him.

Suddenly, with no warning, he came face to face with a heavily armed German soldier, who must have been watching him, concealed in the ruins of one of the burnt-out houses along the shore.

Richard was unarmed. Instantaneously, he knew that it must either be his life or the German's. His knowledge of unarmed self-defence came to his aid, as an immediate natural reflex. Before the soldier could reach for his gun, Richard had dealt him a slashing death blow with the side of his hand, behind the ear.

This was one of the worst moments of the war for Richard. It would come back to haunt him for the rest of his life.

Perhaps it seemed especially shocking, as it happened during a period when there had not been much fighting. The evening before, Richard and some of his crew had been invited on board one of the huge American troop carriers anchored offshore. Some of these ships could carry up to 5,000 men! This special ship was used as a social centre for men off duty. It offered them a chance to relax, with games, refreshments, and even, a movie. Some of the men ashore, also enjoyed visiting the *Samboston*, to which access was easy.

I may be the only person Richard told in detail about this bad war experience. Some psychiatrists to the contrary, talking about it, or mentally re-enacting it, could not erase the shock and horror from his memory. He would have nightmares, and thrash around in bed. His muscles would stiffen, and he'd grab hold of me as though I were the German. I'd have to quickly wake him up. He would then feel very disturbed, as he was afraid that he might have hurt me.

I remember reading, in an American newspaper, a letter from Anne Landers, (the "Advice to the Lovelorn" columnist), in which she answered questions from a woman who had written to her about a similar problem. Anne told her that she should immediately get a separate bedroom, and sleep with the door locked.

I did not take this advice. Richard and I were very close, and he said that if a couple slept in separate rooms, or even twin beds, it was not his idea of marriage. Fortunately, when the nightmare started, he would groan and begin twitching around, so this would wake me up before a steely fist reached out in my direction.

Considering everything Richard went through during the war, I think he got through remarkably well, if it left no other bad psychological scars.

Richard had taken the German's Mauser pistol, as a war trophy. In the man's pocket, he found a photograph of his wife and son, but with no address.

Richard kept the pistol, and on getting home, got a licence for it.

Years later, when we were in the U.S. arranging to get married, Richard's son, who was sorting out things in his father's house in Harlech, found the pistol. The licence had expired. As young Richard was in the Liverpool police, I guess he thought (correctly, I must admit) that pistols, even unloaded, were dangerous to have at home. He took it to Liverpool, and threw it in the river.

Richard felt rather badly about this, as he thought that the licence could have been renewed. After all, it was an historical trophy. Richard was a fine shot, and knew how to look after weapons. He told me he had had another small gun, with which he used to shoot rabbits. (He knew how to skin and cook a wild rabbit. They are very tasty!) This gun followed the other into the river.

At Anzio, Richard had picked up 2 brass shell cases. These made better souvenirs than guns. He had brass handles fitted onto them, so that they looked like mugs. They are handsome ornaments.

On their first trip, after unloading the last of the cargo for Anzio, the *Samboston* left Naples on February 5th with cargo for Malta, which was the life-line of supplies for the British forces. Continuing back on the 15th to

Gibraltar and Casablanca, they sailed on the 25th with Convoy GUS 31, and had returned safely to New York by March 18th.

The Atlantic crossings on their first trip had, as far as I know, been uneventful, but convoys were still necessary. Although U-boats were not so numerous, yet 54 Allied vessels had been sunk in the Atlantic between January- March, 1944 (the last Allied ship sunk by a German sub in the Med. would be on the 18th of May),

Richard, disliking to be reminded of Anzio, had never described these Atlantic voyages, that is why I had assumed that they were uneventful. However, when reading a "Sea Breezes" magazine (of Feb. 1992), I came across the dramatic account of a savage German attack on a convoy which had sailed from Norfolk, Virginia, for the Mediterranean on exactly the same date as Richard, on his second trip to Anzio. This article, entitled "The Ghost of the *Alkinos*", by I.G. Stewart, an Australian writer, tells the history of a Norwegian-registered Liberty ship, the *Viggo Hansteen*, which served the Allied cause until the end of the war. Could Richard have also been on this convoy, No. UGS 38?

Indeed he was! But months were to follow before I could prove it. This was a challenge not to be passed by, as it might reveal an unknown period of Richard's life. Starting my quest, I wrote to Mr. Stewart, who is an authority on "Liberty Ships". The research he had done for his article only concerned the *Viggo Hansteen*, but he sent me a continuation of an account which he had studied. It was in Norwegian!! [4] When translated, I found it contained a hair-raising description of the attack, including the sinking of several of the ships – but no mention of the *Samboston*.

Following this, I sent off letters to various sources of historical military information in London. This resulted in my learning that UGS 38 was an American convoy, but although a few pertinent facts about it were known, none of the British institutions to whom I wrote had a complete list of the ships involved, although I did receive a brief account of the attack, taken from Admiralty files.

The next logical step was to write to the Naval Historical Center in Washington, D.C. They not only confirmed that Richard's ship, the *Samboston*, was in the convoy, but sent me the movement report cards for this ship, from the Tenth Fleet records. Here was all the information I needed: lists of ports of call, dates of visits, convoy designation, etc. It also showed the numbers and dates of other American convoys she had previously sailed in. From these Archives were included documents marked "Secret" (but now, "Declassified"), giving a full list of ships in Convoy UGS 38, including its escort vessels; a report from the Convoy Commander, several messages relating specifically to *Samboston*, reports on crew behaviour, ship-to-shore messages; and, of course, full descriptions of the attack. In all, a magnificent compilation. To top it, came a delightful letter from Bernard F. Cavalcante, Head of Operational Archives Branch, U.S. Navy, concluding:

"Your husband's World War II merchant marine service is noted with appreciation, and I hope this information will be helpful to you."

On March 31, 1944, the *Samboston* sailed from New York in Convoy UGS 38, for Augusta and Naples. The ship's report reads: "Due Cape Henry April 1." She sailed with the "Ocean Section" of the convoy from Norfolk on April 3, ETA, Gibraltar April 20. There were 87 merchant ships in the convoy and 18 escort vessels, "sailing in eight columns about 1,000 yards apart." [5] The ships made an average of 10 knots, considered a good speed under the circumstances, They arrived in Gib. on the 18th. From the "Convoy Sailing Dispatch", the *Samboston*'s draft is given as 25'; Cargo: "General, Trucks, Explosives, Planes"; heaviest lift measurements; 22 Tons; Destination: "Classified". Reports from the Convoy Commodore, Captain Thomas A. Symington, U.S. Navy, from his ship, S.S.*Carrillo*, to Commander, Tenth Fleet, Washington, D.C., reveal a responsibly watchful eye kept on his charges:

General Report on Station-keeping:

> "Fair to good. *Empire Archer* (Br.) bad on station-keeping. *Polarsol* (Nor.) bad on station-keeping, usually way behind." One British Master (not on Richard's ship) was "very bad station-keeper, many times going well ahead of convoy."

Details of any favourable or unfavourable behaviour by vessels:

> "Seven days out nets were ordered astreamed." Two U.S. Masters failed to put nets out. "They reported failure to do so on account of green crew."

Brief narrative of the voyage:

> "Uneventful and pleasant weather until attacked by torpedo planes at 21.00 April 20th."

On the afternoon of the 20th, from advice received from the Escort Commodore, the following signal was sent to all vessels of the convoy:

"Tonight expect air torpedo and bomb attack with flare illumination. . . Must silhouette target to properly locate it. . . do not open fire unless. . . plainly visible and well within range."

Previously, a signal had been sent to all vessels that while in the Mediterranean they must at all times have one A1 Gun manned and ready and to be at general quarters "at least half an hour before sunset and sunrise, to half an hour after sunset and sunrise."

According to a report by the Commander in Chief, Mediterranean, there was an intensive reconnaissance effort made by the Germans during the 24 hours previous to the main attack. Only one of the ten reconnaissance aircraft taking part was shot down. I.G. Stewart describes this: [6] "On April 19, when the convoy was first attacked that night off the Algerian coast, near Bougie, all guns on the *Viggo Hansteen* opened fire but in the darkness the enemy could not be seen and firing stopped after four minutes.

"Shortly afterwards a heavy undersea explosion was felt close by but an inspection of the ship found no leakage." It was presumed that a submarine had fired and missed.

The convoy continued on. The next day, in the afternoon, a submarine was briefly sighted. The main attack came that night. Historian Samuel Eliot Morison wrote that the Luftwaffe attacked in three waves. [7] "As twilight faded, flying close to shore and low over the water, they evaded radar detection until they were almost upon the convoy." 1st wave: "of 9 torpedo planes, attacking 25 minutes after sunset, damaging 3 merchant ships and sank the *Paul Hamilton*."

2nd wave: "of 7 JU-88's (bombers) sank one more merchantman (the *Royal Star*) and damaged a third."

3rd wave: "5 He-III's torpedoed the U.S.S. Destroyer *Lansdale*. . . which sank in 30 minutes."

"This attack on UGS 38 marked the high water for the Luftwaffe in the history of the Mediterranean convoys. . . The convoy encountered superior Luftwaffe technique and was very roughly handled."

The Commander in Chief, Med., attributed the enemy's success to skilful execution, training and timing, and the failure of the convoy to make timely and adequate smoke.[8] I.G. Stewart continues with details: [9] "When three miles off Cape Bengut, some 50 miles east of Algiers, the convoy was attacked. . . first by a submarine, then suddenly. . . by torpedo-carrying aircraft." The attackers missed the *Viggo Hansteen*, but the torpedoes from one aircraft struck the American flag "Liberty Ship" *Paul Hamilton* in the next column, a vessel identical to the Norwegian ship.

"At the time, the *Paul Hamilton* was bound from Norfolk, Va. to Bizerta with a cargo of ammunition and 504 American servicemen, the majority of whom formed part of a special demolition squad on its way to Anzio Beachhead. In the explosion which followed, witnessed by those on board the *Viggo Hansteen*, there were no survivors from the servicemen and crew on board the *Paul Hamilton*" (a total of 580 men lost their lives). "This represented the greatest loss of life at sea among the 4½ million U.S. troops which embarked during the Second World War for Europe and N. Africa."

Here is the official U.S. Navy report of the sinking: "At 21.03 the *Paul Hamilton* in position 42 was hit by a torpedo from a plane, immediately following the torpedo explosion there was a violent explosion aboard, throwing debris and dense black smoke high in the air. When the smoke drifted off there was no sign of the ship. About 30 seconds after the *Paul Hamilton* was hit a torpedo hit the *Samite*, #11, forward, causing her forward two holds to flood.

"At 21.04, the *Royal Star*, #115, and the *Stephen F. Austen*, #94, but at the time trailing column 9 due to steering gear trouble, were hit by torpedoes." This account, signed by the Convoy Commodore, reports that 23 planes were in the attack force, coming in three waves.

I have at hand another vivid description of the battle, perhaps the most dramatic, of the sinking of the U.S. *Lansdale* (DD-426), sent to me by the Philadelphia Maritime Museum.

The Destroyer *Lansdale* was named after my mother's cousin, Lieutenant Philip Lansdale (after whom I was also named). He was a young Naval officer who, in 1899, was killed in a joint American-British defense operation in Samoa. Here is another strange coincidence linking my life with Richard's!

"The *Lansdale* sailed from Oran 18 April to join UGS 38 the next day. Stationed off the bow of the Bizerta-bound convoy, she served as a `jam ship' against radio-controlled bombs, in addition to screening against U-boats."

At the time of the attack, she was "silhouetted by the explosion of *Paul Hamilton* at 21.04. *Lansdale* was attacked from both port and starboard by planes from two and possibly three waves. As Heinkels approached on the port bow and launched two torpedoes that missed, *Lansdale* turned to starboard to repel five JU-88's which had veered seaward from the convoy. Her guns hit one as it passed down the starboard side, but as it splashed well astern, another launched a torpedo 500 yards on the starboard beam before passing over the forecastle under heavy fire and splashing on the port quarter.

"The torpedo struck the starboard side forward about 21.06, wrecking the forward fireroom and opening both sides to the sea. Almost split in two, *Lansdale* immediately took a 12° list to port. Her rudder jammed 22° right, and she steamed at 13 knots in a clockwise circle.

"At 21.12 she again came under attack. Two bombers launched torpedoes on the beam and broad on the bow to port but both missed the still-turning ship. Despite the increasing list her guns splashed one of the planes as it turned from the ship.

"At 21.20 the course of the ship straightened out, but the list increased steadily. Within 2 minutes it reached 45° despite the valiant efforts of her crew to control the battle damage. Her skipper, Lt. Comdr. D.M. Swift, ordered her abandoned when he feared the stricken ship might roll `completely over'. By 21.30 the list had increased to 50° and the destroyer began to break up. Five minutes later she broke in half and the stern section quickly sank. The forward section sank 20 minutes later as *Menges* (DE-320) and *Newell* (DE322) began rescue operations.

"The two destroyers swept the water from 21.55 until 03.30 the next morning searching for survivors. *Menges* picked up 115 men, including two German flying officers who were shot down either by *Lansdale* or *Newell*.

Newell rescued 119 survivors, including Lt. Commander Swift. Forty-seven officers and men were carried down with *Lansdale*." [10]

"At this time the majority of vessels of the convoy seemed to be firing in practically all directions," reported Capt. Symington. "This is accounted for by the fact that the planes from the port bow crossed over to the starboard quarter. . . two planes were sighted above the smoke column caused by the explosion of the *Paul Hamilton*. About four rounds were fired at these planes before sight was lost.

"Several underwater explosions were felt but nothing else seen."

No doubt, Richard had been manning the A1 gun on his ship, as he had trained for just such an emergency.

To conclude, the Commodore wrote:

"The Merchant ships behaved very well and kept their proper formation."

After the sinkings Richard himself had already survived, perhaps witnessing three more such horrible ones was a little too much. No wonder he never mentioned it.

The surviving *Sanboston* then continued on to Sicily and Naples, arriving there April 25. A busy fortnight followed, again going back and forth to Anzio. On May 12, they returned to Sicily, then continued to Algiers and Casablanca, before sailing back to New York. While waiting in Casablanca to join another convoy, Richard could relax a little on shore.

Always interested in people he met during his voyages, Richard recalled walking to the end of the pier in Casablanca one evening, where a man sat fishing. When he looked up, Richard recognised him as someone to whom he had talked to a lot at Anzio – a Welshman, now on leave!

After this, the *Samboston* did not return to the Med. By May 23rd, the Allies had begun a strong offensive and broke out of Anzio. The Gustav Line was broken, and Rome taken by June 4th.

After refurbishing in New York, Richard's ship sailed to the Caribbean. This must have seemed like a holiday to the crew! In July their ports of call were: Macoris and Cuidad Trujillo (both in the Dominican Republic); Guantanamo Bay (Cuba); and Barahona (also Dominican Republic).

Then came New York, and another Atlantic crossing. On July 25, the ship joined Convoy HXM 301, for Loch Ewe. Richard was discharged in Glasgow on August 10th, as the ship was to be taken over by a different company. She was later renamed *The City of Rochester*.

With Richard away for so long, Chrissie had gone to Wales with the children, to get away from the danger of bombing. staying with Richard's mother at "Eryl-y-Don". She found the house full of young nieces, nephews, and cousins, also sent there for safety. so she and her family did not get the help she had expected. Jane and Chrissie had never been congenial, so living at close quarters, the atmosphere was strained.

Chrissie then decided that having two children to care for alone was too much for her, so she asked Jen to take the boy, and look after him.

It is hard to imagine a mother turning over her child willingly to her sister-in-law, so she must, indeed, have felt ill. For Richard, however, this made life increasingly difficult, as he returned to a divided household.

Richard's contract with the *Samboston* had come to an end, and he was now to be ashore for six months before he found another ship. Besides family problems, a lot of unwelcome gardening loomed ahead.

Richard, when he was home, spent a lot of time with Clar (who was to become "Queen of the Family" in later years, after Jane died.) He also felt very close to Meurig, who came from a sea-faring family, and understood boats. Richard felt that Meurig was "the salt of the earth", and that whatever advice he gave should always be followed.

Richard's Aunt and Uncle, Clar and Meurig Griffith, photographed with son William

Meurig's father, Capt. John Griffith, had been the last Master of Barmouth's famous barque, *The Pride of Wales*. This handsome wooden ship had been sadly neglected by her owner. Leaking badly upon a return voyage from the Orient, she was caught in a Force 12 storm near the Azores, and sunk. All hands, luckily, were saved. A fine painting of this vessel hung over the Griffiths' dining room table.

Meurig, himself, was a master cabinet maker, and had his own woodworking shop. He not only made beautiful furniture, but made massive, intricately carved pews for the local chapels. His shop also produced coffins!

Richard never forgot, when still a school-boy, accompanying Meurig to a lonely hill farm, where the farmer had died. The man had been a stern, disagreeable old fellow, and Richard had been afraid of him. He now had to help Meurig carry the coffin to where the dead man lay. It was night, and very dark in the house, which was illuminated only by oil lamps. As they approached the bed, in order to lift the body into the coffin, the corpse raised up his knees. Richard was terrified!

Meurig calmly said that this was nothing supernatural, but simply a muscular reflex that sometimes occurs after death. In spite of this reasonable explanation, the boy remained badly frightened, and was glad when they left the house.

In February, 1945, he set sail again, on another beautiful new ship, the *Samdonard*. This was also one of the "Liberty Ships", built during the war, to help the desperately depleted merchant shipping of both the U.S. and Britain. At this period, the *Samdonard*. (PRO REG, London. Net Tonnage, 4,394; Gross Tonnage, 7,233) was a Ministry of War bare-boat charter arranged by managers, W.S.A. McCowen & Gross Ltd., London.

Richard was glad to get back to sea, and to finally have a long-lasting assignment. He would be Chief Officer of this ship for the next six years. The *Samdonard* became his favourite ship, and he said it was the happiest one.

This voyage (No. 48 on Richard's book) would be his last voyage in wartime. The end of the war was fast approaching.

Leaving Liverpool on February 8, the ship first went to Cardiff, then sailed for New York. From there she went on to Nuevitas (Cuba), and Santiago (Dominican Republic), before returning to New York. She arrived safely back to Britain, and sailed up the Thames, arriving to Poplar dock in London May 4th, where she remained, except for coastal voyages, until the 25th.

The war was finally over!

On VE Day, May 7th, Richard and most of the crew got off, and went to Trafalgar Square to celebrate. The whole population seemed to be there.

What a fabulous celebration, after 6 years of austerity and black-outs. Lights were shining, fireworks were being shot off, and everyone had bottles.

Richard served on the Liberty Ship *Samdonard* and after her sale to the Claymore Shipping Co. Cardiff, for whom she traded as their *Daybeam*. She was his "happiest" ship. *(Welsh Industrial and Maritime Museum, Cardiff.)*

Richard had ship's flares in his pockets, and he climbed up on the fountain to shoot these off.

After all the dismal, perilous years, it felt marvellous to let off steam. Strangers were kissing each other, there was dancing in the streets, and everyone was happy. Like bubbles from uncorked bottles of champagne, lights, song, and laughter rose into the night sky. Yet there were tears shed through the laughter for all the dear ones lost forever.

When the *Samdonard.* was in London, Chrissie had taken Christine to see her father's ship. This was one of the few times that Chrissie visited one of Richard's ships.

They went on board for dinner, then sailed up to Hull at night – very exciting for a child of 6, and Christine has always remembered it.

At dinner, Christine was asked by the Steward what she would like to eat, and she replied:

"Curry and rice, please."

The ship had an East Indian crew, and very hot curry was always at hand. After finishing what was on her plate, Christine asked for a second helping. This made a great hit with the crew! It was unusual for a British child to like such hot food.

Afterwards, they nicknamed her "the curry and rice kid".

Samdonard's next voyage took her to St. John, New Brunswick; then through the Panama Canal, and north up the coasts of Central and North America to Canada. Here they docked in Port Alberni, and Vancouver.

The ship arrived back to Belfast August 29, where she stayed a month for repairs, after which she went to Manchester, and Liverpool.

On October 20 (Richard's third voyage on her), she again sailed, this time for Archangel, far north of the Arctic Circle, in the wake of the Russian convoys.

Richard always boasted that he did a Russian "Convoy", but he never mentioned that it was after VE Day! Merchant ships were now on their own. Both American and British navies had given up escorting ships to Russia in August, although Roosevelt had planned for them to continue to the end of the year. However, when the war ended, Truman, who was now President, decided there was no further need for military escorts. It was, however, of vital importance to keep cargo vessels moving north, as under the "Lend-Lease" programme British warehouses were still full of goods ear-marked for the war-exhausted Soviet Union. Although no longer in danger from German attack, it was an arduous trip especially with winter coming on. Minesweepers had now cleared along the coast, but some unexploded mines without a doubt remained in the sea.

The winter route for these Arctic voyages started out near the Faroes, and went North-East, passing close to Bear Island, before sweeping up past the

North Cape to Murmansk, On this voyage, the ship not only did not have an escort, but I have verified in Lloyd's Shipping Index that she was the only merchant ship sailing from Britain to Russia at the time. It must have been lonely for the men, heading into severe northern gales, with no help nearby in case of break- down.

Arriving safely in Archangel October 30, the *Samdonard* continued on to Molotovsk (which is now renamed Severodvinsk), in the White Sea. Here she would remain for a month. The entrances to these ports, usually only used by convoys in summer months, were already frozen. Ice-breakers now had to lead the way!

The men on the *Samdonard.* were carrying badly needed provisions to their impoverished ally, particularly food, clothing, and medical supplies. Besides this mixed cargo, the ship had a big consignment of gold bars, which, during the war, had been stored by Russia for safe-keeping in the Bank of England. Now, in her depleted state, she wanted them returned. The bars were plentiful enough to fill an empty cabin on the upper deck! Richard was personally responsible for their safety. He had the key to the cabin, which he always carried with him. Every day he went in to count the bars, to carefully check that none were missing. He was greatly relieved when they were safely delivered.

If Molotovsk's harbour was icy, the air seemed doubly so. The ship was so cold that, in spite of central steam heating, the walls inside Richard's cabin were covered with ice! He had to sleep in all his heaviest Arctic gear, with bedclothes on top of those.

Stalin was at this time at the height of his power. In accordance with his isolationist policy, the port was heavily guarded. Military patrols marched up and down past the ship night and day. A thorough search was made for anything that might be considered "subversive". The authorities removed a set of books that Richard had in Welsh. They had never seen the language written before, and thought the books might contain a concealed code.

When an expert linguist examined them on shore, he returned with a big grin.

They were a set of Tolstoy's novels. For once, the joke was on him.

"We read these in Russian," he said. "Very fine books!" The authorities did not want the crew conversing with people ashore. One of the chief inspectors on the docks was friendly, however. He used to come on board, and talk to Richard. He was a worried man.

He confided that he had just been given his position because the place was completely isolated. He could hardly ever, here, come into contact with anyone from the outside world. Shortly before this, he had been an interpreter at the Yalta Conference (Feb.4-11,'45) between Stalin, Churchill, and Roosevelt. He had heard everything that was said there, and that was knowing too much for him to ever again be safe in Stalin's Russia.

He was now badly demoted. He did not know what would happen to him. He would probably be sent to Siberia, or else, "disappear" forever. He felt that he was in grave danger.

Richard was often allowed ashore to stretch his legs. He was told not to wander too far. One day, he walked down to the end of the dock, which did not seem too far.

Here, he found an area enclosed with a high barbed wire fence. When he walked up to it, he noticed many people peering at him through the wire. These were curious local people, who were not allowed onto the dock, but who had been attracted by the ship. They were anxious to talk to foreigners.

He was smoking a cigarette, and they eagerly pointed to this. Richard had put some extra packs in his pockets, and some chocolate, just in case he did meet anyone. He was greeted with excited joking and laughter as he stuck these through the bars, and they reached out to grab the goodies.

At this point, an angry soldier appeared out of nowhere, investigating the noise. He shouted at them to go away, and, in heavily accented English, curtly told Richard that he should not have given them anything, as this just caused dissatisfaction. He said that Richard should not have gone there, anyway. He was not allowed to fraternise with anybody!

Although Richard loved the Russians as individuals, for their warm personalities, their literature, and the wonderful way they sang – very like the Welsh – he hated the concentration camp mentality of the then autocratic government of the U.S.S.R. So he gave a sigh of relief when they laboriously sailed, again with the help of ice-breakers, out of frozen Molotovsk.

Leaving Murmansk on December 7, they arrived safely to Glasgow Dec. 17.

The Long Voyages

11. PACIFIC INTERLUDE

In January, 1946, the *Samdonard* left for the South Pacific and Australia, Richard's fourth voyage on her. He was to sail for the next ten years to this part of the globe. He would now be away for a year. His Discharge Book reads:

    ENGAGEMENT: 18/12/45   Belfast
    DISCHARGE;   17/12/46   Avonmouth

Between these long voyages he rarely got any leave. The first voyage he made on the *Samdonard*, although listed on his Discharge Book as one voyage, really consisted of two voyages overseas, with the ship going to British coastal ports – London, Hull, Belfast – in between. When the ship went to Belfast for repairs the end of August, -'45, Richard was only allowed one night at home before he left on the Arctic voyage.

The Discharge Book is really a skeleton record of voyages, the living body of these is missing. For instance, after the Russian voyage, the ship arrived in Glasgow on December 17th,'45, where Richard's book was stamped *Discharged* for that voyage. However, he continued on with the ship to Belfast, where, the next day, his book was restamped with the beginning of a new engagement. This did not mean that he started out immediately on a long voyage. The ship, with Richard on duty, remained in Belfast for a month, before going on to Liverpool on January 17,'46. She did not leave for the Pacific until the 31st.

A Chief Officer has constant duty and responsibilities when his ship is in port. He has to supervise repairs, oversee loading and unloading of cargo, see to re-provisioning, breaking in of new crew members, and generally looking after the ship. Often, the Captain does not remain on board.

On this fourth voyage, the ship went through the Suez Canal, and on to Calcutta. This was Richard's first trip to Calcutta, and he was invited on shore by the shipping agent for dinner, at one of the city's foremost restaurants. Stepping ashore, Richard was horrified to discover that there was a bad famine in that part of India. A period of drought, followed by floods, had made food scarce. What rice there was available had been hoarded by unscrupulous dealers, and resold at exorbitant prices to the wealthy. People were dying of hunger on the streets.

He and the agent had to walk past dead bodies, and through a crowd of starving people, who milled around the restaurant door, hoping for hand-outs. When they entered the restaurant, it proved to be first class, with good service, and a long menu of the finest delicacies of both European and East Indian cooking. The place was full of well-dressed, obviously well-to-do customers, enjoying their food.

Richard ordered a big steak, and a huge platter of rice, accompanied by all the vegetables he could get, also a pile of "Chapaties". He could not eat, himself, as his appetite had gone away when he had seen the starving throng outside. He got up, when the order came, and carried it to the door. Here he distributed it to the people waiting there, who about mobbed him. In less than a minute, everything had been devoured.

The restaurant's manager hurried up to him, and was very angry. He said that they could not possibly feed all the crowd outside. Giving them a little, such as Richard had done, could cause a serious riot. "But maybe one or two lives were saved," Richard thought.

He left in disgust, and did not eat again on shore that time in Calcutta. From there, the ship contiued on to Colombo, Ceylon (now Sri Lanka), then Australia (Freemantle and Sydney). Returning to Malaysia, with stops at Pinang, Kuala Lumpur and Singapore, she went back and forth again between there and Sydney. On Sept. 21 she sailed for Vancouver. Arriving on Oct. 18, they continued on Nov. 4th to Victoria, on Vancouver Island.

Richard fell in love with Vancouver Island, and often told me that if he could not live in Britain, he would choose it for a permanent residence, as the place is so unspoiled and beautiful, with magnificent forests, and wonderful fishing. Its climate is rather similar to Wales, and, of course, it has preserved its British tradition.

I discovered a funny mark, ✖ on the listing of this voyage of the *Sandonard* in "Lloyd's Shipping Index". This denotes "an accident or calamity". It revealed here that she had struck the breakwater in Victoria, once on Nov. 7, and again on the 15th. It was extremely unusual, for any ship on which Richard served, to have an occurrence like this, much less two!

Going home by way of the Panama Canal, with a stop-over in Curaçao, they arrived back to Avonmouth (on the Bristol Channel) Dec. 16, and to Cardiff Jan. 10, 1947.

While Richard was away, his third child, a daughter, had been born, on June 24, 1946. He did not see her until she was almost 6 months old. Janet, as the child was christened, turned out to be a beautiful baby. Richard immediately loved her. However, when he went back to sea, and Chrissie was again left without help, she felt that she could not cope with the baby, so turned her over to Clar and Meurig in Barmouth. They now had two big boys, who enjoyed having a baby girl added to their family. She grew to be almost like a sister, and Clar became closer to Janet than her own mother. Janet lived with them until she was almost 7. She retains a very special love for this family.

On the following voyage, the ship sailed from Cardiff on January 20, for Halifax, going again through the Panama Canal, and up to Portland, Oregon. From Portland, they went to Singapore, where they remained two weeks, then back across the Pacific to Vancouver and Port Alberni, a logging port which Richard particularly enjoyed.

Arriving back to Glasgow on July 9th, the crew learnt that the *Samdonard* had been sold to British buyers, the Claymore Shipping Co., Ltd. of Cardiff, for whom the Welsh firm of T. Geo. Thomas, Consulting Engineeers & Surveyors, acted as Owners' Superintendents.

The ship would be re-named the *Daybeam*. Now due for a complete refitting, Richard had a long wait until he could rejoin her. He was home on prolonged leave from July 19, 1947 to October 11, 1948.

In "Lloyd's Index", the ship is listed as having returned to London from Melbourne, on October 5, 1948. It is probable that as Richard was due for a vacation, a Relief officer had been put in his place. Whatever the cause, he did not set sail in his old ship again until October 30th, from London. He would remain the *Daybeam's* Chief Officer until April 22, 1952, when the ship was again sold.

The new owner was a fine employer, and more thoughtful of his crew than most. He allowed officers' wives to travel with their husbands, an innovation at the time, although in sailing ship days, it was not unusual for Captains' wives, who must have been intrepid, to sail around the Horn with their husbands, and even give birth to babies on board. The wives who sailed on the *Daybeam* were also allowed to bring their children with them. Chrissie, however, showed no interest in joining them.

She was a big ship, with comfortable quarters, and lots of deck space. The lay-out was good, with accommodation forward as well as aft. Single officers had their own quarters, another part of the ship was given to those with families, and a third part went to the A.B.s.

All the families had their own cats, and some of the single men kept them, too. Richard, of course, had his own cat, a large black and white one, named "Whisky", who used to climb up the rigging, or sit by the wheel studying the compass. The crew thought he was "Super Cat"! Richard told his wide-eyed Indian crew that his cat knew Navigation! Needless to say, rats and mice avoided this ship.

Most ships and yachts today no longer keep cats. Cats will go ashore in ports, and this is against international law, with its now much stricter rabies regulations.

The *Daybeam* had its own cricket team, which took part in many exciting matches overseas, cricket being the most popular sport in what so recently were British colonies. Richard, naturally, was a member of the team.

Mr. J.C. Clay, owner of the shipping company, was, of course, the star cricket player who brought world renown to the Glamorgan team. He arranged for the *Daybeam's* team to be given the special honour of having the Glamorgan coat of arms emblazoned on their jackets. His ships also had the team's colours on their funnels.

They often went into San Pedro, the Port of Los Angeles. The men's first stop ashore would usually be a small water-front restaurant run by an Italian family, who soon knew them all by name, and made them feel right at home, with a warm welcome and good food and wine. When they had time, they would then play matches with the Hollywood cricket team, which was made up of enthusiasts from the large colony of expatriate British movie stars, such as Ronald Colman, David Niven, Cary Grant, and George Sanders. The veteran actor, Sir C. Aubrey Smith, was Captain. He was also Captain of the Polo team, which played in Santa Monica, but the seamen did not attempt to play that.

My grandmother was friendly with C. Aubrey, as he was called, another diaphanous thread connecting my life and Richard's in those early days! When I was a teenager, C. Aubrey often came to Philadelphia with a touring theatre company, and would come to my parents' house for tea. He, who epitomized the English Colonial Officer, or the retired country squire, in his film roles, actually hated acting. He frankly confessed that he did it only for the money. He considered it to be a very hard profession, and was far happier in his free time, on the playing fields.

Richard's itinerary, this first voyage on the refitted *Daybeam*, makes a good lesson in Geography.

Sailing through the Suez Canal, and down the Red Sea, they turned into the Persian Gulf, going to its upper end, to Khorramshahr and Bandar-e Shahpūr (now called Bandar Khomeyni) near Abādān, Iran. They then continued along the coast of Iran to nearby Būshehr.

On December 30, they headed for Karachi. After that, came Bombay, Calcutta, Hong Kong, and Singapore.

At Singapore, I note another ✣ ! "Struck Quay. Feb.23,'49."

The ship never went into Shanghai, as the Civil War was then being fought in China. Richard noted British and American naval vessels in the South China Sea.

Then came Kure, Japan. Kure is near Hiroshima. The *Daybeam* was the first British merchant ship into Japan after VJ Day. At first, the Japanese thought that they were American. When Richard and some of the sailors went ashore, they were hissed at in the street. As soon as the local people realized that the ship was British, however, they became quite friendly. For some reason, they did not hate the British. Although they had fought them bitterly in the grim jungle battles of Malaysia and Burma, and had been very cruel to their prisoners, the Japanese respected the British. They considered them to be honourable soldiers. They had not thrown the atomic bombs.

Richard was taken on a guided tour of the demolished city of Hiroshima, a horribly depressing sight. He also saw some of the living victims of the bombing. The area must have still been radio-active when Richard visited it, but he said to refuse to go would have been an insult to his hosts.

From Kure, they sailed to Yokohama, and Kobe. Then they went again to Singapore, Karachi and Hong Kong, before returning to Osaka and Kobe. By July 22, they were back in Singapore, going on from there to Madras, Colombo, Bombay, and again, Karachi.

Leaving Karachi September 13 for Aden and Suez, they arrived in Port Said September 22, continuing on to Casablanca, and home. They arrived in Glasgow on October 12.

The *Daybeam's* second voyage was less exotic:
- SD. from the Clyde anchorage (Glasgow) Nov. 1, for Swansea
- SD. Nov. 11 for Melbourne and Sydney
- Nov. 16 ✠ "Put back for Falmouth. Engine trouble"
- ARR. Port Said, Nov. 29
- SD. Dec. 7 for Aden
- ARR. Melbourne, Jan. 1, 1950
- ARR. Sydney, Jan.20
- ARR. back to Melbourne, Jan.30

The ship then appears to have stayed in Melbourne a month, before sailing for Alexandria on March 1. Stopping en route at Bona-Bona, New Guinea, and Indonesian ports, she arrived back to Britain (Middlesbrough) on May 31.

Voyage three just went to Australia. Leaving Tyne June 27, and passing Gib. July 3, they arrived to Fremantle Aug. 12; Brisbane, Sept. 25; then Cairns, from where, on Oct. 14 they sailed back to the U.K., arriving in Cardiff Dec. 12.

Richard's first impression of Australian men whom he saw in these ports was that they were very rough, very much like the people shown in "Western" movies. They were uncouth looking, always ready for a fight, and showed no respect for women.

At that time, everyone rushed to the bars immediately after work, as these were only open for a short time right before dinner. They tried to drink as much as they could, very fast, before "closing time". Pushing and shoving to get their drinks, many got into fights.

I understand that this short drinking time has now been extended, so people can enjoy their drinks in a more leisurely way.

Richard was fond of quoting this little seafarers' verse:
"Land of birds without a song,
Land of flowers without a smell,
Land of women without virtue,
Land of bastards,
Fare thee well!"

It must be remembered that the original white settlers, from whom many modern Australians are descended, were criminals, forcibly deported from Britain to start a new life in unknown territory. Some of their crimes were no worse than having been in Debtors' Prison, but to survive in Australia in those days one had to be tough.

Richard later met some really nice Australians. These were recent settlers from Wales. Richard met his cousin John Humphreys (whose father, Captain Jack Humphreys, was Owen's brother). John Humphreys was Captain in the Blue Funnel Line, and lived in Melbourne, where he married a local girl. He later became Chief Harbourmaster and Pilot for Devonport, Tasmania. Another first cousin living in Australia is Richard Williams, whose father was Jane's brother.

"Dick Australia", as the family in Wales call him, is a leading physiotherapist with his own private practice, and has been physiotherapist to the Australian Olympic Team. His wife is lovely, and a born and bred Australian! Pomi went out to visit them, and thoroughly enjoyed her tour of the country, and the people she met.

As in the U.S., no doubt one finds a great variety of people in a fast developing country of such vast size. Unfortunately, the native Aborigines, who belong to one of the world's oldest races, have been treated in much the same way as the American Indians, or the African Bushmen.

Richard's fourth, and final, voyage on the *Daybeam* lasted over a year. Sailing from Cardiff on December 13, 1950, they again found themselves going back and forth between Indonesian ports, Japanese (Moji and Yawaja), and American (Los Angeles). Richard, on one of his many visits to Hong Kong during this period, met his cousin William (Clar and Meurig's son), who was there doing his National Service stint with the British Army. Richard invited him on board the *Daybeam*, where he was entertained at lunch. William remembers this as a nice break from Army life!

By the end of August,'51, they returned to Aden and the Red Sea, going on to Tripoli and Lebanon. Then, turning back to the Orient, they arrived in Moji towards the end of November. By the 26th, when they left Moji, the crew had heard that the ship had been sold. This voyage ended in Rotterdam on April 22, 1952, where Richard was discharged. A fine letter of recommendation was written by the *Daybeam's* Master, Captain Escudier:

S.S. Daybeam,
Wiltons Drydock,
Rotterdam
22/4/52

To Whomsoever it May Concern,
Reference Mr. R. Humphreys, Chief Officer

This is to certify that Mr. Humphreys has served as Chief Officer under my command continuously from November 1948 to present date.

Additionally, although unestablished, he has been treated as a Company's Servant by the owners during the above mentioned period. I can, without question, recommend him as a conscientious – painstaking – sober and industrious Officer to anyone requiring his services. He has had wide experience in general matters of Navigation and Cargo.

He is leaving the Vessel through no fault of his own – the ship having been sold to Panamanian Owners. Subject to any possible provision that may be made by Present owners on behalf of his services to them in the past – he is fit to assume Command of a Foreign going Vessel and it is hoped that such an opportunity will not long be denied him.

U.J. Escudier
Master

Richard then went home for a well-deserved vacation.

After a short stay with his mother, Richard had moved his family to "Erw Fair", Llainfair (close to Harlech). This was a private house. The owner, an elderly widow, took them in as "Paying Guests". She helped Chrissie with the cooking and looking after the children. who soon became fond of her. This summer, all three children were now back with their parents.

Richard's best memories of this period were of picnics on the beach. They would go shrimping in sea-pools at low tide, then make a bonfire from driftwood, and cook their catch. Chrissie would stand at the top of a steep cliff and lower down a picnic basket. She was not much of a beach person, herself. Christine, however, took after her father, and was already a great nature lover, interested in fishing, botany, and outdoor activities.

The Claymore Shipping Company had not replaced the *Daybeam*. There was still a bad post-war slump in Britain, with new merchant ships not being built fast enough, so Richard had to look elsewhere for his next assignment. With the help of Mr. Philip D. Thomas, of T. Geo. Thomas, Ltd., who was familiar with his fine record, he did not have to wait too long. By September, he had found another ship. He received the following letter from his old company:

4th September, 1952

Dear Sir:

We thank you for your letter of yesterday's date and as requested enclose reference covering the period you were employed by this Company. It is unfortunate that for the time being we have nothing to offer you but hope that this position will change in the near future. May we take this opportunity of wishing you the best in your next vessel and to thank you for the excellent service we received from you.

Yours faithfully
F. T. Dewey (Director)

Richard's new vessel was the S.S. *Graiglwyd* (4043 N.T., 6001 G.T.), Idwal Williams & Co., Cardiff. His first voyage on her was September 25, 1952- Dec. 30, 1952.

Sailing from Cardiff October 7th, they went to Gib., and on, through the Suez Canal, to Djibouti (then a French Colonial port), on the Gulf of Aden. Leaving there November 27, they continued down the Indian Ocean, east of Madagascar, to Mauritius, home of the rare pink pigeon, and a tropical paradise (before its beaches had any "development" for tourists).

They arrived home to Liverpool December 29th.

Richard as Chief Officer

12. BALIK PAPEN

Richard's second voyage on the *Graiglwyd* started much like his others to the Orient. Little did he think that it would be his last voyage on this ship.

Sailing January 9th, 1953, from Liverpool to Hampton Roads, the ship left on the 30th for Japan. By February 8th, they went through the Panama Canal, going to Los Angeles, and from there to Yokohama and Kobe. Leaving Kobe March 23, they headed for Australia-Queensland, Cairns, Lucinda and Townsville. By May 18, they had arrived in Jakarta, Java, and by the 27th were in Colombo. Here, we again have this little sign, ✠ ! In this case, "Fouled Propeller".

On June 11 they were in Calcutta, and on July 3 they again headed for Japan, where they went to Hirojata, then left for Portland, Oregon. Staying in Portland 7 days, they returned to Japan. On September 13, they arrived at Otaru, on the northern island of Hokkaido. Here Richard had enough time ashore to look in the shops. He bought a set of six artistically carved bears.

Their next port was Moji (south-western Japan). Leaving there the end of September, the ship headed back towards Java. A week later found them in the South China Sea, far from land.

One of Richard's duties was to periodically inspect the cargo, to see that it all looked safe, with the crates in proper position. Any shifting cargo could be very dangerous.

On October 6th, Richard undertook this routine job. He had sailors remove the hatch cover, which protected the deep hold beneath the deck. Then a board was put across the open top, so that Richard could walk across on it, and look down into the hold from deck level.

Richard walked onto the board as usual, something he had often done safely before. When he reached the middle and stopped to look down, the plank suddenly broke in half, due to a rotten "eye" in the wood, which no one had noticed. Richard fell to the bottom of the hold, landing onto the steel deck, 33 feet below.

The crew thought, as they rushed down to him, that they would find him dead. Miraculously, he was still alive, but had multiple fractures, and was bleeding profusely.

Suffering intensely from broken bones, and from shock, he was carried up to a cabin. They tried to make him as comfortable as they could, and applied the little first aid that they knew. The Captain, of course, had taken a medical course. But there was no doctor on board to set bones, and they could not stop the bleeding. If he was to survive, he needed prompt and skilful medical attention.

The nearest place where they knew there was a jungle hospital with a good doctor in charge was Balik Papen, on the Eastern coast of Borneo. The island of Borneo was then undeveloped, and still inhabited by savage cannibals. A discouraging place to land a desperately sick man! But the *Graiglwyd* had put into the port of Balik Papen before, and the Captain knew the channels through the Makassar Strait. Even so, Borneo was a good 12 hours' sail away. They had grave doubts whether Richard could survive that long.

Richard, however, remained conscious the whole time. He was tougher than they thought! Afterwards, he always remembered how he had to hold his elbow over a bucket to catch the blood.

Arriving in Balik Papen, he was transferred on a stretcher from the ship to a jeep, converted into a make-shift ambulance, that shook him up so much driving on the unpaved, rutted track to the primitive hospital that his wounds seemed doubly agonizing. When he was being carried into the hospital in an almost fainting condition, he heard the attendants saying that they doubted whether he would live through the night. When he was put on the operating table, they asked if he would like to see a priest. It was a Catholic mission. He said no. He felt sure, within himself, that he would survive.

The doctor came to examine him, and found that he had 16 fractures, a broken arm, leg, and pelvis, as well as broken ribs, one of which had pierced a lung.

The small hospital was very short of equipment. The doctor told Richard he would do the best he could to set all the bones, but the hospital was out of anaesthetics, so Richard would have to put up with the pain. When he began setting the bones, Richard, in his weakened condition, found the pain so unbearable that he fainted.

Waking up in bed the next day, he found one leg stretched up in traction, his arms both in plaster casts, with the rest of his body swathed in bandages. He was so glad to be alive that he knew he could gladly put up with the discomfort.

The appearance of the doctor, holding up a magazine, improved his morale. The doctor showed him a big picture of Harlech Castle! Then, Richard knew for sure that he would get well. By a strange coincidence, it turned out that the doctor, himself, was Welsh.

Richard said that he owed his life to this doctor, and to the loving care he received in the tiny hospital, in spite its lack of supplies, and few modern facilities. However, they did, luckily, have the latest (at that time) "miracle drug", Aureomycin, which they gave to Richard to fight off infection. Their biggest worry was the pierced lung, which had bled internally. They did not know how to drain it, but said that the body should be able to gradually absorb the blood, and, if no infection set in, it would heal. Which it finally did.

A bad side affect of Aureomycin was that it took Richard's appetite away. When he should have been eating to build up his strength, he could not swallow anything without being nauseated. The only solid food he could keep down was bananas. Fortunately, the island had plenty of these, and they kept him alive for the three months he was there.

All the time Richard was bedridden he was much bothered by small red ants (the "Fire Ant"), which constantly climbed up the bedposts (in spite of these sitting in saucers of kerosene, which was meant to stop them). They crawled inside his plaster casts, under which they bit him nastily – it did feel like fire! – later causing nerve-wracking itching. With the casts firmly in place, he could neither scratch underneath them, or put any ointment on the bites.

When he finally reached the stage when he was allowed to hobble slowly around the hospital grounds, he used to pass the time talking to an old Chinese man, who daily brought fresh fruit and vegetables to the hospital. This ancient person had visited the United States, and had learnt a little English.

It was a long, dreary convalescence. The doctor did not want to let Richard go before he felt that he was strong enough to make the tiring journey home without a relapse along the way.

The three months spent in Balik Papen would not be the end of his treatment. The doctor had been unable to set his bones properly without anaesthetics. He had only done an emergency patch-up job. When Richard got home, his arm and leg would have to be reset, followed by physiotherapy, before he could get normal use of them again. His left elbow, which had been badly smashed, would have to be reconstructed with wire, and then skin-grafting, both impossible to undertake in Balik Papen. The articulation of his left arm and hand were particularly important, as Richard was left-handed.

At last, he was dismissed from the hospital. It had been arranged for him to fly home. First, came a flight from Balik Papen to Jakarta. This was in an old rattly Army Transport plane, which had no proper seats. The body of the plane was used for cargo. Improvised benches had been put along each side, for the use of husky soldiers. The hard seat really hurt Richard, as he was painfully thin. He felt exceedingly uncomfortable, and became increasingly tired as the plane bounced around in bumpy air currents over the mountains of Borneo. Richard had lost 5 stone (70 lbs.) in the hospital. In a passport picture taken at the time, he looks as though he had just been released from a concentration camp.

He landed, exhausted, in Jakarta, where he had to change planes. He was in no mood, therefore, to find the airport in the hands of military police. Here, he was cross-examined lengthily by truculent immigration officials. Perhaps put off by his appearance, but largely, no doubt, because he had arrived to Java in a British military plane (symbol of hated "Foreign Imperialism"), they suspected that he might be a spy. Indeed, few foreigners were seen here, due to political unrest. President Sukarno's rule was now becoming increasingly harassed by the strengthening Communist forces throughout Indonesia.

No use in trying to explain that he was a merchant seaman, in transit from a jungle hospital, and that he had often been into the port of Jakarta to pick up cargo–cargoes destined for what remained of the British Empire, not for Mao's China!

The cold, impassive faces registered disgust. Night was falling when they finally allowed him to call his shipping agent, who immediately came to pick him up, got him through a road block of soldiers, and drove him to a drab hotel, where he spent a restless night.

The next day, after more talking and repeated explanations, he was finally put on a flight to Singapore, still a British Crown Colony. Here, he made straight for the famous "Raffles Hotel". No, he did not go into the "Long Bar", hoping to see Somerset Maugham drinking a gin-and-tonic! He went right to his room, and fell into bed, exhausted.

Waking up in luxurious surroundings, after a good night's sleep, he felt much better. He found he could eat a big traditional English breakfast, the first meal he had enjoyed since his accident.

Then he boarded BOAC's "Constellation", on a flight to London. He really began to eat and to feel more relaxed on this comfortable plane. By the time it neared Britain, he knew everything was going to be all right.

"Dick Australia" (or, just plain "Dick", as he had not as yet moved to Australia) was at the airport to meet him. Richard spent the weekend in London with Dick and his family, then Chrissie came to drive him back to Wales.

After a short rest at home, Richard went to Gobowen Orthopaedic Hospital, near Oswestry in Shropshire, which specializes in physiotherapy, for his further treatment. His arm and leg were attended to, and as they healed, he was given all kinds of exercises to regain their use, and to prevent the muscles from stiffening up while healing. These exercises were tiring, boring, and painful, but had to be done. Exercising in the hospital pool was pleasant, and also proved very beneficial.

It was lonely, however, far from family and friends, who could rarely go to see him. A tiny little girl, whose legs had been very much crippled by polio, was a cheery companion in the pool. She used to hop along the corridor like a grasshopper to his ward. When he felt low, she would laugh, and say she knew he'd get better, if he just kept on trying.

"That's just what I'm doing myself!" she'd say. Her courage was an inspiration to him.

The doctors told Richard it would take six months before he would be well enough to leave the hospital. Richard answered:

"I'll do it in three."

And he did! By May, 1954, he was home.

The worst after affect he was left with was that tendons had been badly shortened (or tightened) in his left hand, as the plaster cast had been left on too long in Balik Papen. He had been unable to exercise his fingers. He never had the same strength in it again that he had in his right. On the other hand, his elbow, which was marvellously rebuilt in Gobowen, gave no trouble. He was put to work exercising it, and his shoulder, at the proper time.

Unfortunately, as he grew older, the articulation of his fingers in the left hand became worse, becoming increasingly stiff and bent. It did not bother him too much, however, until the last few years of his life, when he had a hard time holding cups steadily, or even writing – very frustrating for a left-handed person. Janet's husband, Don, a brilliant surgeon, kept telling him that he could have the hand operated on easily, to get the fingers back to normal. But he never did. No one really wants to undergo an operation!

I blame this condition more on Gobowen Hospital than on Balik Papen, as they could have made sure that the hand would be alright while he was still there. Another minor condition he was left with was the "seaman's roll", as the broken leg had mended slightly shorter than the other.

He never complained about these after affects, and always emphasized the wonderful care he had had in both hospitals.

Richard's Discharge book had been stamped 7/10/53, at Balik Papen. His last trip on the *Graiglwyd* was marked Voyage 58, the number of voyages he had completed since his first engagement as a young officer in the Merchant Navy. This book was now completed, with a note: "Official replacement has been issued." His new book, issued May 27, 1954, has only 8 voyages listed, after which he finally received his command.

A curious fact emerges here that Ships' Masters do not have "The Seaman's Record Book and Certificate of Discharge" issued to them. Instead, they are taken on by contract, as "Company's Servants".

If a Master does not keep a record of what ships he commanded, and the names of the ports where they went, along with the dates, much research in shipping offices must be done later by anyone wanting this information. Richard himself kept no record. Basically a modest man, he thought no one would be interested in his career.

13. THE BOOTH LINE

Richard, after a short rest at home, started looking for another ship. Undaunted by his accident, he was as keen as ever to return to sea.

He let no grass grow under his feet. As soon as he felt strong enough to work again, he wrote to his old shipping associates, T. Geo. Thomas & Co., enquiring about vacancies.

I quote from a very nice reply he received from them, dated May 22:

"All the vessels are now away and we do not anticipate any of them home for at least a couple of months, therefore, we cannot offer you a berth at the moment.

"We sincerely regret this, as like yourself, we feel after so many years that we do not want the association to end. . ."

"We should be obliged if you would let us know what you now propose to do, and even if you should take another vessel we should still like you to keep in touch with us as we would very much like you to re-join one of the vessels for which we act as Superintendents on the first occasion.

"We should like to take this opportunity of extending to you our congratulations on your recovery and with kind regards from everyone here to both yourself and your family."

Yours faithfully,
Philip D. Thomas

As it was, the doctor thought it would be better for Richard to have a short job nearer home, until he got his full strength back. Therefore, Richard got a fill-in job as First Mate on the Holyhead-Dublin Ferries. He was with them for 5 months, and found it easy work. The company would have been pleased if he had stayed on, and had taken command of one of their ships when an opening came up, but Richard had his sights set higher.

By October, Richard was again corresponding with Thomas & Co. On the 26th, they wrote that the *S.S.Daydawn* (probably the sister ship of the *Daybeam*) was due into London, and might have an opening for him. However, on the 28th, they wrote that the vessel had been sold by the owners, of which they had not previously been informed.

"It is a great disappointment to us that this has occurred as we were looking forward to your rejoining one of the ships for which we act as Superintendents, and in fact, we will do so should the occasion occur in the future."

His old ship, the *Graiglwyd*, was due in Avonmouth in November, but so far had no opening.

Berths were still hard to find! However, these letters show the high regard these shipping agents had for Richard. They obviously considered him to be an outstanding officer.

One cannot keep a good man down! By November 12th Richard had joined the Booth Steamship Company Ltd., of Liverpool. He was to remain with this old, respected company until he left the Merchant Navy in 1967.

The Booth Steamship Company, Ltd. (Liverpool and New York) had originally opened up trade on the Amazon in the 19th Century, sailing up to Manaus at the height of the rubber boom. For many years, it held a virtual monopoly in this area, and was known as "Maggie's", after Maggie Booth, last owner of the name. When Richard joined the company, some people still remembered "Old Maggie Booth", who had run the company with a firm hand. She "took a keen interest in everybody who sailed in her ships, even to making sure the firemen's wives were getting their allotments properly. If not, the husband found himself in trouble." (Quotation from letter to me from Captain Kinghorn.)

The company had been taken over by Ronald Vestey, who greatly expanded the fleet, with ships going all over the world. He consolidated Booth with the Blue Star Line, Lamport and Holt, and many associated companies flying "flags of convenience", into a vast organisation. The ships not only carried lumber and general cargo, but, especially, frozen meat and fish.

Ronald Vestey's grandfather had been an Argentinian beef baron of Jewish origin. His father was the British Sir Edmund Vestey, whose brother William was created Lord Vestey in 1922. Together these two brothers had, in Liverpool, built up their huge frozen food and shipping business. When Ronald, easily an American style tycoon, took over, he increased the family fortunes to such an extent that they were 2nd only to those of the Duke of Westminster. Deeply religious, he gave an enormous sum towards the building of Liverpool's Anglican Cathedral, in memory of his father. He, himself, was a cattle king, and also operator of several experimental farms in Australia and other countries overseas. The Vestey frozen food concern remains one of the biggest in the world. His Blue Star Line alone had 16,000 ton freighters carrying frozen beef exclusively, from Buenas Aires.

The Booth Line promised Richard his command, but while waiting for an opening he still had to accept being Chief Officer.

His first ship with the company was the M.V. *Dominic*, a wartime Hickory Class ship, built by Consolidated Steel Corp., Wilmington, California, and acquired by Booth in 1947. [1]

Richard joined the ship in Liverpool on December 3, 1954. The ship went on to the Royal Docks, London (No. 12, King George V.) before sailing for South America. This voyage marks an important milestone in Richard's

Richard's first ship with the Booth Line was the *Dominic*. She had been built in the U.S. in 1945 as the *Hickory Stream*
(*FotoFlite*)

career, as it was his introduction to the Amazon, on which he was to become an expert.

The following lively account of this voyage has been given to me by Captain A. W. Kinghorn,[2] who served for 37 years in the Blue Star Line before early retirement, and is now with Guan Guan Shipping Ltd., the Golden Line, of Singapore.

"For me it was a fascinating voyage as I had recently completed my cadetship in the Blue Star Line and was now second mate with a brand new ticket on which the ink was hardly dry. I had never visited the Amazon regions before and it was totally absorbing. We sailed from London around the 10th" (December) ". . . for La Guairia, in Venezuela. Thence it was Puerto La Cruz, Willemstad (Curaçao), Cartegena, Belém, Sao Luiz de Naranhao, Fortaleza, Tutoya Bay, Belém, Manaus, Belém, New York; Norfolk, Virginia, Newport news (to take on coal)), Recife, Cabadello, Camocim, Fortaleza, Belém, Manaus, Itacoatiara, Belém, Liverpool, Rotterdam, Antwerp and Liverpool.

"The third mate was nineteen, Tony Roberts, whose brother became a Lamport and Holt superintendent in Liverpool and whose late father had been a vicar – a nice lad. I was 19.

"Your husband was, of course, considerably older than we were. . . Captain G.G. Roberts had been a midshipman in the Battle of Jutland, which dates him! . . . The chief engineer, from Glasgow, was Mr. Watson, and the purser. . . another Liverpudlian, who had an American wife, became personnel manager in New York for the Blue Star Group (Bill Hobday, alias `Hubble Bubble').

". . . Your husband was a kind man – one of the first things he showed me was how to start the Gyro Compass. The old man had told his new and very green second mate to start it and I didn't dare confess I'd never even seen one-the ships in which I'd served my time got by on magnetic compass only! I didn't dare tell the old man this, of course, and to my intense relief your husband came to my rescue when he saw me staring numbly at it. It was a large wartime Sperry model – the ship having been built in California in 1945 for the American Navy. She remained in the Booth Line fleet until around 1962, when she came East, to, coincidentally, my present employers – first as the *Samodra Mas* of Hong Kong, later renamed *Golden Ocean*, which is English for *Samodra Mas*, which is Indonesian. I saw her in drydock here in Singapore, September 1969. She foundered and was lost in the Bay of Bengal a few years later, fortunately without loss of life, near the Andaman Islands. When Dick and I were in her she sprang a leak once – a welded seam opened up! – fortunately in the Engine Room where it was promptly repaired with a cement box applied by your husband and the carpenter.

". . . I never met your husband again after 1955, but was pleased to learn he got command several years later. I recall him telling me about his own apprenticeship, including Spanish Civil War, etc. That voyage in the *Dominic* he taught me a great deal, especially about the special cargo work undertaken in the then busy Amazon trades. When we sailed for New York we had deck cargo piled right up above the mast house tops, and she was never empty; acting for part of our voyage as a feeder ship for the liners *Hubert* and *Hilary*, bringing cargo for them (in Belém) from the smaller outports. The third mate and I – just a couple of kids really – used to play awful pranks on Dick, but he always took them in good part – he was a fatherly figure in our eyes."

This first voyage on the *Dominic* was followed by another, July 5, 1955- Oct. 24.

Richard then served as Chief Officer on three more ships before receiving his Command:

1) S.S. *Sallust*   (G T. 2,993)
   "   "   Jan. 26, 1956 - June 17, 1956
   "   "   June 29, "   - Oct. 6,   "
   "   "   Oct. 15, "   - Jan. 22, 1957
   "   "   Jan. 31, 1957 - Aug. 12, "

The Booth Line steamship *Dunstan* was briefly owned by Lamport & Holt (1956-7) and then sailed as the *Sallust*. Richard was her Chief Officer, later becoming her Master when she was resold to Booth.   *(FotoFlite)*

The *Sallust*, originally named the *Dunstan*, was in 1956 and 1957 owned by Lamport and Holt, but on charter to Booth. She was sold back to Booth in 1958, when she was again named the *Dunstan*.

2) *S.S. Denis* (G.T. 2,990)
Oct. 8,'57- Oct. 28,'57

3) *S.S. Crispin* (G.T. 1,593)
Oct. 29,'57- Mar. 7,'58

Booth Line's *S.S. Denis* normally traded from Liverpool up the Amazon to Manaus, taking more passengers than the company's smaller ships.

(Tom Rayner)

Built in 1956 in Holland the *Crispin* was designed to trade up the Amazon from New York. *(FotoFlite)*

14. COMMANDANTÉ JACARÉ

MASTER AT LAST!

On April 30, 1958, Richard joined the M.V *Vamos* (G.T. 1,090) as Chief Officer. The following day, May 1, he was promoted to Master. May Day, 1958, was a red-letter day in Richard's life. (Curiously, his death also occurred on May Day, exactly 30 years after receiving his command.)

Between May 1, 1958, and July 11, 1967, when he left the company, Richard was Master of the following ships: the *Vamos*, *Vigilante*, *Dominic*, *Sheridan*, *Bede*, *Basil*, *Valiente*, *Veloz*, *Clement*, *Dunstan*, and *Venimos*. These ships all sailed to the Amazon, some leaving from Liverpool, others from New York. Also included in their itinerary were Canadian and West Indian ports, plus many coastal ports in South America, going as far south as Porto Allegre, near the Uruguay border. The *Dominic*, 3,860 Gross Tons, the *Dunstan*. 2,993 G.T., the *Clement*, 1,565 G.T., and some others were too large to go further upriver than Manaus. These ships usually sailed from Liverpool, whereas the small "V" boats, averaging 1,000 to 1,500 tons operated out of New York.

The run upriver from Manaus to Iquitos had not been much used before 1958 by Booth Line ships, due to dangerous swift currents and chances of

Norwegian-built in 1954, the *Vamos* was bareboat-chartered to Booth for 14 years. She was Richard's first command. *(A. Duncan)*

The *Bede* was briefly in the Booth fleet, from 1961-3.   *(A. Duncan)*

being stuck on sandbars, plus lack of good navigational charts. But when Richard successfully pioneered navigation of this region with the *Vamos*, Booth decided that it would be commercially feasible to open up the area for trade. Many voyages to the headwaters at Iquitos were to follow by the "V" Boats.

The *Vamos*, although well-behaved on the River, was by no means Richard's favourite ship. He felt there was some fault in her construction, and that she was very unstable in heavy seas. He was to be proved correct. Sold to a Panamanian company in 1968, and renamed the *Defiance*, she turned turtle and sank in 1969 off the coast of Peru.

The largest ship ever owned by Booth was the *Anselm*, 10,946 G.T. She was a First Class passenger ship, taking cruises to Manaus in 1961-63. Booth, after World War II, also operated three other passenger ships to the Amazon: the *Hilary*, the *Hildebrand*, and the *Hubert*. But by 1964, the company had given up passenger ships. On their cargo vessels, however, 2 or 3 cabins were usually reserved for the more adventurous type of traveller.

Richard himself never served as an officer on one of the large passenger ships, and was very glad he never had to do so. However, one of the cargo ships on which he was Master, the *Denis*, (G.T. 2,990), had additional accommodation for passengers, taking groups as far as Manaus. He only did one brief voyage on her, and this was just as well, as he told me that this experience proved that he would hate being the Captain of a passenger ship. He had to spend too much time being pleasant to people, which took his mind off his work. He was sociable by nature, but not when he was responsible for the safety of a ship. He pointed out that on very large cruise ships such as the *QE 2* there are always two Captains, one to run the ship, and the other having duties more like a Social Director.

The *Veloz*, the *Venimos*, and the *Valiente*, all sister ships, were built especially for the Amazon. After they were lengthened, he was the first Captain to take a ship of this size up to Iquitos, Peru. Later on, Ronald Vestey asked Richard to investigate the river even further up, as far as Pucallpa. Here the river becomes the Ucayali, part of the head-waters of the Amazon (as is the Solimöes at Iquitos). From Pucallpa on, the river turns into a turbulent torrent tumbling down from the Andes and is not navigable. Richard thought it might be possible to take a ship up to Pucallpa, but only during the rainy season, when the water level is high. This project never took place – perhaps because it was not economically worthwhile, since there was too much risk of a ship getting stuck on sandbars.

On December 28, 1960, Richard was again on the *Dominic*, this time as Master, for a coastal run from West Hartlepool to South Shields. On board until Jan. 13, 1961, was a young engineer, new to the company, P. Ronald Duckworth, who writes:

"Those 2 short weeks were to prove most important ones for me as the late Mr. Clatworthy, Personnel Supervisor, remarked. `We were taking a look at you, and no doubt you were looking at us.' This mutual inspection resulted in my immediately being offered Chief Engineer's post on the U.S. Coast vessels. Ever since then I have felt that some favourable comment from your husband helped me on the way."

"Our next meeting was not until 1972 when, and I wonder if you remember this, Captain Humphreys, your good self and 2 young children paid a visit one evening to M.V. *Viajero* in St. Lucia. What pleased me immediately was that your husband remembered me from those few days on the *Dominic*."[1]

This was characteristic of Richard. He always took a personal interest in the people who served with him on his ships, and would naturally remember someone whom he thought was a good officer, or sailor, as the case might be.

Mr. Duckworth goes on to comment "It is a pity that Booth Line records have been destroyed." (All the company's records from the 60's were destroyed when the Booth Line's American office in New York was given up.)

"Indeed, I find it puzzling, to say the least. Fortunately, for myself, I have always kept copious notes on engineering matters, as well as arrival & departure dates of every port visited during my 37 years of seafaring. What a pity so little relates to Capt. Humphreys."

Perhaps, as Master, Richard had so much book-keeping and other duties to attend to that he did not have time to keep his own diary. This has made research into this period of his life particularly difficult.

The M.V. *Clement* went to logging ports along the coat of Brazil and as far North as Montreal. *(A. Duncan)*

By January, 1964, Richard was commanding the M.V. *Clement*, going to logging ports along the coast of Brazil south of Belém: Fortaleza, Recife (Pernambuco), Salvador, Rio, Blumenau, Porto Alegre.

At Salvador, in the state of Bahia, he gave, on July 16, a fabulous cocktail party on board for the local V.I.P.s. Guest of honour was Janio Quadros, a controversial pro-Communist politician, who had been Governor of Sao Paulo, and then (1961) President of Brazil.

For the party, Richard served a powerful punch, which had already acquired a rather dubious reputation in shipping circles. Rumours about the drink had drifted down the coast ahead of the *Clement*. Made from a mixture of rum, whisky, gin, curaçao, angostura, tropical fruit juices, and anything else he felt like adding on the spur of the moment, Richard called it "The Bombe Atomica".

When Quadros, a dark-haired, lively looking man, arrived, Richard immediately handed him a glass.

"I've heard of this," smiled the ex-President, eagerly drinking. After a pause he continued, "But I don't feel any affect."

"Well, try another!" answered Richard.

After chatting for a while, everyone sat down at tables. This was just as well, as by the time the third round of drinks had been enjoyed, the "Bombe Atomica" had done its work.

By November, the *Clement* was in Montreal, then went on to Quebec.

Here occurred an embarrassing episode.

On November 4, a Quebec newspaper reports (translated from the French):

"A cargo ship demolishes a bridge. . . the bridge is a total loss and the damages are evaluated at approximately a million dollars. . . the ship was carrying a cargo of rolls of paper."

The *Clement*, however, sailed the following day with little damage, after a certificate of Seaworthiness was granted by Lloyd's. Richard claimed that the bridge, an old one, was due to be rebuilt anyway, so he had just saved the city some demolition charges!

The only serious accident Richard ever had with a ship during his long career, he was exonerated from any blame. Here is his own report:

(Extract from Official Log, *M.V. Clement*)

"Whilst docking vessel at Shed 19, Louise Outer Basin Dock, Quebec City. The vessel struck Louise Basin Railway Bridge at 0327 hours on 4-11-64. This in my estimation was caused by the main engines operated in the opposite direction than indicated on the engine room telegraph i.e. ahead instead of astern although both bridge and engine room movements both agree. True facts to be ascertained later."

R. Humphreys. Master

In his letter to the Booth S.S. Co. Ltd. management, Richard continues:

"I telephoned the engine room that this was happening and gave Full Astern followed by a double ring of Full Astern. The engines were stopped and just going astern when the bridge was hit bow on. The Starboard anchor was also dropped to one shackle to try to stop the way but unsuccessfully.

". . . The following day I suggested to the Chief Engineer Mr. Beard that now we were at sea we should make every test to see how this mistake could happen. The exact movements as when the accident occurred were carried out. It was amply demonstrated that by tripping the pawl on the safety device this mistake could happen.

"May I state that I hold the engineers entirely responsible for this accident and that everything possible was done to try to avoid it. This is the third occurrence in a short period. First No. 1 Generator damaged, secondly three of the assistant stewards were caught attempting to broach cargo, and thirdly this serious accident. I am not superstitious but this ship has had her fair share of trouble and with a missionary on board as passenger I am not the only one crossing his fingers.

Regretting to make this report,
Yours faithfully,"

In 1964, Booth had begun an extensive program of "jumbo-ising" their smaller ships, lengthening them in order to increase their cargo capacity, plus installing new deck cranes. That spring and summer this work was carried out

M.V. *Veloz*, the first of the small motorships built for the Booth Line's service from New York to the West Indies, North Brazil and the Amazon. It was on this vessel that the Author met and fell in love with Captain Richard Humphreys. *(A.Duncan)*

M.V. *Venimos*, sister-ship to the *Veloz*, also specially built to go 2,300 miles up the Amazon. Shown here after lengthening. *(FotoFlite)*

on the following vessels: the *Valiente*, *Vamos*, *Viajero*, *Clement* and *Crispin*, to be followed, Mar.6-Apr.25, and June 21-Aug.24, 1965, with the sister ships *Veloz* and *Venimos*.

A special word must be said here about these last two ships, as they were soon to find a permanent place of affection in the hearts of Richard and the author. The *Veloz* was the ship on which we met, and the *Venimos* was our "honeymoon ship".

The *Veloz*, a vessel of 1,312 G.T. when built in 1955 especially for Booth, flew the Panamanian flag to avoid high British taxation; the *Venimos*, 1,309 G.T., built in Hamburg for the Salient Shipping Co. (Bermuda) Ltd., a subsidiary of the Vestey organisation, flew the Bermuda flag. She was on permanent charter to Booth. Both ships were lengthened by 60 feet, increasing their gross tonnage to 1,607 each.

Capt. J.D. Igoe, who in 1972 became Master of the *Venimos*, has described her well.

"Quite a small ship for crossing the Atlantic, nevertheless a good sea boat, and very dry in adverse weather conditions. Her size is, of course, ideal for going 1,000 miles or even 2,000 miles up the great Amazon River."[2]

The same words could be applied to the *Venimos*.

Richard had been asked by Ronald Vestey himself to supervise the jumbo-ising of the "V" boats. Some of this work was done in Hoboken, Belgium, near Antwerp; and some in Lekkerkirk, the Netherlands, in the Rotterdam District on the River Lek, where the shipyard, T. van Duivendijk Scheepswerf N.V. had built many ships for the Booth Line. The fact that Vestey wanted Richard to supervise the work was a fine tribute to his excellent knowledge of marine architecture.

Richard greatly enjoyed this interesting job. It kept him busy between his South American voyages, with the company sometimes flying him to the Continent to save time, where he would shuttle by train between the two shipyards. This work was quite an undertaking. The steel hulls of the ships were cut in half, then the parts rivetted together. This was a challenging job even for these top-notch shipyards, as the hulls of the ships, which could easily have been weakened by such work, had to be so strongly welded together with the new parts that the ships would become as good as new, and would safely withstand the worst pressures and buffeting they would get from ocean waves.

When some of this work was to be done, Chrissie sailed from England to the Continent with Richard, not primarily to enjoy a sea trip or sightseeing, but to see their son Richard, who had previously (in 1961) finished a training course in the Royal Military Police. He was now doing his military service as an M.P. with the British Sector of the Army of Occupation in Berlin. (This, of course, was still the time of the Berlin Wall.) He rode on his motorcycle to Holland to see his mother and father.

He had been interested in medicine when he got out of school, particularly surgery, and had watched many operations in a Liverpool hospital, where he knew one of the surgeons. This doctor told Richard that his son should study to be a surgeon, as he "had the gift of the knife". However, this would have meant years of study, which did not appeal to the boy, as he was not studious by nature. He preferred to work in the open air. After his stint in Berlin, he chose, as a career, to join the motor cycle squad of the Liverpool Police Force.

The love of motorcycles ran in the family, as Christine, too, used to zoom all around the countryside when she was studying in Bangor at St. Mary's College of Education. Her father had not only given her and Richard motor bikes, but the black leather outfits to go with! Janet was the only one who did not enjoy this activity.

While doing the shipyard jobs, Richard became friendly with one of the supervisors, who was German. He had a wife and a small daughter. Richard often invited them on board for a meal, which they appreciated, their own food supply being very limited.

After Richard had returned home, tragedy struck this little family. Their child was playing near a canal close to their home, fell in, and was drowned.

The majority of Richard's voyages with the Booth Line went up the Amazon. Some were round trip from Liverpool, but they mostly went from New York, stopping to trade at ports in the Caribbean, and in Guyana, along the way. Richard had an affinity with the people along the river, particularly with the Brazilians, with whom he could speak Portuguese. He soon picked up the words from Indian dialects with which their language was mixed. Most of the other Captains knew no Portuguese, so it goes without saying that Richard became very popular. He could transact business easier and faster than the others.

He treated the river as a navigational challenge, and never got stuck for more than a few minutes on sandbanks, somewhat of a record. Many ships had been stuck not only for hours but for days, and in the dry season even had to have their cargoes removed onto barges to be able to float clear – a lot of time and money wasted for the company.

The sandbanks moved with the tides and the seasons. For that reason, charts had to be constantly renewed. Richard made the charts used by the company. At that time, there were no good official charts available. With each voyage, new notations had to be added. Even the river pilots were impressed with Richard's charts.

Richard, being a nature lover, was fascinated by the jungle environment, not only by the vegetation, but by all the exotic birds, animals and fish, not forgetting butterflies. Some of the English seamen who did this run did not enjoy it at all. They did not like the heat, were oblivious to the scenery, could not communicate with the people, and only thought of getting home. To them, it was indeed a "Green Hell".

Not long after beginning his trips on the river, he heard the local sailors chatting on deck excitedly, but they would stop talking if he approached. He had an idea that they were talking about him, so he listened carefully from a distance, and heard the words "Commandanté Jacaré" often repeated in the conversation. He cornered one of them, and asked what they were saying.

The man sheepishly hung his head, and did not answer. "Come on and tell me!" Richard said. "Were you all talking about me?"

The man nodded, but still did not want to speak.

"Well, you had better tell me – or else!" he said, with pretended sternness.

The sailor then admitted that all the new Captains, when they took over ships here, were given funny nicknames by their local crews. One Captain had been nicknamed "Commandanté Calças" ("Captain Trousers"), as he wore trousers very loose at the waist, and had a habit of often hitching them up!

"Well," laughed Richard, "that's not too bad. What is mine?"

Richard's nickname was "Commandanté Jacaré", meaning "Captain Alligator". This did not mean that they thought him vicious or dangerous like an alligator, but because he could see so much. The alligator's eyes protrude high up as though on swivels, and he can see behind his head. Richard not only could see great distances without glasses, but, like the "Jacaré", could also see what was going on behind his back, things people did not want seen! The seamen and dock-workers were all involved with as much smuggling as they could get away with. Customs officials were even bribed to look the other way when whisky, cigarettes, perfume, radios, TV's and washing machines were quietly put ashore, duty-free. But this did not escape "Jacaré's" eyes!

Within a short time everyone from Belém to Iquitos knew about "Commandanté Jacaré"; but the name was spoken with respect and affection.

Richard's love of animals came to the fore on the river. One day, when they had stopped at a small logging port, Richard was on deck, leaning over the railing observing the activity on the dock. He noticed a man dragging what looked like a large, bedraggled kitten along at the end of a string, which was tied tightly around his neck and almost strangling him.

Looking more carefully, he saw that it was an ocelot kitten, freshly caught from the jungle. It looked half starved, and unhappy. Richard could never bear to see an animal being maltreated. He gave one of the sailors some money, and told him to go ashore and buy the kitten.

"Oh no, sir! You shouldn't do that! That cat's wild," exclaimed the man, much alarmed.

"You just wait and see!" laughed Richard, who had a way with any kind of cat.

The man on shore was pleased to sell the kitten, and the sailor dragged it, struggling, up the gangplank and into Richard's cabin.

"Now bring me a saucer of steak, minced very fine, and some milk," ordered Richard.

The kitten, who had been cowering in a corner, came out immediately when he saw the food, and devoured it.

That same night, the "Wild Cat" made himself completely at home. Richard fixed an old jacket on a chair in his sitting room, thinking it would make a cosy bed for the kitten, but he ignored this, sneaked into Richard's cabin, and jumped up on the bunk. From then on, he always slept with Richard. He grew very fast, getting bigger and bigger and bigger. Soon he wanted the whole bunk to himself. He used to put his 4 paws against the wall and push his body into the middle of the bed, forcing Richard over onto the outside edge.

Richard named him "Wicked", "Wickie" for short. He became a one-man cat, with Richard his master. He used to sit on Richard's lap, and lick his face with a razor-like tongue. Months went by, and he was no longer a cute, although somewhat large kitten, or even an unusually big cat, but had become a healthy, full-grown ocelot, the size of a big dog. The crew would not get near him, although they'd stand in the doorway and look at him with rolling eyes.

Word got around about "the Captain's cat". Going into New York, one of the shipping agents came on board. He walked into Richard's sitting room very cautiously.

"I hear you have a cat," he said in a timorous voice, looking carefully around. When he did not see anything alarming, he carefully put his coat and briefcase on a chair, and then sat down on a sofa behind a big fixed table.

"Yes. Would you like to see him?" asked Richard. Without waiting for a reply, he called: "Here, Wickie!"

The table was covered by a table-cloth which hung to the floor. From underneath this, Wickie appeared, and sprang onto Richard's lap.

The agent gave a shriek, grabbed his briefcase, and leaping right over the wide table, disappeared out the door.

The sad time came when Richard was to go home on leave. No one on board wanted to keep Wickie on the ship. Richard was due to leave in New York. Here, one of the Superintendents, who liked cats, said he lived in the suburbs, and had a small garden. He could make a cage for Wickie and keep him there. Richard was afraid that he would not know how to handle Wickie, who did not take to everybody, and might turn vicious with strangers. After all, he was a wild ocelot! Even much smaller wild cats usually did not adjust well to being captive pets, Richard decided the best thing to do would be to give him to the Bronx Zoo, who were delighted to add this strong, healthy animal to their collection.

A year went by before Richard was again in New York. Right away, he went to the zoo, and stood before the ocelots' cages. There was Wickie, in a cage of his own. Richard climbed over the barrier, and went up to the cage. He called "Wickie!"

The cat came running, and started licking Richard's fingers, which he had stuck between the bars.

At this point, a keeper appeared, and cried: "Hey! get away from that cage. Thats a dangerous wild animal."

"Oh no! He knows me," Richard answered. He told the keeper about Wickie. He then asked whether he could go into the cage, and play with him.

The keeper did not want him to do that. It was against all regulations. He was, however, finally persuaded. He said he would allow Richard to do it, but only on his own responsibility.

As soon as Richard went in and called "Wickie!", kneeling down with one knee up, the animal gave one bound and landed on his knee, and started licking his face. By then quite a crowd had assembled in front of the cage. Richard stayed for a long time playing with him.

"You can't tell me cats aren't affectionate, or forget the people they love. And that goes for ocelots, too!" he always said afterwards.

Richard got into a steady routine of several months going up and down the river, followed by a vacation at home.

His family lived in the early 50's in "Afallon", a house they rented on the hillside near Harlech Castle. Although in a good location close to town, it did not get enough sun, as it had a steep cliff right behind, making the house cold and damp. Later on, they managed to get a modern, comfortable "Council House", at 49, y-Waen, close to the Grammar School, which Janet was by that time attending. In 1965, Richard bought "Llain-y-Grug" ("Amongst the Heather"), an outstanding house built of hand-dressed stone (the last one built of this material in the area). This had been built for the Bursar of Harlech College. It had a spectacular view of the bay. Richard had had his eyes on this house for a long time, and with the help of good friends was the first to know when it came up for sale at a reasonable price. With his increase in salary as Master, he could afford to buy it.

Richard, of course, enjoyed seeing his family, and being back in Wales, but as the children got older they became involved in their own activities. By 1965, young Richard was with the Liverpool Police, Janet was also in Liverpool, studying at the University, and Christine was married. By then, his mother, Jane, had died (July, "Gorffennof", 26, 1961, at the age of 78). She had had diabetes, but neither she, nor any of the family, had realized this. Without any treatment, she suddenly went into a coma. Richard arrived home from sea only a few hours before her death. Although she appeared unconscious, when he held her hand she squeezed it.

Her death left an empty place in his life. Therefore, he did not want long vacations at home, as he was rather at a loss for interesting things to do. By preference, he used to take the *Queen Elizabeth* or the *Queen Mary* from New York, instead of flying home. The company paid his fare, and he said this was his real vacation, although "a busman's holiday"! He enjoyed relaxing on the sea voyage, in luxurious surroundings, without the responsibility of looking after the ship. Here he could pick and choose with whom he wanted to talk, without hurting any feelings. He became so well-known and popular with the crew and officers on these voyages that a special seat was saved for him in the First Class bar. "That is the Captain's chair," warned the bar-tender, if anyone else tried to sit there. Passengers used to think that he was the Captain of the ship!

By 1966, he could see no change occurring in this routine. In a few years, he would be of retirement age, then would follow a comfortable, but dull and unexciting life at home, brightened somewhat by renewing contact with old school pals, and some other retired sea Captains who lived nearby – but no gardening for him!

He also had friends in the Masonic Lodge in Barmouth, of which he was a member. He had never risen high in the hierarchy, due to being away so much, yet he enjoyed the meetings when he was home. Although the Masons have come under criticism for being too exclusive, and for their secret rituals, scorned by our democratic society, yet their mysticism attracted Richard's Celtic temperament. It has now been revealed that down the centuries the Masonic Societies, in Britain, particularly those of the Scottish Rite, have preserved extraordinary, generally unknown facts concerning the early history of Christianity, which otherwise might have been lost.[3]

But Merlin the Magician had other plans for Richard. He never suspected, when he prepared to sail from Brooklyn on the *Veloz* in the summer of 1966, that on this voyage, with a wave, perhaps, of Merlin's wand, his life would be turned upside down, and completely change its course.

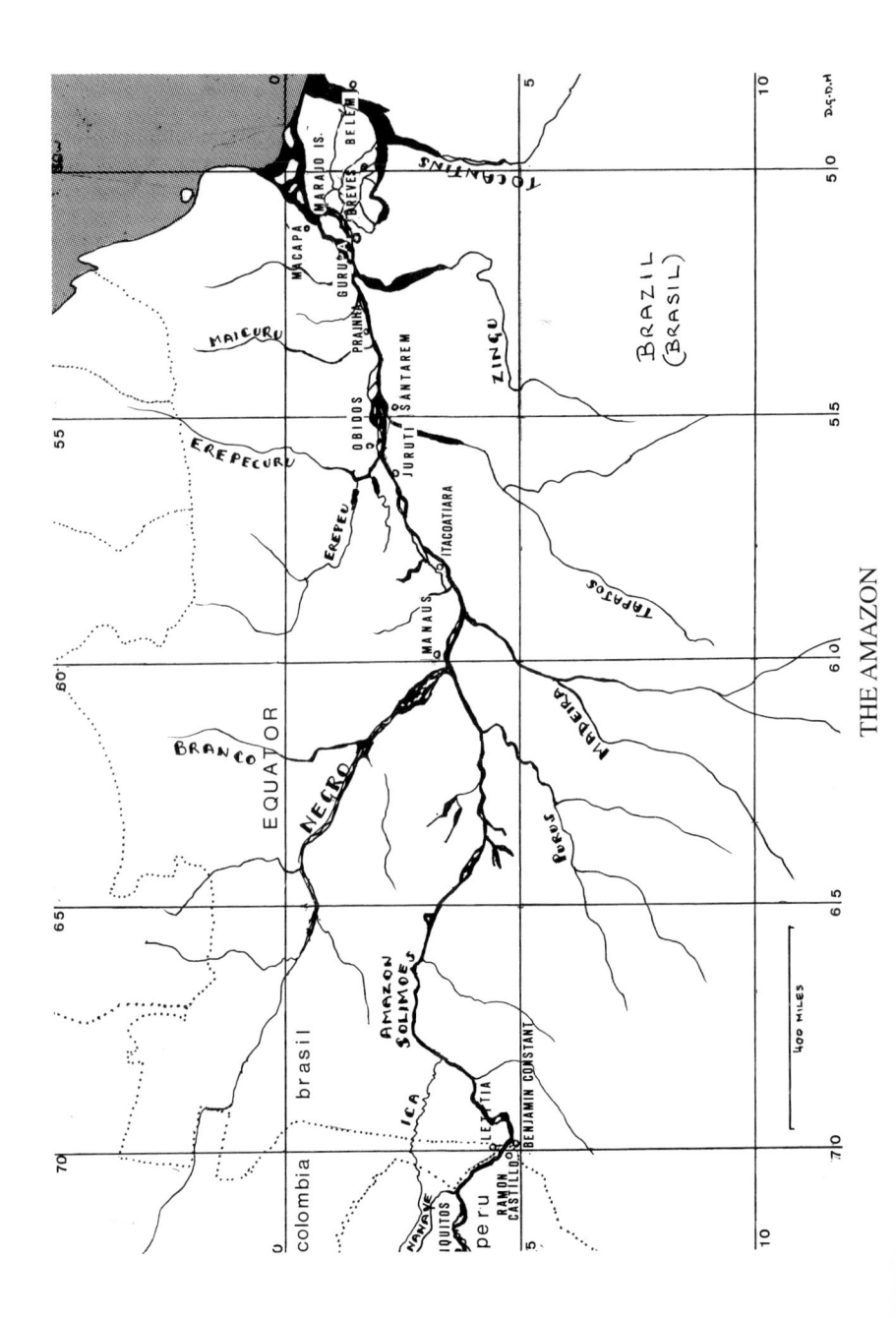

THE AMAZON

Part II.
THE AMAZON MERMAID
Her Story

Some claimed that the mermaids who lured sailors onto sandbanks on the Amazon were really Manatees. "If so, sailors must be dumber than I thought," said Richard.

PREFACE

If it had not been for George, I never would have thought of going up the Amazon. Although a seasoned traveller to places such as France, Spain, Italy, Greece, and even Mexico, I had always considered the Amazon to be the exclusive realm of explorers, head-hunters, missionaries, and botanists.

George Podbereski, my Polish husband, 19 years older than myself, had been born and bred in Kiev, where his father was an engineer with the Russian Railroad. In World War I. he had been the first to receive the highest military award, the "Virtuti Militari", in the newly formed Polish Airforce. He became a lawyer in Warsaw between the two wars, and had escaped with some of the armed forces when Hitler attacked his country in 1939. He made his way to England, where he served as Squadron Leader in the RAF during the war. After the war, he emigrated to the U.S., where he became Head of the Polish Department of the U.S. Army Language School, in Monterey, California.

Tall, good-looking, with a shock of grey hair, he always stood out in a crowd. Intellectual, distingué, well-versed in current affairs and the arts, he was a lively addition to any group.

I had gone to California from Philadelphia (my "home-town"), where my mother and father were leaders in cultural circles. When I was young, I felt dominated by them, and felt I should be independent, to find my own way of life. With a musical education, I became associated, as composer-pianist, with a theatre group in Ojai. When this folded up, I went to Carmel, where, of necessity, I took, what was to me, a dull job as Assistant Bookkeeper in a gift shop.

When George appeared at the door, with an introduction from mutual friends, my life became more interesting. I was fascinated with George, whose background had been so different from mine, and listened, spellbound, to his stories about life in Russia and Poland. I soon believed that this was love, or, let us say, it seemed like love until things began to go wrong.

George, however, before looking me up, had, cagily, asked our friends: "Does Dale have money?" ("Dale" is the nickname by which I am called by many friends.) My solid background in Philadelphia is certainly what attracted him, when it came to a serious relationship.

I would have been horrified if I had known this at the time, as I thought our love was mutual. I have never had anything but contempt for the antiquated concept of marrying for money or social position. To me, a true romantic, love is the only good reason for marriage.

After retiring from the Language School, George became President of

"The Friends of Poland" (the "Free Poland" of the Government in Exile). He also occupied himself with painting, sculpture, and designing and building houses.

We had been married for 17 years when my story begins, and had two children, Eva, a rebellious, difficult 16-year old, typical of the Hippie, "drop-out" generation, who believed that travel with her parents was a dull waste of time; and Jerzy, age 12, an enthusiast about any kind of travel, and interested in what he saw. We always travelled with them during school vacations, believing this was part of a good education, and we, ourselves, benefited from the trips. However, with children of such different natures, things did not always go smoothly, especially as George, who enjoyed cafés and nightclubs, thought children were more or less of a nuisance.

George had gradually become dissatisfied with Monterey, which he considered to be a provincial dead-end. He also thought most Americans were provincial – not very flattering to me! He complained: "I have come as far West as I can go without jumping into the Pacific. Will I be stuck in this miserable Monterey for the rest of my life? Böze! Böze!" ("God! God!")

I, on the other hand, by this time was making a place for myself in the musical world, as well as writing music criticism and travel articles for various newspapers. I enjoyed the people I met, and made good friends.

Looking back, I do not believe the Poles adjust as well to being "displaced persons" as do the Russians, many of whom seem to start anew optimistically, remaining cheerful and unembittered. There is a saying that when 3 or 4 Poles get together, there are always 3 or 4 differences of opinion, with angry voices raised. The same goes for 2 Poles! When George and his son by his first marriage, a promising young architect, got together, they were constantly shouting. (And Poles, unlike the Welsh, do not bother to translate what they are saying.)

As time went on, it appeared that George and I were temperamentally unsuited. We started to have heated arguments, particularly about love, and the meaning of life. George's gloomy attitude, so different from mine, wore me down, like the affect of a continuously taken depressant, until I, too, thought that I had reached a dead-end.

"What is Love?" George would ask. "I'm not sure there is such a thing! As for life, what meaning does it have? And after death? Just- nothing."

Travel, therefore, became a good escape from troubles at home. Wondering what our next trip should be, George suddenly said: "What about the Amazon?"

He had had a friend in Poland who had gone there, and who had told him the jungle was fantastic, and that it was the trip of a lifetime. George and I both liked hot weather, and loved tropical vegetation and wildlife, so I answered "Why not!"

We soon found out about the Booth Line, which had freighters going from New York to Iquitos, taking 4 passengers. The trip took 6 weeks, and went 2,300 miles up the Amazon, at very reasonable prices.

It still seemed like a rather frightening challenge. We would need smallpox, typhoid, and yellow fever shots. What of malaria, dysentery, sleeping sickness? Would it be safe to take the children? We attended a lecture in San Francisco by the controversial German, Dr. Binder, a specialist in tropical diseases. He and his wife ran a jungle hospital on the Ucayali, one of the headwaters of the Amazon, for the benefit of the Indians. He was trying to help them fight disease, and also encouraging them to take a pride in their own culture, and not succumb to the missionaries, or other exploiters.

Peruvian government officials in Lima were opposed to his work, and spread rumours that he was a Nazi. They did not want to help Indians. They wanted to grab their land. No financial aid was given him, and he had to spend months every year lecturing abroad, in order to raise the money to keep the hospital going. We were invited to visit the hospital, if we got that far up the river! "The Booth Line ships are very clean," he said. "You should be in no danger. But, be sure to take Entero-Vioformo daily," (a drug then considered to be the best protection against dysentery), "and continue doing so for another three weeks after getting home," the good doctor advised. "And wear long-sleeved shirts in the evening against mosquitos!"

What about snake bite? We hurried to buy heavy knee-high jungle boots. I was still apprehensive. What about vampire bats, Tsetse flies, leeches, and jiggers that got under the skin? But when we were packed with all our protective clothes and medicines, plus cameras, binoculars, and lots of film, I found myself eagerly looking forward to the trip.

15. AN AMERICAN AT SEA

July 18, 1966, Monday

"Don't know why you want to take a boat like that! Six weeks on a freighter! No! It would be too dull for me. Hope you took along lots of cards and chequers." The cab driver's words floated back to me on a 90-degree wind, as we rushed along the East River Freeway towards Brooklyn.

"Isn't there any other ship that's faster to South America?"

No use to explain that we looked forward to lazy days on the Caribbean, that we welcomed idle days floating up the Amazon, surrounded (as we hoped) by exotic birds and butterflies.

Janek (my step-son) had asked for our lawyer's name and address.

"Farewell!" he exclaimed, as he went off to work, as though we should disappear forever into the jungle, like Fawcett.

4 PM We are settled in our cabins on the *M.V. Veloz,* of "The Booth Steamship Company, Ltd.", also called the "Booth American Shipping Corp." by their New York office.

The fans are blowing, and fly and mosquito repellant are on the tables. It seems as though we are in an exotic port of call already. We have met the Chief Engineer, a short, humorous, friendly man, who introduced himself as Arthur Resson. Now he takes us down the hall to meet the Captain, who had been occupied talking to some businessmen when we first came aboard. George remarked to me later that he thinks Captain Humphreys has a forbidding look, like someone who would be very hard with his men, but I disagree. He looks like a tower of strength to me, someone who could cope with any emergency at sea. Yet I detect a tremendous kindness underneath, and I feel absolutely reassured about the unknown, perilous voyage which lies ahead.

"Are you both English?" I ask.

"No, only one of us," replies the Captain. "I'm Welsh." The Chief Officer is Polish! And served in the Polish forces in England during the war.

One other passenger is expected, an unknown named Pendleton, who will leave the ship at Dominica.

After 3 weeks of delay, due to labour strikes on the river in Brazil, and another delay last weekend (when the refrigeration broke down), we are delayed again. We'll not sail until tomorrow. However, as we're booked on the ship from 1 PM today, we may remain on board. I recollect Tomlinson, and how he sat on his ship waiting in the cold and rain in some Welsh port.[1]

6.30 PM The Chief Officer's name is Ogonowski (Joe). He and George talked Polish in the "Smoking Lounge", over a beer. He knows the husband of George's old girl friend, who lives in the Bahamas. (He was George's superior officer during the war.) Joe says another Pole lives in Iquitos (the late Mayor of Iquitos!) The Amazon is magnificent, he says. The first time one goes up! This will be his sixth.

"Any place becomes monotonous after a while." New York last week, he adds, was hotter than the Amazon ever gets. It was 106 degrees here!

This happens to be Jerzy's 13th birthday. No cake! I had no time to arrange one, although before getting on the ship I had thought I might ask the cook to bake one. At dinner we had English pudding with custard sauce, and strong black English tea!

We are flying the Panamanian flag, but on a life preserver our home port is marked "Liverpool". We are 1,300 tons net, 3,000 tons gross (this is with cargo). There is still another tonnage called "Dead Weight", but Ogonowski can't remember what this is! The ship is 11 years old, and last year was lengthened by 64 feet. She is over 300 ft. long, narrow, with sleek, stylish lines, painted pale grey, sparkling and beautiful. We were built particularly for the Amazon, and are the largest sized vessel that can go up to Iquitos.

The Captain also tells us the Amazon trip is magnificent. He often lectures to school children and their teachers about it in Wales. He says it will be a better education than school for our children. The ship will go so near the shore we will almost be able to touch branches of the trees. We'll see monkeys, parrots, macaws, butterflies, moths.

"I never get tired of it," he remarked. "Every time one can see something new. If one is looking, of course."

Mr. Resson emphasizes stars, and cloud effects. "Stars one never sees anywhere else, and cloud effects particular to the Amazon."

"I've been all over, Africa, Malaya, and have never seen such vegetation," adds the Captain.

A cargo of apples, biscuits, frozen foods, chicken, fish, perfumes, clothes, machinery, prefabricated housing. Almost anything. Looking over the side into the open warehouse, I see cargo unloaded from the last voyage; unrefined rubber in grey, corrugated bundles, and stacked cartons marked in Spanish,"Manteca"("fat"- meaning butter or lard). Later, we learn that our cargo is worth several million dollars! In the lounge we watch on TV the ascent of Gemini 10. (The TV will go ashore when we sail, as will the telephone.) The lounge is cosy. Two card tables with chequer-board tops, chintz-covered chairs, a small library.

Mr. Pendleton appears on deck. He has resigned after 19 years with the American Express, and is headed for Dominica (a British island), where he has bought 55 acres of coconut plantation. He uses hairless sheep to keep down the grass.

"Do you shear the sheep?" he said he asked his native manager.

"No", the man replied. "They are born that way. Is there a different variety?" When told that wool comes form long- haired sheep, he remained silent.

The next day he returned, and said: "Yes, you were right. It is true that wool clothes are made from sheep's hair. I have asked the school teacher, who has agreed that this is true!"

We sit in the cool breezes of the stern deck (which is gaily bedecked with coloured lights), and watch the lively East River traffic. A ferry crosses from the Battery every five minutes to Staten Island, and in the background looms the Statue of Liberty. Many barges go by loaded with freight trains. Several large cargo boats, tugs, and a small passenger steamer are sailing out to sea. Helicopters bring commuters from the airport, and suck the water up into frothy waves as they come in to a landing platform near the harbour. The view of lower Manhattan from across the water is that of a fantastic Space-Age fortress with no point of entry. The sun sinks behind its turrets and lights glitter on. The highest building has a translucent green top. George takes a colour time exposure, but can a photo capture the flavour of the scene? We feel we are on a luxury yacht, but Onassis or Niarchos would never appreciate this. They would be too busy worrying about finances!

Tuesday, July 19

Loading most of the day. More apples, cabbages, olive oil, and machinery. Several tractors on the forward deck. One weighs 8, another 11 tons. One in the hold weighs 21 tons. All for Antigua. The officers are worried how they will unload the heavy one, which was loaded on by a barge. The *Veloz's* crane is only meant to handle weights of up to 20 tons.

We walked to the Brooklyn Post Office, which is guarded by policemen. There were race riots last night. One woman was killed. It is unpleasant walking back to the ship through the warehouses. The stevedores are rough and resentful of passengers. One has the feeling that they would like to ban passengers from freighters, as the Longshoremen's Union might be responsible if a passenger got hurt. One man stopped loading a truck so we could get by.

"Go on, you beautiful woman," he grumbled.

4.10 PM   Sailed at last. New York shimmered in a hazy glare. Rounded the East side of Staten Island, where a row of freighters from all over the world lined the shore. We were cornered on deck by a young drunken crew member, who lent George two books, one about the First World War, and another about the treatment of Jews by Poland during the Second.

"You just read this, and we'll get together with Ogonowski one night over a bottle of whisky. I'd like to hear what you'd both say about it. It'd be fun to hear you argue, and I'd just sit back and listen!"

"I just got 7 bottles of Tequila last night," he continued, "from the Mexican freighter that was berthed next to us. Think I'll go down now to the cabin and have a drink. You should see Ogonowski when he's drunk! Last time out he got a big board on the end of a rope, hung it over the side, and smashed it into Resson's porthole. Did the same on the new 10-story building in Belém."

"How many times have you been across the Equator?" asks George.

"50! Off Belém there is a small island which crosses the Equator. All you have to do is to run around a rock there which is exactly on the Equator. You can cross it as many times as you want. But I don't know why you want to go up the Amazon. I've been there 7 times myself. Hope you have plenty of insect repellant. I made an insect collection last time for a friend in New Jersey. Caught them right here on the deck. Beetles as big as your hand, with snapping jaws! I've just signed on for another year. Must have been crazy!"

The skyline has faded. We are following the channel marked by a row of groaning buoys. A choppy sea and a high wind as the pilot climbs over the side near the Amboys.

After dinner (here called "Tea"), we are invited into Mr. Resson's cabin to hear the short-wave BBC news, direct from England. The Captain is writing down the soccer (which the British call "football") scores, as he, George, Mr. Resson, Mr. Pendleton and myself all sit around a small table. We hear how Queen Elizabeth received King Hussein of Jordan and his wife. "She was a typist in London once," somebody says. "Buckingham Palace was a bower of sweetpeas," says the announcer. "That's all our money," says Mr. Resson, waving his arms grandly.

"And does she ever receive us?" asks the Captain, with mock humour. "But she is good for the Commonwealth, something it is hard for Americans to understand."

The porthole is shut, and the air thickens with cigarette and cigar smoke. Conversation turns to politics: how England lost Suez thanks to American pressure, "when we should have just taken Egypt and avoided this whole mess in the Middle East," says Resson, a retired British Naval officer.

"You Americans are too young in political experience. Now you are trying to lead the world, and look at the mess in Vietnam!" the Captain continues.

The ship is rolling and pitching. "Excuse me, please, I feel very tired," I say hastily.

"The poor girl is tired!" Resson says, in mock sympathy. I rush up the ladder-like stairs in the dark (no one has turned the hall light on), and just make it to the bathroom. Seasick!

Wednesday, July 20

Seasick! An ignominious beginning to the great adventure. Lie in the bunk all day.

I have insisted on taking the upper berth, although George complains that its "unladylike", There's more room to sit up and write my journal, and read in bed. Its hard to get out of with a rough sea, though.

A grey sky and high swells. I'm ashamed of myself, as I don't think she's rolling as much as the *Saturnia* the day they strung ropes around the lounge (in the Mediterranean) and I wasn't seasick at all. I feel very tired and just want to sleep. I think I'm having a reaction after all the excitement of getting off. Or maybe its after eating too much lobster when Janek took us out for dinner!

"Get up, Dale! There's no excuse for you to be tired," shouts George.

Excitement occurs about the children's key. They have locked it in their cabin, and there's no duplicate! A sailor has to cut the screen off the porthole and climb in to open the door. Then he fixes the door so that its impossible to lock. A subtle revenge!

I begin to feel a little better, and go out on deck in the evening. Eva sees a school of dolphins.

"Porpoises!" says the Captain. "Americans call them dolphins. Dolphins are fish. These are porpoises – mammals."

I notice a flock of small birds following the ship. But, being no naturalist, I do not know their names.

Thursday, July 21

Higher swells, and much rolling and pitching.

"We skirted a hurricane last night. Winds up to 70 miles an hour. This is the hurricane season!" announces the Captain, cheerily.

The air is warmer. The sun is burning through the overcast, and the water is dark blue under a steel grey surface. We are south of the Gulf Stream. Jerzy sees the first flying fish.

Talk at the breakfast table turns to the Amazon and its wildlife. We tell how we saw a coiled boa-constrictor about 6 feet long under a stump on the beach in San Blas (Mexico).

"That's nothing!" exclaims the Captain. "I myself saw a watersnake 20 feet long in the river at Manaus. The sailors caught it and brought it up hissing. The scientists now think its possible for an anaconda to grow to 60 feet. I have heard of them 135! Anything is possible on the Amazon. We do not really know what it contains."

He takes us into his cabin to show us a collection of moths (from New Jersey!) he is taking to exchange for an Amazonian collection for a New Jersey couple who made the trip on the *Veloz* last January. The moths are all sizes, and coloured like flowers. Some are iridescent.

"I like dead ones better than live ones," I say gloomily.

"But they can't hurt you!" he laughs.

Nevertheless, I hope that someone puts up the fly-screens, which I found under the sofa, on our portholes before we reach the Amazon.

"She is afraid of moths! And I can't understand it!" explains George.

The Captain lends us an extraordinary book with fantastic photographs of the Amazon, "The Amazon" by Emil Schulthess. (Simon & Schuster, 1962)

The lazy days have started. We are sitting in deck chairs at the stern, our feet stretched out on the railing. Mr. Resson has had two fishing lines put over the side. They are really ropes, tied to the railing, some 150 ft. long, with an old piece of dirty shirt as bait. One is the Captain's, the other Mr. Resson's. They are having some kind of contest as to who will first catch a fish. Mr. Resson hopes to catch a kingfish or a dolphin ("Dorado"). But the Captain says he won't get anything until we reach the islands.

In the afternoon, George, Eva, Jerzy and myself walk along the lower deck to the bow. The ship is still pitching so that every few minutes the screw comes up out of the water, and slaps back with a peculiar squelching sound. We crawl past the huge tractor lashed to the deck, and up the ladder to where one can look out over the edge of the high bow. One feels like a figurehead of an old sailing vessel, with only the vastness of the ocean as horizon. Plenty of small round pieces of seaweed float by, golden through the blue water, and looking like sponges on the surface. A sure sign that we are in the Gulf Stream.

After "Tea" the ocean becomes calmer. Blue sky overhead, and a new moon high up to our left as we look over the stern. This is bad luck to George's mind, who has a half- serious superstition that one should see it over one's right shoulder for the coming month to be good. In this case, Jerzy alone saw it correctly, as he was leaning with his back to the stern at the time.

The sun goes down behind a dark cloud, and lines it with gold. Pink glows on silky aquamarine waves. The Captain comes out for an evening stroll, and tells about the Sea of Saragossa (south of here), which the sailors on the old sailing ships used to think was inhabited by sea monsters.

"In 24 hours, the sky will be blue and the sea absolutely calm," he adds.
George joins Mr. Ogonowski on the Bridge, where he has the watch. They talk for about two hours in Polish. Mr. Resson takes the children on a tour of the engine room. They come back very quickly, saying it was like Dante's Inferno, hot and dark in the lower regions. Mr. Resson appears from the depths about ten minutes later.

"I seem to have lost the children somewhere along the way!" he says with mock disappointment.

At 8 we listen to the BBC news again. The astronauts are safely down.

Friday, July 22

I was awakened at 7 this morning by sounds of slamming and banging. Looking over the edge of my upper bunk, I see our bathrobes (on hooks against the wall) flying out at odd angles, and the floor wet with water. Rain is pouring in the forward porthole, which we had left open. Books, table cloth, sofa, and George's clothes are drenched!

"The same hurricane we have been skirting ever since leaving New York," say the officers at breakfast. "They usually blow themselves out in about a fortnight!" There is rather a high sea, but I seem to have found my sea legs. However, there is nothing to do but to sleep in the cabin. By afternoon the rain has stopped. It is windy, but warm.

We have lifeboat drill. From out of the depths appear gnome-like creatures we have never seen before, spindly dark legs under bright red football-padded life preservers. Once in a while, a dirty figure has been seen up the rigging arranging a rope, or else, scrubbing down the tops of the hatches. Now they are all lined up in front of two lifeboats, over a dozen deck hands, some black, some yellow, some half-way between; all are Portuguese speaking Brazilians. In greasy work clothes, with greasy black hair and moustaches, shifty eyes look obsequiously away as one tries to catch their glance. The young (20-year old) Third Officer, British, in impeccable white shirt and shorts, with a smiling blonde face, blows a whistle, and the slaves are gone in a flash, running single-file down the ladder and along the main deck, where they are seen, a minute later, squirting enormous fire- hoses out to sea. One more minute, and the deck is again deserted.

What are they thinking of the array of British officers in their crisp white or khaki summer uniforms? Or, of us passengers in our clean airy cabins on the upper deck near the Bridge? Perhaps, like in a Conrad story, one morning they will confront us, a solid phalanx, machetes or axes in hand?

There are 26 men in the crew altogether, of which half seem to be officers! Besides the three senior officers (including the Captain) who sit at our table, there is the Chief Steward (a tall, good-looking, but rather unbending Englishman named Mr. Curtis), and at least 6 junior officers in their 20's. There is also the Radio Officer, "Sparks". I don't yet know which one he is. Then, indispensable in our section of the ship, is the dining room steward, Alfredo, small, black-haired, Portuguese (from Belém), to whom George speaks Spanish.

"But he speaks English!" protests Mr. Ogonowski. The cabin steward, husky, perspiring, is usually seen with a bucket and mop, and speaks little, except when bringing in one's early tea or coffee. Then he just exclaims, pointing at the cups, "This tea! This coffee!"

Below him in station, there appears to be a kind of cabin-boy helper, small, wizened and moustachied, with no English at all.

Mr. Curtis one hardly sees at all. He cannot arrange menus all day! Perhaps he also doubles as cook? [2]

The meals are heavily boiled-pudding English, of the liver, steak-and-kidney pie, dumplings, cabbage and boiled fish variety. Not tempting to the appetite when one feels seasick! However, good enough to stoke up the seamen's private furnaces, and certainly good quality food.

The passengers are merely a "mal necessaire", one presumes. No frills such as dressing for dinner, or sitting around over a cocktail. Here "the witching hour" is a private one in the cabin, No one seems to congregate in the lounge. No one drinks anything at table. George is afraid to order a bottle of wine (even if they have it, which we doubt), as he'd then have to treat everyone in the room! Anyway, meals are at such odd hours and so close together that one scarcely has time for a before-dinner drink. Breakfast is at 8.30, followed by Dinner (the main meal) at 12.30. At 3 PM tea-and-toast appears in the cabin. 5.30 is "Tea", really a heavy supper – for which I never feel hungry, but George manages to eat it alright!

We still have a bottle of "Haig and Haig" that we brought with us, in the cabin. George and Mr. Ogonowski polished off half of this in one sitting. Once I tried some, but for a slightly seasick person it was pretty unappetizing, served without ice, and with Schweppes Club Soda, which was warm and without fizz.

Later in the afternoon I am sitting on deck and Mr. Resson starts to fill my ears with eery stories about the Amazon. First, he says the Captain's description of an anaconda 135 feet long is quite true! He says he bought a photograph in Manaus of a giant anaconda 44 metres in length, half in, half out of the river, but its body visible, with huge jaws open. The photo showed a number of natives trying to pull it onto the river bank. He said he first wondered if the photo wasn't a fake. He showed it to a professional photographer, who happened to be a passenger on the *Veloz* at the time. This man said that although it was a poor photograph, he was certain that it had not been retouched or faked in any way. He was sure that it was authentic!

"I can show you the photo any time," added Mr. Resson. "Have it in my cabin."

"Once, some years before I joined the ship, an anaconda got one of our officers. We tie up to a floating pier in Manaus, and have to take a small boat to shore. One night this officer was returning to the ship late, around midnight. It was very dark, and he was standing at the foot of some steps by the small boat landing, waiting for the boat to pick him up. Well, he never got into that boat! Anaconda came and carried him away."

"Wait until you meet this Maxwell woman," he continued. "Queer American living up in Iquitos. She has plenty of stories about the jungle. Takes people out on safaris. Came here several years ago to write a book about modern uses for native medicines. She was paid by some American pharmaceutical company to do it. She learnt native dialects and went and lived among the Indians. Called her book "Witch Doctor's Apprentice", but the publisher didn't like that. He changed the title to something like "The

Jungle Search for Nature's Cures". She found out a lot of things. Indians have a cure for toothache. They stuff the cavity with some leaf, and the ache stops immediately. A little later, the tooth disintegrates and falls out."

"At first I wondered why the Indians have comparatively few children. Well, this woman discovered that they mix up some brew from a native plant" (author's note: the Passion flower) "which will prevent a woman from having babies for 8 years! If she changes her mind, she can later take a different brew, and then have a child. Better than The Pill, eh?"

"This Maxwell woman came on board last time. You'll see her. Funny looking gal, tall and thin with buck teeth, and a long cigarette holder. I'm sure she'd know your Dr. Binder. We had a kind of party on board. She came with that Polish-Belgian woman (who also arranges to take people out into the jungle). Several of the young officers came with very pretty girls. One Peruvian girl was particularly pretty. Only 24, and imagine, she said she was a doctor! You can never tell from looking at a girl!"

"Yes, you can never tell what people do from looking at them. I met a very good looking young Englishman last time who said he was a scientist. He didn't look like a scientist atall! He's hunting for bugs out in the jungle, something to do with tracking down different viruses. Asked me to get him six electric machines in New York which he could attach to trees, to make the bugs come out of their holes. Can't get anything like that here. He gave me the money, but I'm not bringing back his machines. When we were in port in Brooklyn the money was stolen from my cabin. Over one hundred pounds."

Later we learnt that the Captain had also had $1,200. stolen from his safe at the same time. He could not prove who did it, although he suspected that it was an inside job. The Line may make him personally responsible for this money, although it really wasn't his fault that it was stolen. For this reason, he is very insistent that we keep our cabin doors locked when we are in port.

Saturday, July 23

We have gone in a straight line between New York and Puerto Rico. We are now nearer to Puerto Rico than to Florida, says Captain Humphreys. It is a beautiful day, a high sea running, deep brilliant blue. Very warm, though windy. Blue sky and puffy good weather clouds. Mr. Pendleton saw flying fish before breakfast. He is always peering over the side with binoculars.

I have finally done some "washing", and it is hanging over the Engine-room catwalk to dry! Here is the story of "Mr. Resson and the Washing":

We had wondered several times before our departure what one does with dirty laundry on a freighter? With 4 of us, there would be a lot! "Don't worry," said the majority of our friends. "A reliable British line like that carrying passengers will have a laundry room with washers and driers. The Steward will iron things for you! After all, on a 6-week voyage, the crew will have to have some arrangements to keep their own things clean, too, you know."

Frankie Bell, a friend who had gone to Sweden on a freighter, had a different opinion. "I just washed things out in a basin, and they gave me a iron and an ironing board."

Well, I thought, that was a short trip, only 10 days, and I'm sure the *Veloz* will have better arrangements. "Better take a lot of drip-dries to be on the safe side," I kept telling the family. For some reason, George refuses to buy drip-dries. Every summer before starting off somewhere I bring up the subject.

"I've plenty of shirts, and I don't want to spend money to get any more," he insists. This year I forced him to get two sport shirts, a tan and a blue, which "never need ironing". However, after two washings, they are already full of wrinkles. He still won't buy a white Dacron shirt.

"I have plenty of white shirts," he keeps repeating. Jerzy is still young enough to be pliable about clothes. I just went out and bought two for him, one white and one red checked sport shirt (which so far haven't wrinkled). Eva, the most stubborn member of the family, refuses to buy anything, blouse or dress, even vaguely resembling a drip-dry.

"Oh, Mom!" she says, in a deriding tone, "That's all you have on your mind! I don't want to hear another word about it. I'll wear what I want. After all, its a freighter."

Eva's permanent wardrobe is an old pair of faded jeans, with uneradicatable rust stains and holes in the knees, worn with an alternate choice of two boy's shirts (once bought by me at a rummage sale for the purpose of house-painting). One is an ancient colourless check, the other green and looking like a maternity blouse, both of which are always in a crinkled condition, as she never irons them.

The first day out at sea, when I was feeling so seasick, and was just crawling out of our cabin for a breath of air, Mr. Resson cornered me in the companionway. With an energetic cheery smile he said:

"Well, I guess you'll be wanting to do some washing!"

"Oh, yes, I suppose so," I answered unenthusiastically. "What are the arrangements?"

"Oh, I'll just have the men leave a bucket for you by the Engine-room door, and some soap. They can string up a line at the head of the stairs on the deck – you'll see it."

"Thank you very much," I gulped, beating a hasty retreat. Next day, he accosted me again. "Well, done any washing yet?" he asked.

"No, I'll get around to it, but I'd rather wait until the sea calms down," I answered firmly.

In my rambles around the deck I later spied a long coiled rope, bright orange in colour, hanging on the rail at the top of the stairs leading to the Bridge. In my mind's eye I untwined the rope and strung it, like a maze, around the upper deck. Would I have to do this every time I hung something up to dry? Wouldn't it get in their way on the Bridge? And wouldn't the orange colour run?

The following day, Mr. Resson said: "Have you found the line yet? Sorry we don't have any pins."

Immediately, I visualised the wash flying out to sea. "Is that the line at the top of the stairs?"

"Oh, no! Come with me and I'll show you." He led me through the Engine-room door. There was a white line strung over the catwalk. Furnace-like waves of heat enveloped me as I stepped on the transparent walk, suffocating blasts mixed with the overpowering fumes of diesel oil. Looking down from the height of a 3 or 4 story building, one dizzily sees below a jumble of engines, pipes and ladders. A narrow railing without sides separates me from the void, as I stagger along to examine the line.

"Thank you very much!" I manage to articulate. "This will just be fine!"

Coming out the door again, I look up at the orange line, and notice that one end is attached to a life-preserver!

The wash is now done, but how about the ironing? "I have an ironing board in my cabin," says Mr. Resson, "but I've lost the iron! Must be around somewhere."

"Hey!" he continues at lunch, "did you ever use that liquid starch? Just tried spraying some on my shirt, but it got all over the floor instead!"

"Who likes to sew here?" teases Mr. Oganowski. "And who likes to do ironing?" Everyone looks at Eva. She turns her face away without the trace of a smile.

Sunday, July 24

A very high sea, hot sun and showers alternating. Small flying fish, the size of sardines. I sit on a deck chair this morning, my feet on the stern rail, and hear more stories. This time from Mr. Pendleton, about life in Dominica.

"I bought my farm (55 acres, now planted in coconuts) from a Swede, Mr. Bloomquist, one of the big land-owners on the island. He struck it rich right after the war. All through the islands were stainless steel portable landing fields (actually, strips of steel fitted together), which were of no use when the military bases were given up. They were going to throw them in the sea. so this Swede bought them cheap. Thought he'd find some use for them. Well, then along came the war in Korea, and he sold them right back to the U.S. Army! Made a fortune on them, and bought a huge property in Dominica.

"Ever since then, he's been trying to make another fortune overnight. But it wasn't so easy! First, he imported a herd of cows from Europe – not just a dozen or so, to see how it would work, but several hundred! Had them flown in. A terrible job getting them. Then he turned them loose on the island. Imagine cows on a tropical island! They gradually all died. Skeletons all over the place.

"Next, he decided pigs would be the thing. Ordered hundreds of pigs! They all ran loose again in the hills, except for feeding time, when they turned up back of his house to be fed. He fed them ground up coconuts, and they loved it. Everything was going fine until one day he decided it was time to have some roast pork. Didn't want to slaughter one near the house, so he took his gun and went up in the hills to shoot one. Got one alright, but everyone heard the shot. First thing you know about 11 of his men had appeared to help him clean the meat and carry it back to the farm. By the time he arrived there, the whole village had turned out to share the roast! You know what happened after that? Everyone went up in the hills to shoot themselves a pig! Next thing, there wasn't one left.

"Well, after that he decided to give up livestock and concentrate on bananas. Perfect climate for bananas. But instead of planting a few acres to try it out, he planted hundreds of bananas. But then came the problem of how to get them out? There're no roads in there, you know. He decided to load them by ship. Had a nice deep water cove on his property below a sheer cliff (this point with the cliff now belongs to me!) and he spent a fortune building a derrick to load the bananas over the edge of the cliff. It cost plenty to bring in all this heavy machinery. All went well until the bananas were lowered down on the deck. Then the strong tidal swells lifted the ship up and bruised all the fruit! Bruised bananas are no good commercially.

"Then, he tried taking them out by jeep. He ordered two heavy jeeps and had them welded together to make one vehicle, with a raised platform for the driver in front. Two things were wrong with this idea. First, the jeeps bounced around so much (there wasn't any road, of course) that the bananas got bruised anyway. Second, the British authorities wouldn't give him a license to drive this contraption!

Right now, he's been trying to start a real estate boom on Dominica. That's when I bought my property from him. No roads into my place, of course. Don't know how I'll get out during the wet season. My house came all pre-fabricated from New Guinea. There was no piece longer than 18 feet. But we thought we'd never get it around the mountains, even by jeep truck.

"The first thing he did in his real estate venture was to build a hotel. Thought all the tourists would love it. It has a beautiful view and all, but its on the wrong side of the island! The tourists all arrive on the Leeward side, and if they only have a day or so to spend, don't want to stay way out over a poor road on the Windward side.

"This is when he hit on the idea of selling lots in Sweden. Hundreds of Swedes back in Sweden bought them from his ads, sight unseen, encouraged by the descriptions of "a tropical paradise", etc. Last summer, he had a bunch of them flown in, 120 of them on a chartered flight, to examine their property. Imagine 120 Swedes on this little island! There was hardly room to put them all up. Well, he showed them the lots, and what did they see? Thick, impenetrable jungle, with no roads, no electricity, no water! They all started demanding their money back!"

A lazy Sunday. Roast duck with orange sauce for lunch, and fresh rolls, which smelt good baking all morning. The First Officer had a drink with us before lunch in our cabin, and talked with George about mutual Polish friends. Imagine, they have dozens from the war period!

I tried to get some Club Soda to go with the Scotch, but its a hopeless struggle. Nothing but Schweppes again, without fizz! Probably no one ever asks for it, and its been sitting on the shelf too long.

The Chief Steward appeared, looking very harassed, with two bottles of Quinine Water in his hand. "These were on ice," he said. Seeing my doubtful face, he added: "Scotch is really very good with Quinine Water. Everyone drinks it that way in England!"

"Aren't you thinking of Gin-and-Tonic?" I ask. "How about some gin?"

A blank look comes over his face. He probably can't supply us with any gin. (Later, I find out there's really plenty of gin. Maybe he just hadn't wanted to go back down to get it.)

Mr. Ogonowski brings his siphon to the rescue. Much shaking and flourishing of the bottle, but when poured, the water looks very flat.

"I think I'll just drink plain Quinine Water with ice," I say.

Eva sits on deck and talks to the young Third Officer all afternoon. He has brought up a battery-operated record player and folk records. He walks with bowed legs and arms like a veteran sailor, but he's only 20. In Eva's opinion, he is an intelligent young Englishman.

The sea is getting rougher, the wind stronger. In the evening, Jerzy floods the bathroom, by leaving the shower curtain open. On purpose, I'm sure! Several inches of water swish from one side of the floor to the other. As we share the bath with Mr. Pendleton and, I think, the Radio Engineer, we have to clean it up. George takes a plastic scrap basket and tries to scoop it up that way.

As we go down to hear the news, we see the lights of a ship crossing our stern, far to the horizon. "The ghost of the `Santa Maria'!" I exclaim.

For several evenings while sitting watching the sunset on deck (as we always do), I've thought of how Columbus sailed these same seas, and how, although it seems so long ago to us, when viewed from the point of view of geographical history, its hardly been a minute. The sunsets and cloud effects look like paintings from Columbus's time. Clouds like Baroque angels, or Winged Victories. The sky subtle blue and rosy tones like the Florentine masters.

On BBC we hear that several members of the Argentine team hit the referee, in the first International Football ("Soccer") Match of the World Cup, in an argument about England's winning point. Said the Captain of the

Argentine team: "We play a different kind of game in our country." (As they still were doing in 1990!)

Monday, July 25

Its hard to stand up this morning. Plenty of grey clouds full of rain, which scurry away in a minute, then the blue sky and sun reappear.

"I'm tired of this weather," complains George. "We haven't had one clear, calm day since New York."

"There's a new hurricane reported 60 or 70 miles east of Puerto Rico," report the officers at breakfast. "This is Eileen. We have already skirted Celia and Dora since leaving New York. We're anxious to pick up more about it on the radio. They can switch their course very quickly."

"I thought we were going through a hurricane last night," grumbled George.

"Oh, no," answered Mr. Resson. "Then you wouldn't be able to stay in your bunk. You'd have to be lashed to the deck!"

I have lent Mr. Pendleton Mother's book, "Behold the West Indies", as there's a whole chapter about Dominica.[3]

"I enjoyed it very much," he told me, his round sunburnt face beaming under a little checked pork-pie hat. "Of course, some of the estates have changed hands, and the older owners have died off. The son of one of the owners she mentions, the nephew of an old Democratic Senator, is still there. He owns four plantations, with four different houses. Can you imagine, he has a different "wife" (or "house-keeper") in each one, each with about 10 children! He isn't married to any of them, but he supports all of these families, which is something in his favour!"

2 PM   The Captain asked us all up to the Bridge to see "Sombrero", the first glimpse of land! Its a very flat small rocky island, with a tall red lighthouse sticking up like an oil well in the middle. Long before I could see it with a pair of binoculars, the Captain said he saw it with the naked eye – and that the lighthouse was red! I could scarcely believe that he really saw it. Was he teasing me?

All ships that pass this light have to pay a fee. While on the Bridge the Captain let us read the radiograph from San Juan about Hurricane Ella (not Eileen). Ella is 500 miles off Guadalupe and heading Northwest, therefore, towards us! Much excited discussion; later, Mr. Resson says she's passed by far away from us.

8 PM   We have passed "Dog Island" (to our Port), then St. Bart's, and St. Martin's (which is half French, half Dutch). To the Starboard, looms the extinct volcano "Saba", looking like a cross between Gibraltar and Capri. The main town is called "Bottom" (of the crater!) It is Dutch. Its inhabited mostly by women (of mulatto colouring). The men go to sea, or work in the oil fields of Curaçao.

We are now in the Caribbean. The sea is calming down. We sit on deck and look for the Southern Cross, but cannot find it. The moon is too bright, and there are many clouds.

Due into St. Kitts at 11 PM.

Listen to the BBC. West Germany has beaten the Soviet Union in Football. A bomb exploded on the airfield at Recife. King Hussein is visiting Scotland. And the International Bird-Watcher Society says Great Britain is still a fine place to observe many different species of birds.

Anchored in the harbour of Basse-Terre at exactly 11 PM. It looks mysterious, with rows of lights down by the water, but one cannot distinguish the buildings. The population was 9,000 when Mother was writing her book in 1951, and it doesn't look much bigger now.

Tuesday. July 26

Up early, and take the first boat to shore at 7 AM – a small motor launch in which they unload cargo. This little boat went back and forth between the pier and the *Veloz* all day.

The island is impressively tropical. Green sugar cane grows high up on volcanic hills, to a point where the fields meet dark jungle. The tops of the hills are hidden with moist clouds. From our first steps on the pier walking down to the Custom House, where a young, inky black policeman in startling white jacket and sun-helmet waves us on, it is strictly British Colonial. I almost felt I was in India under Queen Victoria – from the type of architecture and vegetation, not the people. Architecturally, one actually thinks of the period of Lord Nelson. Small, intimate buildings have several tiers of wide verandas.

We eat breakfast at "The Palms" (once called "Shorty's Bar"), which overlooks the main square. It has a big, airy bar and lounge decorated with comfortable cane chairs, fans, and pictures of Queen Elizabeth. Its probably the centre of English and American activity in the late afternoon. At this hour, it was empty, except for an English woman (the owner?) giving snappy instructions to the bartender, who was prefabricating a variety of cocktails. She ignored us (poor psychology!) We were given a huge breakfast in a rather formal diningroom, and paid too much for it.

Then we took a taxi (a Chevy station-wagon) around the island. It has the most lush tropical vegetation we have ever seen! And we saw plenty in Mexico.

Huge Flamboyant trees, Breadfruit with their fantastic leaves, and Frangipani of exotic connotations (I've never seen either of these before). There are lots of abandoned windmills without their sails, with crumbling chimneys. These were the private sugar refineries on the sugar estates. Today, all sugar on the island goes to one factory. Is this more efficient, or is it a step towards Communism, as Eva suggested? The Labour Party has again been voted in (its been in here for 15 years), but its never done anything for the people, according to our driver. He speaks in a very intelligent way, and is most polite and helpful.

We drive through a lot of villages, where there is obvious poverty. Most people live in tiny prefabricated houses, some on stilts against floods. But I think the people look better off and certainly more cheery than the Mexicans. Everyone looks very cleanly (and gaily!) dressed. The younger ones have a hopeful light in their eyes, in contrast to the depressed underdog look of the Mexicans. They don't show any feeling of inferiority just because they are Negro. They have their own self-respect. One doesn't feel any segregation here, and whites and blacks mingle quite freely. But there are mostly blacks! In every village is a large school, attended even now, in summer. Mr. Pendleton told me that under the education system its all free to anyone, even University. Mr. Pendleton added that now it is quite the thing for young English girls born in the Islands to marry young Negroes on their way up.

We went swimming at a "private club" (actually a café, with bath-houses). Rather dirty and primitive, Mexican style. Saw some huge kind of water-fungus. At first I thought it was coral. The girl in charge came rushing out and waved us away from that section of the beach. Maybe it was poisonous. Or did it shut up and trap one if one stepped on it?

We noticed rather large boys around Jerzy's age swimming naked. No Catholic puritanism here. Most of the population belong to the Church of England. They laughed with natural humour when George struggled with bare feet across the burning sand! George said I've put on a lot of weight on the ship, and that I look like "an overblown vegetable" in my bikini. Eva and Jerzy both shouted the same. Darn that heavy English boiled-pudding food! I'm always afraid of not eating it for fear of hurting the cook's feelings, and here's the result!

We ate lunch on the waterfront at the "Sea Beach Hotel". Sat at the bar on the 2nd floor, and drank rum-and-coke. Eva wanted some and George would have let her have it, but I put my foot down. Jerzy said: "What's wrong with it?" And Eva said I'm as bad as my mother and father, who disapproved of drinking. I saw her going into a funk, and, of course, I got a guilty feeling (as my theory about wine has always been that the children should be allowed to have some.) I offered her some of mine. She said: "No! I'll order my own if I want some."

However, I still think 16 is rather young to have a rum- and-coke!

Talked to three Englishmen, businessmen from Antigua; and two Americans, tourists from Missouri. Otherwise, there were crowds of Negroes, some staying at the hotel, others eating lunch there, some looking as though they were waiting for buses. We had an enormous lunch, served at long tables. Of course, it was extravagant, when we could have eaten free on the ship, but this was atmospheric. We could look out the windows of the dining-room, and see the *Veloz* looking very romantic in the harbour. Pictures of Queen Elizabeth, Prince Philip, and Kennedy hung on the wall. George says it always makes him feel sick when he sees pictures of Kennedy.

A tropical downpour as we were leaving. We had to go back into the hotel, and George drank another rum-and-coke. The fellow who sat next to George kept insisting a hurricane was coming our way. With rolling eyes and flashing teeth he insisted we'd better not return to our ship, but go down into a cellar!

Returned to the *Veloz* safely, there was no hurricane! A spectacular red sunset lit the horizon, interspersed with dramatic rain clouds. We saw our first Man-of-War or "Frigate" bird, with immense bony black wings and tail, and white body. Two pelicans flew low over the water. They look smaller than ours in Monterey. Another freighter, or tanker, is anchored near us. She is rather rusty, smaller than us, and is flying the Norwegian flag. She left early in the evening. Our ship sneaked out of the bay at midnight. George and I had gone to bed, but were suddenly awakened by the engines starting up. We just left without even one toot on the horn. No one was on the forward deck, and only a few dim lights were burning on the masts. We didn't even hear the anchors coming up. We went out on deck and saw the lights of St. Kitts getting smaller and smaller, as our speed increased.

Much later, George got up again, then returned saying he has seen the Southern Cross. As he said it doesn't look like much, that its rather dim and insignificant, I did not bother to get up. In the morning, everyone decides that he has seen the "False" Southern Cross.

Wednesday, July 27

St. John, Antigua. We've been anchored since 6 AM way out in the bay. The town, across an inner harbour, can just be made out through binoculars. Its too shallow for us to go further in. To our right is a white sandy beach with one bungalow, where Princess Margaret stayed during her honeymoon. Queen Elizabeth and Philip were here on the island only two months ago.

Very light green water, with darker blue streaks farther out. We are unloading the heavy machinery here – several tractors and some "grinding machines" (whatever they may be!) for the airport. Barges have to come alongside to get them. The barges are heavy, but primitively made. Swarms of dark-skinned men arrive with the barges, and crowd on our deck. Most of them don't do much, but lounge around looking over the edge all day. One man, who stayed on a barge which is tied to our side, starts to fish, and another lies down on the bow and goes to sleep. I can see this will be an all day operation!

We get on a little boat, which had pulled one of the barges, to go ashore. Have to hang onto the sides the way we did with the Venice "Vaporettos", except there aren't any railings or sides! We just grab the outside wall of the tiny cabin, and hope for the best.

St. John is a lot more sophisticated than Basse Terre. It has a city atmosphere. The women dress as for any city. It still has a mixed population, but we see no wildly-coloured nor fantastically shaped dresses nor mounds of things piled on heads.

The island seems less lush than St. Kitts. Sometimes there are severe droughts here. It isn't mountainous, and there is little fresh water, except from wells whose water is brackish. One has to drink beer during a drought, and wash clothes in the ocean!

"Are there poisonous snakes here?" I ask the cab driver.

"Oh, no! We have an animal, the Mongoose, which eats them all."

We did see the deadly Machineel tree, with its small acrid green apples here fallen on the ground, near the entrance to "Nelson's Harbour". The Caribs extracted the tree's poisonous milky sap to put on their arrows. If one stands under the tree in a rain, one's skin becomes badly infected.

"Nelson's Harbour" was quaint and Valley-Forge-ish, a well cared for National Monument, but I preferred the modern yachts, for which the harbour is now used.

Then we drove to a fabulous South Sea Island type beach, with sparkling white sand, and crystal turquoise water together with waving palms, and a free bath house. The taxi left us, to return in an hour and a half.

"Ten minutes would be enough for me," complained George. "We are wasting our time!" Only the top of his head showed through the water, and the rest of us splashed like fish around him until his complaints died down.

In the middle distance floated the *Veloz* , like a tramp steamer; in the foreground sailed local fishing boats, stockily built, with red, asymmetrically curved sails. "They look like boats on the Nile," came George's voice from the waves.

Jerzy discovered a porcupine fish (is this the correct name?) dead on the sand. It is large, fat and grey, with a big head and eyes, and it is covered with white quills – a nasty looking customer! Later, the Captain told us this is called a "Sun Fish".

Back to town, and to the "Kensington Hotel, Bar & Restaurant". This is British Colonial in style. We sit in a delightful garden under palms, accacias, and bananas, and sip rum. This is $2.10 a bottle in the stores, BWI money, for the best. (Their dollar is about half ours.) I have a Pineapple Daquiri, all whipped up and frozen, in a huge goblet. Later, I remembered this drink with particular pleasure, although George called it a "Ladies' Drink". Although I asked for one many other places, I never could get another. George takes a movie of us, and of everyone else in the café. Its a stylish looking mixed group. Several very pretty dark-skinned girls are sitting with young American men. We couldn't stay long as we had to catch the little boat back at 4.

Tonight is Carnival here, and they will choose a Queen.

"I could sit here all day!" sighs George.

Back on board, we're starving at 5.30 for once, as we hadn't eaten lunch. I eat all my ox-tails and boiled potatoes (in spite of their being fattening.)

"I had the most wonderful Daquiri," I tell Mr. Pendleton. "Made with marvellous fresh pineapple juice, probably right from the island."

"That wasn't fresh juice!" he laughs. "That was Dole's, right out of the can, and its not even juice, but the slices of pineapple. They put it through an osteriser."

This evening we are late for the 8 PM news. George and I become involved in watching the last heavy machinery being unloaded. George had had a shower, and goes down to the bow of the ship in his orange bath-towel material beach-robe, which he uses as a dressing-gown. It makes an odd contrast with the black, dirty workers! Our crew members are just standing around also, watching the local people do the work. Eva goes into a funk, and sulks alone on the deck aft. Something is going on in her head about women being useless, and that she feels ashamed to be watching while the men do the work. However, our officers don't do this physical work, either. I shouldn't think she'd want to be a stevedore in Antigua!

"Well," I say to Mr. Resson, who has appeared next to us, "we'll have an empty hold for the Amazon."

"Oh, no, we won't!" he corrects me. "We're taking on 1,800 tons of cement in Trinidad for Iquitos, Peru – plus assorted fresh vegetables!"

Thursday, July 28

Arrive at Roseau, Dominica, at breakfast time (8.30 AM). A long (47 miles, 18 wide) island, volcanic and mysterious. High sharp peaks inland are hidden by rain clouds. The day is a scorcher, and I put on my bright orange Japanese hat, bought in Big Sur (California), which Eva says looks Peruvian.

Thick jungle vegetation on this island. Mr. Pendleton says the little towns (there are no big towns!) are all on the water, and boats are the main means of transportation. Roads are still largely undeveloped. Bananas are the main crop, and a "banana boat" (of the British Geest Line) stands off shore a little way down the bay. Mr. Pendleton says land still goes very cheap (about 8 shillings an acre!) if it can't be planted in crops or trees grown on it. Then, the foreigner can buy it! But no roads get into it, of course.

Mr. Pendleton's property is 15 miles away as the crow flies, but 45 by road. Rather, not by road, but by trail that a jeep can get over, and the last 5 miles doesn't even have that. Mr. Pendleton will lead a lonely life. His nearest neighbours, the Bloomquists, live only a mile away, but everyone else atall intellectual live much farther, and communication is next to impossible. Perhaps he is trying to escape from something? George suggests jokingly that we buy some property, and get in by helicopter.

Mr. Pendleton gets off here, so we say farewell – and good luck! – on the lower deck, as we shall take another small boat to shore. He has to go through Customs.

We have to anchor close in, as the bay is too deep farther out. However, a shallow shelf extends here part way, and we will drop the anchor onto that, which is a tricky manoeuvring job for the Captain. While this is taking place, we watch a garbage truck come and dump its entire contents into the sea, next to the main dock! For a long time, there is no other sign of life from the dock.

The Captain comes on deck, and says impatiently: "They must all be asleep." He disappears, and a minute later a tremendous blast is sounded on our horn, enough to wake the whole town!

Roseau is another charming town with an atmosphere which is completely exotic. Not sophisticated like St. Johns; more like Basse Terre, but less Colonial. There are no white people on the streets. Even the Baggage Master and the Shipping Agent are French-speaking Negroes. The people are less colourfully dressed than in St. Kitts, but the houses compensate by their colour. Each one is painted differently, with pink, blue and red predominating.

There are three tourist sights in Roseau: 1) the St. Mary's Convent "Home Industries"- straw baskets, mats, and grass rugs. Here several French-speaking Belgian Sisters greet us. They are very worldly Sisters. One smells of Yardley's Old English Lavender!

2) The Botanical Gardens. Small, intimate, and very tropical, right on the jungle's edge. Yet, we notice on the hill above, which is thick with vegetation, a large white cross, so someone has penetrated up through this jungle! Actually, that is the cemetery.

We become very thirsty walking around the gardens, and immediately, a cleanly dressed young man appears by magic from nowhere, and gives us ice-water!

Here Jerzy picks up the fruit (or is it a seed?) of a "Canon-Ball" tree. Its the size of an 18th Century canon-ball, and weighs as much. We discover a Banyan, or "Eternal" tree (as I call it). The kind Buddha sat under in India, that perpetually puts down new roots. It never dies!

3) "Marjorie's". A popular bar on the waterfront. This is closed. We go to the "Fort Young Hotel" instead, for a rum- and-coke. Its on the site of the old fort. Unfortunately, it has modern motel architecture, with an inner courtyard built around a swimming pool. It reminds me of places in Mexico, but George says Mexico probably copied the West Indies in their resort-style hotels, which is turn, were copied from the U.S.! Some Hindu teenagers are cutting up in the pool, and a washed-out blonde Englishwoman watches two baby-doll frizzy-haired daughters, while gossiping with a fat woman with a poor figure, who is stuffed into a bathing-suit too small for her. The "Canon-ball"

stinks! George asks two waiters to throw it away. They admit that it does stink, and say it isn't good to eat. A somewhat similar variety is good, they say, and tastes something like an apricot.

"This one is rotten!" they say, laughing. Jerzy dissolves in tears. He says it is the most interesting fruit he has ever seen, and he thinks if he kept it it might dry out. George relents, and tries to get it back, but they have already thrown it away. Despair!

An obvious American with a black beard and Mexican sandals approaches me. "Are you in the ketch anchored in the harbour?" he asks with undisguised curiosity. A shift-clad girl with long blonde hair under a big straw hat lurks in the background.

"Yes," I reply, aimlessly, without thinking.

"Where are you from? Do you own the boat?" he inquires too eagerly, a calculating gleam in his eye.

"No, no!" I quickly correct him. "We're not in that yacht. We're from the freighter."

A cold look of disgust comes over his face. He quickly moves away, his girl-friend following wordlessly.

4.30 PM We were meant to leave at 12 noon, but we're still here. All unloading is over. But I saw the two French- speaking agents come on board quietly in a rowboat some time ago, carrying a bottle of rum. Maybe the Captain and officers are all sitting drinking! It seems more like a Conrad story than ever.

Eva and "Rick" (the 3rd Officer) are sitting on the floor of the deck near the forward stair, to catch some breezes. Everyone else must be below. It is stifling on deck. I wanted to sit in a deck-chair with a book, but it was so hot I didn't even bother to open up a chair. I go in and do a big wash instead. and hang it over the engines below. Eva said she and Rick got a good laugh about my line last night when our bathing suits were out to dry. The laundry looks comically domestic over the engines!

I'm afraid we won't see Martinique. Jerzy and I both want to see Mont Pelée. The Captain said if we left here at 2 PM we'd reach St. Lucia by 10 – already too late to see Martinique, I fear. This trip we only stop at the British West Indies. On alternating trips the *Veloz* stops at the French islands.

Too bad Mr. Pendleton is no longer with us, with his drink in hand, and his supply of scandalous stories about local inhabitants. He told me a great one about Mary Pomeroy, the "Segregationist of Nevis". She sued Queen Elizabeth because the St. Kitts-Nevis ferry would not wait for her when she was sitting in "Shorty's Bar" having a final drink. She once appeared on an American TV program as a "Segregationist". She is against mixing with Negroes, although she is one of the very few white people living on the island of Nevis. She inherited some property there, and has started a beach hotel.

Our ship is covered with salt. All the walls are salty when one touches them. There must be an extra large amount of salt in the Caribbean. We noticed the water was especially buoyant when we were swimming yesterday, almost like the Salton Sea. One hardly has to make any movement to stay up.

The *Veloz* sailed at 10 PM! Before this, we all sat on deck and looked at the town (and people) through binoculars. The Captain's are stronger than ours. George wonders if this is an infringement of people's privacy? (There has just been an article in "Time" about privacy.)

I wake up in the middle of the night, because the ship is tossing and rolling like mad. Our forward port is banging back and forth, and so is our closet door. The empty bottle fell over, but not the full bottle of rum.

Friday, July 29

Mr. Ogonowski denies at breakfast that we had a high sea. "Just a little swell," he says.

I am afraid for my wash, some of which I had left last night. I go to look, and find Jerzy's shorts have fallen way down, where they hang over a railing. Jerzy is afraid to go down the ladder, and Mr. Resson rescues them.

We arrive at Castries, St. Lucia, before breakfast. A pilot comes on board. The harbour channel must be narrow. We dock at the main pier in the centre of town, beside a British Navy Frigate. Her crew look very smart and jaunty, in their military shorts and blue shirts. Perhaps they look better than our sailors as their hair is definitely longer! (This is Eva's observation.)

St. Lucia is not a success, as far as George is concerned. He finds the town to be commercial and unattractive. It reminds me somewhat of Monterrey, Mexico – the same throng of shoppers eagerly bustling through hot dirty streets. (Little then did I dream that in a few years' time, St. Lucia would become like a second home to Richard and myself.)

We wander around aimlessly for a while. We go to change some money at a bank, then take a taxi up "Morne Fortune". Its worth the drive just to see the lush vegetation, and there is a spectacular view on top of the whole town and harbour, (although George insists that it looks just like Santa Barbara, due, I guess, to all the private villas on the hillsides).

The driver manages to charge $5.00 "Beewee" (British West Indian currency) for the drive, which lasted only 35 minutes. George says we have been taken. We tell him to leave us off at a good bar with a garden; but instead of taking us to the "Saint Antoine" (which Mother described in her book as one of the most famous hotels in the West Indies) he deposits us at a dusty place on the 2nd floor of a business building. The waitress is surly-looking, and so are the customers. It looks like a cheap sailors' bar – but we did come from a ship!

After this, we walk to the market, which is interesting. Plenty of bananas (this is another "Banana Island") and limes, but not such a variety of fruits and vegetables as in Mexican markets. Plenty of mats, baskets and straw hats. Also dozens of hand thrown pottery grills ("coal pots") of an unusual design. They look quite modern! I would have gotten one, except that it would be hard to carry. A crowd of people were bargaining around the pigs' feet stand (although the meat is not refrigerated).

George's camera, the movie one, won't work. The switch seems to be stuck. He can't take any pictures in the market.

We get back to the ship by 12, when we were supposed to sail. But Captain Humphreys, who is standing on deck as we climb up the gangway, says we won't leave till 6.

After lunch, and George's nap- (he only takes a 40-minute one today, instead of the usual 3 hours!) we start out again. I insist that we should wear our bathing suits under our clothes, although George says 3 or 4 times: "I don't want to swim! Go by yourselves!" And, "Swimming is a complete waste of time."

First, we go back up the main street to try to find a photographic shop, and to have someone examine the movie camera. We ask at a bookstore, and they send a young man to show us the way. He leads us up a dingy stair, to a barber shop. A barber, of Hindu descent, is cutting a man's hair.

"Come right in! Come right in! Wantee barber?"

"No, I want my camera fixed," says George.

"Ha! Ha! Ha! You want your camera fixed? Camera doctor be here, just one minute. You waitee! Ha! Ha!"

He leaves the man in the barber chair, and goes into another part of the room, which is empty, but has several photos on the wall. He returns with a big, black cloth, which he spreads in the air in front of George's camera.

"Ha! Ha!" He whisks it around like a magician. "First I'm barber! Then I'm camera doctor! Ha! Ha! Ha!" he laughs.

"Do you know how to fix this camera? Something's wrong with it."

"Oh, ha ha! I thought you wanted to take the film out without getting it light-struck. Let me see! No, I never saw this kind of a camera before! I don't know what's wrong with it. You come from that boat down in the harbour, don't you?"

"Yes. Isn't there someone else here who knows about cameras?"

"Yes, yes! Camera doctor, thats me! I fixee camera! A little while ago some other people came from big boat in harbour. They have camera that doesn't work, too. I don't know whats wrong, but I give it several shakes, and then it work OK! Lets do samee with yours."

"Thank you very much," George says hastily but firmly, walking towards the door. "Maybe I come back later and get a haircut?"

"Ha! Ha! Yes, siree, you come back for haircut. Me cut your hair. Ha! Ha! Ha!"

We take another taxi and go to the beach, out by the airport on the other side of the harbour. A row of shade trees overhang the sand. Rather rough waves, with an undertow, and the sun keeps going under so that its hard to get a suntan. Still, the water is refreshing. Its almost cool! A lot of native boys are on the beach, and a few English people.

Back on board. We sail at 8. At dinner someone says: "Put away all your bottles in the drawers tonight, and be prepared for a lot of pitching, and waves breaking over the side." A strong wind is already blowing in the harbour.

As the ship leaves the dock, a crazy woman in a colourless skimpy cotton dress and a big straw hat rushes from one end of the ship to the other holding up a carton.

"Bye-bye! Bye-bye!" she shouts. "Who'll buy paw-paws?" She holds two up. "Cigarettes! Give a poor woman a cigarette! Bye-bye!"

George throws her a coin, but it rolls under a pile of lumber. Someone from below throws a cigarette. A young boy near her grabs it. Another one is thrown and another boy catches it, but gives it to her, laughing.

The ship has reached the harbour's mouth, and the pilot is already returning. The small figure of the woman is still seen on the dock, waving desperately. "Bye-bye! Bye-bye!"

The moon comes out, and we watch its reflections on the water. For more than an hour we follow the long shoreline of St. Lucia, until the two volcanos, "The Donkey's Ears", loom close but sinister through darkness and clouds.

Saturday, July 30

Bridgetown, Barbados. We dock at the end of a long breakwater, constructed 4 years ago. We are berthed next to a French liner, the Companie Général Transatlantique's *Antilles*, a vast cruise ship, at present emptied of passengers. We walk to town, a long windy, showery walk, during which we are assailed a dozen times by taxi drivers trying to persuade us to hire them, or, at least, to tell them where they can pick us up later!

A downpour as soon as we reach the shopping centre. We take shelter in the "Hong Kong Café", up on the 2nd floor. Its decorated with tinselly Chinese ornaments. George orders "Planter's Punch", and doesn't like it. He says its too sweet. A bunch of English people are listening to the football game. The big play-off is today (in England). An excited British voice describes it play by play, but all I can understand over the static is the word "ball".

Go down again to the main street. A pretty, French-speaking native girl, wearing a sun-top dress just like my latest fashion California shift, admires Eva's pendant. Eva designs and makes her own costume jewelry and is quite good at it.

This is meant to be a "Tax-Free" port. It's where Jerzy is sure he can get

$100. tape recorders for $15.! He swears he's heard the crew on the ship talking about such bargains. It still looks like a pirate town to me, from the type of architecture, the jostling crowds, and the cheap stores advertising tax-free merchandise – but inside, showing expensive stuff. We go into a radio shop and price their smallest battery-run tape recorder. "$130.," says the clerk, "but you don't have to pay it all at once."

"My son wanted one for $11.!" comments George. The clerk's mouth falls open, and he stands there speechless as we hurry out. Jerzy starts crying on the street. I go into a bookstore, and buy a book on "Tropical Trees" for $3.00. George gets infuriated, and shouts that I am wasting money. "You have spoiled the whole day! You, and Jerzy."

He stalks ahead to an open square, where we all stand on the sidewalk, immobilized. "Taxi! Taxi!" comes a chorus of several energetic voices. The heat bakes down, and I believe I feel the ship rocking under my feet. We stand and stand. Three 2-masted "Island Schooners", loaded with bananas, sugarcane, etc., are docked at the inlet beside us. They look like buccaneers' ships. "Go and take a picture of those," I tell Jerzy, through disgusted tears (hidden, I presume, by my dark glasses, although my chin has probably lengthened to the size of a mule's.)

"Taxi!"

"Well, what do you want to do?" growls George. "We can't stand here forever. I think we'd better go back to the ship."

"Why don't we go out to that beach Ogonowski recommended?" I ask, timidly.

"How would we get there? And how much would it cost?"

"Only $5.00, Bewee money, sir," comes a smooth voice beside us.

"How far is it?"

"Only 7 miles, and there's a hotel and bar out there."

"Alright!" agrees George, "if everyone wants to go." This turns out to be the "Coral Reef Club", a very swish Acapulco type luxury hotel, with private cottages, beach, and yacht club. Only open to the public in summer, Oganowski had said. We sit under a beach umbrella on a shady terrace by the sea, and sip "Planter's Punch". (I have it this time, George has rum-and-coke.) We see the coral formations through the clear green water.

"If you just put a piece of coral under fresh running water, it will come out pure white and pretty, like this," says the waiter, showing us a round filigreed piece. We have a swim. With waving palms, and beautiful water George's humour improves, although he is bitten by some insect that must have been in the water on a rope he was hanging onto. A painful red botch shows on his side. I step on a piece of coral, and sting my foot slightly on something spiky. (Coral can cause a bad infection.) A big grey fuzzy fly bites me on one arm!

We eat lunch on the open-air terrace. A buffet with chilled Vichyssoise, cold roast beef, all kinds of salads, and coconut meringue pie (extra good); plus a bottle of "Nuit St. George". George does not mind paying for this!

There are a few Americans eating here, and some English, all in beach clothes. Lots of waiters, very attentive. Its a relaxed, glamorous, international style hotel (seeming more European than American). Flocks of small birds fly through the dining area, landing on chair tops and tables, and eating the scraps.

"This would never be allowed in the U.S.," laughs George. "We are too regimented as to sanitation for that."

"I really love this place," he adds, his good humour now completely restored. "And, particularly, the wind-swept palms hanging over the water, which make one think of all the South Sea islands one has ever heard of. Its amazing to actually be seeing them!"

We start talking about writers at lunch, and I tell about the man who lived on the Amazon for 30 years, and had explored all the major tributaries, had shot the rapids in native canoes, and had lived amongst the most primitive Indians, and "still I don't know enough about it to write a book!" he had said, pugnaciously, to the author of one of the recent books I had read on the Amazon region, whom he had met at the bar of the leading hotel in Belém.

"All those people who go up the river for two weeks on a Booth Line boat and then write books!" he sneered. "You're not an author, are you?" he challenged, a dangerous gleam in his eye. "Every man who calls himself a writer here deserves to be knocked down! What do they know about the Amazon?!"

"No, no, no!" my author quickly gulped. "Certainly I'm not a writer. I'm a scientist. Studying bugs."

"All the same," commented George, "I could look at this ocean here, even if I don't know the region, and still write plenty about it. As I look at this empty horizon, all kinds of thoughts come to mind. I think the fact that this man who lived on the Amazon for so long didn't write about it shows that he didn't have any imagination; whereas, the other one, who had just arrived, did have imagination, and therefore, he had plenty to write about."

People seem for some reason to get very possessive about their trips to the Amazon. I remember Theodore Roosevelt's explosion about people who go up the river, and call themselves "explorers", when in reality they were just simple "travellers", he said. He alone was the great "Explorer"!

On the way back to the ship, we buy a half gal. of rum, "Mount Gay", 10-years' old "Sugar Cane Brandy", Barbados' best! It is $7.80 Bewee, very expensive. Later on, we decided the lighter, less expensive rums are better. This one is too sweet.

England has beaten West Germany, and has won the World Cup! The score: 4- 2. Hurrah!

Sunday, July 31

Arrive at Kingstown, St. Vincent, at 7 AM. Heavy rain clouds hang over the mountains. The largest peak, behind the town, must be the volcano, Soufrière. We dock. The waterfront looks empty, as its Sunday. Its a small, sleepy town. Not much of a business centre, except for one warehouse for "Arrowroot", the island's main product. Villas are scattered amidst the thick, tangled vegetation on the hillsides. Cliffs come steeply down to the water. No bathing beach in sight. Maybe there's one on the other side of the island? But George says no taxi rides today! Cost too much.

We wander along the waterfront. "Good morning!" say the few people we meet, impoverished looking Negroes. "Enjoy your stay!" one says, politely. And adds: "This is a very peaceful place." He smiles a toothless smile.

By the time we have walked the length of the waterfront and turned a corner, going uphill past the War Memorial (from World War I), it has become very hot and steaming. We stand undecidedly, looking around.

"Want a taxi?" immediately comes a voice. "Only $5.00 an hour. Show you the Fort, the Governor's Mansion, take you up the mountain to show you a panoramic view."

"No, thank you! Just take us up the hill to the Botanical Garden, and leave us there. $1.00, and no more! We'll walk back."

"I can come back to pick you up!" he answers, persistently.

"No, thank you."

The Botanical Garden was founded in 1765 by Captain Bligh (of "Mutiny On the Bounty" fame). It is the oldest one in the New World. He brought many seeds from the East Indies and India. Here a lot of the tropical plants which now grow on all the Caribbean islands were started, such as the Breadfruit, Nutmeg, Clove, and Cinnamon. A tall Canon-ball tree stands in the garden. This one is covered with flowers, so poor Jerzy can't find any fruit lying on the ground.

We spend about an hour walking about this tropical paradise, under "Umbrella" palms, and other shady trees. The gardens in Antigua are more impressive, as they are laid out with a formal plan, like a park, with each plant having space around it. The planting here seems haphazard.

It gets muggier and muggier as we slowly wander back to town. People are getting out of church. There are three, the Methodist, the Church of England (or Anglican, as they call it), and the Catholic. Most people here are Catholic, due to a large number of Portuguese settlers. We pass a burnt out school, burnt recently as a vengeance by some frustrated politicians who had not succeeded in getting elected.

We only meet one white woman on our walk, a discouraged looking person with hair in curlers, leading a small child by the hand. Another white, a man with a camera, walks aimlessly in the other direction. A tourist? He must have come by air, as no other ship is in the harbour.

We reach the "Blue Caribbean Hotel", facing the harbour, and painted blue, a Somerset Maughamish looking place, whose owner, a thin Englishwoman, sits at a table on the terrace. We cross the street to a pavilion in a garden, preferring this to an empty air-conditioned bar. A waiter brings George a "double" rum-and-coke. Then the tropical downpour begins, which had been threatening all morning. We put on our plastic raincoats, except for Eva, who had left hers on the ship, seeming to feel that it was beneath her dignity to take it. The rain really freshens the air. Lots of green lizards rush up the trees, and Jerzy catches a tiny frog. In the gutter by the street a crab hurries along. We slop through the rain towards the ship, as it is nearly lunch time.

An old Englishman with a cane, in shining white shirt and bow tie, is taking refuge under an arcade. He accosts us as we walk past. His bald head is covered with insect bites.

"Do you know Count Dziednuszycki?" he inquires, when George tells him he had been with the Polish Airforce. "I put him up in my home for several weeks during the war. He slept with me and my wife – not in the same bed, I don't mean that! He gave me a present of some fine cigarettes. Never heard of him again. He may be dead. . . You from the *Veloz* ?"

He shakes our hands several times. Then asks us for a match to light his cigarette. He talks in such an incoherent way that I think he must be slightly crazy, but George says he's probably just had several Sunday drinks.

5 PM   Slept until 3.30 after a heavy Sunday lunch. It is still raining steadily. The hatches are covered and no work has been done all afternoon. I wonder if we will really leave at 6? Sit around and read "Zorba the Greek". Our cabin is draped with yesterday's wet bathing suits and beach towels, wet shoes and raincoats. Can't hang them over the Engine Room in port. Mr. Resson says everything would be stolen. Two mangoes have gone bad, and give the cabin a fermenting odour. I throw them overboard, and they sink heavily to the bottom. A large pile of delicious bananas are becoming over-ripe on the table. No one eats them. We have too much to eat!

Go for a damp walk on deck. The air is cool and refreshing. Awnings have appeared over the Boat Deck, against tropical rain and sun. Showing that we are nearing Equatorial Regions!

8 PM   Sail. Sit on wet deck and watch the desolate island grow smaller and smaller under grey enveloping clouds. Another distant island shows two lonely lights. We wonder who lives there?

Monday, August 1

The Pitch Lake, Trinidad. We had to put in here to refuel. 100 tons (20 gal. to the ton) of Diesel Oil. This will save George a 60-mile (& return) trip by taxi from Port of Spain, as I am determined to see Pitch Lake,   We have sailed in through the narrow channel between Venezuela (to the right) and Trinidad. From the distance, Trinidad does look as though three separate peaks stick up from three separate islands. I guess this is why Columbus called it "La Trinidad". Our first glimpse of the mainland of South America showed rocky cliffs and jungly vegetation. To think that only a little further south is the mouth of the Orinoco! We are only 10 degrees north of the Equator.

The day is a scorcher, with cloudless sky. The water is calm and oily. It looks unnaturally green, and we think it must contain oil. Maybe we just think this as we are so near the oil fields of Venezuela. This is the first completely calm day we've had. Later, as the sun gets higher, we enjoy sitting in the shade of the tropical awnings, while watching the sun rays dancing on the water, like shining drops of rain.

About 11 we arrived at the Lake, which we can't see from the pier. There are 3 or 4 oil derricks standing on stilted platforms in the bay. We dock at the end of a long, rickety pier, which is the end of a conveyor belt of the "Trinidad Asphalt Lake Co., Ltd." The pilot has to manoeuvre the ship several times, like a tricky parking operation. as the tide is against us.

After lunch, we start off to walk to the lake with Mr. Ogonowski, who has visited this place before. He carries our raincoats in a basket, as an inky black rain cloud is piling up nearby. The water has turned pale turquoise, almost white. We pass the *Aristotelis*, from Monrovia, a dirty, rusty freighter tied opposite us. The crew look like a combination of Greek, Italian and Jew – except, says our Captain, the Jews never go to sea.

George shouts over to them: "Where are you from?"

"Greece," one shouts back; then, on second thought, he shouts: "Texas!"

The ship flies a flag with red and white stripes, like the U.S. flag, but with one star. The Lone Star? No! When we check it in "All About Ships & Shipping" it turns out to be Liberia.

The sailors seem interested in Eva. She is wearing her long, colourless shirt, under which nothing else is visible. Actually, she does have on her white shorts. But the sailors thought she didn't, Rick tells her later.

Farther down the line is another freighter, from Hamburg, with a Germanic crew of clean, husky, blonde young men, who put on bathing trunks later, and take flying high dives off the end of the piers, showing off for Eva's benefit, we're sure.

We walk up an asphalt road. Jerzy notices that the asphalt has melted, then rehardened into patterns like abstract paintings. We go up a long hill in the heat. It feels particularly hot, as we've just had a heavy lunch. Past the Club for Company workers (tennis, and rum-and-coke, says Ogonowski). Past the well-kept workers' houses with their neat gardens. One even has a swimming pool. A golf course comes into view, and then a soccer field. We have reached the top of the hill where we see the expanse of Trinidad Bay spreading below us, now darkening under storm clouds.

"Imagine being condemned to live in a place like this!" groans George.

"Oh, I don't know," replies Ogonowski. "They have good houses, a fine climate, free recreation."

"Its a lot nicer than New York City," I add.

"Not to me," grunts George.

We arrive at the Asphalt, or Pitch, Lake. From the distance it looks like a large parking lot. Rain-water stands in puddles, as the surface is not quite even. Some boys are splashing around in this. George steps out onto mud, rather, asphalt that has not quite hardened. This is the only thing that impresses him. Mr. Ogonowski insists there is nothing like this in the world, but George keeps repeating that he has seen something like it.

"Don't you want to walk over it?" Ogonowski asks. Eva is already far ahead. "Once I walked completely across. Its as hard as a road."

"No!" George firmly replies. "We can see it from here, and there's really not much to see."

It has started to rain, and we take refuge under a shelter for Company machines. The aerial railroad ends here at the Lake, but there is no sign of anyone working. Some other tourists have gone in ahead of us, but locked the gate. A sign reads: "All Trespassers will be prosecuted."

"Well, its not raining too hard, so lets start back," suggests George.

Half-way back the torrent descends, and we put on our plastic coats under a convenient bus-stop shelter. Eva is walking ahead again, her raincoat over her head, but her body getting drenched. Jerzy and I follow single file, watching huge pelicans fly in geese-like formations. George and Mr. Ogonowski stroll slowly behind, rain pouring off them, conversing in Polish.

Our ship pulls out at 6. The Germans are still swimming (one has snorkelling equipment), and they have to be called out of the water so the ship won't hurt them. A labourer, with dark skin and bright yellow helmet, then reprimands them for sitting on some pilings too near where our ship will pass.

The storm is over. A flamingo pinkish-red sunset. Pale calm turquoise water. We recross the Bay to Port of Spain – 20 miles. Going at our speed of 10 and a quarter knots an hour, it takes us two hours. It is dark when we arrive. The full moon is dramatically piercing some storm clouds on the Eastern horizon. We have the festive chain of coloured lights – "Fairy Lights", the Captain calls them – turned off at the stern, in order to again try to see the Southern Cross. This time we are looking directly South, so should not miss it. As the light fades, and the stars strengthen in intensity, we seem to see 5 or 6 crosses in the sky. Several of the young officers join in our search. Each one sees a different Southern Cross! One launches into a discussion on Castor and Pollux, which he thinks is part of the Cross. Finally, Mr.

Ogonowski points knowledgeably (from years spent in southern seas) at the real one. It gleams faintly, partly concealed behind clouds low on the horizon.

"Look! There are the 2 bright stars pointing to it. Mr. Pendleton showed them to me. And thats how it looks on the Australian flag, slightly leaning to the right," cries Jerzy, with final authority.

8 PM The News. A student in Texas killed 9 people. More riots in Chicago and Omaha. India and Pakistan won't agree to peace talks until the problem of Kashmir is settled, etc., etc. In other words, nothing cheerful.

The rum and the gin is brought out, and we sit until 10.30 drinking in celebration of Mr. Resson's 38th wedding anniversary. "To two red-heads!" says Mr. Resson, gallantly including me in his toast.

Captain Humphreys waxes eloquent, and discusses his war experiences, how he was sent on a secret mission to blow up part of the Danube, and how three of his ships were sunk by German subs. He also talks about Wales and the history of the Welsh people, something I never knew much about.

"They migrated from the foot of the Himalayas, back in prehistoric times," explained the Captain. "There's a connection between Sanskrit and Welsh, believe it or not. Betcha with all your knowledge of Polish, George, you can't pronounce this – " and he says an unpronounceable (to us) Welsh word. He goes on to explain that all the Celtic people come from the same stock: the Welsh, the Cornish, the Irish, Scotch and Breton, and even the Basque.

Well, I have a lot of Irish and Scotch blood, so here we have a mutual bond. Captain Humphreys comes from Harlech (where the song "March of the Men of Harlech" originated). Incidentally, the Captain is wondering if the Welsh will accept Prince Charles as their next Prince of Wales? Preparations for his Investiture in Caernarfon Castle in 1969 are already under way. As part of the ceremony, Queen Elizabeth will have to go down on her knees, and beg permission from the Welsh people to confer this title on her son. I'd like to see that!

Mr. Resson has told me he thinks Captain Humphreys is "the greatest Captain I've ever sailed with". (And he's had 40 years at sea.) "He and I get along fine," he added.

Tuesday, August 2

Two weeks on our way! Wake up to see the harbour of Port of Spain. Its a large port. We're berthed way out on Pier 6, far from where the passenger ships come in. A long dock with a big warehouse meets the eye. The harbour seems inactive, except for a few tugs, and a queer contraption near us, half house-boat, half dredger, puffing out black smoke. A few tankers are anchored in the distance. Where is "the glamour of Bombay and Hong Kong" and the teeming waterfront life which impressed Mother in 1951? Here we are three miles from town, down a dusty, commercial street, devoid of life save for a few trucks and cyclists.

The centre of town, Frederick Street, is teeming with life, of many descriptions. Negro, Hindu, Chinese and English predominate, with a strong Spanish touch, if one can judge by the noisy men lining the sidewalks a little farther down in the warehouse region. The more Latin they get, the more uneasy I feel, due to their attitude towards women. I felt more relaxed among the cheerful Negroes of St. Kitts. Peddlers are shouting on the sidewalks, selling cheap silver bracelets (@ 20 cents each), or Bingo tickets. They are very aggressive. "The Oriental touch," says George, "but you'll soon get used to it."

Although one can see a lot of different types here, all mingling freely (which is good), they aren't nearly as colourful a crowd as I had expected. A few Hindu women wear long saris, but many dress in a conventional way, with just the addition of a cheap gauze veil over the head. A lot of them don't even bother with this.

From a taxi we see one holy man, in a white turban and "dhoti" cloth, with a long beard, carrying a bundle. "Some religious nut," says the driver. The Hindu temple is not visible from the centre of town. We observe many poor-looking Chinese restaurants. We go to a photographic shop to leave the movie camera, which again has stuck. Then we struggle through the crowd to Barclay's Bank, Ltd., to change some money. After this, wandering around the square looking in shop windows, we become overcome by sizzling heat reflected up from unshaded pavements. I had the feeling that George was worried that they wouldn't be able to fix the camera (they had sounded very doubtful), and he did not want to have to buy a new one. One could scarcely find a good camera in a place like this, even if one had the money. He was thinking of this, rather than of sightseeing. Eva looked bored and hot. Jerzy was clearing his throat all the time, and I thought he might be getting a cold. As for me, I kept thinking I should be taking picturesque shots with my own camera, but either did not see anything photogenic; or else, the family had gone so far ahead that I didn't dare stop for fear I'd lose them; or, the sun seemed to be in the wrong position for my picture to turn out well. I kept thinking how mother had raved about this city. She wrote that one could spend weeks here without even bothering to go out of town on excursions.

Right now, to me, Port of Spain just seems hot and over-crowded. The main street is very tiring, as there is such a crowd one can hardly push one's way through. If one hesitates and walks a little slower than the mob, one hears the old refrain of "Taxi?" from a hopeful voice. The stores have cheap-looking merchandise, and no typical items seem to be sold to attract the more discriminating visitor. There is nowhere to sit down (no open-air cafés), except dingy 2nd floor bars, which exclude children. "An Anglo Saxon touch," remarks George in disgust. "Exactly the same thing in London."

We drive out to Maracas Beach, on a winding mountain road (made by the Americans during the war, in return for Navy bases). Its about 15 miles out, through jungle scenery. Huge bamboo, the most gigantic we've ever seen, typifies the place. The jungle is inhabited by parrots and monkeys (invisible, but present, says the cab driver), and many poisonous snakes (fer-de-lance, bushmaster, coral snake), but these only in the interior.

"Do you know how we catch monkeys here?" the driver asks. "There is a tree which has big roots around it out of the ground. These have hollows which fill with water during the rains. Well, if we want to catch a monkey, we empty out the water and put very strong spirits there instead. Then, when the monkey comes down to drink, he gets very drunk, so drunk he can't climb back up. You just take him by the hand, and lead him away! Several hours later, he's furious when he finds he's in a cage!"

We have a swim at the beach, a spectacular stretch of white sand, lined with tall, windblown palms. It is kept like a state park, so that everyone can enjoy it. It even has a modern bath-house. "The Government wouldn't allow anyone to build here, even a hotel. It would have spoiled it."

The waves are very strong and knock us down, in spite of its being a protected bay. A Calypso singer with a guitar serenades Eva and myself on the sand – rather a touristy touch. We eat lunch, fresh fried fish, in a tiny beach restaurant, accompanied by a tropical deluge. One cannot see the water through the rain.

"This is the kind of fish my wife likes," says our cab driver, who is eating with us. "Once she asked me to get her some really fresh fish, so I came here, where there's a little fishing village. I asked a fisherman who was just coming in with his boat to give me a fish. Man! That fish was really fresh. When I got got home it was still jumping. Every time my wife thinks of it now she says: "That was a fresh fish!"

On the drive back, he gives us two mangoes. They feel very hard, but when I try them, they turn out to be delicious, even sweeter than the Mexican ones, and with a slight lime-like flavour. George doesn't like them. He prefers papaya.

The driver launches into another story. "Do you know the one about the boy who saw a ripe mango hanging from a tree, just out of reach? He threw a rock and sticks at it, but it would not fall. Finally, he climbed up the tree to see if it was ripe. He crawled along a branch until he could touch it. He felt it. It was just right to eat. Then he climbed down again, and started throwing more rocks at it. It still didn't fall. "That's awfully funny," he thought. "Its ripe enough to fall any time!"

We drive past the Country Club, an area of exclusive modern houses, completely California-style, with the exception of the extra-luxuriant surrounding vegetation. Here we have a flat tyre. "I knew this was going to happen," exclaims Eva. "Things always repeat themselves." (We had had a flat in St. Kitts.) We are looking at a flamboyant tree, covered with vivid red blossoms. "I often ask my wife," says our driver, "who painted these flowers? Who? And who painted the birds? They certainly look as though an artist had painted them!"

"Too bad you're not staying until Sunday. I'd take you to a Hindu wedding. You'd never forget it. The groom is all dressed up in silks, with a crown on his head, and lots of jewelry. Everyone comes up and looks at him, and tells him how handsome he is. It is his day. No one looks at the bride. She stays somewhere in a corner!"

"One good thing about this place," he continues, "is the mixture of races. Have you noticed? A Chinese girl may have dark skin, or a Hindu slanting eyes. There's nothing prettier than a girl with Chinese and Hindu blood. In one neighbourhood Chinese, Negroes, Hindus and whites all live in good relations, and invite each other to their parties. Its all a question of educating people right from the start. Our President is very fine. A man from the People, a man of my complexion" (dark). "He came from a very poor family, but was bright in school. Won all the scholarships. He went on to Oxford, and won all the scholarships there, too. His teachers said he was one of the most brilliant boys ever to graduate! He has a PHD in Economics. He can hold his own with anyone! He is putting the country on a sound economic basis. He's gotten loans from everyone, including the U.S. The only country he didn't get a loan from was England. He went there particularly to ask for one, but he didn't like their conditions. Why should he meet them? He got angry, and left."

George said privately to me later: "I'd like to see this country in 5 years. I bet it will have collapsed economically, and they'll be begging Britain to come back. Its ridiculous for an island this size to stand alone."

When we told Captain Humphreys about our conversation with the cab driver, he said: "I don't agree about the mixture of the races. That is only on the surface. An Englishman would never marry a girl with a trace of dark blood, no matter how pretty. Some of these girls are stunning. What figures! And well-dressed. But they might have a dark child! Some white men in the islands have 6 or 7 dark children, but they never recognize them."

We drove up to the "Hilton". "Just to show you!" said the driver. "So you'll know what people are talking about."

Its called "the upside down house". It has a beautiful location, up on a hill above "Queen's Park". Unlike other Hiltons, it has lovely planting, so most of the building, which is large, is concealed back of trees and bushes. However, when George took a look in the lobby, he saw a showy group of low class tourists, and this was enough for him. "Why come to Trinidad to see types like these?" he demanded.

9 PM We start out again, to do the "night-life". (Jerzy stays on the ship, and goes to bed.) First, we are driven up a mountain road (the "Lovers' Lane" of Trinidad, says our driver, the same one we had earlier), to see the view at night. A full moon is shining down. "Its too early to go to a night-club yet!" says the driver.

On the way down the mountain, I hear a shrill whistle from the bushes. "What's that bird?" I ask.

"That's not a bird! That's a frog," he laughs. "One night I was walking along a lonely road at night and I heard someone whistle at me. Then, again. It was the darnest thing. I didn't see anyone. Then I saw a little frog. He was making the noise!"

We are taken to a club, "The Gay Caballero", the driver's suggestion, on the outskirts of town. This place, although nearly empty, and so dark one cannot see one's drink, has a very good dance orchestra with local character. Electric guitars and bongo drums dominate (unfortunately, no steel drums). The music has a lively rhythm of the South American variety. "They can sure play sweet," is how the cab driver expresses it.

One or two couples, good-looking young Negroes, with a fine sense of rhythm, start dancing the Cha-Cha. Several pretty girls are dancing around by themselves near the bar. It is too early for a floor-show, and when a juke box was turned on, to give the orchestra a rest, we left.

"What were those single girls at the bar for?" asked George, when we got back in the cab.

"Those girls are for many purposes!"

We drove through the dark, deserted streets to "The Penthouse", which everyone says is the best-known, the most popular night-club (and the most expensive). It is the only one to have steel bands and Limbo dancers on week nights. The show here does not start until 11.30 PM.

"Are women safe walking along the streets at night?" asks George.

"Oh, yes. There are many policemen guarding the streets. See, there's one now on the corner. Anyway, there isn't much crime. If there are fights, its usually something local, like several boys fighting over one girl. Our boys wouldn't think of attacking foreigners! I always tell my wife its a terribly cowardly thing for a man to attack a girl. Its an unsportsmanlike fight. Anyway, where do you hit a woman? You wouldn't hit her on the face! Thats what attracted you to her in the first place. You wouldn't hit her on the hands. These hands cook and sew and care for you! You wouldn't hit her on the feet. These feet take her from one place to another while she's doing chores for you, these feet run errands and minister to you. You wouldn't hit her on the body. This body bears and nurses your children. So where can you hit her, I ask my wife?"

"Have you lived up to this with your wife?" I ask.

"Oh, yes indeed. Been married to my wife for 23 years, and have never regretted it once. I asked God to choose a wife for me. When you do that, when you put the choice in God's hands, you can't make a mistake!"

By this time, we had arrived at "The Penthouse", through a narrow passage in a dingy office building. At the door, one has to pay $2.00 (Bewees) admission, go past a group of men blocking the hall like "bouncers", then up 5 flights in an elevator. Then, climb up one more flight of dilapidated stairs. One enters a dark, crowded bar, with lots of small tables, and a minuscule dance floor. A 2nd rate duet is playing for dancing (piano and snare drums), Viennese waltzes, and "Mac the Knife". A 3rd rate singer begins to croon. "Just like dance time on the old *Saturnia*, in the Second Class lounge," whispers George.

He orders a rum-and-coke.

"We don't have any Coke." says the waiter.

"Oh, then bring me a Pepsi." replies George.

"We don't have any Pepsi." growls the waiter. "I'll bring you a 7-Up."

When it comes, he can hardly taste the rum. "This drink doesn't have anything in it," he says in a loud voice, when the waiter brings the bill.

"You get what you pay for here!" answers the waiter, in a surly tone. Several people turn around to stare.

"You'd better not shout," I whisper, "this looks like the kind of place where people would enjoy starting a fight."

"I'll shout if I feel like it, and I feel like it now! This place cheats," George says loudly. "and I don't like to be cheated."

I am drinking a Daquiri, in which there doesn't seem to be any liquor. It just tastes sour.

The place looks like a clip-joint sailors' bar in any port. In reply to my thoughts, a big group of U.S. sailors file in. One, a huge burly fellow, immediately asks Eva to dance. "No, thank you," she says. Then he asks me. I also decline.

"Well, that was nervy, when I was with you," I say, disgusted.

"Oh, I guess anything goes here!" comments George, quite unconcerned.

Most of the customers, not including sailors, a few " bar girls" and some Negroes, seem to consist of a large group of Dutch tourists (of a 2nd rate variety) from a cruise ship, the *Prinz der Netherland*, which we had watched docking near us this afternoon. They seem to be having a good time, and are dancing like mad on the jammed dance floor.

The entertainment is poor. No steels drums! A Calypso singer named "The Mighty Sparrow" (well-known, someone on our ship said) sang extremely dirty songs. Some, improvised, were aimed at the people from the Dutch ship, who screamed with delighted laughter. They seemed to understand his English alright. Fortunately, I thought, there was something wrong with the microphone. It made terrible buzzing sounds, so it was hard to understand him. I don't mind risque songs, but he didn't have any style or sense of artistry (maybe that's what lowbrow people like about him?) It was plain muck, such as: "I see 3 men sitting there alone. How are you going to make love without any girls? You'll have to make love amongst yourselves!" Well, this isn't really very funny – but the Dutch howled.

Next, came the limbo dancers, 2 men and a girl, who wormed their way lower and lower under a stick held parallel to the floor. "Just to show off the lower part of the girl's body," was George's cynical comment. The grand climax was when one of the men jumped and rolled on a pile of broken glass, to the frenzied beating of drums. I suspected some kind of Voodoo here. Maybe he worked himself into a trance, and the glass didn't affect him? George suspected some kind of trick, as he noticed that each time before he did it he shook the glass so it would be in a loose pile. Maybe if it was loose, it didn't cut him? Anyway, it was rather sickening to watch. We noticed that this act got hardly any applause.

Shortly after this, we left. We were sorry we hadn't stayed longer at "The Gay Caballero", which might have been very interesting later in the evening. At least, it had seemed like a more natural place.

Wednesday, August 3

"Want to do some ironing?" the Chief greeted me bright and early.

"Sure! I was wondering whether you had found the iron."

"Oh, yes. I have an iron and an ironing-board. When do you want to do it? Before noon?"

"Well, I'd rather do it tomorrow! Don't want to waste the morning when we're in port." (I was to regret these words!)

At 9 AM we were back in town, via the same taxi driver, who seemed somewhat subdued after his talkativeness of yesterday. He did not try to persuade us that he should take us anywhere this morning except the photographic shop. Probably, we've actually seen all the sights.

The movie camera is fixed! The clerk held it up triumphantly when George entered the shop.

We go to the Museum, as I want to see Columbus's anchor, which, our driver yesterday said was in the basement. But, there is no sign of any basement! Downstairs is a display of snakes, pickled in alcohol; and alarming pictures of what to do in case you're bitten. The Captain told us later that in Trinidad the Mongoose has gotten tired of eating snakes, so the Mongoose and the Snake have divided the island between them, each taking half for himself!

There is also a display of moths, of a frightening size. One measures a foot across! There are also local birds, looking very dead and moth-eaten. On the 2nd floor are some poor paintings by native artists, and a lot of gaudy costumes for the Mardi Gras. It is very hot, and we are overcome with fatigue. (Its queer how one usually feels this way in museums.) After sitting limply for sometime on a sofa, we find a door marked "Exit", which takes us outside. There, by the side of the building, are two rusty anchors lying unmarked in some straggly grass. We go back and ask whether these are Columbus's anchors? "Yes!" came the quick reply. Its more likely these anchors actually came from some 20th Century wreck.

Have lunch at the "Normandie", which is meant, both by Mother and the taxi driver, to be a gourmet French restaurant. It turns out to be a commercial hotel, with an ordinary-looking air-conditioned dining room. The food is heavy and expensive ($4.50 Bewee for lunch). Its not French, and not even particularly good. George orders a bottle of Pomard, which turns out to be watery and nothing special.

4 PM   Back on board. We sail at 6. Almost all the bags of cement are loaded. plus a lot of ice-cream, brought by another Booth liner all the way from England! The ice-cream is for Iquitos, and is kept at a -5 degree temperature.

The other Booth freighter, only 3 years old and slightly bigger than us, is Mr. Ogonowski's old ship. She is anchored a little was up the harbour from us. We can just see her funnel. Mr. Ogonowski had spent the day visiting her. In fact, he says he likes her better than the *Veloz* , and would like to get back on her.

The port had suddenly gotten livelier. Five or six freighters are now anchored in the harbour "roads", as Mr. Ogonowski calls them. "You can't just anchor anywhere," he explains. "Sometimes there are underwater cables which interfere; the water is too shallow; or explosives have been dumped. Also, a free channel has to be kept for ships to come and go. We have to pay something for anchorage. In a place like Port-of-Spain, almost as much as tying up to the dock."

Right next to us, the *Spenser* had docked. It is the "L and H Line" (Lamport and Holt). The *Spenser* is a good deal smaller than us. An officer from this ship walks over and watches our departure. He has a hard-boiled look. (We are particularly fortunate in our officers, who are unusually pleasant.) First, he drinks a can of beer, then throws it into the water. Then he lights up a cigarette.

"Its funny how people always have to have something in their mouths!" exclaims George, who rarely smokes.

It is dark by the time we clear the harbour. We are going through a narrow passage (locally nicknamed "The Hole in the Wall"), and Mr. Ogonowski comes, binoculars in hand, from the Bridge, to ask me to draw the curtains over our forward porthole. The bow of the ship must be kept in darkness, so they can see the rocks! We are very close to land on each side, and a particularly large and vicious rock stands out on our port side, just visible in the night as a slightly darker spot on the water. Right near the horizon, as we lean over the stern railing, is the Southern Cross. Now we know where to look for it. It isn't as bright or as spectacular as I had imagined when reading poetic descriptions. The lowest right hand star seems rather dim – but maybe that's because the whole constellation still hangs low in the sky.

Thursday, August 4

A rough sea again! Going through many rain-squalls. We are somewhere off the coast of Guyana (formerly British Guiana), where it is now the rainy season. I stagger on deck and slump into a chair, feeling very squeamish.

"Good morning!" comes Mr. Resson's energetic voice. "All ready for your ironing?"

"Oh, no!" I groan. "Just let me wait until it calms down a little. One can hardly stand up today."

The three officers at our table all have hang-overish looks. Mr. Ogonowski was drinking with his former pals on his old ship. "Would like to transfer back to her," he keeps repeating. "She's nicer and newer than this ship. This ship is surprisingly seaworthy, though, in spite of the weight of our cargo." If he has old friends on the other ship, its reasonable that he would prefer her.

Mr. Resson and the Captain say that they fell in with the only passenger on the *Spenser*, a woman whom the Captain recognised as being a friend of a former passenger on this ship. She asked them yesterday to the "Hilton", where she had taken a room while the *Spenser* was in port, at $16.00 U.S. for one bed.

"Isn't that rather extravagant, when she can sleep on the ship?" we ask.

"Oh, a lot of passengers do that!" replies the Captain. "The last ones we had, some missionaries with 2 children, always went to the best hotel when we were in port for one or two days. They seemed to have plenty of money, very expensive cameras, and everything, so why not?"

"This lady had invited all the officers of the *Spenser* yesterday evening to the "Hilton" for drinks. Cost a lot of money, but she wanted to do it. We all sat around the pool, and you should have seen the beautiful girls! All the bigwigs from Trinidad congregate at the Hilton bar. Its the place to be seen!"

"What kind of woman was this?" asks George, suspiciously. "What age woman? One woman, alone on a freighter!"

"Oh, she's old enough to know the ropes! She's been around and knows all the answers. She's going down from Canada to visit a friend near Rio. Seems to like to travel like this."

I lie on the bunk most of the day, not actually sick, but feeling very heavy. My mind doesn't function. When I try to read or write, the letters dance in front of my eyes and I feel dizzy. Then I have to lie down again. Even George is sleeping a lot.

No more listening to the news in the evening! Mr. Resson tells us that the short wave radio he had was only borrowed from the 4th Officer, and that he had to return it. He had ordered a similar one from England, which he was to pick up in Port-of-Spain (it was shipped by Booth Line), but he received a cable that it was stolen along the way.

"This is an unlucky trip!" he says.

"I also had over £1,000. stolen in New York!" the Captain reminds us.

At 3.15 PM this afternoon an awful grinding noise had been heard in the engine. Suddenly the motor stopped. We were drifting at the mercy of the waves!

"This happened to me during the war, going from England to Canada," said George. "We drifted for 24 hours before it was repaired, and lost 1,000 miles. Not so funny, with all the German subs around."

"Now we'll have a Mutiny. The food will run out, and the sailors will all come up from down below, machetes in hand, and take over. They will make you their slave, and murder the rest of us."

"No," I reply, "I think they'll eat me, if there isn't any food!"

"But they'll rape you first!"

After 10 minutes, the engine started again. "Nothing to worry about," said the room steward, cheerily, as he brought in tea. "Just some water in the engine."

Friday, August 5

It was so rough during the night that we were tossed from one side of our bunks to the other, as the ship rolled. We were rolling so much we had to shut the porthole which opens onto the port side deck. Waves were splashing in.

"Was that anything unusual in the way of weather?" asks George at breakfast.

"Oh, no. Wait until we really get some rough weather!" answers the Captain with a wink.

"Its always choppy along here," explains Mr. Resson. "Won't get calmer until we round the hump of South American."

The big sea is gradually easing, the breezes are cool and delightful. I am even wearing long slacks without feeling too hot. Imagine, so near the Equator, the breeze from the water is cooler than any we have felt since leaving New York.

4 PM   When going out on deck, I suddenly see some sailors in life jackets. The alarm sounds. Life-boat drill! The second one we've had, which shows that the Company is a responsible one. We all line up obediently by the life-boats. The dark grimy faces under the jackets today look smiling and familiar. Personalities are gradually emerging from the mass.

6.15   Sunset. The rain clouds have drifted away. The stars come out, and by 7 o'clock shine brightly overhead. Far on the horizon a ghostly light blinks. "The Flying Dutchman!" I exclaim.

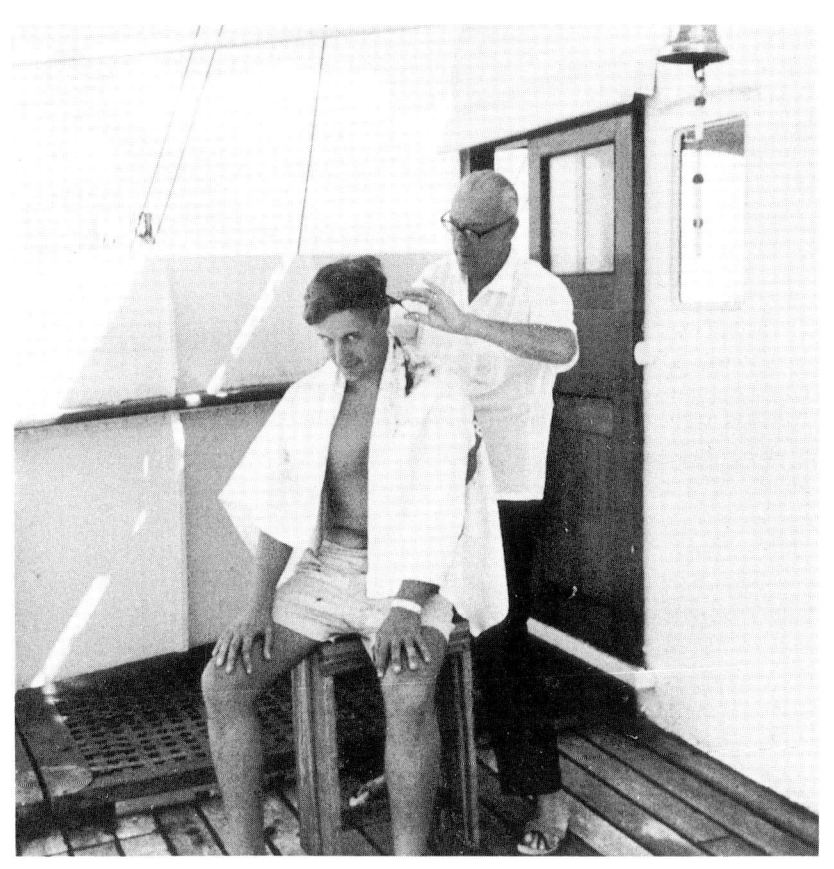

The Captain cuts hair on the Bridge of the *Veloz*

Saturday, August 6

A glorious day! The waves have calmed, the sky is blue, and sparkling sun rays dance on blue-green water. We spend a lazy morning on deck. Porpoises are seen, jumping single-file quite near the ship. Then, in the middle distance, whales start to blow.

George has a hair-cut on deck. The Captain doubles as a barber! Jerzy refuses to have one (he already looks Beattle-ish). Everyone says he'll get lice on the Amazon. "Oh, no!" he says, defiantly.

I do more wash. George sleeps all afternoon, after drinking a substantial amount of run-and-coke before lunch. Later, we discuss where our next trip will be, by freighter, of course! Jerzy says Egypt.

Everyone, except us, is late for "Tea". They were listening to the fights- Cassius Clay versus London. Clay won in 2 and a half rounds.

"A great fight!" sighs the Captain.

"Are you interested in wrestling matches?" someone asks George.

"No!" he answers. "Generally, I'm not interested in sports atall." Dead silence at the table. This has shocked the sports-minded British.

George launches into a long story about French Canadians. No one was interested. People started filing out one by one until George was the only one left eating. I guess the rum-and-coke had made him too talkative.

The stars seem particularly bright tonight. The Captain is watching the sky, and sees the Telestar moving slowly across. It is very dark by 7. The sun always goes down by 6 in these tropical regions. Tomorrow we shall set our clocks forward one hour.

We discuss what the scientific word is for the Milky Way. The Captain thinks its "galaxy". Just then we see a shooting star.

Mr. Ogonowski explains that we are going against the Equatorial Current, and that is why the Trinidad-Belem run takes 6 and a half days. In the other direction, it is only 4. We had not realised how strong this current is. He starts talking about ocean currents and how they form a chain: the Equatorial Current links into the Gulf Stream, which, in its turn, becomes something else off the coast of Ireland, etc.

Around 8, Mr. Ogonowski sees a satellite. The Captain explains that it is really the same one going around again! It takes exactly 93 minutes.

Sunday, August 7

A quiet, noisy Sunday. The power sander, which has been going for the past two days on the lower deck, is now hard at work above us. on the mini deck that goes around the funnel. This little deck is reached by ladders, and doesn't seem to be used for much. Right aft of the smoke-stack is a large cage-like structure, made of strips of heavy wood, with a big door which can be bolted from outside. When we first saw it we thought that it must be used to transport wild animals from the jungle – maybe a panther, or a wild boar. But upon inquiry, we found out that its just a bin for potatoes! However, no one ever keeps potatoes in it.

The noise of the sander is so loud one can't talk, and it is accompanied by penetrating sawing, scraping, and hammering. Thousands of particles of dried black paint fly down on deck and cover us and our chairs with a soot-like coating. I decide to go into the cabin and wash out some clothes in the wash basin, in hopes that they will have finished the work by the time I have done this job. They've already scraped the lower deck, where the crew sit around and play dominoes in the evening (usually to the accompaniment of hilarious laughter). In fact, they get so excited over the dominoes that it sounds like a circus. (This is the only time one ever hears anything from them atall.) The floor, formerly black, is now a blazing yellow, with the imprints of several feet immortalised in the middle.

When I take my wash into the Engine Room to hang up, the noise is so terrific, as they are working directly overhead, that I can't stay in there. Now I understand how one's eardrums could burst from a loud enough noise.

To escape this, we walk to the bow. It is the calmest day we've had, cloudless except for a few good-weather clouds, and the ship is scarcely rolling. George has the movie camera, and takes some pictures. It is quiet and peaceful here. No crew members are around, one can't hear the sander, nor even the engine. One just glides silently through the water. Big ropes are coiled in the bow, near the winch used to raise and lower the anchors. Two anchor chains go through holes in the deck. Its rather frightening to peer down these at the moving ocean.

George and I drink rum-and-coke again before lunch, and lament the fact that the meal won't be gourmet, with a bottle of French wine. We imagine that no one objects to the rather plain cooking but us. Its probably the kind the English are used to at home. The trouble is its too heavy (and certainly too fattening!) Three different kinds of potatoes are served every day, plus a heavy soup (usually good, I must admit); plus some kind of bread-and-butter pudding (which always tastes flat, as the cook forgets to add salt and sugar).

Everyone is late for lunch today, except us. We are always right on the dot for meals (having nothing else to do!) We imagine that the two chief officers are having a Sunday drink with the Captain. In fact, I saw Mr. Ogonowski disappearing in that direction, ice-water bottle in hand.

The regular Sunday joke is brought up. Mr. Resson says he's going to pump the organ after lunch for Church Services, the Captain will read the lesson, and Mr. Ogonowski will sing. The first Sunday they told us this I thought it was true. Then they all laughed and said this took place in their dreams, during their Sunday siestas! The missionaries (their former passengers) were shocked by this joke it seems, and said it wasn't a Christian ship.

We saw a group of 3 or 4 dozen flying fish in formation for several hundred feet along the water.

Mr. Ogonowski, whom I met around 4, coming up from the lower deck with a huge grin on his face, said the water was turning a golden brown already due to the influence of the Amazon. I thought he was kidding (we're still 2 or 3 days away from the mouth of the river), but George said he had noticed that the water wasn't so blue this morning, and had seen a brownish tinge where the waves broke.

"The Amazon is so huge," said Ogonowski, "that it influences the whole coast of South America."

Later, currents are pointed out, showing darker and lighter streaks in the water. We are skirting deeper and shallower channels. The depth reading at 3.30 was 50 fathoms, or about 300 feet (not very deep for the ocean). When we hit the current over a deeper section, the ship gave one big roll. Otherwise, she's been steady.

Beat Jerzy tonight at 3 games of dominoes. Jerzy learnt by watching the crew. He stood at the head of the stairs and looked down at them as they were playing. Our set, a family one, is dated 1890.

Monday, August 8
Finally ironed two of George's shirts and one of my dresses down in Mr. Resson's cabin (he has a convertor for the electric current). The ironing-board is propped up against his desk.

Cut, and washed my hair this afternoon. Quite a job with the ship rolling a little, the door shut, and curtains over the ports for fear someone might see me in my bra with goop all over my head. It was stuffy and stinky in the cabin, due to all the shampoos and rinses, although I had the fan going. Put on my good suntop, for fear someone might come in (I usually do my hair stripped to the waist). I was doing it in Eva and Jerzy's cabin, as its more private (the steward brings tea into ours at 3), but the kids kept bursting in, to see how I was progressing.

8 PM CROSSED THE EQUATOR!
No ceremony. The officers had left the deck, and we just waited around in the cabin, without going to bed early as we usually do. We had wanted to get some champagne to treat everyone as a surprise, but they don't have any on the ship, very much to George's disgust. He says the British have gone down in his estimation. However, he forgets this is a freighter – no frills!

Previously, at 6, when we were watching the sunset, it was quite cool. A strong wind came up, with rain clouds. A huge black cloud started to stream across the sky, in the shape of a hippo standing on his hind legs, then elongating into an alligator, then growing a long beak, and looking like a heron stretching his neck to catch a fish; finally he turned into Woody Woodpecker in gigantic size! Later, Walkyries rode across the sky, or wild men on horseback; and again an enormous elongated alligator reached across a quarter of the horizon, where the Amazon must be, held up by a monstrous fist. The stars were obliterated, and flashes of lightning were seen far off. Big waves splashed up, and the ship rolled and pitched.

The Captain made fun of me when I went in to put on slacks, and came out with a windbreaker around my shoulders, as did Jerzy and Eva. Its meant to be 86 degrees, but it feels cool.

Mr. Ogonowski said the crew would come up and tie us to our bunks, so we should not roll off as the ship manoeuvred the deep chasm of the Equator! Maybe we'll have to be tied in anyway, on account of the rough sea. Spray is coming in our ports, and the curtains are flapping wildly. One can hardly believe one is on the Equator.

The *Veloz* enters the Amazon with a load of American cars for Belém

16. THE RIVER WEAVES ITS SPELL

Tuesday, August 9
Approximately 4 AM, George wakes me up, excitedly announcing: "We're on the Amazon!"

I look out and see black water under a sky with dimming stars. The water is quiet, and our engine has stopped. We must be taking on a pilot.

To the right, from our forward porthole, is a flashing lighthouse. It must be on the Island of Marajó. To the left, a ship with blazing lights goes by. The water, no longer so salty, smells fresh.

6 AM We are all on deck examining the Amazonian water, here pale blue on the surface, but tannish underneath. Far on the horizon is a low shoreline. Later, through binoculars, we distinguish tall tree trunks, which first I had thought were cliffs. A solid mass of tree trunks. It must be the jungle!

We spend the morning peering through the binoculars. A few fishing boats appear, then more and more. They have spectacular sails of a rich, almost black, brown; a few dyed rusty red, and one or two blue. These remind me of the sails in Brittany when I was a child (no fishing boats with sails remain there now, alas). The shape of these Brazilian sails is different – sharply asymmetric. I think they look Chinese, but George insists the Chinese have square sails. Anyway, they look like "strange shores and foreign lands". The boats are small, roughly constructed, and lie low in the water. Their prows are slender, pointed, and painted gaily with red or blue stripes, sometimes pink.

The Captain calls them the "Suicide Squad", because they have no lights to speak of at night, only a dim red candle or lamp which is scarcely visible. Several years ago our ship ran down one in the dark. Two men were rescued from the water, but the third drowned.

"The others didn't seem very upset about it, although he was a relative," he dryly remarked..

At 11.05 we have dropped anchor. No hope of getting on shore for lunch, although we are ready and anxiously pacing the deck. Now both shorelines are quite close. In the distance we can see the "sky-scrapers" of Belém. It looks like a moderate-size commercial American town somewhere in the Mid West, from this distance, that is!

On our right we have passed several islands in the Bay of Marajó – or, what is actually the mouth of the Para River. Belém is 80 miles up this. The area is still considered to be part of the Amazon Estuary. We passed very near to the islands, so that we could see thick jungle, with all sizes and shapes of trees squeezed tightly together. The foreground is lined with packed rows of mangroves, whose copious roots stand out of the water. Curious slender

Floating islets of bric-a-brac drifting downstream can be a hazard to shipping

palms grow in profusion against a background of taller trees, with very thin trunks and small round balls of leaves at the tops. From a distance we thought these were orchids. Flimsy fishermen's huts on stilts are occasionally seen through the trees.

On our left, magnificent white sandy beaches, private villas, and beach clubs. I guess there are no piranhas here! With closer knowledge, it does not seem so luxurious, as no road goes there and one has to commute by boat. "The Sightseeing Tour of Belém", a tourist leaflet recommended by the "Grande Hotel", says:

"Mosqueiro Beach: (Chapen Virado)

"Only recommended on Sunday and Brazilian Holidays when it is possible to make the return trip in one day as hotel accommodations are difficult and very poor."

A marvellous perfume wafts from the jungle to the *Veloz*, smelling like a cross between gardenias, orange blossoms and the flowers of the Cannonball tree. This, mixed with the scent of river water (slightly brackish) reminds me of Southern Mexico, south of Vera Cruz, (the only really tropical place I have ever been to). The colour of the water has changed to a shining gold. First, the children said "Pea-soup", but now under the noon sun it is gleaming gold. Contrasted with clear blue sky it is beautiful to see. Later in the day, Eva says it has turned to weak iced coffee!

In the morning we had begun to see the famous bric-a-brac that is continuously carried downstream – a huge tree, or smaller ones stuck together like a solid mass glide by.

"Why, that's just a little branch," remarks the Captain. "Wait till you see the trees upriver!"

We are anchored for the Custom officials to thoroughly search us. We have been warned to lock the cabin doors, as innumerable people (hangers on, asking for favours, or trying to steal something) swarm on board. They are nosing into everything, and are a motley looking bunch. They look like a typical Hollywood crew of corrupt S. American officials! But which are the officials, and which the "hangers on"? Their skins are all shades of brown, they are all dressed in long trousers, tropical jackets, hats – very formal – and are carrying many brief cases and bundles. They occupy the lounge, drink coffee on the deck, and crowd into the Captain's cabin. Some eat lunch in the dining room.

By evening, we have learnt that they have confiscated a vast number of TV's, radios and other small appliances, which the crew (most of whom are from here) were trying to smuggle in tax-free. The items were found hidden in potato bins, laundry closets, etc. Alfredo, the dining-room steward, seemed to be the worst culprit.

"There are a lot of gloomy faces around here tonight!" says Mr. Ogonowski. "But, with a little bribery, they can buy all this out of hock tomorrow."

Later, the Captain explains that such smuggling is to be expected, but if anything is found smuggled in the hold with the cargo, then it is a more serious offence, and the Company is held responsible. They are always on the look-out for smuggled drugs, of course, particularly the New York Customs, who go over any ship coming from South America with a fine-toothed comb.

When this "official" bunch leaves, another bunch arrives, the stevedores, arriving on a puffing tug with "Booth" written on it, which is pulling 3 covered barges. As they swarm on deck and stand waiting for the barges to be tied alongside and uncovered (a lengthy procedure), I think what a characteristic photo this would make. However, with nothing else to do, they are all staring up at Eva, in her short shorts, and me, in a bright yellow dress.

"Mom, you would have to wear the brightest dress you have!", says Eva, accusingly.

What with stares and restless mumblings from this throng, I'm embarrassed about taking a photo. It might be resented. I'd never make a good press photographer! But, actually, I could kick myself that I let this one slip by. Later, George tries with his movie camera, but the camera gets stuck again! Later, when one man sees the camera, he takes off his hat, respectfully, a nice, picturesque straw that would have been great in a picture! A half naked black stevedore wears a white cloth tied around his middle, instead of shorts, that looks like diapers! This man is directing the other ones, and is quite a personality.

They are unloading huge, unwieldy bunches of steel wires (used to fortify cement buildings), and dumping them messily on the deck. Enormous heavy crates are being lowered into the hold (containing contraband machine-guns, I whisper!) Next morning, round cases are being loaded, looking as though they should contain brandy. "Nails!" laughs Ogonowski. "But there's no point really in their doing all this building in Iquitos, where we're taking these supplies. The water rises 31 feet during the rainy season, and undermines everything!"

While we are waiting, we watch the Brazilian Navy having target practise on the river, right next to our ship! Targets are set up on the water near our stern, and two military planes keep swooping down and bombing the targets. Boom! They explode in the water, and red flames and black smoke flare up. They never seem to manage to actually hit the targets, and the explosions happen in the water too near the ship for comfort! A typical S. American army manoeuvre! Little fishing boats keep going back and forth, quite unconcerned. Near the shore opposite us is a gunboat; later, a larger Navy ship passes us, going out to sea. From where we sit on deck, we also see a ship-repair yard, with what looks like a Mississippi show-boat being repaired. An old, dilapidated, stern paddled-wheeled boat is anchored nearby. Just like a view of the Mississippi 100 years ago! Farther up, is an oil refinery belching black fumes. A Brazilian tanker flies a red flag, "Dangerous Cargo".

We don't pull up anchor until after dark, nosing up past the refinery, then past masses of fishing boats moored for the night. Little lights glow, and people are seen to be living, or, at least, eating supper on board. I smell a dreadful smell, such as pigs or fertilizer.

"Is this the sewage of Belém seeping into the river? Or, is someone keeping pigs on these boats?"

"I think its the smoke from the refinery," someone suggests.

We dock far from the centre of town, near a rusty old freighter from Rio, the *Rio Prianco*. One woman is on board her, a dark-haired beauty in a tight red dress, talking to an officer. Jerzy notices the *Prianco*'s rudder is out of the water. "A sign that the ship is poorly cared for," he announces with authority! (More likely, she is sitting on a sandbank!)

The lights are very dim on the dock, and, indeed, in the whole town. The big "sky-scrapers" have shrunk to grey, undetermined shapes. The place now doesn't look more impressive than Mazatlan by night.

A pretty woman in pale blue slacks comes on board with her husband, an Englishman, the Booth Line agent. She is carrying a yellow kitten, with such long thin legs and long nose that I first thought it was a monkey. This is a present for Captain Humphreys, who loves cats.

Wednesday, August 10

Belém from the distance may look like a modern commercial city, but seen near to, only the main street is atall bustling or urban. The main street is wide, with decent looking stores. Lots of people are on the sidewalks. The women are surprisingly chique, in summer dresses. (I even saw one of the cut-out shoulders "Mod" dresses, the rage in London, which are hard to find yet in New York.) The men all wear long trousers, but not jackets, as its too warm. The fact that George and Jerzy both wore shorts attracted terrible attention. Also, the fact that we had 3 cameras. Plus, my red hair! Its quite unknown here. Our skins are much lighter than most people's, too.

In the West Indies, all men wear shorts, the British influence, I guess. Here, almost everyone stopped walking, stood where they were on the pavement, and stared at us with amazement. Their faces were slightly shocked, but otherwise blank. Not exactly friendly, however. It wasn't a pleasant experience. I'd like to try walking without cameras, and with the "boys" in long trousers, and see if we'd still attract attention. Maybe as we're a group of 4 we're particularly conspicuous. Even small children coming out of school stopped dead in their tracks and stared. I must admit that we were the only English-speaking people on the street. There seemed to be no Americans at all. However, there are several curio shops, selling snake-skins, imitation shrunken heads, and "Morpho" butterfly trays (all priced at twice too much, we were informed), which shows there must be some tourists.

We stopped first at the Booth Line office. They own their own building, an impressive older building on the corner as one starts up the main street from the waterfront. We inquired about mail. Only one clerk spoke English, and that very poorly. Hardly anyone here understands English.

The main street has a slightly European flavour, of Naples or Greece. Stretched across it are large banners advertising "Cinzano" and "Martini and Rossi" (maybe that's why I think it European!)

We changed money at "Jake's", a curio shop whose owner gives Black Market prices – $2,200 Cruceiros for one $ U.S. But George had been offered $2,250 by a steward on the ship. The Cruceiro goes up and down every day. A clever person could make a lot by changing at the right moment.

George took a dislike to Jake. When he told Jake that we came from the *Veloz*, he just snapped "2,200!" without any attempt at pleasant conversation. Besides the curio shop, he owns the "Acapulco Restaurant and Bar" across the street, where we ate lunch (not knowing that he owns it).

George stood on the sidewalk and took some movies of life on the street. (The camera is working again.) We became conscious of the fact that a suspicious-looking young man had been following us. Wherever we walked, there he was. He was dressed better than a beggar.

"Maybe he wanted to guide you around," someone on the ship later suggested. However, he didn't try to come up and speak to us. We turned a corner, and tried to shake him off, but he still stuck right at our heels. Fortunately, just then a taxi came by, and we got in, to escape. Taxis are very cheap here, and charge by the meter. There is no bargaining, as in the West Indies.

We drove to "El Bosque Gardens", quite far out through many suburbs. In this way we saw a lot of the town. The residential part is full of old Spanish-type houses, with blue, yellow, or green tile fronts, such as one sees in Mexico, only more numerous. The streets are wide, with many trees, and the houses all have gardens – full of more exotic, luxuriant and unknown (to me) varieties of trees than in Mexico. They're covered with orchids, and in profusion, the brilliant red ephidytes, "Bromelias". Philodendron vines strangle them – giant "Monsteras" climbing up the trunks.

The city, as a whole, reminds me strongly of Mexico. George thinks its more Spanish and Portuguese rather than Mexican, and is inclined to like the people better. The Mexican Indians don't appeal much to him, he prefers people of European background. I'll reserve my judgement. I'm not keen about the Latin men's approach to women. The men here seem more aggressive than the Mexicans (who are more used to Americans).

The "Bosque Rodrigues Alves" is described, in "Suggestions for Tourists in Belém", as "A bit of Amazonian jungle, some birds, and a small orchid garden." It is just that. One pays a small admission fee, but it seems quite natural inside, not too slicked up, and does contain a real jungle of native trees and animals. Paths have been cleared, however; and in the middle are playgrounds, ping-pong tables, picnic tables, refreshment booths, and ornamental walks over artificial lakes, all quite empty and unused. I suppose people come here on Sundays, and holidays.

Multicoloured macaws sit on perches in the open near the entrance gate. The first thing we noticed were several enclosures with a species of wild rodent (the world's largest), the "Cabybara", about the size of a boar. These are a main source of meat for native hunters. Then, suddenly a huge grey form walks down our path. A Tapir! Quite loose, unafraid, and friendly. We penetrate further into the woody area, and discover an abandoned sugar mill. it has a tall brick tower completely covered by orchids (not in bloom at this season), and is surrounded by fantastic ferns. The tower has a date, 1903, but it looks much older. I suppose "jungle rot" has set in! Inside, one can look up to the sky from many holes in the ceiling, through which one sees more orchids hanging. A fire is smouldering in one corner. For what purpose?

Outside, on the path, we see our first "Leaf-Cutting Ant", carrying a huge section of leaf, quite a few times larger than himself. The ant is quite small. Jerzy picks up a large leaf chewed by the ant; it is perforated evenly over its entire surface, with small, perfectly round holes, as though a paper cutter had punched them out. "Pacas", rodents the size of hares, are scurrying through the underbrush. They have small ears, long legs, short fur (brown, tinged with red, especially in the rear), and look more like ground squirrels or prairie dogs than rats. There are also agoutis, another form of rodent, rather resembling a guinea pig.

We discover an English-speaking couple, probably Canadians, peering into the leaves on the ground. They say they saw a snake! We look up a tall tree and see a very small monkey with a skinny tail climbing to the top. The climax of our prowl in the garden is a huge bird, standing on a little island surrounded by water. He is the size of a Marabou stork, white, with very long black spindly legs, and has a long fat neck, black, edged with rose; his ferociously sharp beak is several feet long.

George starts to take movies of him, and a guard comes up and irritates the bird with a stick to make him fight. First, he puffs his neck up to larger than normal size, puts his beak up in the air, and makes a sound like two pieces of hard wood being struck together (like Maracas). Then he grabs the stick, and wrestles with the guard, then flaps enormous wings energetically. The guard motions us back. I guess the bird is quite dangerous. We have never seen a bird like this before.

Leaving the "Bosque", we go to Hotel Vanja for a drink. This is the taxi driver's suggestion. It is a new, modern building in the suburbs. We have the bar to ourselves. It is decorated with unusual plywood, light yellow, with dark irregular streaks. This must be a local wood. The floor is a dark red hardwood, something different from home.

George asked for a drink, "Muy forte Brazilianas!" He got a "Creoula" daquiri. It tasted something like Tequila to me, but George thought it was better quality. "Creoula" is made from sugar cane.

A tall young man kept going in and out of the bar, gulping down strong drinks. He looked like an alcoholic. George asked who he was, and the bartender said he was the Air Force Squadron Leader. Too bad for the Air Force! If their leader sets this example, no wonder they can't hit the targets.

Back to the main street, and the "Acapulco" for lunch. It is very hard to find a restaurant in Belém. There don't seem to be any. The bartender had told us there weren't any first class restaurants. This one was open to the street, crowded with people (men, there were only one or two women). It was dirty, but atmospheric, something like a lower middle class restaurant in Greece. The food was very good, and they served good inexpensive Brazilian wine.

An old woman (whom George thought was Hindu, and I first thought was a Brazilian Indian) asked me with sign language whether we came from Argentina? She had gold earrings, her hair hung down her back, and she wore a voluminous skirt to her ankles. I decided that she must be a gipsy.

Three young men at the next table ogled Eva all through lunch. Eva kept saying: "Come on! Lets get out of here!"

George says it is a compliment for a woman if men give her appraising looks. However, we do not like it! If I have come here to learn something, to study the place and absorb its atmosphere, I don't want people making me think about myself all the time by staring, mumbling personal remarks, etc., as this takes away the pleasure of the surroundings. I'm not here to sell myself! George says: "Phooey! What woman seriously wants to study a place? She must take her place as a decoration for a man."

Eva says: "I'm tired of being with you guys! We don't see anything. I'd have much more fun by myself, or with a friend. You don't do anything."

George replies: "I'd like to see you walk down that street alone. You wouldn't get more than one block without being surrounded by men!"

Eva is a beautiful looking girl, with regular features and long brown hair, but disguises her assets by going around in sloppy clothes, and using no make-up.

5 PM   Back on board. We are pulling out to anchor in the bay at the same place we were before. A German ship needs our space to load. We have to wait for the *Bernard* (Ogonowski's old ship which we saw in Trinidad), in order to take some cargo from her for Iquitos. She is too big to go so far upriver. Rumours fly around that we may be here until Sunday. No one knows when the *Bernard* is coming in. So much the better for us, as it will be a good chance to get to know the town. We had planned to go ashore tonight to some local bars (just George and myself), but decide against it. There is a boat to shore, but no one knows if we could get back at around 1 AM. "I'd like to see you down at the dock then, all tired out, and having to pay £5.00 for some little rowboat that would take two hours to get out here," warns Ogonowski.

Instead, we sit on the deck, where its pleasant and cool, with the three officers, and the men bring out bottles of Scotch. The Captain becomes nostalgic, and spins tall tales about his years sailing through the Greek islands. He was carrying a cargo of wine- and drank wine with Ataturk! He even carried pilgrims from India to Mecca. He has had 40 years at sea, but is only 57! Of course, all the men ended up discussing their war experiences.

Ogonowski quite happily opened up a bottle his wife had given him for his birthday. Then he told about an old Welsh sea captain, who used to sail on clipper ships. His love and knowledge of the sea reminds Ogonowski of Conrad. He became a Captain in the Brazilian Navy. He is retired now, and lives in Belém, with his Brazilian wife, the daughter of an ambassador to Paris. Captain Humphreys knows the family very well, and always goes to see them when the ship is in Belém. "Its like home away from home," he explains.

We sit there until midnight, in the soft tropical air. Its better than a nightclub, everyone agrees. Suddenly, a huge sail, dark blue, silently swishes past, towering above our boat deck, almost touching the railing. A fishing boat, with a tiny dim light. I've now decided they look like gondolas, except for the sails. "What a beauty!" George exclaims. I almost cry thinking back the next day about the evening – the conversation, the entourage, but above all, the stimulating company of these adventurous seafarers.

George throws an empty bottle overboard, and it crashes against the rail. We have drunk enough! And all go to bed.

Thursday, August 11

In Brazil, we are told, the bus and taxi drivers never stay around if they have an accident and happen to hit someone. They jump out of the car, and run for the nearest bushes as fast as they can, leaving all responsibility behind. If they can hide for 48 hours without being found by the police, they may return and won't be prosecuted, even if they killed someone!

We stay anchored in the harbour all day. We decided not to go ashore, although several small boats are taking various crew members back and forth. We drank too much last night. George has a stomach ache. Ditto Eva, although she did not drink! Maybe its something we ate ashore. We're all tired, from so many new impressions, all except Jerzy, who is raring to go! I write cards, and rest. Eva does a lot of drawing.

Rick brings a letter for us from Hebe, which proves that the Brazilian mails do function sometimes, in spite of the many rumours we have heard to the contrary.

Rich tells Eva that he is leaving the ship, and going home to England, as he has a stomach ulcer. This is dreadful for such a young man. He had already had one before, and must be very unhealthy.

Rumours fly all day about when we'll dock. First, we hear that we're going to dock at 5, then at 8, etc. Then, we're spending the night again at anchor. Then, half an hour later, no, we're not! We see the *Bernard* , which came in during the night, through binoculars, docked where we were yesterday. Next to her, a small German ship. We have to wait for the German ship to leave before there will be room for us at the dock.

The kitten ("Ginger") is 10 weeks old, and very lively. She sneaks into the kids' cabin. Jerzy has to entice her out with a string. When she pounces on it, George grabs her. Last night, she sneaked into a cupboard when the Captain and the "Chief" were having two extra gins (nightcaps after the rest of us had gone to bed). Then the Captain couldn't find her, although he kept hearing a distant mewing. This morning, the steward even came into our room and looked under the sofa for her. Then, when he went to the cupboard in the Captain's sitting room to put away some clean glasses, out she popped! She's all over the place, and sneaks into my bunk at night and creeps under the covers. She bites, but it doesn't hurt very much. She's good fun.

Tonight there is a spectacular sunset, with the queer rayed affect of light (pictured in the Captain's book of photos of the Amazon), which must be peculiar to the region. Over the water, is a huge mushroom-shaped cloud, with dark rain falling down straight underneath, like a thick stem. Dark grey colour, graded to crisp white, with another cloud on top, of bright orange.

Slowly, the whole formation gets rosy, with golden rays streaming out on the sky as though painted on canvas. When the colour dies, it suddenly turns black and sinister, with heavy rain falling underneath, hitting the water like a veil. On another part of the horizon, heat lightning is playing. But the sky immediately overhead remains clear blue. Jerzy launches into a scientific discussion on how the different kinds of lightning are formed.

Ogonowski comes on deck, and gives us some Brazil nuts someone gave him, "But we carry 6,000 tons of them every trip!" He suggests that George and I join him ashore tonight, as we'll dock at 8. Just at that moment, a little boat appears full of stevedores, and inside an open doorway by the pilot we see a man cooking in a tiny kitchen. The man looks very Mexican in colouring and tropical dress (most are stripped to the waist), but these men are gloomier looking than the Mexicans. Mexicans look gloomy, but when you speak to them they become cheerful. These people never smile.

We are all sitting in a row along the railing again, and the Captain is brought a note saying we don't move tonight after all. The stevedores will work here until 11 PM, unloading several barges. Already, the decks are overflowing with heavy machinery, and we seem to be listing to Port.

The Captain has a huge pitcher of fresh chilled coconut juice, and invites us and Mr. Resson to join him in a drink of this mixed, with rum. The coconut juice is palling, if you're not very thirsty, due to its flat, though somewhat salty, taste. A little lemon might help. Maybe I was too timid, and did not add enough rum to mine.

We watch an old DC-3 circle the airport, and then return close to our ship. It goes through this manoeuvre for about an hour. It is very slow and heavy, and looks as though it will run into our ship each time it comes around. Some student pilots practising, we guess. It never seems to land.

"A plane crashed just over there in the jungle a little while ago," Mr. Resson points across the harbour. "It took 4 days to find them, the jungle is so thick."

We see the lights and the mysterious shape of the German ship, passing us on her way out to sea.

"Just ten years old, and I went through her on her maiden voyage here," comments the Captain.

Now will they bring another letter with orders to dock? The little boat is spotted again, with its green and red navigation lights, and a white light on the mast. It comes alongside, but the orders have not been changed.

Friday, August 12

At 9 am we go ashore in the tender. Its a 15 minute ride to the dock. There's no room here to come alongside, and we scramble onto an old river boat, which is tied up, the *Rio Amazonas*, and walk over her to the pier. She's a small craft, low in the water, and open at the sides, her deck full of perspiring half naked men unloading rubber. Some have towels wrapped around their heads like turbans. Somehow, the scene looks oriental. The big, black balls of rubber are piled in the warehouse. Their surface is rough and dirty, like elephant hide. George thinks it looks repulsive. To me, its just jungly looking.

We walk along the waterfront towards the market. A square with flowering trees runs parallel to the street, behind it a row of 3 or 4-story buildings, covered with gay tiles, with big windows and balconies, reminding me of Vera Cruz. Near the market is an ancient Spanish church, its stones grey and time-worn in comparison to the big double-towered white church which looms above the fishing harbour. The market, held in and around a bright blue ornamental market building, is teeming with life. Rows and rows of stalls, with crowded narrow aisles between them, stretch to the water's edge. It is similar in purpose to Mexican, or even, European markets. Some stalls sell cheap clothing, some hardware, but the more interesting sections sell fruit and vegetables. One entire aisle has onions, hanging in heavy bunches from the stalls. There is a large variety of vegetables and fruit: tomatoes, different kinds of lettuce, root vegetables, small cactus fruits, lots of papayas, limes, avocados, mounds of oranges with greenish skin (undyed!), watermelon. We had some of this for breakfast, and it wasn't very good. The meat is pale, not dark red as we are used to, and it doesn't taste very sweet. On a hot morning, it is still refreshing, however.

The most pictorial section was of bananas. Piles of green ones are stacked, as tall as a man, at the edge of the water, where they have been delivered by boat. My mouth waters for a small, ripe banana. A boy selling them picks out a perfect one for me, so sweet you wouldn't dream of putting sugar on it. George goes to pay him, but he won't accept any money. This was his way of welcoming strangers! In Mexico, such a boy would have grabbed the money.

At the end of the bananas is an open space with pottery, big orange-coloured bowls for baking, mostly. Not as refined as the Mexican. A stand of calabash (used as soup bowls, I later saw) tempts me, but George hustles me away, saying that they're not interesting. He doesn't want me to have too much to pack at the end of the trip. They are brown, with a wide black stripe, and glazed. I regret I did not get some. Near these, are mats of all sizes made of woven palm fibres, and big bamboo screens (probably very cheap). Some stalls in this section display medicinal herbs, snake-skins, turtle shells full of powder, and small boxes of incense. Little vials hanging on strings contain perfumes from rose and sandalwood oils. Some contain oil from the fresh-water porpoises and dolphins. This is considered to be a powerful aphrodisiac.

We came to the end of the stalls, and there was the harbour for fishing boats, the most fascinating part of all the market. Boats were jammed side by side by the dozens, full of brown or black men, again stripped to the waist, loading or unloading. Most were unloading fish, which was then sold on the spot. Some were cleaning their boats. These were the gondola-like boats with beautiful sails, but the sails were now furled. Several men were loading big blocks of ice into them.

The crowd was so thick that no one paid any attention to us, and I even took photographs without anyone turning to look at me – very unusual! I got a close-up of a woman wrapping up her newly purchased fish, and she didn't stop wrapping it or look up as I clicked the picture. Some of the fishermen had finished work and were lying down or sitting in their boats, resting. Around the boats, wading in the shallow garbage-strewn water, were flocks of the variety of buzzard we call "our friends" (as we got very fond of them in Mexico). In Mexico, they are called "Zopilote". They are large, black, turkey-like in shape. This Belém species is smaller and thinner than the Mexican. Actually, they are all varieties of Condors. Here they are called "Urubu". People welcome them, as they keep the streets clean.

At the far end of the pier, in an open space, they were selling large black crabs, wrapped in bundles of palm leaves. Some broke loose, and started to run around. A drunken, half-crazy woman sat on the edge of the pier, haranguing a sailor. She had frowzy, blondish hair, and had been pretty once. Now she was dressed in a dirty colourless dress, with a slip hanging below the hem. George said she looked like a down-and-out street walker. I suppose she was.

Unfortunately, there are a number of miserable beggars and disease-ridden cripples in Belém; blind men who shuffle into the cafés begging, and such like. One old woman, with her swollen leg wrapped in a filthy bandage, and dressed in rags, had a very distinguished regular-featured face, and neat grey hair in a bun. Dress her well, give her a chauffeur and a Cadillac, and she'd be a "grande dame" of the old school! We saw her first while eating lunch, and George gave her some money, against the judgement of the waiter, who was trying to shoo her out. Later in the afternoon, we passed her much farther down the street. Around 10 that night, we saw her stationed outside a movie, as the show was getting out. She probably had more energy than one would suspect- in fact, maybe nothing was wrong with her leg at all!

From the market, we took a taxi to the "Museum Goeldi", "A very interesting zoo and a museum with a good Indian collection", says the Guide. On the way, we passed more Spanish-style houses, and quiet, shady plazas.

Crowds of small children, all in uniform, thronged out of the museum as we were arriving, ushered by a pretty Latin- type girl, in a chic blue and white dress with a scarf of the same material tied to the back of her long hair. She would have been smart in Mexico City or even Paris. The only difference here is that the girls wear no eye make-up atall. Dresses are of simple cotton materials, gaily coloured. Shoes are still largely high-heeled pumps, of the same colour as the dress (a very Spanish style). Eva's and my flat leather sandals were looked at curiously. Even George noticed girls looking at our feet! Many girls wear big Spanish earrings. Dresses are tight-fitting, and form-revealing. The shift is not popular. Most women have good figures, and few are overweight.

The Museum is in a garden of the same variety as "El Bosque". The trees are marked by name here, but I prefer the wilder "Bosque". Huge brown and white eagles were the outstanding feature of this zoo, with shining fierce eyes; almost as large as Condors. It was feeding time, and the monkeys were shrieking with weird intonations. The macaws, of course, were especially splendid, and looked brighter and healthier than ones we see at home. Here we saw two "Hyacinth" macaws, blue with yellow underneath. This variety is becoming rare, and is the most prized. Jerzy looked in vain for the Anaconda, and the Sea-Cow ("Manatee") in the Aquarium. The Aquarium was shut to the public, for some inexplicable reason, and an old man shooed us away as we peeked in the door.

The Captain's favourites, the "Cats"– ranging from small wild cats up to the Jaguar – were enclosed in small cages, and looked angry and unhappy. He told us that the last time he was here, he put his hand inside the bars, and scratched one of these beasts on the head! He is not afraid of any kind of cat.

The Museum has a fine collection of photographs of wild tribes, along with head-dresses, bows and arrows, drums, etc., particularly from the Isle de Marajó, and the Xingu region, which is not far from here. We did not stay long, although there is also an interesting collection of stuffed snakes, birds and insects peculiar to the area. It was getting muggy, and Eva felt terribly tired. She is not a good sight-seer, and says she has never liked zoos, anyway. Before leaving, I enjoyed looking at the different varieties of rubber trees in the garden, and was straining my neck in search of monkeys. I was reluctant to leave.

We went to the Grande Hotel for a drink. I thought we owed it to them, as their little Tourist Guide is very good (it was given to me at the Booth Line office). But the hotel is shut up! It is the only representative-looking building in the way of a hotel, on the main square, opposite the Opera House (yes, they have an Opera!) We hear that the plumbing was old-fashioned, and that there wasn't any air-conditioning, and that's why they shut it down. George says that in a town like this there probably weren't enough tourists to support it- it takes up a whole block.

We go instead to the Excelsior bar. The Excelsior Hotel is a modern, apartment-house looking characterless place, reminding one of the "Jolly" chain hotels in Italy (always good for a hot bath, comfortable bed, and safe ice-water, but lacking style and local atmosphere). Two or three people are sitting in the 2nd floor lounge, where drinks are served. Not very lively! They refused to serve George "Creoula", and the waiter looked disgusted when George asked for "Muy forte Braziliana". He had to drink rum-and-coke and paid twice as much as at the Vanja.

We eat lunch at the Florida (pronounced Flo-ree-da) Bar and Restaurant, similar, and next door to the "Acapulco". Later, we learn that "Jake" owns this, too! After lunch, we wander through some side streets hunting for a bookstore where we can get a map of "Amazonas". We find many narrow streets with old buildings full of small, high-class shops (one very fine jewelry and silver store, for instance) that actually reminded us of Paris on the Left Bank. We decide that it is a beautiful city. George thinks much more cultured and in the old-world tradition than Mexico City. He keeps mentioning how dignified the businessmen look (must be the Portuguese touch). Actually, the people here are a mixture, and many have Irish and German blood. On the street, one sees labourers and road-workers of Negro and Indian descent, as well as the more dignified Portuguese and Spanish types. To see a half-naked Indian in a battered straw hat (looking slightly oriental) carrying a heavy burden, next to a soberly dressed businessman, gives the place dramatic contrast.

On our way back to the ship, we stopped at the Booth Line and found out that the *Veloz* is now tied up to Pier 10. While we were wandering around town, we found a café, not on the sidewalk, but with open doorways. It is very humid, and is sprinkling now and then, so we stop in for a beer. This is a bar, strictly speaking, not a café. It has little tables full of men – no women – and most are drinking beer from huge quart bottles, one per person! Or else, Pepsi-Cola. A coffee bar near the door serves demi-tasses of strong black, sweet coffee. This is crowded with men, who stand while they drink it. The Radio Engineer and another young officer from our ship appear, and join us. They say the ship is due to sail at midnight, but they hope she won't sail for a week, as they are enjoying this place so much! George teases them about what kind of adventures they can have here with girls, as the local girls evidently are just waiting to be picked up.

6 PM   Back on board. George is so tired at "Tea" that he almost goes to sleep at the table. He blames it on too many drinks, and goes to his bunk for a nap. Right then, our first real torrential cloudburst on the River occurs- without any warning, although there had been rising humidity all afternoon. The heavens open, and a sheet of rain descends. I rush to get George to see it, even if I have to wake him up. The sky and everything around it is enveloped by a thick grey cloud. It was black, like a thundercloud, two minutes before it broke. When it broke, it was like a grey fog. The rain is even stronger than in Acapulco. It's blowing in on the Port side, in the open doorway to the deck, and runs down the hall which crosses the ship. I can feel it when I stand in the doorway to the Starboard side. It's cool and refreshing, and we don't mind getting a little wet. Everything outside the ship is obliterated by water. One can only see the river for 2 or 3 feet.

"This is why I felt so tired!" mumbles George, and staggers back to his bunk. He always feels a pressure on his head when a storm is approaching. Several days later, he doesn't remember having seen the rain atall. He must have been mentally asleep when he came out to see it.

Sheet lightning flashes all around, but there are no loud claps of thunder. I'm usually afraid during terrific thunderstorms (such as we have in Philadelphia- or, Texas!) when the thunder cracks and stick lightning hits the ground all around. I used to actually feel the electric charges in the air! But this Amazonian storm doesn't alarm me atall. I actually enjoy it.

By 7.30 the storm is long past, and the last few drops of rain have fallen. By 8, George has come back to life, and we set out to mail some cards and to see the town at night. The ship isn't sailing now until 7 AM.

The dock and our decks swarm with stevedores, who will work all night, transferring the cargo from the *Bernard* to our holds and decks. Already one deck is so piled up that its hard walking around the crates. The workers appear unsmiling and hostile as we pass. In this world, passengers don't count, and get in the way.

We walk down the long dock, past the *Bernard* , which is tied next to us, a tall, rusty ship, with a black hull decorated with red stripes. She looks dirty, and more "cargo-ish" than we do, with our graceful line and fresh grey paint. She is unloading still. Farther down, the *Rio Amazonas* is leaving; next to her is a large Brazilian passenger ship from Rio, whose high windows on her promenade deck tower above us like a sky scraper. She is white, and is being scrubbed down. No sign of passengers. Potatoes are being brought over the side, and the bags are dropped too heavily. Some break all over the ground. Jeers are shouted from onlookers at the two unfortunate stevedores in charge. A rat runs along the wharf and disappears over the edge. We are glad to pass the gate, and get out onto the main street into the world of "civilians"

The streets have emptied. Only a few women are hurrying home, or getting on buses. Otherwise, there are mostly men, of a rougher variety. A few women stand in doorways, waiting for pick-ups. A pretty, smartly dressed, dark skinned girl waits by a lamp post.

"A professional!" says George.

"How do you know? I think she's too attractive. She's just waiting for a bus."

"Oh, there's something suspicious about her." We slosh along through puddles, looking for an interesting bar. There should be an open-air café on the plaza, but there isn't. We turn back, and investigate "Parao", a cellar-bar we were told about on the ship. Empty, and dull-looking inside. "Strangers In The Dark" is coming loudly from a record-player. "We'll come back later,"

George tells a pompous doorman.

The girl at the lamp post has not taken a bus. She is slinking down the street ahead of us, rolling her hips as she walks. I guess George was right. However, these girls have no customers, people are too poor. Two characters lurk under a building. I thought they were girls, but girls don't wear tight sailor pants here. They are young men of the "3rd Sex".

We decide to drink some coffee at "Acapulco" (where we had lunch the first day), which is brightly lit, and full. But only men! George walks ahead looking for a table. I'm about 10 or 12 feet behind. Suddenly I feel my arm grabbed, and I'm pulled down by a young man. I squeak in a startled tone, and pull back, like an old-fashioned lady who has seen a mouse. By then, he notices George. He lets me go, bringing his hands up in the air in an exaggerated fashion. The whole table shrieks with laughter. I rush after George, with offended dignity. He has not seen anything.

When the Captain hears about it the next day, he says I should have put one finger under my nose, parallel to the mouth, which is an insulting gesture, and everyone would have been put in their places. Ogonowski, on the other hand, says I should have been complimented that they wanted to attack me, as it is definitely complimentary to a woman when men act like this!

I did not take it this lightly. In the café, after it happened, I went off into a tirade to George about how women are treated here. There are absolutely no "decent" women out at night, even with men. Where do they go? The young ones can't agree to stay home the whole time, and never go to a café or restaurant. Actually, there seem to be no high class men around, either. We decided people must go to private clubs, as certainly there are signs of considerable wealth here, and I'm sure the wealthier ones must want to go out, sometimes, but there are no public places where one can enjoy oneself. Later, some of the young officers told us they went to a "family" nightclub far out of town, where whole families go, to eat and dance.

We leave the Acapulco, and walk back down the sinister street (so lively in the daytime), attracting the eye, I feel, of every passer-by. Through the gate, and back down the long dock, deserted now, except for a few sailors leaning against railings in dark corners. I've never wandered around docks at night before, and certainly never around South American ones.

"Docks are meant to be the most dangerous place you can walk at night!" George announces, cheerily.

I feel like a character from Conrad, or Jack London. How many people have wandered around strange docks at night?

Around our *Veloz*, there is still a lot of activity. Heavy boxes are swinging in the air over her side. Coils and coils of Trans-Atlantic cable in monstrous round crates taller than a man are lined up by the dozens.

"Surely we won't take all that. We'll sink!" George groans. But this load was not for us.

We slink along the gang-plank, and down onto the cargo deck. Dark faces and black suspicious eyes watch us unblinkingly from the shadows. My tentative "Good evening!" smile disappears before it forms. We quickly climb the ladder to our own quarters. Outside our cabin, loading, shouting, and bright lights never cease all night. Eva and Jerzy's voices are heard in the background. They seem to be wandering on deck, watching, until very late. The atmosphere is restless, charged with hidden drama.

Around 1 AM I hear Jerzy: "Eva, turn the light off. Turn the light off!" He must have gone to bed.

Saturday, August 13
7.30 AM. We leave Belém. The *Bernard* goes five minutes before us, heading for Macapá, a logging port on the main channel of the Amazon. We leave the harbour through a narrow subsidiary channel between two islands, and then turn left up the River Para.

Eva's friend Rick stands on the pier with a Company agent. He stays watching the ship until we are so far out that we can no longer see him. It is a gloomy departure. On Sunday he will fly back to New York, then to London to have another operation. Eva looks as though she has been crying. We

Typical bamboo house on stilts as seen near the "Narrows" from the *Veloz*

hardly see her all day. The Captain, when questioned by George, did not seem concerned. "Oh, he was just an apprentice, and he had had this trouble before."

George concludes the ship is run like the Army, without personal concern from the officers about their crew. There was, however, more to this story than met the eye. To keep a ship running, a lot of discipline is necessary. Captains may be caring, but they also have to be tough.

We spend the morning in a wide section of water which is like an enormous lake. The shore is merely a green line on the horizon. So many sailboats are out that it looks like a regatta. From the stern, the water again is pure gold, the bronze gold of paint in medieval paintings. It shimmers and sparkles, small choppy waves giving it the quality of very thickly applied pigment.

We must have quickly passed the mouth of the Tocantins, which comes in to our left, but with no land near, it is hard to tell where the two streams meet. Later, we go through another narrow passage, like a canal, where the banks are so close we can see every tree in the jungle. Here, the forest is as thick and as varied as in the "Bosque"; but the amazing thing is that its all wild, not cultivated, although it looks like a vast botanical garden. Little shacks are half-hidden along the banks, on stilts, made of bamboo, with palm-leaf roofs. Right before coming to this section, the Captain shows us places where 4 ships at various times were wrecked on sandbars. "There can be a sandbar in one place, and water 60 feet deep right next to it," he explains. "That is why we need two river pilots. Navigation is very tricky here, as the river conditions are always changing. Right now, the water is low."

"All this is tidal. The tides go 200 miles up the river, as far as Obidos."

I ask whether the tides make the river water brackish?

"Oh, no. The natives just scoop it up and drink it. It is pure fresh water. The sea only acts as a stopper, pushing the river water back upstream."

We come back to wider waters. This evening, we'll reach a long, narrow channel which takes 8-12 hours to navigate. This is known as the "Narrows", and is noted for its exotic beauty. There, we'll really be able to study the jungle close to.

We are sailing on the southern side of the Ilha de Marajó, the island in the Amazon Delta which is the size of Switzerland! And, like Switzerland, it has herds of cattle, the only place on the river where they do well. We'll head west from here through the Narrows to the main part of the Amazon. On my large map of the region, which I bought in Belém, and have pinned up on the wall, there is no channel marked here atall! Mr. Ogonowski shows us where it should be. All maps of Amazonas seem to be inaccurate.

As we watch the shore, it seems quite irregular, with many islands and tributaries branching off. There is no straight shoreline of the Ilha de Marajó.

It is easy to understand how one could lose one's way, and why the Conquistadores were afraid to penetrate far up the mouth of the river. It has been hinted by historians that King Solomon may have been more courageous, and that his famous wealth came in part from the Amazon, but that he wanted the source of it to remain a secret (as did the Spaniards and Jesuits when they started looting the Inca gold). The upper part of the River, across the Peruvian border, is called the "Rio Solimöes"- the Solomon River. This is the original Indian name. For what reason?

The Spaniards later renamed it the "Amazon", as they thought that a race of female warriors inhabited it, corresponding to the Amazons of pre-Christian history. Early records from the period of Spanish exploration describe this tribe in great detail, from eye-witness accounts. They go into detail about their courtship habits – how these women allowed men into their villages only for the purpose of giving them children; and how each woman had only one breast, having cut off the other, as a sign of fortitude. However, a recent book on the Amazon states definitely and flatly that the Spaniards mistook men warriors for women, as a certain tribe here wear head-dresses of fibres hanging down their backs, which give them the appearance of women. Each story is convincing. Which one is right?

When darkness descends, we anchor near a small lighthouse at the entrance to the Narrows. Clouds have come up, visibility is poor, rain is predicted, and there is no moon. Safer to stay here for the night, the officers say. The night breezes are fragrant and balmy. We sit on deck late, watching the constellations, which appear in different positions than at home. We see 3 or 4 shooting stars, and then a satellite. The steward reports having seen two more from the Bridge.

Sunday, August 14

George woke me early to see the sunrise. We had already started up again. I staggered on deck barefooted and bleary-eyed. The sky was getting light. On the Eastern horizon only a thin sickle moon and the "Morning Star" (probably Venus) were visible. The water was dark and still, like a polished mirror, reflecting every tree along the banks. A cool wind blew, and I shivered in my shortie shift. Flights of parrots flew across the sky, high above the treetops. Their shapes were heavy and stumpy, and they were so high that they looked black. They fly with characteristic short wing-beats, and always in twos or threes – a couple, or a couple and one child! Later, Jerzy saw one bird closer, flashing red, green and yellow in the sunlight. Then we saw macaws, in twos and fours, recognizable by their greater wing-span and long tails.

In the water appeared our first Manatee! A dark, hippo-like form barely sticking out of the water, heavy and cow-like. The Manatee thrives on water-hyacinths, and some of these creatures have been exported to the Florida

Left: Our ship enters the "Narrows"

Below: Dale pictured on the deck of the *Veloz* on the Amazon

Everglades to keep this growth under control. Later, we saw two more, and could make out their pinkish colour. There is also a rare pink dolphin on the Amazon, according to the marine biologists. (Here the bottled-nosed porpoise is called a"dolphin".)

Jerzy saw a moving shape under some bushes on a muddy bank. "An alligator!" he shouts, peering through the binoculars. It has gone before the rest of us see it.

By now, the sun is rosily up, and it is much warmer. We have entered the "Narrows" proper, and can see the trees and underbrush on each side distinctly. The "Jungle" is not, as some writers describe, "a solid wall of green". One can distinguish all different shades of green in the trees and bushes, and recognize their shapes. First, solid blocks of water-hyacinths and mangroves. Then, taller bushes, reeds and ferns of all descriptions; behind these, small trees with aerated roots, under which you peer to catch glimpses of muddy ground where alligators might lurk. Bananas, both cultivated and wild, plus innumerable varieties of palm grow near the water. The Captain says there are over 200 varieties of palm! Then come medium sized trees of every shape. Some, no doubt, are rubber. In the background loom the forest giants, with immensely tall column-like trunks, usually whitish in colour, topped by an umbrella-burst of foliage. Some of the tallest are nut-bearing. Vines in profusion twine around these (often causing their death), while rope-like lianas swing to the ground. These trees are laden with orchids, particularly near the tops. There must be millions of orchid plants, but not blooming at this season. I only see the Bromelias, with their red, sword-like flowers, in bloom, but Jerzy spots one white.

On a tall dead tree the Captain, who had come on deck with a cup of coffee, spies 4 shapes climbing up.

"Howler monkeys!" he exclaims.

By the time I found them through the binoculars they were just four dark forms sitting hunched at the top, like vultures.

"They climb up to get an hour's sun, one hour before sunrise, and one hour before sunset," he explains. That's the time to look for them."

A few minutes later, I see another equally large dark shape in a tree. "No," says the Captain, "that's a hornets' or bees' nest."

Vultures are also flying around. George and I spot a beautiful black and white one. It must be an eagle of the same variety that we saw in the zoo, from the shape of its head. Jerzy sees two small monkeys climbing trees. Of course, it is not so easy to see them. One has to wait patiently, all the time watching through the binoculars.

There are not many flowers. One vine has purple-ish blue flowers in small clusters. There are occasional trumpet-shaped large white or red flowers, on a tree that looks like an acacia. But all the time is wafted the marvellous perfume of the tropics, heavy on the morning breeze.

"The smell of rotting wood!" says the Chief Engineer, in a scoffing tone, as he comes on deck, eating an apple.

If its rotting wood, it must be sandalwood, rosewood, or camphor!

As the sun gets higher, the birds disappear into the dense foliage. When looking for birds, we notice many hanging nests of the brilliantly yellow Weaver Bird (who is similar to the Mexican Oriole).

The jungle here is not virgin forest. It is quite inhabited. Every few hundred yards are little shacks on stilts, very primitive, open to the elements, with very little inside except a few kitchen utensils and a hammock. Usually there are a few clothes drying on a line in front. The queer thing we observed is that many people have potted plants by their doors.

"The baby factories!" says the Captain. "Every house has about a dozen." Infant mortality here is about 50%.

"Why feel sorry for these people? They have free food; plenty of fish in the river; bananas, corn and manioc by their front door. No need for clothes! And no taxes or rent to pay."

I notice that the cultivated clearings around these houses are not our idea of "cultivation" atall. A clearing is made by burning off the size space desired, but leaving all the burnt tree stumps in the ground (these remain thick and close together). Seeds are then dropped in between. In a few weeks, jungle growth will have taken over again!

These people keep pigs (immune to snake-bite), and ducks and chickens. Also dogs, a protection against alligators. Only at one settlement during the day, a large centre with a sawmill, did we see cows. These were a cross between Zebu and Jersey. There were 3 or 4 such little centres, with a church and school (the children come in for miles by canoe). Here were a few heavier-built houses of painted boards. Lumber is a local industry, as we saw logs being towed in a long line on the river; several places had piles of neatly cut wood.

The people – particularly the children, and the younger boys and girls – are out on the river in their dugout canoes most of the day. These canoes, each made from a single log burnt out by fire, are of balsa, the lightest wood. They sit very low in the water, and are easy to upset. But even very small children take them out alone, paddling with curious round paddles dangerously close to our ship. They shout like little monkeys, and wave. But they do not want to be waved to in return. They want us to throw them empty beer or coca-cola cans! They use these to collect liquid rubber, or to make primitive oil lamps. Soon the crew's collection of used cans had been thrown on the waters, and quickly grabbed up. Someone threw some saltines wrapped in wax paper. These, also, were rescued.

The pure Indian children, with dark skins and black hair (usually cut short with bangs) are beautiful children. When little, the boys go naked, or almost so; the girls have colourless sleeveless shifts (colourless from too much washing in the muddy water). As the girls get to be teenagers, dresses are more colourful; some girls even wore modern head-bands. "A trading boat selling materials goes up and down the river," it was explained.

The children with mixed blood ("caboclos"), of which there are many here, are less attractive. They are overly serious, even gloomy. But I would not agree with the writer (for "Paris Match") who called them "the most miserable people in the world". George says he has seen equal poverty in Poland and Russia, and certainly we have in Mexico. And, what about India?

Near the settlement with the sawmill is the wreck of an old schooner, high on a sandbank, with trees now growing out of its bottom.

"Its been there for about 70 years," said the Captain. "They probably stripped it of machinery, and used this in the mill." Its a wonder no one tried to refloat it.

About 1 PM we slowed to let a huge Italian tanker pass: the *Oceanianica Elena*, from Genoa.

"Oh, for Italian pasta and wine!" sighs George, as she steams by, handsome Italians leaning over the rail looking at us curiously. "If they would only invite us for lunch!"

"Near where this ship passed us, are some very wild Indians," the Captain later says. "I was walking in that region once and met two braves on the warpath – they wore funny pointed caps made from palm leaves, which meant that they were warriors. Completely naked, except for G-strings, and carrying spears. Gosh, I was scared! Didn't want to show it, though. I traded a pack of cigarettes for their hats!"

"Just recently, a Belgian couple who were staying near the mouth of the Tocantins (which we passed yesterday) decided to go 20 miles up the river, just to see it. The woman got an arrow through her throat! Fortunately, it just went through the fleshy part and did not kill her. They got out of there mighty fast, though! And it was only 20 miles upriver."

"The Xingu!" the Captain continues, as we lean over the rail, chatting. "Forbidden territory still. Some of the most savage of all the tribes live there. If you ever go up the river and come across 3 crossed spears, this means stay out! They hate the white man, not only because the Spanish, Portuguese, Dutch, French and English grabbed their land and killed many of them, but because the missionaries put clothes on them, which made them get pneumonia and die. Any close contact with a white may give them a fatal (to them) disease, such as measles, or the common cold. Can you blame them for wanting to be left alone? They are happy by themselves in the jungle."

"Fawcett? Just a couple of years ago some bones were brought out of the jungle, which were meant to be his. Fakes, of course. And a shrunken head!

No one will ever know what happened to him. He thought he'd find a white-skinned, blue-eyed race of Indians out there, the descendants of refugees from Atlantis. I don't believe they exist! But he was convinced of it, and so lost his life."

At sunset, the river gets its famous "muddy" look. But as the clouds become flamingo pink, it, too, takes on a pinkish glow. Every kind of cloud appears at sunset. Under colourful fair-weather clouds are black, ominous thunder clouds, laced with sections of double rainbow. Overhead is bright blue sky. Off in the north are puffy, mashed potato clouds. The sun sinks behind a small dark cloud, immediately casting up huge, rosy rays, almost like the Aurora Borealis. I have watched this effect for three nights now, and marvel at it each time. The flame colour in the sky dims, then heat lightning flashes from all sides. Rain is seen down river, and a cool breeze stirs in our direction. But, it does not rain. The stars come out, with the Southern Cross higher up tonight, and the Milky Way glowing brightly. The same "Sputnik" we saw last night appears on its evening round. On the port side the lights of a town wink faintly in the distance.

"Gurupá," the Captain explains. The river is wider here, and lights are scarce and dim. The place has its own weak generator.

"That place may look small, but there's a lot of history behind it. There's an old fort to the left of the town, from the Spanish times. The English were occupying it about 200 years ago. They thought everything was peaceful, and they were all asleep one night. The Dutch took them by surprise, and massacred everyone. They're all buried there in the cemetery. After that, the Dutch held it for a long time. If you were here in the daytime, you'd notice a lot of Dutch influence in their houses. . . Yes, this river has seen a lot of dirty business and bloodshed."

We had noticed earlier a small graveyard, in the sawmill town, its simple white crosses nearly choked by jungle growth.

"Last year half of it slipped down the bank and into the river."

Going into the cabin to write, hundreds of grasshoppers are attracted by the light. They are very small, bright green, with dark wings. They go all over the cabin, into our bunks, onto our clothes, in our hair. Out on deck, hundreds of them sit on the white accommodation walls. How did they get here? We have left the Narrows, and are now in mid-stream of the main river, where it is very wide. These insects only seem to hop, not fly. The screens are still not on our portholes. The officers make fun of me, and say not to put the screens up, as I'm threatening to do. It will make the room too hot. There aren't many mosquitos on the river is their opinion!

In order to escape the grasshoppers, I move to the sofa, and spend the rest of the night there, where I am joined by "Ginger", who chases them, climbing clumsily up the back of the sofa, then dropping down on my head, all claws out! I put her under the sheet, where she curls up fuzzily next to my body, and goes to sleep. In the morning, the grasshoppers have disappeared from our room, but are still thick in the bathroom. I have to flush a bunch of them down the toilet, before I dare use it.

Monday, August 15

We woke up early, having gained an hour last night. I was especially wakeful on account of the grasshoppers. Who can sleep with 100 grasshoppers? The final straw last night came when a large moth got into my bunk (large to me, I suppose small or medium-sized to anyone else), and this is what really ejected me onto the sofa. It was extremely muggy all night. The cat, besides using me as a mountain on which to chase grasshoppers, now has a new habit, which is to bite, affectionately, but sharply! Even Ogonowski said his cabin was so close he couldn't sleep. And he always says he loves the heat. Anyway, it wouldn't be right not to be hot on the Amazon! Actually, its no worse than Philadelphia. From 3- 5 PM are the hottest hours. Evening and early morning are delightful.

Yesterday, we saw several large butterflies playing around the ship. Black with vivid green and white stripes. Later, I thought I saw another species, even bigger, with long points at the ends of its wings. I approached it enthusiastically, calling everyone to see it. It flapped away crazily towards a deck light that had been left on. A moth! I tell the "Chief" George's favourite story about me and the moths at "Villa Juarez". At the same time, I hear George telling the Captain the same story, in a highly exaggerated and derogatory way.

Once, when driving in Southern Mexico, we had arrived late at "Villa Juarez", a jungle hotel. It was already dark, and a strong light was burning over the door. George went in to get the key to our room, while the children helped me get the bags out of the car. As we walked up to the door, I noticed what looked like hundreds of moths flying around the light. They seemed huge, some the size of bats!

I could not bring myself to walk through them. They were flying so crazily, I felt sure some would land on my face, or in my hair, and no doubt be squashed to death there. Are they, to me, a symbol of death? I know it sounds stupid, but I am repulsed by them. I don't want one to touch me. Its some kind of phobia, which seems ridiculous to everyone else.

George got a blanket from the car, and put it over my head. Then I rushed safely through the door, and up some stairs to our room.

The room had a very high ceiling, Spanish style. The lighting was dim here, so we saw no moths. However, after I had gotten into bed, and looked up at the ceiling, there in a corner was a dark shape which I was sure was a large moth with folded wings. I pulled the sheet over my head, and slept with it like this all night, much to George's disgust.

In the reassuring light of morning, we saw the "moth" was still there. It had not moved. In reality, it was a bunch of feathers from a feather duster!

The river is extremely wide today. George estimates 6 or 7 miles, and each bank is quite far from us. However, we do go closer to one or the other occasionally. We have long since passed the mouth of the Xingu. At lunch time we passed a small town with a church, Prianha.

"All these little towns are exactly the same," explains Ogonowski. "Just a church, a school, and a few houses."

The colour of the water has become muddy brown. Every now and then one distinctly sees sandbars, noticeable by a streak of lighter colour, and by wavelets continuously breaking in the area. No parrots, monkeys, or seacows! The terrain has changed considerably, no longer thick jungle. It is flat, with semi-cultivated marshy fields. Only along the banks are tangled bushes, but these look more Californian than Equatorial. Numerous large white herons wade along the shore. Some better-tended farms, whose buildings have tiled roofs, are set back from the water. The most surprising feature of the landscape is a row of low mountains to the North. One table-mountain even has rugged orange-tinged cliffs. Far off on the foothills, one sees a wilderness of forest. These mountains are left over from a far distant geological period, before the Andes were formed, when high mountain ranges ran along the Atlantic side of South America. Then, the table-land tipped down towards the Pacific – the exact reverse of what it does today. We wonder why the vegetation here is poor, in comparison to yesterday? Maybe due to the vestiges of old mountains, the soil is rocky and lacking in proper nutrients.

Ogonowski remarks at lunch that the river is very "clean". We have noticed a few "floating islands" of growing grasses and tightly packed mud drifting downstream, and a few branches, but not as much debris as we had expected.

I sit in the cool breeze on the starboard side all afternoon, and read "The Jungle Search for Nature's Cures", or "Witch Doctor's Apprentice", by Nicole Maxwell, the woman the officers know in Iquitos. This book at least proves that one woman has been courageous as an explorer! However, as I get farther into the book, I decide that her explorations have been superficial, as well as the method by which she collected her specimens. If she had lived longer in the places to which she went, she might have greatly gained the confidence of the people she met, and not have been taken in, as she obviously was in many cases.

Mrs. Maxwell, the ex-wife of a U.S. Airforce man, is a U.S. citizen from San Francisco, who evidently has lived in Paris as well. She has lived in all sorts of adventurous places, such as Ecuador, Columbia, Peru, Gallapagos, Indonesia, China, the Philippines, and Hawaii. She makes one remark that I like and which I found refreshing, that "home is where I happen to be". Right now, however, she has just bought the biggest house in Iquitos, which somewhat neutralizes the impact of her statement.

After "Tea", the mosquitos come out on deck as though they mean business. Almost as bad as the New Jersey coast before they sprayed it with DDT. We are still passing close to a flat, marshy-looking region, now cut by canals which lead to a lake (of 100 sq. miles), invisible at night. Here President Vargas of Brazil raised rice, as an agricultural experiment. The area is now in disuse.

We rush in for the 6-12 Insect Repellant. Whoever said Amazon mosquitos just lap up repellant was right! I had put on my jeans, a long sleeved shirt, and sneakers. But they bite through the jeans! My jeans are of the light-weight stretch variety. These mosquitos would only be discouraged by the heavy-duty stiff kind of Levi. I start spraying repellant on my jeans. The Chief says he just puts "Fly and Mosquito Killer" (6% Strobane-DDT Thanite) right on his skin. On the bottle it says: "Prolonged use of this on the skin may cause toxemia." Soon, however, they don't bite so badly. George thinks the repellant is working after all, but I notice that we've left the proximity of the shore, and are now in the middle of the river, where the mosquitos don't bother to go.

The stars are putting on a show tonight, as it is a cloudless sky. We notice the Southern Cross has again climbed higher in the sky, but the right side of the "bowl" of the Big Dipper is lost below the horizon. Fireflies, brighter than in the U.S., fly around the ship and skim the water. We see lots of shooting stars. Pass the blinking airport light and the dim town lights of Santarém, one of the oldest settlements along the river. It looks like a small place at night, but Ogonowski says it is a big town for here. It has roads and cars! He emphasizes (being Catholic) that it is the seat of a Bishop. This is the largest Bishopric in the Catholic Church, as it includes all of Amazonas in the diocese. Right past the town, the Tapajos River joins the Amazon from the South.

"Too bad you couldn't see it by day," says Ogonowski. "The river water is clean and transparent, of a lovely blue, and you can see the difference where the two streams come together. We used to go up it a little way to get drinking water."

Tuesday, August 16

This morning we pass another small town, Juruti, which again reminds me of Mexican towns. Eva is reminded of Corfu, I don't know why! Perhaps because it has a new church with a clock tower and red tile roof. The churchyard is decorated with coloured decorations and lights for the 15th of August. The market building by the waterfront is also new, the Captain points out. Another large building still under construction will be a hospital, he thinks. The place is evidently thriving. A broad muddy track leads up the hill from the market. It is strange to see no cars, but there are no roads here. Communication is by radio-telephone. The river is truly the highway.

The wealth of the little centre comes from jute, grown on all the local farms. We are surprised how populated it is. The land is quite flat and open, with many prosperous looking farms lining the riverside. When I say prosperous, I mean by lower-middle class Mexican standards. The houses in this area are not like the palm-thatched huts of the Narrows. Those here have walls made of boards, and tile roofs. Some others nearby are very intricately and beautifully made from local grasses, with walls and overhanging eaves against the sun. A few farms even have fences. Some cows and a few horses are seen. Kapok is plentiful. The kapok trees are small, at present leafless, with oval red seed-pods. These contain the kapok, which looks like thistledown. We saw some blowing on the wind.

Many inlets and lagoons are passed, the abode of fish and alligators. More conspicuous are the huge white herons we noticed yesterday. One single tree must have had several dozen perched upon it. Cormorants fly in groups of 5 or 6. These are longer in body and more slender than the variety numerous on the California coast. I see the yellow and green flash of a parrot's wings – for the first time really distinguishing the colour. We notice plenty of the unique Amazonian seagulls (tern-like in form). There are always several of these swooping close to the stern. A grey dolphin jumps near to shore. Hundreds of butterflies fly around the ship, particularly across the cargo section forward. They are mostly white, yellow, and orange. The white and yellow resemble the ordinary European "Milkweed", the vivid orange is a little larger. One, especially lovely and unusual, is pale green with bright green stripes.

The whole scene has rather an African look, due to the open spaces now covered with blossoming trees. One tall tree is topped with thick fragrant blossoms, which are white when they come out, then turn yellow, and finally red. Thousands of birds add to the African look.

"Its one of the most magnificent mornings of my life!" exclaims George, who has been enthusiastically taking movies.

Before lunch, we start drinking rum-and-coke. It is muggy, clouds have appeared on the horizon, and this drink tastes heavy to me. I would have preferred a gin-and-tonic. However, George decides that we should empty the bottle, so we can clear off our table by throwing the empty bottle over the side. There wasn't much rum left in it anyway, so he decides, after that, to drink some Scotch. I start telling him a story (read in Maxwell's book) about a poor Indian up an uninhabited river, whom she met when she was on her travels collecting herbs. He had had several deaths in his family due to natural causes, but he thought a witch doctor had put a curse on him, and that a "Ghost Tiger" would kill him and his two children.

I wanted George's opinion about how you could help a man like this, without laughing at his beliefs, or by sending him to a missionary. Missionaries are the only people out in the jungle with supplies, teachers for the children, medical knowledge, etc.; but, if one doesn't believe in what the missionaries are teaching, should you send a man like this to them for help?

George suddenly said he really was not interested in such Indians. He said he had seen enough of the river already. It would not interest him to penetrate further into the jungle. What difference did it make if this man's children did die?

I replied that it did make a difference, because they were his children and he loved them; just as it would make a difference to us if Eva or Jerzy got sick and died.

George said it might make a difference to us, but who would care in the outside world? Maybe birth and death were of no importance. I replied that it shows a lack of feeling to make such a statement. If one does not feel sorrow when a child dies, any child, it is because one is callous. And how about Dr. Binder, who is trying to cure such diseases as T.B. in the jungle?

George answered that Dr. Binder's hospital has some value as it eases suffering. He said he did not like to see people in pain. But as for T.B., didn't Chopin die of it? And thousands of other people in Europe? And so what? What did it matter if they did die?

At this point, I said that I thought I would go out and sit on deck. I felt dreadfully depressed by the conversation. Insulted as a human being. I went out, and was explaining the discussion and my reaction to it to Eva and Jerzy – why not discuss it? – when George appeared, and said in a fury:

"I'll never forget what you just did, NEVER! I'll never forget that you left me sitting there ALONE!"

The lunch bell jangled. At lunch, George was talking in a loud, fuzzy voice, and spilt his beets all over the table-cloth. The officers knew he was drunk, from their shocked faces. They drink a lot, too, but the Britishers, with their "stiff upper lips", never show it, and even if they've had a few, always remains cheery. In this case, Ogonowski looked at George with consternation.

I have never seen George so obviously and pugnaciously drunk. He suddenly turned to me, and repeated loudly, so all could hear: "I'll never forget what you did, as long as I live!"

Dead silence at the table.

The kids and I, the Captain and the Chief, all go upstairs. Ogonowski and George remain at the table. Besides the emotional storm, a real storm is about to break. From the deck, we watch the rain approaching. The ship is heading into it. It's the same effect as in Belém, a thick woolly curtain of rain. One minute we're out of it, with a blue sky overhead; the next, the world is blotted out. The rain is preceded by cool, refreshing wind. Then the rain hits the brown water with an impact like hail, and each drop bounces on the opaque surface of the river.

A word about drinking. As this voyage progresses, it is sad that George is getting testier and testier. True, there are moments when he is thrilled by the environment, which in its exotic beauty exceeds even his expectations. However, heavy drinking during the heat of day, which he then has to sleep off, is no help to our morale, as a family.

Normally, George has looked down on people who drink too much, but on this vacation, he seems to think its OK for him. Its very hard on those who witness it.

It is a well-known fact that people need to drink more liquid in the tropics, as the body quickly casts it off – but the liquid doesn't have to be all alcoholic. If one overdoes the alcohol, this can be disastrous. The crew all like their drinks, and the Captain has to keep an eye on this. He himself enjoys social drinking, and as Captain of the ship he has to be a genial host, but only in off hours when everything on board is going smoothly.

I have to nurse one or two drinks along slowly, just to be sociable. If I drink more, it makes me sick.

George has appeared again three quarters of an hour later from the dining room, and goes directly to his bunk, where he sleeps until "Tea". At Tea he scarcely remembers that there was a storm, and also seems (fortunately?) to have forgotten his argument with me. Can it be the "Tropics" are getting us? That, as the weather gets muggier and muggier, and more electricity forms in the air, nerves get more and more tense, and therefore, more liquor is consumed? A la Conrad, or even, Graham Greene?

George was the one who was first fascinated by the thought of seeing the jungle. I was the one who would never have thought of coming here! Now everything is reversed. He doesn't seem to have an interest in getting any deeper knowledge of it, while this little taste has so appealed to my imagination that now I could even imagine myself visiting the wildest tribes without any fear!

All afternoon the sky has remained leaden, and the air cool. The river is dark, and full of eddies, and floating debris. The Chief laughs at me when I say that it looks "swollen". "That little bit of rain doesn't make any difference!"

As darkness falls, the low banks have their trees silhouetted against heat lightning. Gigantic patches of lightning illuminate grotesque cloud formations. It plays in all directions. The whole earth, sky, and water look like a scene from an artist's conception of the beginning of life on earth. One could easily expect to see a dinosaur's head emerging above the tree tops.

Some explorers of this region have even told of rumours about the existence of some form of dinosaur here even today. An American travel writer, Leonard Clark, (author of "The Rivers Ran East"), as recently as 1946 reported such a story, heard 2nd or 3rd hand. Unfortunately, such stories always originate with an Indian who said he saw a huge animal moving among the trees, but he was so frightened that he ran away, and could not really describe it. But these tales wet the appetite!

Wednesday, August 17

Two exciting things happened today. First, George saw people in a canoe, a man of about 28 or 30, with a boy (maybe his son) of 12 or 13, hunting for fish with bows and arrows. The bows were very large. The people were standing in the boat aiming the arrows, in case any fish appeared. As our ship passed by, George had the feeling that one of them might send an arrow through the air at him!

George rushed to get me. It was early, and I was still in bed. By the time I could get out on deck, the canoe had disappeared, and no more hunters of this variety showed up again.

Later, while still looking for hunters, we saw a large eagle, with black and white wings, holding a snake in his mouth, which he dropped as we went by. We thought he had dropped it because he was afraid. That was not the reason, we later learnt. He dropped it to kill it, and would then swoop down to eat it. (An eagle with a snake in his mouth is on the official Mexican flag, but we have never seen it before in real life.)

Many dolphins were putting on a show near shore. The Amazon fresh water dolphin, small, grey, with a whitish stomach, has a beak-like snout.

Right after breakfast, we passed a thriving commercial town, Icacoatiara, another big jute centre. The Captain says this industry (and crop growing) was started less than 10 years ago. Jute was not native to the region, but it did very well here. It looks like tall marsh grass. Next to the factory, the jute is hung on racks to dry, much like tobacco. It is used for making bags.

This town is so prosperous that a road, opened only a year ago, was constructed from it to Manaus, through the jungle. The Captain has driven on it, and says its a fine place to see snakes, "cats" (he means jaguars!), etc.

Not far from here, the Rio Madeira (described by Tomlinson in "The Sea and the Jungle") joins the Amazon, but we did not see the actual junction. There is a long island here which blocks the view. The whole length of the Amazon is such a maze of islands, auxiliary rivers, inlets and mudbars that to be a pilot on it must be very difficult. The Captain says he could pilot the ship alright as far up as Manaus, but he would not like to take her further up, where the water gets shallower, without a local pilot.

We went close to shore most of the day. It is extremely agricultural here, more so than yesterday. One farm is right next to another. Houses are bigger and more imposing, with many fences to keep in livestock. There are large banana plantations, as well as other fruit orchards with oranges (the green-skinned tropical variety), lemons, papayas, bread-fruit, and other fruits with which we are not familiar. Kapok trees, with their leafless branches, and hanging red seedpods, continue to line the riverbanks, and Kapok, of the consistency of milkweed down, continuously flies through the air. Life preservers are made from this.

George is disappointed that the area is so populated. It almost could be a farming region in the U.S. or Europe, except for the thick jungle always visible in the background. These farms do not penetrate far into the wilderness. The Captain says an area larger than Europe is waiting to be opened up. It could feed the world! But the Brazilians are too lazy. It's not only the heat, and the fact that their civilized centres are far to the South. It's the fact that they look down on this region as being wild, and still savage, so they don't want to bother with it. "Mañana!" they say.

"I'd like to see it in a hundred years," says the Captain, optimistically. (Author's note: Now it has been opened up in the wrong way, its natural resources cruelly exploited. Before his death, Richard was horrified by reports of the destruction of the environment, and said he would not like to go back to witness this.)

My Journal continues:

The river has been like polished glass all day. Grey clouds over the whole sky give it a dark, heavy appearance. It is unusually cool for this region, everyone comments, only 77 degrees. Tonight, we'll anchor off the oil refinery on the Rio Negro.

"I brought up all the material about 11 years ago myself to build that refinery," says Captain Humphreys. "The oil does not come from here. It comes from up or down river. No oil deposits worth working have been found anywhere near here, although prospectors have been all over."

"The *Veloz* was sunk right off the refinery on her maiden voyage," he continued. "It was also the Captain's first trip on her. No, it was not me! Was he embarrassed! He ran into a big barge, and got up on a sandbank."

The Captain continues, spinning tales of people finding huge nuggets of gold: "I knew a farmer myself near the northern channel in the mouth of the Amazon, who was working his field with a hand plough and oxen, and dug up 15 nuggets of pure gold. He went to Rio and lived like a millionaire for two years! Plenty of men are still looking for diamonds. You see them going up the river near Santarém, in long dugout canoes, pistols in their belts. If they find anything good, it's usually stolen from them! They try to smuggle the diamonds out through F.G. (French Guyana). They'd have to pay too much tax here. There used to be plenty of smuggling going on – coffee, cars! Yes, anything's possible on this river!"

17. JUNGLE FEVER

Thursday. August 18

"A stinking, disintegrating cadaver!" is George's opinion of Manaus.

"Once fabulous capital of the Rubber Boom, the jungle is now reclaiming its own." "Forgotten jungle city." "Dazed thousands, with a lost past and no future, rot on the side of the river." "Why does anyone stay?" "A town living in a dream of a once-glorious past."

These phrases, remembered snatches from innumerable sensational magazine articles come to mind. Then again, Simone de Beauvoir, who considered it an equivalent of "The Black Hole of Calcutta": "A steaming, hot blanket descended on me. We could not breathe. The hotel air-conditioning was off. We lay suffering in our beds in pools of perspiration. The jungle reared up, a solid green wall on all sides. No plane out for 3 days! No phone or cable communications with the outside world! We walked hopelessly up and down the little plaza. No escape!" (Re-written from memory from one of her journals.)

Is all this true? It depends on your mood, your health, the weather, and your natural point of view. I love small, sleepy, forgotten towns. The smaller, the more relaxed, the better. But can anyone imagine Simone and Sartre anywhere but Paris?

Here is how Manaus appears to me:

Waking up before sunrise, on a cool, almost cold, cloudy morning, mist, like the San Francisco fog, is rolling over low hills. We are pulling up anchor, and are going upriver about 10 miles from the oil refinery. The refinery, on an elevation near the mouth of the Rio Negro, is very small and non-polluting in comparison, for instance, with the huge refinery in Ventura, California. Only a small, slender stream of smoke, accompanied by a slight smell of burning, pollutes the atmosphere.

Around a curve in the river, we see the houses of Manaus, along the waterfront, and on low hills. We have been discussing and examining the water of the Rio Negro. The surface does look black, but one must remember it is reflecting a grey sky. Later, when the sky partially clears, it appears blue-black. The water is supposed to be clear, not muddy like the Amazon. In the wake of the ship it is dark amber. This is caused by some chemical reaction of the earth it has flowed over. The officers say it is very good drinking water. The Booth ships always refill up above the town. They tell us that up to 3 months ago when the last "Revolution" took place, a "floating city" existed in the harbour of Manaus; a city of houseboats and huts on rafts, much as in Hong Kong. People washed in the river, used it as a toilet, and as their source of drinking water. Also, their garbage disposal! Little children were tethered on long ropes, and when they fell in, they were just pulled out again. It was really picturesque. Much more interesting and characteristic than the modern town. Now, with a new energetic port authority, all these people were ordered to leave. "Or else I'll burn them and sink them!" He added it was a danger to navigation. Where did these poor people go?

We passed several large white factories for processing jute. Tall, industrial smokestacks loomed in the distance. One turreted, heavy, 12-story building "used to be a brewery". A large wrought-iron ediface is the market, designed by the architect of the "Tour d'Eiffel".

From a distance, the Opera House, dominating the city, is a shock, a large, rectangular building, with a huge green tile cupola in the Italian style. The fact that it is covered with shining tile makes one think of a mosque. It looks pretty in the soft light, but is overly magnificent for the impoverished town.

As one sails into the harbour, the waterfront does look impoverished. Dozens of flimsy board houses run parallel to the water, on very high stilts. They are all painted in soft pastels, but mud and rain have made them streaked with dirt. They somehow remind me of Oriental scenes. Is it Java which has such houses, or Malaysia? Red tiled Spanish and Portuguese style houses pile behind them on higher levels. A few broad muddy streets run straight up, steeply. All kinds of small motor boats and canoes, used as local ferries, constantly move in the foreground, carrying produce or people. The whole place does look slightly dirty and in disarray, as though the humid atmosphere had seeped into the materials. It is a large, lively town, however, and not sleepy like Roseau, Dominica, or Kingstown, St. Vincent.

The Booth Line dock is a well-known feature of Manaus harbour. It is a floating pier, on huge metal barrels. Three ancient derricks stand on it, and all cargo is swung from them along metal wire some 500 yards to the shore. Heavy tractors swinging along this aerial railway on thin wires look very precarious! The derrick and warehouses are 80 years old, and are monuments in themselves. They have gone through the Rubber Boom, when the Booth Line had a monopoly on river traffic. It was meant to have been a Booth Line ship on which a British botanist smuggled rubber seeds to Malaysia, thereby ruining this industry on the Amazon. Actually, the Booth Line is 100 years old.

We take a rowboat, bobbing from side to side as we climb in, and go about 300 yards to the main pier, a long boardwalk on pontoons, which has a narrow section for pedestrians, the remainder containing a little cog railroad carrying freight.

"Imagine all this freight mixed up with pedestrians in the U.S.!" exclaims George. "The Stevedores' Union would have a fit."

We climb from the boat up 5 or 6 steps. This is where the anaconda carried off the man from our ship several years ago! Except, that it wasn't an officer, it was a stevedore, George says someone told him. This morning, with dozens of boats and lots of people coming and going, I don't think there's much danger. But maybe late at night! The shore is quite built up with warehouses, but, of course, an anaconda could lurk under the pilings of the pier, and then rise up to seize his prey.

The main street of Manaus nearby is crowded with vivacious South American types. Here, however, we notice very few pure-blooded Indians or Negroes. Spanish blood is obvious, particularly in some coquettish girls, standing in a laughing group at the end of the pier. And the distinguished older man (in the usual tropical wear of a shirt and tan pants) of whom we ask directions, seemed Portuguese. There are many of these courtly, old-world types (who could equally well be Polish) here, as in Belém. Many men, particularly a mixed bunch in large straw hats whom we noticed on the dock, who did not look quite right for stevedores, looked in our eyes like small-time crooks, the kind who make all kinds of underhand deals. As no wealth of any kind is apparent here, I don't believe there are any big-time crooks. In spite of wild talk of diamonds, gold and fabulous wealth in the jungle, this place hasn't seen any big money for years.

Speaking of crooks, we have the *Viajero*, practically our sister-ship, docked next to us. She is Booth Line, but registered in Panama, and has a West Indian crew. A year ago, there was a murder on board. When she arrived here, the cook killed another crew member. Well, he was sentenced to 18 months. But, as he also runs a small business in Manaus, and the jail is in Itacoatiara (over 200 kilometres away), they let him stay here and look after his business during the week, and just spend every Saturday night in jail!

This town has life on the streets, but is better mannered than Belém. We only got a few stares at our feet, and very few stopped dead in their tracks to look at us. There are lots of shops, for a small town, although they sell extremely cheap quality merchandise. But the side streets and plazas all have charming artistic details. Most houses are covered with the patina of time. Their proportions are graceful, with tall French windows and balconies. Rococo details catch the eye, such as sculptured pineapples or mermaids on roofs, balustrades carved with baskets of fruit and fanciful coats of arms. The main square has a green fountain, with many tiers of golden cherubs. No water flows in it, alas. I think Baroque would be a good term for the town. Its extravagance suits the lavishness and warmth of the surrounding jungle. The fact that houses are falling down, that they're half empty, with broken windows, or that new apartments are started and never finished does not bother me. One notices the same in Mexico. George says Mexico is dirtier. I'm not so sure.

The Opera House, "Teatro Amazonas", built in 1896 (and its heyday over by the 1920's, I would say), is also Jungle-Baroque. Severe and stiff from the outside, as first viewed from an empty plaza over whose curly black and white mosaic pavement (à la Rio) two nuns in floating white garments hastened, inside both the architecture and its decoration struck me as happily imaginative. It may have been started as a copy of La Scala, but it turned out to be something quite different. A reporter [1] has listed an international medley of fabulous decorations: curtains from Damascus, ironwork from Glasgow, marble from Carrara, tiles from Alsace, and a proscenium curtain "painted a century before by the Comedie Françaises's designer, Crispim de Amaral".

The stage, trod only in fantasy by Caruso, Jenny Lind and Sarah Bernhardt, is small and intimate. Sadly, no artist of world renown ever appeared there. By 1909, no more operas were performed at the Teatro, and it would soon become "a sporadic venue for operetta, circus and cinema."[2] Standing on this stage looking into the hall, one has the impression, due to its rosy pink walls and boxes, and pink and blue murals (painted by a French artist), of real warmth of spirit. Instead of conventional wine-coloured plush seats, or heavily gilded balustrades, we note light elegant cane chairs of a lacy pattern, harmonising with wrought-iron balconies, these painted a golden shade of yellow. Over the boxes, one glimpses big windows, which bring in the soft tropical air.

The main stairway to the Foyer also has handsome wrought-iron balustrades, fashioned in a French style reminding me of New Orleans. The Foyer combines a native wood parquet, columns with marble pedestals, painted tapestries of Amazonian subjects (one panel depicts a scene from a Brazilian opera), Venetian rainbow glass chandeliers, and an Italian mural overhead, which has some trick perspective (highly admired and its worth exaggerated by our guide).

"What a nonsense!" What a nonsense!" George keeps muttering.

Of course, with tens of thousands of Indians dying as slaves to the rubber barons, it was worse than a nonsense. (These Indians were ruthlessly shot if they could not carry their quota of 50 kilos a day, while their exploiters were enjoying the opera.)

On the other hand, as mansions in Natchez revive pictures of the old South of pre-Civil War days, so this building is filled with the ghosts of rubber barons and their ladies, dressed in French imports and longing for the culture of a Europe which scarcely recognized their existence.

Perhaps these ghosts have not completely gone. Some older men who remember the period are said to still haunt the bar of Hotel Amazonas. But they are now engaged in such activities as coordinating entomologists' research of strange insect life in the jungle. We went to this bar, but only met two young officers from our ship, who were also there looking for local characters!

Now the opera has fallen on bad times. "The next performancee here will be a Military Policemen's benefit," said our guide, the Custodian.[3]

A taxi ride on the road to the "Japanese Settlement" was not as interesting as we had expected, and the driver (no meters here), overcharged. The road was a commercial thoroughfare. Although we went 10 kms. out of town, we did not find the "Virgin Jungle", as we had been led to expect. Little "Sports Clubs", football fields, etc., lined the way.

Lunch, in a tiny restaurant on the main street, was nervous, as George did not have enough Cruceiros. They refused to change U.S. dollars at the restaurant, and all banks and shops were closed, at 11.30, for "La Siesta". The banks, we soon discovered, take a long siesta. "They do not re-open until Mañana, Señor."

A speculator, sitting at the next table, offered to make change, for 200 cruceiros per dollar, less than the bank had given us. We decided just to eat less, and carefully add up to see if we could pay the bill. We ordered "Milanese", which turned out to be fried pork, mostly gristle, and not salted properly. With this, came some rice. When one added salt and hot piquant sauce, it was quite edible. The French bread is good here, also the little cups of strong coffee. A radio blared, playing scratchy records. George said he couldn't stand the noise.

"Hurry up! he said, "I want to leave. This place doesn't have any atmosphere, and I don't like being cheated by crooks."

However, I'll remember this restaurant for a large brown butterfly that flew around, and, when they tried to catch it, landed on the back of the waitress's skirt. She didn't know it was there until we told her. Then she took it quite gently by the wings to show us. When she put it in George's hand, it flew happily away.

The drinking water, in carafes on the tables here, comes from the Rio Negro, and looks brownish grey. We drank beer!

Walking back to the ship, the sun came out. Then you really feel the weight of the equatorial sun. Most men wear big straw hats, women don't. Walking down the ramp (past the marking on the high retaining wall which shows where the river rose 31 feet in 1953), Eva says she's had a slight headache, or a kind of pressure on her head, ever since coming on the river, even indoors, if she gets up or moves too suddenly. Eva has never especially liked heat.

We have to be back on board ship by 3, the Captain had said, as he planned to sail at 4. "If you're not back, we'll go without you," he threatened, and I believe he would! Passengers are unimportant on freighters.

"I want to get started up river as soon as possible," he had continued. "A ship has just gone aground (a Booth Line ship) about 200 miles down from Iquitos. The river is getting very low. I draw 15 feet, and I don't want to take any chances. I have the record so far. I haven't gone aground yet, in 14 years on the river."

Two new pilots have come on board, Peruvians from the Peruvian Navy. One can equal Richard's record of 14 years experience up and down the river.

"They're Syndicate pilots," someone says, "and don't take the same chances as the Company pilots. These are the best there are! But the Company pilots used to take the ship so near to shore that you could almost touch the trees, and this was more interesting."

George, who has been talking to the Captain, comes up with another version of the anaconda story.

"The Captain says that it didn't happen at the stairs we used at all, but at those stairs over there." He points to a steep flight of about two dozen steps leading up from the river to the warehouses across the water, at the terminal of the aerial lift. The warehouses are built high, at least 50 feet over the water, on a double layer of wooden pilings. Cavernous empty spaces yawn underneath, a perfect hiding place for snakes.

"And it wasn't even a member of our crew, who was eaten, much less an officer! It was just some workman who went down there to wash his hands."

This is the way stories go on the Amazon. Everyone has a different version. Now we wonder whether anyone was really eaten at all?

To the right of the warehouses, over near the long walk with the cog railway, big trucks are unloading something which I thought was brown gravel. Men shovel it over the side into barges.

"Those are Brazil nuts!" exclaims the Captain.

The Second Officer, just before we sail, has a whole stack of packages wrapped in green paper delivered by the little rowboat.

"My stores!" he says, "about 6 pounds worth. Just in the nick of time."

He is feeling pretty good on Pisco, and confides in me how to make a little money really easily. "First, buy about 5,000 cigarettes. Then, when we get to Peru, I'll sell them for you for twice as much. Then, go and buy a gold ring. They have very good heavy gold, and it isn't expensive. Buy one with a ruby or diamond. When you get back to New York, sell it there for twice as much!"

"Not a bad idea!" I laugh.

A beautiful rain cloud, grey, mushroom-shaped, lined with gold, hangs upriver. As we've now seen several times before, a curtain of rain falls below it, like the stem of a mushroom.

"When you see a rain cloud 30 miles away on the Amazon, anchor immediately!" exclaims the 2nd Officer.

Instead, we turn around and steam downriver. The frightening cloud dissolves. Blue sky enfolds us. The river is navy blue, but when one looks directly at it, it appears inky black – the "Rio Negro".

"But pure water!" comes a voice. Next time, when this "pure" water, grey

A mushroom-shaped rain cloud threatens the *Veloz*

in the carafe, and tasting a little different, appears, I will drink it.

The bell rings for Tea, but we stay on deck with the Captain to see the junction of the Rio Negro and the Amazon.

"You can have Tea any old time, but when would you see a sight like this?" he asks, going on to explain that there really is a distinct line between the two waters. One can tell which river is low by the position of the line. While we're waiting, a superb "Swallow Tailed" butterfly swoops by, black and green.

"I've collected over 300 of the Amazon butterflies alone, not including moths," says Captain Humphreys. "Got them for the children when they were little. And beetles, too. The collection is now in my uncle's school. I knew a man up here who had grown up on the Amazon. He lived in Manaus. A German butterfly collector. Very famous."

"Farbre?"

"No, Farbre was French, wasn't he? Can't remember his name. Used to come on board all the time. Gave me one of the rarest butterflies of the jungle. Black, its wings lined with blue. Beautiful! I still have it at home."

"One of the transparent blue kind was flying around the deck today when I was taking my nap," laments George.

"Did you see the funny cricket-like creature that was on deck, which had a soft, feathery head?" asks Jerzy. "Its meant to walk, hop, fly, swim, burrow- and, it chews material!"

We have come to the meeting place of the waters. From a distance, we have been approaching a dark line (like the wake of a motor boat) stretching across the whole river. The water on the other side of it looks higher up (an optical illusion.) Closer to, we see the water on the far side is lighter in colour; for that reason, it looks unnatural, like a plastic sheet. When we come up to the line, straight with a few scarf-like streamers, the black water we have been sailing on suddenly ends! The sun has come out low on the horizon (it is 5.45 PM), as though to light the water for our benefit. We say farewell to the black Rio Negro, and rejoin the golden brown muddy waters of our old friend, the Amazon, from here up called the Solimões. I had admired a dramatic photo of this junction, taken from the air (in the Captain's book); but one always suspects, in colour photography, that the colours may be exaggerated. In this case, they weren't. We saw it with our own eyes. We were looking at the meeting of the waters with such absorption that we forgot to take our own photographs!

After Tea, we take our evening positions on the deck chairs. A crimson, burning sunset tonight, with a new moon hanging right above on a luminous sky. The same rayed affect as always! Banana plantations and huts with little glowing lights beckon on either side. The stars complete a brilliant show, along with competing fireflies.

"Sparks", usually very silent, is in a jolly mood (after Pisco?) He has cornered Eva, and I hear his excited voice describing Vampire Bats, while his arms wave like phantom wings through the air.

An army of vicious mosquitos zoom down on us, and we hasten to our cabins, leaving the Captain and the Chief discussing the old movie stars and popular singers.

Friday, August 19

Last night I did not sleep very well, as we had received a letter in Manaus saying that an artesian well that we were having dug on property in Villanova, Pennsylvania, that I had inherited from my mother, had now been taken down to 305 feet. Even so, only a fair amount to water had been struck. 100 feet was the original estimate, at $1,800.

"Crooks!" shouted Eva and Jerzy. "Don't you think they chose this location on purpose to make you pay more?" (The children seem to have inherited their father's cynical attitude about business.)

Now all the worries about taking care of 4 properties came back, and guilt about the fact that I had sold an old trunk, found in an attic, full of my great-great-grandfather's letters, which dated from 1780, for $100. George had goaded me on, as this had seemed like a lot for "a bunch of old letters". I didn't want to read all those musty papers! I had shed such worries the moment we had gotten on the train to New York to take the *Veloz*. But now, in a nightmarish way, I imagined various "Historical Society" members crying:

"They might have been of tremendous interest to us!" These letters described a walking trip through Pennsylvania. Will they now end up being made into lampshades? I could sense my mother's horror, had she known!

Continuing the nightmare, different pieces of inherited furniture appear before my eyes, which might be fine to get rid of, but would break up the family tradition.

"It ties one down to have material possessions," said the great Indian teacher, Krishnamurti. How true!

But what to do with the property itself? Steinbeck has said: "A farm that is no longer self-supporting is poor business, and if it has to be boosted up by outside money is a rich man's folly and not in the dynamic American tradition." (Loosely paraphrased from "Travels With Charley".)

As the night wears on, I toss heavily in my stuffy upper bunk (which I would insist on having, even although George did want to take it). Its more comfortable for sitting up and reading than it is for sleeping. My head is bored through by a rock-like pillow.

Am I, myself, a failure? I recall stern voices of old teachers: "Make something of yourself! Make something of yourself!" Had I wanted to be a composer for the wrong reasons? Sad, chiding voices repeating in the night: "Women are discouraged too easily, that's why they don't get anywhere." "With all that talent and training, Lansdale, do you mean to just throw it away?" A real nightmare! All these voices and their exact inflections come back to me from years ago – but I cannot remember one note of a Chopin Nocturne I have played as a music student in recital.

Floating on the night waters, on the ship of my dreams, for whom should I "make something of myself"? And for what purpose? Rather to relax, to exist like a tropical flower, a thing of beauty in itself, through no effort of its own. Just to be liked (or disliked!) for oneself, for one's own perfume.

At 6 AM I am finally sleeping a heavy, exhausted sleep, when George wakens me to see the sun, blood-red, creeping over the horizon.

We seem to float all day in a globe of sky, trees and water. With eyes strained, I peer endlessly into the ripples and the foliage for any sign of wild-life, an occasional arch of grey dolphin's back, or the flash of a King-fisher's feathers. The King-fishers' nests are in holes bored in the muddy banks, now over 12 feet above the diminishing water-line.

Long sandbars reach tentacles out of the water. They are full of uprooted trees, long since dead, or mammoth pieces of mouth-watering driftwood, which would make great decorations, if one could only transport them home! Sometimes we go as near as 50 feet to shore. As the day progresses, it becomes extremely hot. Then the forest is very still. Later, no wildlife is visible as we have arrived at an area of many huts and clearings. The people who live here are probably hunters. The only beast that doesn't mind human company is the Amazon gull. Three or four follow the ship all day, and swoop around the stern in big circles, squawking, probably looking for castoffs from the galley. At close range they are bigger than I thought, with handsome wings, heavy black markings on white. Their beaks are particularly long and fierce for their size, parrot-like yellow and slightly hooked.

In the forest we see a tall tree with smooth hot red bark. "That's Mahogany", explains the Captain, "but a poor type, not used commercially, as its too brittle."

However, to see mahogany of any kind shows that we are in the middle of the most exotic, steamy jungle! My inner eye has been turned outward today, outside of the round bony trap of the brain. I'm no longer conscious of myself, but only of the new impressions of the strange world around me. I could almost say I am this world! And, in becoming part of this new, pulsating life I have discovered joy. Suddenly, it's a shock to think that we have only 5 more days on the *Veloz*, a voyage which in the beginning had no sense of time. If I could only stay here, in this golden moment.

One rebels at returning to the prosaic world of humdrum activity, the competitive world, the world of petty worries such as "Will I have another cavity in my teeth when I get home?" "Will Jerzy and Eva make out alright in school this year, even if they're late in starting?" Or, "How can I bear to think of cooking and cleaning the house again?" Then, thoughts about money: "Will I have to use all my savings to pay for the well? And, if so, will I have to take out a loan in order to pay the taxes? And would this not mean we could not take another trip in the near future?" The world of conformity: "I've noticed your boy stands on one side when the fellows are playing ball." (Actually, he had a broken arm at the time.) "Your son is uncoordinated." "With ideas like your son's, does he have any friends?" Or, "Jerzy just doesn't fit into 6th grade at Hilltop School."

Eva has just remarked: "Mom, you are too direct and straight-forward in your thinking." This in connection with my descriptions of things which happen on the trip from day to day. In other words, "Mom, you have no imagination", because I see things the way they appear on the outside. She thinks I don't put my subjective thoughts into inanimate objects, and this makes what I say dull.

Well, that is the way I am. She may not realize that when alone I am often philosophic and introspective, but I try to to be completely objective when it comes to describing our travels. One thing has struck me, though, that to take a trip like this is the perfect way to relax (one has to, on this ship) and leave all one's troubles behind. One can live exactly in the present minute, and really get the flavour of life without the worries of one's job. American business men should all come here and just glide aimlessly on jungle rivers with no communication with the outside world. (What brought on my sleepless night was the fact that I had received that letter in Manaus. I should never have given any forwarding address.) They might see themselves and life in a different perspective after this experience. Some of them might disappear into the jungle for good. It has been said that jungle people never have ulcers or high blood pressure.

9 PM   This evening was the most beautiful we've had. A fiery sunset, as red as the rising sun, with a prolonged after glow in the sky, and the usual fantastic clouds.

"Although that's nothing for the Amazon!" jokes the Captain, when we point it out.

A shining clear sky with bright stars. A quarter new moon gleaming on the water. Warm balmy air (not much breeze). Heat lightning putting on its dramatic display around the horizon. And dim mysterious kerosene lamps and wood fires burning on shore. Mosquitoes? Just enough to be atmospheric!

The "Capo Verde", however, a delta-winged fly, had made its appearance earlier in the day, accompanied by much slapping the deck with towels by the officers, whose ankles are chewed already. One way to treat the sores is to put a drop of nail polish on each bite! A tip from Nicole Maxwell's book, and it really works. It kills the eggs, which the flies lay under the skin, and also takes away the itch. The men scorn this treatment as being too feminine, and prefer having welts on their ankles.

This is a perfect night for a glass of cold beer. George and I have some before turning in.

"Do you realize where we are?" asks George, wonderingly.

"On the full Amazon!"

Saturday, August 20

Today, which dawned heavily, with dark clouds spotted across the sky (in spite of a fiery rising sun reflecting in crimson splendour in the water), has been noted for heavy tempers, and much insect activity. George has been giving me the silent treatment all day. Nervous tension was aggravated by the fact that the movie camera stuck again, just as he wanted to take some pictures of the forest. Almost every time he uses it, the film sticks inside. He has to open the camera to adjust it. I'm afraid the film he did succeed in taking will be light-struck. I can't help repeating: "I told you so! You never should have bought this camera!" And continue by saying: "If you had listened to me in the first place, we shouldn't be having this trouble now."

Then he gets really angry! I had wanted him to get a $300. German make, the latest model – particularly as he said this was the one time he wanted to take really good movies, so he could show them, perhaps even accompanying a talk on our trip. Instead, he bought this old junk for $70. at an auction, goaded on by a man we had met at different rummage sales, who had been a photographer. He insisted this was a great bargain. (Moral: one can outsmart oneself.)

I think this is the hottest day we've had. There isn't a breath of air, and the Capo Verdes are buzzing. We have 3 cans of "Fly & Mosquito Killer" on deck, and I'm spraying with my 6-12 also. None of this bothers them!

Mr. Resson, in blue and white swimming trunks, and a bath towel with which he mops off the perspiration, every few minutes slaps at them with his towel – to no avail. The Captain gets up and stalks each individual fly along the deck, then stamps at it with his foot – but it flies merrily away. Jerzy catches one by putting a glass over it, and it flies around inside, a prisoner. He has brought my "Iridescent" nail polish out, and is putting dots of it on my bites. George's bites have formed big welts, but he doesn't want any polish, and keeps on scratching. I'm afraid they'll get infected.

Today, many new varieties of butterflies are swooping around the ship; some land on the railings, the life-boats, or the deck. Two sad little ones with white speckled brown wings with orange stripes are asphyxiated by the DDT. Or so we presume. They are found stunned on a big wooden chest which sits on deck (full of life preservers). They spread their wings and remain immobile, even when we come close to them. After an hour, one regains its strength and flies up on the awning. But the other folds its wings and slips unconscious down a crack.

A huge speckled one we hadn't seen before lands on the deck, another tremendous one marked with orange on the lifeboat, where he folds his wings. On the outside when folded the wings are dark. He is the colour and exact shape of a dead leaf! The pale green variety, with bright green stripes, which we have seen before, is one of the prettiest. Another has bright red markings.

A monstrous grasshopper, pale green with translucent wings, flies (not hops!) around the railing, and also lands on the life-boat. He is twice the size of a normal grasshopper.

Jerzy and I saw two macaws flying across the bow. We saw their scarlet colour distinctly. When the parrots take off from the trees one can also see the green sheen of their feathers. We are going very close in most of the day. The jungle is now a dense, vine-covered tangle, with immense trees from whose tops huge eagles, and an occasional heron, arise. Looking into the underbrush, it is very dark. There are now fewer settlements. In the afternoon, I finally saw a man fishing from a canoe with a bow and arrow. He was dressed disappointingly, though, not as a naked Indian, but in khaki pants and shirt.

One large colony of neater looking farms is settled by the Japanese. Yesterday, we thought everything looked Japanese. Particularly at sunset, when smoke from brush fires drifted along the ground, never rising on account of the heavy atmosphere. The humidity must be 100 percent today. Even I feel a "pressure" on my head, and sit taking catnaps in my chair all afternoon. To add to the weight of the atmosphere, we ate one of those extra-heavy lunches the cook seems to delight in making. Rabbit pie (with thick pastry), a double portion of mashed potatoes, and white beans stacked high; rolls; and a jam-filled pancake for dessert. All starchy! One can feel the fat forming as one sits in one's chair. I've taken three showers today in hopes some of the fat will melt away. (The cold water has something wrong with it, and runs hot, so it does not really cool one off.)

Rain clouds are all around us by Tea (tonight suddenly called "Dinner" on the Menu). We are sure we are in for a storm. Rain is falling far away at our stern, and part of a rainbow is visible. It seems to be doubly thick. I guess everything is larger than life on the Amazon!

The rain doesn't break, but a cooling breeze at last blows in our direction from the threatening clouds. Standing at the bow, my hair blowing, and watching the clouds swirl over eddying water, with an unbroken line of forest as far as I can see on every side, I think: "This is the kind of scenery I love! Not one tract house in sight. No pressures of civilization."

Bats start to come out of the forest, and fly crazily at the ship. I think they're going to fly at us on deck, but they always swerve off at the last minute. They are the largest we've ever seen. Twice the size again of a normal North American bat.

"They are attracted by your white pants!" jokes George. Since a breeze has come up, he is more cheery. In spite of the breeze, the mosquitoes are now making their evening rounds. We all start spraying like mad. Can you imagine, by 7 o'clock there is such a breeze that the Captain says:

"I'm going in. I'm cold!"

All day we have noticed more and more dead uprooted trees piled up in a tangle on the banks. The banks are still showing a 12 foot drop in the water level. High water was May 15th.

We are coming to a place about 10 PM where there are so many logs in the water that we may have to stop, if the night remains dark. The moon has a ring around it, and may go under the clouds altogether.

Sunday, August 21

Our last Sunday aboard ship! The Captain, to celebrate our successful voyage, invites us for a drink in his cabin before lunch. He has a special bottle of Guiness stout for me, as I had told him that I liked it. George has "Pink Gin", the Captain's favourite (Gin, with Angostura Bitters – a secret formula from Trinidad – and water).

Of course we get on the subject of Wales, and how the Welsh are so poetic.

"Did you ever know Dylan Thomas?" I ask.

"Yes! And his wife, too."

"What did you think of him?"

"He was mad! I didn't like him at all. But they say there's a narrow line between madness and genius."

"Well, he was a drunkard, wasn't he? And I never could understand why he wanted to drink himself to death."

"Because he was mad! And he was a sex maniac, too!"

"Oh," puts in George, "now I know why Dale likes him! She's read everything about him and all his letters. You ought to know whether his descriptions of Alexandria are correct."

"You're thinking of Durrell!" I shout. "Lawrence Durrell. Do you know him, too?" I ask the Captain.

"No. I've never heard of him. He's not Welsh!"

"But to get back to Thomas," I say,"I liked reading about him more than his actual poetry. Some of it was so morbid, all about death and worms and winding-sheets."

"Well, that's the Welsh! When they get gloomy, no one anywhere can be gloomier."

The Captain looked at me and decided that I must have some Celtic blood, (knowing him, this is the biggest compliment he could give me). I do, as I have plenty of Irish and Scottish. He says the line between my nose and upper lip is in just the right proportion!

Everyone gets very gay, and all three officers suggest that we should go back to New York from Iquitos with them on the *Veloz*.

"We'll be in Iquitos for 10 days. Enough time for you to run up to Pucallpa, Cuzco, and all around."

"The jungle's better than the high mountains, anyway," I say, falling in with the mood.

At lunch, the jolly mood continues. They tell about some recent passengers, a couple so fat that they couldn't fit into the bunks. They occupied the cabin Eva and Jerzy have. "They used to sleep on the floor, stark naked!"

"They were travelling with overweight luggage, too. Over 200 pounds of it, including hamsters and white mice!"

"The woman was fat when she got on, but you should have seen her grow on board ship! Every meal her plate was piled a mile high, and there was no room for salad. Had to have it on another plate. And she kept Gregorio (the steward) running back and forth for extras and second helpings. Cereal, bacon and eggs, salad and fish for breakfast, and mounds of toast. She was disappointed not to get steak. You should have seen her eyes gleam when she sat down at the table and started to read the menu!"

At this point, I, who always worry about my figure, particularly now that we eat all this starchy food and don't get any exercise, decided not to finish my dinner – bananas with cream and sugar!

"When we were several weeks out she started to split out of her dresses, and she threw them over the side!"

"How old was she?"

"Oh, not old. Only 39. And was intelligent and well-informed when you talked to her."

"That's a real tragedy," commented George.

Speaking of overweight luggage, Nicole Maxwell has said that the sign of a rank amateur, whether traveller or explorer, is to take too much luggage. This time, we really did it, but, of course, all the blame falls on me – "and you have travelled enough to know better, Dale."

My suitcases are full of hot-water bottles, wool stoles, dinner dresses, silver slippers, evening purses, unnecessary medicines and such things that I've never used, and never will use. George has 2 dozen shirts, but only wears the same two drip-dry ones.

We decided to completely reorganize. If we want to take the local riverboat to Pucallpa, and then go over the Andes by "Camionetta"(bus), there won't be room for so much. We certainly can't carry it all ourselves.

The steward carries away a huge pile of shirts, my "Beat" Magnin's coat, which weighs too much, etc. We fill my largest suitcase with stuff we won't need but want back home.

George's big case is empty except for the heavy bag of Brazil nuts, a present from Ogonowski. George says its silly to send them home; however, they'll come in handy at Christmas time, and will be nuts with a personal touch! We'll send both cases back on the *Veloz*, but probably won't get them for months, as from New York they'll have to be shipped to California by Railroad Express. My case contains coral, and a pearly-white conch George found at Antigua – even he thinks we should keep that.

My main trouble was not knowing what to take on this trip. Actually, on the ship I have lived in two pairs of shorts, and two blouses. One does not even bother to put a dress on for Tea! One pair of jeans, and a long-sleeved blouse against mosquitoes. Sometimes I put on white slacks and a dressy blouse in the evening. A windbreaker is good for sunrises, or the days at sea; of course, a sun-top instead of a blouse for the hottest days. A shorty shift (pyjamas are too hot) to get back and forth to the bathroom completes my everyday wardrobe (one sleeps naked). Two or three summer dresses are necessary for going ashore, and, of course, a slicker. Sandals, sneakers, and one pair of heels are enough in the way of shoes. We have never needed the jungle boots! We'll give them to someone ashore.

Today we saw something typical of the Amazon, a whole bank caving in. Huge forest trees were toppling into the water, one by one, with lots of earth following them. There was no wind, no movement of the water at all, yet suddenly it happened before our very eyes. Sometimes, a tall tree just slides straight down a curvy bank, without even falling over. The water is full of such uprooted giants. Many whose roots remain in the water continue to grow where they fell. We saw two making little islands of themselves, with just their green tops out of the water. Bubbles like soapsuds floated downstream along the banks, and powdered sawdust made scummy streaks farther out.

"The river is down 6 inches since yesterday," reported the Captain. "We learnt it from the daily reading in Iquitos. We're glad to say that the ship that ran aground got off the sandbank and will reach Iquitos tomorrow."

Today was noted for a flight of a dozen parrots an hour before sunset, up from the treetops and over the water near our stern. For the first time I really could fully appreciate their gorgeous colouring; in the sunset glow they were soft green, mixed with gold. The Amazon parrot also has touches of deep blue and red, but this is hard to see when they are in flight. Their squawking is unmistakable, too. I'm getting familiar with them, and can now pick them out from a great distance from their short, fat bodies and quick wing beats.

This evening handsome blue and white herons were a dime a dozen, one every few hundred feet. And manatees were flashing pink in the water. These are shy and do not like to show too much of themselves. They are not show-offs like the dolphins.

At one small settlement we saw a group of teenage boys playing "football" (soccer) on a sandy beach. A strange sight in the jungle! Every few minutes several would fall flat to the ground and rest, overcome by the heat (they played in the full sun). One or two others went down to the water and slopped some on their faces, arms and legs. But we noticed that no one ever went in more than ankle deep. Nowhere have we seen anyone swimming. "Too dangerous!" says the Captain. The danger comes from piranhas, electric eels, and anacondas.

Tonight the stars are out in their full glory, although the moon is so bright that the stars seem far away, not close to touch.

We are discussing the latest U.S. satellite orbiting the moon.

"What was the first animal to go into Outer Space?" quizzes the Captain.

"Didn't two Russian dogs go up first?"

"No," says the Captain, "it was the Cow Who Jumped over the Moon!"

We have gained another hour today. The sun set when we were in the dining-room around 6. I noticed that the water was wine-red. The Chief insists that the clouds and the sunsets we've had on this trip are nothing for the Amazon, but we could not imagine anything better.

Later this evening, the Captain gives me a little talk about astronomy, and points out Arcturus and Vega, important to navigators. He explains how in navigation one makes triangulations from one star or constellation to another. Jupiter is now the Morning Star. He says one can see at least 3 of its moons here with the naked eye. He adds that he has, three times in his life, distinguished the rings around Saturn with his naked eye. "but one can hardly ever do it." He has amazingly keen long distance sight.

While we slide over the glassy surface of mirrored moon and star light, and watch the ghostly silhouettes of trees, 3,000 people have been reported dead in an earthquake in Eastern Turkey. It makes one wonder by what stroke of luck we are here, not there? Is it the same good luck that allowed the Captain to survive his three wartime sinkings?

It was more than luck, it was Fate, in which old Merlin had a hand, Richard told me later. We were destined to meet, this had always been in our stars. He knew now, for sure, at this point in the trip, that this was why he had survived so many dangers which otherwise might have been fatal. But it remained for both of us to fully recognize this.

When he had stood close behind me, pointing out the constellations, he had wanted then to put his arms around me, but, of course, couldn't. He said later he had had to go into his cabin to keep from doing so. He thought he had fallen in love with me when I had first appeared on the ship, but as the feeling grew fought against showing it. I was there with my family, he was a married man, and an honourable ship's Master.

I, also, had been sensitively aware of his presence from the beginning, and as time went on, increasingly so. Ever since I had been married to George, I had never thought of having a love affair, even when it became apparent we weren't getting on too well. But I could not help feeling a great strength and steadfastness coming from Richard. It was more than sexual attraction, although we certainly had that. I knew he was a person in whom I could have absolute confidence. The difference in backgrounds was unimportant. In fact, he knew little about me, or whether I had money! We had not even had many private conversations. "We just belonged together, and that's all!" Richard was often to repeat, afterwards.

At the beginning of the voyage, he and Mr. Resson (who also liked redheads!) used to discuss me, and they both thought that I seemed mismatched with George. I did not even look right as the mother of the children! A strange family, they thought.

I do hope, however, that in spite of having to follow my star, I have not been a failure as a mother. The attraction between Richard and myself, and the tense situation that grew from this, was impossible for children to understand. No doubt I appeared aloof and distracted during this period of upheaval. They did know that their father and I were constantly arguing, and this was upsetting in itself. But it was impossible to explain that I had reached a serious crisis in my life.

The river had exerted its magic, and I had undergone a sea-change. Richard thereafter was to call me his "Amazon Mermaid".

Monday, August 22

This morning we were up at 4.20 AM to see Jupiter. The night sky was magnificent. Three planets were conspicuous, but none were in the right position to be Jupiter. I went back to bed.

At 5, George called me, and said that Jupiter had risen. He had seen a glow on the horizon, but had thought that it was a plane. But it did not move. Then, slowly, the tremendous planet rose, so big that it almost looked like the moon. As I came out the door, the sky was turning dusty pink in the East. On this background, low over the black forest, Jupiter reflected in the water.

We looked and looked, but could not see the moons. Through our binoculars, its light twinkled and blurred. (Later, the Captain said that we should have gone up on the Bridge and borrowed his powerful glasses.)

I again went back to bed. When I went out on deck about 8, it was already hot. The sky was cloudless, and the air still. Sunlight reflected with such a glare that I needed both my dark glasses and my big hat. The family make fun of my hat, but I find that is a great help when peering against the sun into the forest. This jungle-watching, which we do constantly, is very tiring to the eyes. One never relaxes on deck with a book, nor snoozes in one's chair, as one does on an ocean voyage. One is always on the alert, one's muscles tense, binoculars in hand, waiting for the rustle of a leaf which might reveal a monkey or bird, or a widening ripple on the water from which a mantee or dolphin may arise.

This morning the jungle was quiet and abandoned by wildlife. It was too hot for them to leave the sheltering regions of the forest's depths. Only a few immense "Fish Eagles" sailed majestically in the upper atmosphere.

As we get nearer to Peru the people look different. Today, most people we see lined up in front of their houses to watch the ship go by, or sitting in canoes fishing, are definitely Indian. They are more suspicious of contact with outsiders. Even the children do not respond when we wave. No one paddles out shouting for beer cans. We watch three men in a canoe spearing a fish. They all throw spears at the same time, and as one spear sticks out of the water, it must have hit a fish. As the water is full of mud from the constantly crumbling banks, we wonder how they can see any fish to aim at? Their canoes slide along under these towering banks, whose quaking, oozing sides may at any moment collapse, sending a toppling tree on top of them. One canoe has 4 women, one with a bright purple umbrella shading her from the sun. The women here all wear straw hats as well as the men, and the tall, rectangular shape of these give a Peruvian touch.

We notice one characteristic of all the houses. Each one has a lot of wash in front, spread out on the ground to dry. Drying laundry must be a major problem, in spite of the strong sun, on account of high humidity. I cannot resist remarking that it would be an American businessman's nightmare to see so many houses without washers and driers. Such a vast, but untouchable market!

Small house and clearing on riverbank near Leticia.

George wonders why Brazil has been so backward in developing such a source of unimaginable, untouched, unlimited natural resources.

"I'm sure it is possible to develop this land. Surely, with modern methods of construction, roads could be opened up, on stilts in the water when necessary for the rainy season. The United States would have done it long ago. And divided big blocks of land into smaller sub-divisions. Opened it all up for homesteaders." [4]

"Sub-divisions! And what would happen to the beauty of the endless, untapped jungle which still appeals so much to the imagination? What would happen to the remaining `savage' tribes, who want to be left alone? Or, even to the settlers already along the river, who manage to live on the natural resources, still free to all?"

"A lot of artistic sentimentality!" he scoffs. "One must sacrifice the picturesquely primitive in order to help those poor people who live here now. Not that I'm not glad that I saw it as it is! But to think that all this exists – and at the same time a satellite is going around the moon!"

At that moment, a little two-decker river boat puffing a lot of blue smoke from a small smoke-stack, passes, going downstream. She is freshly painted, and I notice a big Red Cross on her bow. I also notice that she is flying a red and white flag.

"The Peruvian Navy!" explains the Captain. "Its their Hospital Ship! It goes up and down river, a floating emergency clinic."

I wonder how the Brazilians feel about the Peruvians invading their waters in this way? To me, it is a reassuring sight, as it had looked as though there were no medical help for hundreds of miles.

We notice waves breaking far out in the river, in the wake of our own ship. It is a sign that the water's very shallow. Tremendous sandy peninsulas, obviously belonging underwater, have been left high and dry, except for protruding skeletons of driftwood.

Mr. Resson announces: "We've just heard from Iquitos that the river has fallen 3 feet in two days! And look how hard the engine is working in these narrow places, where the current is stronger. This morning we are losing half of our power."

The river is not really narrower here. It still looks like a swollen mouth of the Mississippi. But here it is cut up by many islands, where even seasoned navigators lose their way.

"What happens if you get up to Iquitos and the river falls so much that you can't get back down?"

"This can happen! We just have to wait for it to become swollen. We have been known to have to wait in Iquitos for as long as 6 weeks!"

"A huge log hit us last night!" continues Resson. "Stopped the propeller."

Before lunch Mr. Ogonowski comes into our cabin for a rum-and-coke. He is very jovial, and has been drinking with the Chief Steward since 9 AM. He shows us his Master's Certificate, giving him permission to be Captain of a "foreign-going" ship.

"Just like Joseph Conrad!"

"Except that Conrad had trouble getting his. He had a hard time with the English language, and that held him back. Did you know that Conrad only finished secondary school? I'm one up on him! I went to the University."

"Some of the greatest writers never went to college. Hemingway! Dylan Thomas! But they had it within themselves, the power to turn everyday events into their own magical creation."

"You sound interested in writing. Would you like to follow in Conrad's footsteps?"

"Yes, I have often thought of it! I have seen things, too, you know. I have travelled."

"Have you ever done any writing?"

"Never! But as I have been to the University, I would have less struggle with English. But Conrad! He had more than genius!"

The sky has clouded over. We are so heavy after lunch that we have long, exhausted siestas. I had only had one beer, so should not have been sleepy. Everyone predicts a storm. At 4 PM the heat is unbearable. At 4.30 we progress downstairs to the Chief Steward's room, where we were invited for a drink. There, we find the Radio Engineer, the Second Officer, and still a third young officer – all in shorts, with naked tops or under-shirts, drinking beer or rum.

"This is a drinking ship!" someone announces. "Nobody's stiff and formal! No dressing for dinner, or that kind of thing. However, one of our last passengers was shocked seeing us going around in our shirts. Didn't like it when there was a power failure in Iquitos, and all the lights went off, either!"

"That's the one who complained because she didn't have her personal steward? Can you imagine? She and her husband parked their car on the Brooklyn pier when they got on the ship. When we returned after 3 months, of course it was gone!"

"What were they doing?"

"Oh, the husband said right away that he was writing! The wife wouldn't say what she did. Was very secretive like. But in the end it turned out she was a writer, too. Wrote for some woman's magazine."

"I'd hate to see what she wrote!" I laughed.

"Tell me, Madam," asks the Chief Steward, formally, "has there been too much bad language used on this ship? Maybe we get very loud down here, and you hear us?"

"Oh, no, I've never heard anything," I reply, truthfully. (I'm wondering whether the "New Tribe" missionaries complained?) "But, anyway, when a lot of seafaring men get together, you must expect some swearing and noise!"

"Have some good Barbados rum? The very best!" he offers it to George. It is close in the cabin, and the perspiration streams from all of us. The talk turns to home leave.

"Don't get any! We are all signed up for 1 year before we can go home. Just go up and down this river. Might as well stay on board, too. One gets into too much trouble ashore."

"Well, I don't really want to go home!" the youngest one says. "As soon as I'm home, I want to start out again."

"I guess its only hard on the married ones," I suggest.

Talk turns to drinking-bouts in African ports, where some of them have been with other ships.

"Want to come ashore with us the first night in Iquitos? We'll show you the town!"

"Yes," answers George, "but without Dale. She'd better stay in the hotel." He gives a warning frown in my direction, much to my disgust.

As I had gradually been taken over by the spell of the river, and, more important, by the personality of Richard, himself, an unspoken undercurrent existed and grew stronger, which George without a doubt felt, and was baffled by. I had probably put up an invisible psychic wall between us, which he could not understand. Although Richard was always formally courteous to George, the two men from the start were antagonistic. Richard told me afterwards that he never had any use for George.

George felt my interest in the river and involvement with the crew of the ship was going too far. It was no reason to neglect him, and he thought the hot climate was affecting my reasoning. His sleeping all afternoon after too many drinks, or going to bed at 7 and leaving me alone, while the children occupied themselves with their own games, did not count. To him, the river was like a picture one quickly walks past, which does not involve one emotionally, or change one's life. "When we get home, we'll talk a little about it, show some photographs, and then start planning our next trip to some other place."

One night, towards the end of the voyage, as we were nearing Iquitos, George decided that my neglect of him had gone too far. He became infuriated, and very violent. I was sitting in my bunk writing my journal when he shouted: "That's enough! You are forgetting my marital rights!"

He pulled me forcibly out of the bunk, and pushed me brutally down on the floor. Not my idea of romantic love-making. It would have amounted to rape if I had not been his legal wife, an object with which he felt he could do as he pleased. I don't see anything wrong in making love on the floor if both partners want to! But in this case, there was no love in it.

The next day he told one of the officers that I was a sex maniac! This was repeated to Richard, who, much later, after I had split up with George, told me he had been so furious that he had had to control himself not to go and knock George down.

After Tea, we plump ourselves heavily in our deck chairs. Inky clouds are everywhere, and a wind is starting to blow, "a sure sign of rain". Even the mosquitoes have been blown away. The sun has set unnoticeably, and darkness falls. Then a wild electrical display begins, something like the Northern Lights. Giant flashes of heat lightning, illuminating all shapes and sizes of storm clouds, like several evenings ago, but on a bigger scale. Forked and stick lightning also flashes down, across, or from under clouds, but without a sound. The light is at times blinding in intensity. It all has a theatrical, unreal effect. I am usually terrified of electrical storms (perhaps it is the noise?), but this just looks like a heavenly performance put on for our benefit. George takes several photographs, but is afraid that he snapped each a second too late. Its too dark to fix the tripod for a time exposure.

The wind increases in strength, so much so that we hasten to fold up the deck chairs. I have put on my heavy "sweat-shirt", the first time on the river that I've needed it, as the temperature must have fallen 30 degrees in 5 minutes. A sweet smell as of aromatic grass floats on the wind.

Finally, the blackest clouds pass overhead, a general grey overcast appears, and rain begins to fall – not a torrential rain, but gently at first, and then increasing to moderate strength. The pressure is removed, and one can breathe again! George goes to bed at 7, a mistake, I think, as he'll get up at midnight, wander around for hours, and then feel exhausted again in the morning.

"But I see things at night I would otherwise miss!" he says.

By 9.15 the rain is over, and moon and stars are peeping out of the clouds. Our engine stops for 5 minutes. Did we hit another log? I go out on deck, and can see nothing unusual. Just a faint glimmer of water, and a long line of trees quite close.

Tuesday, August 23

A dramatic incident at night! I had finished writing my journal last night, read for a while, and had just turned out the light, when George, who had gotten up and had been wandering on deck, came in in great excitement. It was about 11 PM. I noticed that the engine was off again, but thought we had stopped to let another log slide past the propeller.

"Come outside!" he cried. "I think we've hit a sandbar!"

I pulled on pants and a shirt, and dashed out. We were very close to shore. One could distinguish the black forms of trees, in a sinister line obliterating the sky. The moon was under clouds. Below the steep bank, the usual jumble of prostrate trees, reaching skeleton limbs out of the water. We weren't more than 25 feet away! The ship seemed to tilt slightly towards the bank. The engines went on, and churned up a lot of water, but she did not budge. Everything was silent and dark on deck, like a derelict ship. Suddenly, she started to go astern, in a manoeuvre to get her bow free of the shore. We were standing directly by the stern, and saw the shore coming quickly towards us. The bank reached up much higher than we had thought, higher than our deck; above it threatened the solid wall of trees. Then came a scrunching, sickening sound of the hull hitting one of the fallen trees. The ship gave a shiver. The engine stopped; but we were still drifting backwards. We were now so close that all the night noises of the jungle hit our ears – giant katidids, tree frogs, and other innumerable nocturnal voices. The ship looked as though she would surely hit the bank. I imagined her lurching crazily onto a sandbar; or, the impact with the bank creating a landslide such as I had previously seen. Those trees towering over our heads were indeed ominous, as they could crash on deck, reducing the awning to a pulp.

"Don't you think we'd better run to the front of the deck, or go inside?" I asked, nervously backing away from the railing. In an emergency like this on a freighter, its every man for himself!

Silence from George. He leaned over the rail in mute fascination.

"What do you think we should do?" I repeated. No reply. I went back and peered over the railing again myself. Lights appeared on the deck below, and stewards' heads. Just at this point, the engine started, and with wildly foaming water, the *Veloz* slowly nosed her way from the danger zone. Then, she stopped again. Little bells signalled. Dim lights flickered, and shadowy figures moved on the bow. The Captain's voice was heard from the Bridge. I went to wake up Eva and Jerzy. No need for them to miss all the excitement. They would be angry if I did not wake them.

Jerzy got up right away. Eva showed no sign of life. But two minutes later, she appeared on deck, complaining: "Why did you wake us up?"

The engines started throbbing very hard, but the ship remained in one place.

"We're on a sandbar! I just know it!" Jerzy said, gleefully.

"They've done it this time!" I shouted (meaning the pilots). "The poor Captain! He was just boasting that he held the record on the river, for never having gone aground in 14 years."

"Shhh!" whispered George. "He might hear you and feel badly. Maybe he doesn't want anyone to know."

"Well, on a night as dark as this even the best pilots could go aground. And the Captain said they were the best on the river. But with the water so low, it certainly is tricky."

"Do you think we'll have to go ashore and walk for help?" one of the children asked. I sized up that impassable bank. Just to climb up through the mud would be hard. On top is a thicket of vines and underbrush. To walk along the top edge would be dangerous, as it might collapse.

"Don't worry! We're not too far from Leticia. They'll send help."

"No, we'll have to wait for rain, to get off."

More grinding sounds from the engine. No change of position. Then we heard the clank of the anchor chain. The mast light and the forward lights came on.

"There's the anchor. That means we'll stay here for the night. Let's go back to bed."

At dawn, I am awakened by the first vibrations of the engine being tuned up. "Come on and let's see what's happening," I tell George. I pull on some clothes, in the meanwhile hearing the anchor come up. By the time I come out on deck, we have slowly started to move, and are gradually making headway. We go cautiously for about 15 minutes before picking up speed. During the night we must have floated free, with the help of the current. The Captain is sitting on his perch on the Bridge, eyes glued to the channel. We see now we are headed due East, whereas we generally go West. We're in a section of the river where it curves around and is full of islands.

Looking over the side, after the sun comes up, we notice a small brown bird, with a white stripe on his tail, about the size of a sparrow, flying up and down the length of the ship just above the water. He beats his wings quickly, like a hummingbird, but looks as though he is looking for a place to land. He is down too far to find a perch, and only sees the perpendicular side. Back and forth he darts.

"I think he's hypnotized," George comments.

Finally, he falls into the water, exhausted. His feathers look crumpled. He's obviously not a water bird. The quick current carries him away. We are sure he has drowned.

"I saw him, too!" the Captain says at breakfast. "I thought he must have been a fledgling."

"Well, we almost ran into a sandbar last night!" he continues.

"You mean we didn't?"

"No, but we almost did! The pilot was going too near the shoreline for such a dark night, and he didn't turn quite quickly enough. But its awfully hard to do."

Everyone looks quite impressed by the night's events. After breakfast, we line up in the deck chairs in our usual positions, to watch the jungle float by. It is particularly splendid vegetation today, with the giant trees I especially love that are festooned with lianas and philodendrons. Beneath them, "elephant ears". A new kind of graceful feathery palm has appeared, laden with heavy bunches of small yellow nuts.

"Buru-buru," says the Captain. "They each contain 3 waxy nuts. People here use them for wax. We used to take some as cargo."

We pass plenty of enchanted South Sea Island palm-thatched huts. "There are so many here because the land is high," he explains.

George still keeps telling me that the people look Japanese, because their clothes are so bright and clean looking! We pass several big missions, with imposing churches, schools and living quarters. These buildings are much bigger and more solid than their secular neighbours, the grounds better looked after, and are incongrous oases.

This morning we find a huge rare moth on deck. About 10 inches across its wings. It is sleepily sitting on the flagpole. Mr. Resson rushes to get a butterfly net, and George catches it, with the help of the Captain, and Eva and Jerzy, who are all crowding around. All except me, as I still don't warm up to moths! However, in the daytime, in its captured state, I must admit that this one is beautiful. The finest we have seen. It is brown, with a soft pink design on its wings, and looks like a flower. The Captain takes the poor thing to his cabin to chloroform. He will add it to his collection for the New Jersey couple.

Right before lunch, the little speed-boat is launched. It zooms brightly away carrying the Chief Steward, the 2nd Engineer, and the 2nd Mate to the border town across the river, to pay port fees for Leticia.

"And, there'll probably be plenty of drinking all around. They won't be back until around 4.30!"

We are anchored off Tabatinga, a military post on the border of Brazil and Colombia. Across the river is Benjamin Constant, Brazil, and Ramon Castilla, Peru. All three borders are within sight of Leticia, Colombia. A gambling ship used to be anchored here in the middle of the river!

Indians come alongside in dugouts, two miserable families. An old woman without any teeth, who looks partially paralysed, is paddled by a young boy. These seem to have nothing to sell. In the other canoe is a very slender younger woman, with a childish figure, but a work-worn face, accompanied by a year-old baby, a girl of about 8, and also a young boy. She has two men with her who behave as though they are both her husbands! They hang onto the gangplank to keep from drifting downstream, and have a few bananas and Brazil nuts to sell. We throw them some coke bottles. Then we notice how miserable and ragged they look. Their clothes have enormous patches, yet still are full of holes. Their faces remain hopelessly impassive. The women in each canoe look subdued and listless. However, the men and boys have keen, bright expressions. Its a man's world here! We hand down some clothes over the side: my green dress for the young mother, my kimono for the old woman, a shirt for one of the boys. I am almost ashamed to look at them. They take the things and look them over very carefully, appraisingly, even. The old woman hides hers under a bag. But no expression of thanks or of any other emotion shows on their faces.

"Why are you upset?" asks Eva. "We have equally poor people in the United States."

"Not quite," I explain. "At least, we have Welfare and Relief, and other philanthropic organisations. I don't believe these people do."

George hands down a full can of coke, and then another. They eagerly drink this, passing the tins around. The baby loves it, and holds out her arms for more. The little boys opened the cans, we noticed, with practised hands! Only when they had drunken everything, a half-smile formed on the lips of the boys, and the young woman got up enough courage to look up at us. The men remained impassive, as they hadn't shared in the coke.

A wind has come up. The water is getting choppy. Down river a curtain of rain slowly moves in our direction. Even with the first drops we stay on deck, welcoming the change in temperature. The wind is now quite strong, and bears the intoxicating fragrance – as of orange-blossoms, gardenias, and all other exotic blossoms rolled together – that always makes me stop in my tracks and sniff the air in a blissful trance. Even George, whose sense of smell is poor, smells it.

Equally suddenly as it came, the big rain cloud veers off to the South. We have only received 5 minutes of rain.

By the time we have docked at Leticia, it is time for Tea. At least 15 "officials" come on board to "clear" the ship. They all go into the Smoking Room, where liquid refreshment is combined with business.

Immediately after this, we go ashore.

George is annoyed with me, as I had put on a dress, but as the mosquitoes were beginning to bite at this time of day, and it looked very muddy in the port, I went back and changed into slacks, and Eva did the same. I made the mistake of talking about whether people would stop and stare at us the way they did in Mexico when we wore slacks. This annoyed George. Later, he made fun of me by acting out the part of me getting off the ship and looking anxiously around as though afraid to show myself. Not true!

The sight of an obvious young American intellectual, with a serious face and glasses, and a Peace Corps or Bug-Hunter look, shirt opened to the waist to show an expanse of hairy chest, á la Trinidad, helping out of a boat a native girl who was wearing slacks, reassured me. They looked perfectly self-possessed. Its funny how this type of young American can be spotted right off. It is true that I am not a typical coolly collected American, much as I'd like to be. I always do feel self-conscious in a new place if I notice people looking at us, no matter how much I may have travelled previously.

Leticia is very simple. A small town on the edge of the jungle, much as one would imagine such a place to be. The dock is a floating one, less than half the length of the ship. Stretching from this over the water to the muddy bank is a primitive bridge made of loose boards. The bank goes about 100 yards up a steep incline of hardening mud; at the top, a dirt road goes further up the hill to the main part of town. Parallel to the ship along the banks are small cafés, markets, warehouses (for "Pieles" or skins), and money changers. All these are built in the roughest way, with open fronts. During the rainy season, the ship would be on a level with the top of the high bank, and actually look down on the shops.

All around the dock, near our ship, are tied tiny boats with open sides, and wooden roofs under which are small kitchens or cabins. Their decks are cluttered with collections of large metal gasoline barrels. Over these are slung hammocks. At night, kerosene lamps dimly light reclining figures, or people eating at make-shift tables. Some canoes, with palm-leaf rooflets against the sun, are also moored nearby. And ditto, the Columbian Navy! This consists of two toy gunboats of a peculiar square shape (flat bottoms for shallow water), whose duty it is to keep the borders quiet. There has been frequent fighting here between the three countries (later it was to become a major outlet for cocaine dealers).

As we get off, deer skins by the hundreds are being carried on men's

People live and trade on small boats such as this one photographed from the *Veloz*.

shoulders down the hill to load onto the *Veloz*. A shocking sight for animal lovers. A boy leads a small, miserable-looking monkey on the end of a rope. He yanks and pulls the poor creature along "30 Pesos, Señor," he says – about $1.80. I should have liked to have bought the monkey to rescue him, but what could we have done with him?

The town has plenty of wide, open squares; lots of trees; small houses open to the streets, where people sit chatting in their doorways. It is family orientated. Girls of all ages walk around for evening strolls without being molested. Some even wear slacks and ride motor cycles! Motor cycles ridden up and down by young sportsmen constitute a menace to the pedestrians, who prefer walking on the street than on the narrow pavement. Cars are few. The existing ones seem to be filled with teenage joy-riders. One jeep full of soldiers drives without lights, and George shouts at them.

We are conducted to the hotel by a quiet, middle-aged man who attaches himself to us at the wharf. We can't shake him off. One or two other hangers-on follow, Mexican style. But the man turns out not to be a native in search of a tip – he's a Jew from Czechoslovakia, who has long since forgotten his Czech! He has lived here for 32 years, and now thinks and speaks in Spanish.

The Hotel Victoria Regia, Marcy Elden, Proprietor, is an imposing brick building, which used to be a market. It, and its surrounding grounds, occupy a whole block, with a fine view of the river. The office is full of Indian masks, blow-pipes, beads and snake-skins. The proprietor appears from an inner room, a young, dark-haired, attractive divorcée from Laguna Beach, California. She is sophisticatedly dressed in immaculate white slacks, and sleeveless low-necked top. I had read about her in an article in "Sunset Magazine" last year, and had thought that as we're fellow Californians we should say "Hello".

"I've been here about two years," she says. She came up river working with a company making a documentary film, fell in love with the place, and stayed. (We wonder privately how one woman alone can run a business in such a place? And, particularly, a foreigner?) She has been on a lot of treks into the jungle. And knows Nicole Maxwell. "A very amusing person."

We follow her into the bar, tastefully decorated with a palm-leaf ceiling, local style. We order "Aquardiente", an indigenous drink, tasting like paragoric, and reminding me of "Ouzoo". She tells us about a tribe of Indians living three miles from here.

"They are Catholics, but still keep their own customs. When a girl reaches puberty, they have fiesta for 3 days. They dress up in fancy outfits, with masks, and dance and drink. They cut off the girl's hair very short, and she's a woman! I had them all here and fed them. In return, I got these masks."

We wonder if she gets many tourists? She has 14 rooms, but at present the hotel looks empty.

"Oh, now 5 planes a week fly in from Bogotá. Some tourists come here to see the river. And starting next week, we'll have a boat service from Iquitos."

All the time we've been talking, an eager young man with a few words of English has been playing records, very loud.

"Have American records! Yes, also Columbian music! Bolero!" (This sounds like an Hawaiian bolero!) Mrs. Elden speaks very softly; it is hard to catch what she says over the noise. The conversation lags. We feel she is thinking of something else. Probably its nothing special for her to have visitors from California.

"Monkeys make very good pets," she is saying. "I've had four myself. They never bit me."

Later in the evening, walking back over rutted streets, we are reminded of Salina Cruz, in southern Mexico, "but this is cleaner," insists George, "and less Mexican!" We see no poor Indians in town. The people look Spanish. All the little boys wear shoes and socks, or rubber rain-boots, a significant sign of prosperity.

A church bell rings. We follow people hurrying up a street where there is a Catholic church of artistic, modern design.

"I can't go in," I say. "I'm in slacks, and have no head scarf."

"To Hell with Religion!" Jerzy suddenly shouts, in a loud belligerent voice. "Just go in there and shock them to death."

"But that wouldn't be right," I say, in a conciliatory tone, trying to explain that although I'm not a church-goer myself, one must respect others' feelings, particularly when entering a church.

"I'm going in, come on, Dale," says George, although he is a Catholic, and should know the customs.

"Not in these slacks," I insist. "And Eva should not, either."

Inside the open door, I see a woman with a white lace mantilla on her head. We are left standing on a dark plaza outside, with groups of young men circling around ogling Eva. When George comes out, he says the congregation consisted mostly of pupils from a girls' school, escorted by a very young nun. The catechism was being said by a layman.

Jerzy is still in a rebellious mood. "Why didn't you just go in? Why do you care? I'm not religious!" he keeps shouting. Eva senses a scene approaching, and is stalking ahead. Later, she says to me in private:

"I am fed up with you guys! I am fed up travelling with my parents! You never do anything. It is dull, dull, dull! All I do is walk around the ship or sit in the cabin. I just want to get off on my own and have some FUN."

George criticizes me as we continue down the street: "I don't like the children's attitude one bit. They are ignorant savages. And its all YOUR fault, Dale."

That's when the jeep without lights again bears down on us, and he shouts a warning. I pinch Jerzy angrily, and push him off the middle of the road, where he is in danger of being run over. Then I slap him. Yes, I do! Although its wrong, unreasonable, and won't help. "Why do you always talk so stupidly in such a loud voice?" I add.

In reply, he hits me like sledge-hammer on the shoulder. He is getting stronger and stronger. Do I have a moron son – or, am I a moron mother? The others have walked ahead. Jerzy starts crying. At that point, I see a huge frog leaping in the grass, and lag behind to examine it. Everyone turns around, saying all together "Why are you walking so slowly?" George continues: "I hate these moods! You spoil all these places worrying about clothes. You changed your clothes 3 times before getting off the boat."

Jerzy is still sniffling. I am overcome with remorse. Why are all these beautiful places we have travelled so far to see spoilt by arguments? The same thing happened on an earlier trip to Italy, when Eva was too "superior" to show enjoyment of anything. She and Jerzy were fighting all the time in the back seat of the car. At least they get along better now.

"Jerzy," I say contritely, "do stop crying. Do you realize you are in one of the most interesting places you'll see on the whole trip? I was angry with you with reason. Even if we're not religious, we must act decently if we go into a church. These people believe. Let them believe. We can have our own ideas, but don't insult theirs."

"I didn't understand," answers Jerzy, in between sniffs. "But you shouldn't have pinched me. It hurt."

"Yes, I shouldn't have, I know it. But you were so exasperating," I add rashly, adding oil to the fire.

"Why? What did I do?" he starts up again. However, later, he volunteers to me that this was the most interesting town he has ever seen, and that, actually, he was taking in a lot.

Before walking back to the ship, we find an open-air café on a corner, with tables with beach umbrellas, and a dilapidated rotisserie puffing out rancid fumes! We drink cups of after-dinner coffee, delicious light Columbian coffee without the sickening taste of sugar and chicory that they add in Brazil. These only cost us, for 3 cups, 6 cents, U.S. money! A lizard catches a fly on the wall. A large friendly brown dog wants to climb into Jerzy's lap. And George sees a huge rat climbing the wall inside a dry-goods store next door. After leaving the café, George is sure he's seen the local house of prostitution. In a brightly lighted room one man sits surrounded by several girls. One of them plays the guitar. The place looks clean and cheerful. I'm more inclined to think its a private home. Anyway, what does it matter, one way or the other?

Wednesday, August 24

George and I were up at 6 AM, and off to the market. The ship, which dominated the shore with her looming form and brilliant lights against the evening sky, this morning has receded to normal size. Cargo is being unloaded, and a gnome-like procession of bent figures hurry up the hill, their shoulders laden with 10-gal. tins of "Aceite de Cerdo" (lard), and bags of cement. No modern transportation methods here. Gallon bottles of "Vino Tinto" (from Portugal), wrapped in basketwork, stand in rows waiting to be carried away. We're sorry we can't taste some.

On the upper bank the market is in progress. It is chiefly fish. Canoes parked side by side in the water are full of shining silver fish. More fish are piled on leaves on the steep bank. People swarm up and down the muddy slopes. A few stands sell strange skinny bean pods, limes, and roots (which must be Manioc). Under one stand are 3 or 4 small monkeys (with whitish faces and yellow legs – very appealing), in a cage with one turtle. (Do people eat monkeys here?) Another stand has a boy in a white chef's cap selling French bread! We walk until we reach a dead end – a loose plank bridge on high pilings tottering over a deep canyon. The jungle confronts us. We hear the morning noises of birds, mostly parrots and parakeets, coming from lofty trees. Walking back, we notice several small restaurants with families eating breakfast.

After returning on board, and having coffee, we start out again with the children, who are upset because we hadn't called them at 6. "But I thought you weren't interested in going around with your old parents!" I challenge Eva.

"Oh, I just said that because I was angry!"

"You know we don't want to miss anything. I'd like to take photographs, too," Jerzy adds.

This time we walk along the other bank. Here are a row of frame shacks marked "Fauna Tropical"; "Zoological Gardens"; "Pelts, Skins, Animals Stuffed and Alive". This is the enterprise of Mike Tsalakis, an American-Greek, entrepreneur of many enterprises in Leticia. "If you want anything, just ask Mike!" the saying goes. (Everyone calls him "Mike", unusual in formal South America.) Besides catching jungle animals for zoos in the U.S., he organizes hunting trips and expeditions into the jungle. He advertises in Bogotá, and even in New York. An article about him appeared in "Readers' Digest" last spring, and in another periodical a picture showed him wrestling with an alligator!

Four young men, standing near the buildings, accost us. They offer to take us to the "grande" zoo, up the hill. They cut across a jungle path, under elephant-ear bushes, through which parrots flit. The narrow path is so muddy that planks and logs have been put down, but they have long since rotted and sunk beneath the mud and slime. I slip and slide in rubber Japanese sandals, and have to take them off to get up a perpendicular bank. On top, we find an open space, with a big, shed-like structure housing snakes, monkeys and parrots. The poisonous snakes, "Jacaranda" (or "Fer-de-Lance), one could not see plainly behind two barred and screened doors. The next cage housed monstrous anacondas, glistening in the sun. Two lay coiled together. They looked like one, but had two heads! They were 18 feet long (short for these!) Their bodies and heads were broader and fatter than I had imagined. They looked so powerful that it was obvious that they could easily crush your bones. I have seen them before in zoos, but never so fresh, so powerful, so healthy. In the same cage, iguanas crawled or sat. One was laying a white egg right next to an anaconda. She wasn't afraid.

The monkeys depressed us. There were cages with hundreds, their side touching as they sat in long rows. They were the same kind we had seen in the market. They were playful and lively, having just been caught. They, unfortunately, were all destined for the laboratory. I read recently that there is such a demand for monkeys for labs that they are in danger of being exterminated. No wonder that we have hardly seen any along the river. One cage containing a few was marked "sick". Another cage had a sloth, and 2 dark grey woolly monkeys. "Rare", said one of the boys. We didn't catch the species' name, mentioned very fast in Spanish. "Black and White Whisky" were the only English words these boys knew!

Outside, were cages of birds, particularly the huge blue heron we have been seeing, which would be a show-piece in northern aviaries. A tank of "Cayman", (the Amazon alligator), which comes in two shades, white and black. The black are the more dangerous. Here they only had small, young ones. A tank of electric eels was rather repulsive. They are large, slimey, and black. They are one of the menaces of the river for humans and animals alike.

A sign on the shed reads: "Tarpon Zoo, Field Station". On another small shed we find the information that it is the Field Research Station for the Bowman Gray and Louisiana State University Schools of Medicine.

I am sorry that Mike himself did not appear. He is 35, a live wire, and willing to help fellow Americans in little things such as changing money. We did need to change some at this point! George had left his dollar bills on the ship. Actually, Jerzy was the only one of us who had single dollars. George did not want to change a $20. bill he had in his pocket, as we did not need a lot of Columbian money. Therefore, how to tip our guides was a problem.

We all started to walk down the main road to the ship, passing a man pushing a wheel barrow with freshly caught "Tiger Fish" (a medium size fish with black stripes). George and one of the young men from the zoo launched into a political discussion. The oldest and most intelligent-looking one, tall, well-dressed, with dark glasses, said:

"I've never been to the United States, and I don't want to go! I don't like the United States!"

"I am a Nazi! And I think Hitler was great!" another youth said, enthusiastically.

"They say he is still alive in Argentina," someone said, excitedly.

"Well, if he is he would be over 80 today, and no longer a menace," laughed George, in a soothing manner. "But how can you say you like Hitler?"

"Germany will come back, Germany will reconquer Europe!" another voice shouts. "I love Peron!" yells still another. "He is an intelligent man. He should come back and conquer America."

At this point, we see on a building the emblem of the U.S. Consulate, a consoling sight. "I think we'll go in and pay our respects," suggests George, to put an end to the inflammatory conversation.

Inside. a young Spanish beauty sits behind a desk, surrounded by Indian masks, beads, drums, blow-pipes, poison arrows, and modern primitive paintings in the style of Miro.

"We just came in to pay our respects to the United States!" says George, gallantly, in Spanish.

"I don't understand, Señor," she says, in a bored tone. The young men, who have followed us in, explain: "It seems this is no longer the Consulate. It is just a Consular Agency." (Mike again?)

Down by the steep bank above the wharf we wait for Jerzy, who has gone on board to get his dollars. The most "intelligent-looking" young man has disappeared, probably thinking that he wasn't going to receive a tip. The political argument rages on with the others.

"Franco is great!" roars a voice.

"De Gaulle, there is a great man!" shouts another. Well, at least we could look a little bit more enthusiastic about him.

A big flock of parrots fly across the road.

"Parrots! Look, look! You can see their colours!" I wave my arms in the air ecstatically, but George did not look up, and forges ahead with the conversation.

"What do you think of the Negroes? I have noticed that there aren't many in this town."

"Negroes!" The Hitler-lover's face contorted with rage.

"If I had a machine-gun, Boom, Boom, Boom! I'd shoot them all like that."

"Parrots!" I jump up and down on the road, and dance around with joy, as another flock swirls past. No one notices.

Suddenly I have it. The Klu Klux Clan! All three young men look like members. Tense, sharp faces, mean mouths, crafty eyes.

Jerzy is back. He can't find the dollar bills. An argument starts about how to get some change. Eva says she has one dollar. "That will be enough!"

"May I change one dollar?" George asks.

"How about $10.?" they say greedily, all at once. "Or an Express cheque? I change Express cheques!" One of them sticks a greasy letter of recommendation under George's nose.

"How about changing the $20. into Peruvian Soles?" I suggest. "Do you take Soles?"

"Sure! Sure! We'll make change. Any kind of change."

"May I help?" an elderly man wearing a hat steps forward, holding a U.S. passport. "I'm headed for Iquitos. Going up by Navy plane. I went from Belém to Manaus in the paddle-wheeled SNAPP Line boat, then flew here. The whole thing only cost $50. Booth Line wanted $180. Don't let these guys gyp you! I have the official rate of exchange here." He holds up a printed card. "26.50 soles for an American dollar."

One of our Nazi boys has already drifted away. The others exclaim: "No! No! We'll only give 24 to the dollar. The soles have changed value since you got that card."

George looks disapprovingly at them. The American looks very stiff and proper under his hat. For a minute the crazy idea comes into my mind that he may be a missionary travelling to a mission (as he mentions that he knows about the "Linguisticas" near Pucallpa – who are translating the Bible into 26 different Indian dialects). But he turns out to be a mere tourist, a Dane of U.S. citizenship.

Two young American girls appear in tight pants, low-cut blouses, and big fancy straw hats. A blonde and a brunette from California! They have flown in from Bogotá, and are going for a 2-day hunting trip. They are Hollywood's dream-girl safari-goers.

We look around. The last two of our young men have vanished. George looks relieved. But I don't feel right.

"They did guide us around, and they did deserve a tip, even if they were Nazis! Not giving them one will give the U.S. a bad reputation. The next people who want to see the zoo won't be treated well.

"Don't you worry! These fellows weren't connected with the zoo. They just happened to see us, and wanted to contact some Americans."

I walk back to the ship feeling uncomfortable. After all, everyone expects to be paid for favours here.

The "American Intellectual", who we had previously noticed getting out of a boat, is standing again wistfully near the *Veloz*. Is he longing to leave Leticia? Yesterday, when we saw him, he was just returning from an expedition by motorboat across the river to a lagoon, where the "Victoria Regia" grow – the mammoth water-lily pads. His opinion of the Hotel Victoria Regia is that the food is awful! Beans and rice for breakfast, beans and rice for lunch, beans and rice for supper! But maybe the local people like beans and rice?

On board the ship a small, pretty-ish, but dirty Indian woman stands by the gang-plank, holding a baby close to her body, wrapped, papoose-style, in a shawl. She has on a long, tattered skirt, and wears several strands of red and yellow beads, which brighten her rather miserable appearance. She is selling a case of rings, very cheap factory-made merchandise.

"Couldn't we buy her colourful beads, just to help her?" I suggest. "Cuánto?"

"500 Pesos. This all real coral, Señora. Each bead is threaded by hand. Mucho trabajo!"

"How much is that?" I ask George.

"Why, that is about $30.!"

"Thirty dollars for that junk, and it isn't even real coral! I thought it might be 2 or 3 dollars."

"Better not buy it," says Ogonowski, loudly, coming out a door. "The price is so high because I take 15%!" (He said this to scare the woman, and to warn us, he tells us later.)

"Have you any radios?" asks the woman, crudely.

"Yes," answers George, "we have a radio, but just for ourselves."

We climb the stairs to the upper deck, feeling disgusted. A poor Indian degraded by the border town. "She's probably got a radio and a TV at home in her miserable shack!" I meanly think. "Maybe she just dressed like that to get sympathy, like a gipsy." A horrible suspicion arises that those poor Indians we gave the clothes to were also just acting a part.

We are leaving Leticia. The heat is oppressive. "The temperature of the water is 84 degrees and the air about 88. Not really so hot. Its the atmospheric pressure and the humidity. Phew!" groans Mr. Resson, mopping himself with his wet towel. He is in a bathing suit. I still have on my slacks and feel most uncomfortable.

Conflicting thoughts about Leticia crowd my head.

Fascinating, free; anything goes, like an American frontier town of the old West. Smuggling, diamonds, dope – anything! Arms! Castro plots. Nazi revivals. And the Indians are the victims.

"Now I know why the Peruvians won't support Dr. Binder," says George. "The Spaniards feel the land is theirs. They want the Indians out of the way. The fewer Indians that survive the better."

I go in and plunge, head and all, under a cold shower. Perhaps this will help sort out my thoughts.

"The clouds, the water, vegetable and animal life! This is the real Amazon, and from this comes its sense of freedom," I think later on. "And Indians living as they are used to, part of the natural environment. Greed and the worst cruelty came with the white settlers.

"But the law of the jungle is kill or be killed. Isn't this also true of human life? The Indian tribes fought each other. Nazis killed Jews. Russians killed Poles. Why not Spaniards (or Peruvians) killing Indians?

"It may be a natural law, but I refuse to accept it," I answer myself, stubbornly.

For me, at least, this is the moment of freedom, floating in enchantment. Enjoy it while you can, I think. Soon it will be over. Back to tract houses, super-markets, freeways, TV, P.T.A., Republicans, Democrats, and all the rest of it, such as trying to be friendly to your neighbour with whom you have nothing in common. Possessions. House-cleaning. Income Tax.

"All that does not worry me one bit!" says Eva, when I tell her what I've been thinking. "I just go my own way."

"You're lucky if you can," I grumble.

Storm clouds have covered the sky. Lightning flashes, stick lightning shoots down. This time we hear thunder. "Exactly 3 and a half miles away," George has timed it.

Birds fly nervously from trees. Trees have gotten taller as we sail upriver, many are real giants. Even the palms are immensely tall and spindly. Emerald-green steep hills emerge, covered with palms, á la Gauguin. Here cattle keep the grass cropped. Primitive rafts are being pulled up stream, almost submerged by their loads of 20-gal. gasoline tanks. We pass our Booth Line tug, with barges. The tug is called the *Stemwinder*, a funny name! We salute each other by 3 blasts on our respective horns. Our 3rd blast goes way up off key, and really made me laugh. (I had rushed out on deck, thinking it was boat drill again, for sure!)

The temperature has fallen, and now there's a steady, quiet rain. We are going very slowly. There are only 3 feet to spare underneath our hull! The officers explain that in case we do go on a sandbank, the barges we passed will come and take off our cargo. Then the tug will push us off.

"Once one of our ships spent 40 days on a sandbar," says Mr. Resson.

"I'm a witch!" I exclaim, gleefully. "Today I said I hoped we'd go on a sandbank so that we'd have longer on the ship!"

"I really think you'd enjoy it, at that," he replies, thoughtfully.

At dinner, we laughed like mad. Tears rolled down my cheeks. I can't remember when I've laughed so hard. We were discussing pills, and how we have a suitcase full of 600 anti-dysentery tablets but haven't used one yet! 600! Dr. Binder had told us to take them for 3 weeks after getting home, also.

"Two of our former passengers used to take pills all the time," said the Captain. "`Where does this water come from?'" they'd ask. `New York', I'd say. Plump! two tablets went into their water. Breakfast, lunch and dinner! Pills before meals, and pills afterwards. Later on, `Where does this water come from?' again. The river, I'd say. Plunk! in went the pills.

"I bet that doctor who recommended those pills just wants you to give them to him for his patients when you get up to Pucallpa. He just needs some pills. Any kind! As for me, I hate to take pills, and never do if I don't have to."

"We had two horrible children here once," someone continues. "Children of missionaries. They were born out in the jungle. Never saw regular food. `I don't like that!' one would say, and throw his food on the floor. `I want monkey!' `I don't like that! I want snake!' the other would cry, also throwing his food on the floor. Nasty little tykes."

"Yes, we've had some pretty horrible passengers. Like the crazy flutist," continues the Captain. "Was a retired flutist from the Philadelphia Orchestra. He really played beautifully. But he went berserk when we got into a little fog out of New York harbour. Was rushing all over the ship bothering us. Thought we were going to sink. I had to tell him to stay in his cabin, or we would lock him up! Later, when we went past his door we saw him and a missionary fellow he was sharing the cabin with both on their knees, praying!"

"Of course, we consider you to be the model passengers!" adds Ogonowski, quickly. "Never in our way. No special demands. As for me, the less I have to do with passengers the better. They're a nuisance. Served on a big passenger ship once and hated it. All that organized entertainment, and dressing for dinner, and having to be pleasant all the time. Give me a freighter any day!"

"But you're pleasant to us!"

"Yes, but this is a freighter. Our life isn't geared to the passengers. The passengers here are incidental, and they can take us or leave us."

Thursday, August 25

We have been packing all morning, as we are due in Iquitos early tomorrow. We have filled the two largest cases with things we don't need, to be sent back to New York, including the useless movie camera! So part of us will go back with the *Veloz*. We are getting sad and sentimental about leaving her. She has been our happy home for almost 6 weeks, and the crew our friends and companions in what to us has been high adventure. I'm still hoping she'll get stuck on a sandbar, so we won't have to get off tomorrow! Mr. Resson says he wouldn't mind her getting stuck in Iquitos for 6 weeks, as long as he could go ashore. But the Captain says it wouldn't be any rest for him, as he knows too many people, and he would have to do too much drinking.

"You mean you are invited out a lot? I suppose South Americans are very hospitable?"

"No, it isn't that. They all swarm on the ship, and they'll drink anything!"

Last night we anchored from 2 AM until 6, as they were afraid of sandbars, and the visibility was poor. The steady, quiet rain turned into a torrential downpour right before breakfast. George had gone to take a shower, while I was still in my bunk, when it swept in through the forward port and drenched a letter George had been writing, which lay on the table. Its so blurred that he won't be able to send it.

He takes this as a sign that he shouldn't really have written to this particular person, whom he hadn't seen for 35 years. So, he won't rewrite the letter.

The motorboat was launched in the middle of the morning, with Mr. Ogonowski at the tiller, and 5 other men with him. They started out on choppy waves, and the boat was bobbing around so much while they were trying to start the motor (which gave them trouble) that we were afraid that they'd crash into the side of the ship. They were all in raincoats, as it was still pretty bad weather. (The temperature has fallen to 70 degrees, really cold for here. Actually, one could hardly imagine that it could ever get this cool.) No sooner had they gotten started than the motor died again. In one minute, the little boat was drifting downstream. It looked overloaded, and there was no sign of life-preservers. Fortunately, they got it started soon again, and went speeding away upstream until they disappeared around a misty bend. They had been sent out to take depth readings to see the condition of the channels ahead. The river is still dropping 6-7 inches a day, in spite of the rain. Today, due to the rain, we saw several waterfalls gushing from side streams over the banks.

We sat at anchor until about 1 PM, waiting for their return. Their report was that one channel (the one that is usually shallow) now has 17 ft. of water, while the other (which is usually deeper) has filled up with sand – which proves the rapidity of the changes here. We need 16 ft. to get through safely – so we only have 1 ft. to spare! George says this isn't very much, but

Ogonowski says its plenty.

"Even if we scrape bottom a little it isn't serious!" Just after anchoring during the worst rain, George said that some poor Indians were alongside in a canoe. "Really authentic-looking Indians, this time," he added. I had a bunch of clothes I had weeded out of my suitcases: 3 straw hats from Arizona (which none of us had ever worn!), a faded sweat shirt, and my old yellow Japanese rubber sandals. George dropped them over, and the Indians caught them. I didn't go out to see them, as I was busy packing at the time, but George reported that they were definitely "real" Indians.

About an hour later, the steward came to our cabin and said that the Indians were back, and wanted to see us. They had presents for us!

This was the most touching experience of our trip. Such a contrast to the corrupted Indians in Leticia. We found a huge dugout canoe tethered to our stern, containing a family of about 12 Indians; young boys, teenage girls, little girls, a baby; and a middle-aged woman who must have been the mother. They all wore colourless clothes full of holes, rags, really; but they were looking up at us with joyful, happy faces. Their boat was full of bananas, oranges, fish, parakeets, and a monkey. "They say they've brought you this in return for the things you gave them," the steward called from below. A rope was lowered, and a huge stem of small ripe bananas (the best!) was pulled up and deposited at our feet. Then a bucket was lowered, and came up with a basket of gleaming, silver fish!

Jerzy rushed in, and found two more of his shirts that he didn't really need, for the boys, and threw them down. They landed in the water, but were quickly retrieved. Then the bucket went down again, and up it came with oranges, the green jungle kind (unwaxed, uncoloured, and very sweet), plus two bunches of large cooking bananas (plantains). All their faces were beaming. The first happy Indians I think I've ever seen! As a family, they closely resembled each other, and all looked healthy, energetic, and physically attractive. Even the older woman did not look too careworn, but looked as though she still enjoyed life, even although poor. We enjoyed them all so much that George rushed back into the cabin, and got a white foam cooler box (which he had used to protect the movie films from dampness), and threw it down. Then they pointed to the parakeets. There were a dozen loose in the boat, and some in a basket – all brilliant green and gold. But no! we couldn't take one with us. We had to shake our heads. Finally, they held up the monkey, a small, cuddly looking one, which sat on the lap of one of the girls like a cat, while she patted it. I would have loved to have had him. But we really couldn't travel with a monkey! People say that they get pneumonia very easily. I'm sure he couldn't have stood going over the Andes, or even adjusted to our Monterey climate. Again, we had to shake our heads. By now, the crew were leaning over the edge bargaining for birds. A basket load of parakeets went up over the side, and then another. Our dining room steward got three for his wife.

"I don't see much point to them," said Mr. Resson. "They don't talk." However, they are beautiful!

Paper money floated down to the canoe. Some rolls with butter were thrown to the children.

To find such warm, generous people did our hearts good, after our experiences at Leticia with glum and mercenary people. In my memory, these will always be "our Indians", the first ones with whom we had friendly contact.

Here is the real heart of Amazonas. There are fewer inhabitants than near Leticia. When we anchored, I only spotted one little palm-thatched roof far across the river. The jungle looks impenetrable, with huge forest trees, vines, lianas, etc. It is also quite hilly here, which makes communication difficult. And to get into a boat from the shore one has to climb about 15 feet down a perpendicular wall of slippery mud, from which the river has recently receded.

The fruit we were given is enough to share with everyone. And the fish

The heart of Amazonas' impenetrable jungle, viewed as we sailed close to shore.

was fried for Tea. We all ate it at our table. The Captain and Ogonowski ate theirs on the Bridge, where they are watching the tricky channels. This variety of fish is "Pucu", very good eating, said the steward. Small, round. flat, with many bones, but scrunchy and tasty when fried. However, this special batch was terribly salty. It had come salted (which I hadn't realized when I asked the cook to fry it.) He said he couldn't get all the salt out, unless he boiled it. This is my introduction to "salted fish", the only way people have of preserving it here. I don't know why writers, such as Mrs. Maxwell, think that its so bad. If one likes anchovies, its not nearly as salty as that.

We anchored again in the middle of the afternoon. There was not a house in sight. We gave three toots on the horn, and pretty soon a speedboat appeared around a bend. Four men in uniform climbed on board the *Veloz*. The Peruvian Army! Just as they were going in the door, one of our stewards was seen trotting along the deck after them, carrying 3 cases of beer. They disappeared into the Smoking Room. Pretty soon our passports were called for, the first time anyone has asked to see them on the whole voyage. (I suppose this is because we are leaving the ship in Iquitos.)

Later on, we, ourselves, gathered for a drink, in Mr. Resson's cabin, with the Captain. A kind of farewell cocktail hour. But we don't have to prepare ourselves to leave too early tomorrow, as we won't get in to Iquitos now until around 4 PM, the Captain thinks. The *Veras* (the ship that ran onto a sandbar) is ahead of us, and even at 4 o'clock may still be at the berth (there is only room for one ship at a time).

Another boat has now been sent out to measure the depth. It didn't take so long this time. Right after tea, we start moving along at half speed. The rain has stopped. A wet- looking moon shimmers through the clouds. Fog hangs low on the banks. The water is indistinct, with black streaks – sandbars? The mosquitoes have come out, too, and we spray ourselves every few minutes.

"Well, I'll go and keep the Old Man company over his gin. He might be lonely," says Mr. Resson. He calls the Captain "The Old Man", although Richard is really a good deal younger. Mr. Resson was retired from the Royal Navy, but although past retirement age, then joined the Merchant Navy. He enjoys the life at sea, and does not want to just sit at home.

When we go into our cabin, George opens a bill from the Chief Steward. Here it is:

Mr. Podbereski- summary

	£.	S.	d.
84 Coca Cola	4.	4.	0.
27 Beers	1.	4.	9.
5 Pepsi Cola		5.	0.
7 Soda		9.	0.

1	Vermouth		12.	6.
7	Whisky	7.	17.	6.
3	Rum	1.	17.	6.
1	Gin		12.	6.
		£ 17.	2.	9.

£ 17. 2. 9. @ 81 d to 1 dollar
= 50 dollars   78 cents

So ends our last night on "The Drinking Ship".

18. THE HEADWATERS

Friday, August 26

Woke up to find that we had navigated the sandbars successfully, and that we were in Linares, within sight of Iquitos, before breakfast.

Linares has an oil refinery, with oil from Pucallpa and Oriente. This has neat little houses for the workers. There is also a sawmill. The *Veloz* takes loads of veneer down river from here. Linares looks too modern to be interesting. However, the Linares River has crystal clear water, and is safe for swimming. The Navy School is also at Linares, across the Linares River by ferry from Iquitos.

While we were on deck, waiting for breakfast, Scrunch, Scrunch! We scraped bottom. First I thought it was a log hitting the propeller. The ship shivered. The propeller is damaged. It will have to be examined when the cargo is removed. Anyway, the ship will have to get back to Belém even if she has to go into drydock there. But the officers think they can get back to New York OK by compensating with the motor.

Upon inspection, the propeller does turn out to be damaged in two places! Just when we were thinking we had gotten up here safely.

At 8.30 AM we had arrived in Iquitos, where the Amazon headwaters mingle.

All we see is a sawmill of the most primitive variety. Logs are floating in the water. and one man in swimming trunks pushes them one by one from the water to a conveyor belt. We anchor here. Several hundred yards ahead is the *Veras*, busily loading. There is nothing else in sight but a few moored palm-roofed boats, and a 2-decker riverboat, badly in need of paint, having her propeller repaired (she must have struck bottom, too!) A man is working on her waist deep in the water, although the water here is opaque and full of garbage, and he would be unable to see snakes or electric eels. This is one of the riverboats that go up to Pucallpa, on the Ucayali, and we'll take it, or one like it, if we go. It does not look encouraging.

Iquitos, what we see of it from here, is unimpressive. The only large building – elongated, one-story, with a corrugated iron roof – has a cross on it. Missionaries! The main part of the town is up a hill out of sight, a little further upriver.

The river is now down about 25 feet from the high water mark, from the looks of the banks. One sees the high water line clearly on tree trunks. A girl climbs up and down carrying a container of water on her head. She is dressed quite decently, and wears sandals. Another girl scrubs clothes in a wash basin on the deck of a houseboat. Small speed boats rush up and down, and 2 barges pass carrying drums of oil.

"The 40 Thieves" come on board, as the Captain jokingly calls them. Actually, there were 15 or 20 men, just to clear us with Customs and Immigration! Our passports and vaccination certificates were examined, our private store of liquor checked and OK'd. Then we – our family – were officially admitted into Peru.

The officials all leave the ship laden with presents (cartons of cigarettes, whisky, etc.) on the tug *Samuel*. I guess its good to keep them all happy. Later, the *Samuel* returns bearing the news that the *Veras* won't sail until 6 AM tomorrow. We are given our choice as to whether we want to leave on the *Samuel* now, or stay until the *Veloz* docks. We decide to stay.

Later, the Captain receives the news that the *Veloz* won't leave Iquitos before Sept. 15th, as the *Veras* has taken all the cargo, and there won't be any more until then. They will have to wait for a load of lumber to come down river from Pucallpa. Time for us to go up to Pucallpa, he says, cross the Andes, see Cuzco and Macchu Picchu, then fly back here from Lima, and get back on the ship. On her return trip, she will stop at British Guiana (now called Guyana), but skip the West Indies. Very tempting! We are playing around with the idea of going back on her, in case there are no other passengers booked – we have to find out about that from the Shipping Agent. It would be a lot more fun than the plane. The only hitch (and this is what worries George) is that the kids would be much later in starting school.

Cold salmon for lunch, a farewell delicacy. George comments that he'd be more enthusiastic about returning on the ship if the food was real gourmet French cooking! He seems pretty serious about this, but I think that's a minor point myself.

Everyone off duty is flat out after lunch for "la siesta". This does not include myself. I think a siesta is a waste of time, when I could be watching what's happening on the river. I restlessly head for the deck, walking along the hall past the Captain's cabin. His door is open, and he beckons me in, then shuts and locks it.

In less than a minute, without anything being said, we are in each other's arms. When we come up for air, Richard says that he had left it as long as he could, but it was now or never. He had to tell me that he loved me. He could not let me go! I answered that I loved him, too.

What a nerve-wracking situation! There was no time left to talk. How would we ever sort things out? We could, however, arrange to meet on shore, as the ship would be in port for so long. By good fortune, we had planned to remain in Iquitos for about 10 days. I had previously suggested having the Captain and the two "Chiefs" for an evening get-together in our hotel. Richard said when they came, that he and I could arrange how to meet alone.

Later in the afternoon, several dramas occur which have a depressing influence on George. First, he receives a letter saying that Jadwiga (his ex-wife, who lives in Poland) has been in the hospital for almost two months with eye trouble – something wrong with the nerves, and that she's almost blind. As she is an art restorer by profession, this is really awful. He still cares for her enough to blame himself that we have been on the ship all this time and had not received this news before. However, we did get mail in Belém.

Second, the matter of tipping. George tips the two main stewards, the dining room steward and our room steward, who are the ones who did the most for us. He wanted to be really nice to them, and gives each $20. American money (although Ogonowski says that $5. would have been enough). In addition, he had added about $10. in Trinidad "Bewees" that he wanted to get rid of. They seemed overjoyed, he said. The room steward even brought me a cup of coffee along with the officers' in the middle of the morning – which he had never done before! And signed the check himself when George ordered 3 Coca Colas.

When he brought in our afternoon tea, he very gloomily told George that he wanted to give his whole tip back, mumbling in Portuguese-accented English something about the Chief Steward. George could not understand, and went down the companionway to find out what was wrong. It seems that the two stewards had told an assistant steward, who sometimes brought in our tea, but whom we rarely saw, about their tips, and this man wanted a share. The stewards said they would share equally with him (maybe that's the system on these ships) but looked glum about it.

We told the Captain and Mr. Resson about it. They both said to let the stewards sort it out themselves, that we had given enough.

George, when mulling it over, decided this might cause a dangerous situation, that in South America, where people are inflammable, the neglected steward might even get someone to attack us on shore! (Shades of Jack London!) He decided that he had made a mistake neglecting this man, and went down to tip him, too. On the way, he met the Chief Steward, who told him not to. So he didn't, and came up again, looking even more worried and depressed. I told him he had done his best, and now he should not think any more about it. But this is the kind of episode that always gets him down.

Third worry: Ogonowski was on deck, and had been talking to Eva. When she wandered off, I asked him whether Eva had given him the drawing of hers he had asked her for to send to his daughter. Eva had decorated the walls of her cabin with her drawings, which were much admired by the officers. He answered no, but he would not bother her about it. I said she had kept it out for him, and that it was in her room. He repeated not to bother, that there was plenty of time in the future. I thought his voice sounded very cold and wondered why? Later on, he asked us to his cabin for a drink of wine before tea. Then he said he'd better tell us something about Eva. He had thought that she was a lovely girl, but now he did not think so anymore. The Chief Steward had gotten a paper-back from Eva (which she gave him for the ship's library), and in it was written her name, Eva Podbereski, and the "Peace Sign". Well, that part was OK. But underneath, in the same handwriting, was "Fuck the Birchers". The Chief Steward couldn't believe his eyes and took the book to Ogonowski. (The Chief Steward was the one who had been worried that I might hear bad language on the ship!) Ogomowski couldn't believe it either, but we all looked at it, and it definitely was in Eva's handwriting.

"Well, I think this isn't very nice," said Ogonowski. "But maybe she just wrote it childishly, and it doesn't mean anything to her."

"I don't think she wrote it childishly, but I know why she wrote it!" I say. "In California so much has been said about freedom of speech! Freedom for writers to say anything. I agree that writers should have freedom. But swear words should be saved for some more expressive purpose, when a writer is describing some tough sailors' conversation, for instance. I have never used such words in everyday language, and neither has George."

George says grimly: "Dale, you don't know anything about California trends of thought or what the young groups of Hippies in San Francisco believe. You just sit at home and never meet these people. You just philosophize! Eva has picked this up at school. It is not childish at all, it is deliberate, and I don't like it."

Ogonowski replies: "I think its better not to mention it to her," but his voice is cold. I see that we have gone down in his estimation, as we have revealed ourselves to be parents who haven't properly educated our children.

George tears out the page, and sticks it in his pocket with a frown on his face. Later, he tells me it is much worse to write such a word than to say it. He himself says "Shit!" sometimes and thinks nothing of it (that's because he does it humorously). I think just the opposite. If you write such a word, it isn't in thoughtless anger, but for some expressive purpose. "But to use such a word for a political movement doesn't make sense," he adds, puzzled.

Unfortunately, the whole episode struck me as being funny. If I read and defend Henry Miller, who has been called the greatest American writer of the 20th Century, even the greatest writer in English of the century (which I don't agree with, although he had to exist and be recognized in order to clear his era of literary stagnation, as Lawrence did for the earlier generation) then this fuss about words is comical. But George would not understand this kind of humour. On the otherhand, I do not use such words myself, not because I consider any word to be immoral, but for esthetic reasons. But can one teach a proper use of words? If one does not have an inner sense of balance concerning this, then just saying its wrong to use a word won't help. Some people might say that Eva does not have the right values because she doesn't go to private school, or to church. Others would say that we have made a mistake in living in California (Many residents of the East coast of America still think of California as being crude and wicked.) But none of this has anything to do with it! Eva thinks swearing is smart, modern, and expressive. As long as she thinks this, it is her own honest opinion which others can't change. Of course, a lot of people won't like her for it, and they will blame us as her parents.

On top of all this, nervous tension has spread amongst the crew. A sailor, a tall Negro, has come down with a fever, maybe malaria, and has had to be sent to the hospital. Ogonowski says that a lot of people born in the tropics, particularly Negroes, catch fevers easily when they change climates by going to northern ports, even to New York in the summer; therefore, they are unreliable as sailors.

This evening, we sat on deck until about 8, then had a drink in the Captain's cabin – without Ogonowski, who has disappeared.

Our last night on the *Veloz*. George is gloomy. He doesn't drink much, and says he is sleepy, and does not want to sit up late. He says he doesn't know if he wants to take the ship back after all. He uses Villanova and the well as an excuse, but I don't think that has anything to do with it. Tension has spread over all of us.

To lighten the atmosphere, the Captain started talking about cats, and told us about his pet ocelot, which finally ended up in the Bronx Zoo. After a year's absence, he visited it, and the ocelot recognised him – like Elsa! He says he thinks the story "Born Free" is absolutely true, and that cats never forget. He likes cats particularly; actually, he likes all animals.

Saturday, August 27

When we looked out at 6 AM the river was covered with fog. One could not see more than a few feet. This condition must be caused by our nearness to the Andes. I've read that the airport here is often closed by fog.

Around 8, it burnt off. The *Veras* has pulled out from the dock, and has anchored in the river. By 8.30 we tied up to another floating dock as in Leticia, with a steep bridge leading from it up the high bank. There are warehouses at the top. The bridge here is a permanent steel structure, with a cog railroad for freight in the middle, and walks for pedestrians on each side.

This port does not have the charm of Leticia, which seemed completely free and unregulated. Here, the Military and the Customs give a heavy feeling to the place. The dock is separated at the top of the bridge by barbed wire, behind which silent people stand watching. One woman started to walk down towards the ship, but was rudely sent back by a guard. Watch towers (as for concentration camps) guard each side of the bridge. At present, they are empty, but their look is ominous. The officers say that up to a short time ago, girls could come and go freely to the ship – to do washing and ironing, or for

Iquitos – the Floating Dock, with Pat Nicholls, the Booth Line agent in the foreground looking up at our ship.

any other purpose – but no longer, sad to say. I do not like this feeling of constraint, but perhaps strict vigilance is necessary, due to increased drug smuggling.

Going ashore is like cutting an umbilical cord. George has definitely decided not to return on the *Veloz*. (I never really believed he would want to.) He is afraid it would be "too much of a good thing", as he expresses it. He says its better not to repeat the same experience right over again. Additionally, its more reasonable not to keep the children so long out of school. I sense, moreover, an annoyance with our life on board the ship. As I got more enthusiastic, he became less so, feeling increasingly uncomfortable.

At 9 o'clock we say good-bye to the officers. We stand rather stiffly on deck, shaking hands all around. George's voice sounds very formal and correct, expressing "our wholehearted thanks for having contributed so much towards making our trip the most magnificent one we have ever taken." Ceremonious bows and smiles are exchanged. The suitcases are already deposited on the deck below. My feet feel nailed to the deck. Do I really have to climb down the gangway? If it weren't for the fact that we have all spontaneously made a date to meet in our hotel room tomorrow evening for a party, it surely would have been impossible to budge. Whose idea was the party? I'm sure it was mine. Several days ago I had mentioned it to the officers. Now I hear my voice reminding them about it again. All three promise to come.

The moment had arrived to leave the lovely ship. With heavy feet we file down the steep companionway to the lower deck, then down the gangplank to the dock. Did the others look back at our friends watching our departure? I couldn't. I stood on the rough ground, staring blankly at the side of the ship, noticing big gashes like wounds, where she had scraped against the docks. Immediately, we were surrounded by custom officials dressed like Army majors, again demanding our passports – then not bothering to examine them. They just do this hoping for a present, George had previously cynically remarked.

No porters! A small, miserable stevedore carried our heavy bags all at once up the hill, piled mountainously on his back held by a strap across his forehead. He bent double under the weight, but reached the top long before us. A taxi was waiting there. We disappeared inside it, cut off as by rigid walls from the water, the ship, and our friends.

Outside the big gates leading to the docks stretches a broad, dusty road lined with cheap sailors' bars. Right next to them is a large Catholic convent and mission! Farther along are empty lots, where dozens of black condors ("urubus") fight over garbage, or lurk ominously on trees.

Town centre turned out to be 3 miles farther up the road, which runs parallel to the river. We drove past military posts the whole way. Before leaving the dock we had noticed two Peruvian Navy patrol boats, similar to the Colombian, flat-bottomed, with square frames and enormous funnels, tied up near the *Veloz*. Our hotel itself, on the promenade by the waterfront, is next to a barracks. Soldiers are seen at attention outside all day, manning machine guns. Navy, Army, and Military Police make us feel under siege. Penetrating sounds are wafted daily to the hotel rooms, during the flag-raising ceremony, from what must be the world's most out of tune brass band.

"Hotel Tourista", meeting place of the town, is expensive, (by 1966 standards!) $20. U.S. for the 4 of us. I must admit that we have the best suite, that occupied by multi-millionaire sportsman Harry Payne Whitney a couple of weeks ago, when he came here to catch dolphins. But it only consists of one fairly large bedroom with private bath, plus an enclosed veranda which has two extra beds. However, it has a balcony overlooking the river. When one realizes that this is not just any river, but the Solimões, I suppose this should compensate for the price.

We are, indeed, standing at that mysterious place on the National Geographic map which denotes the end of navigable waters for ocean-going

At Iquitos, "The Headwaters of the Amazon", the river is still wide.

vessels, and is the "starting point for many jungle expeditions", and "the Head-waters of the Amazon".

A boulevard with scarcely any traffic stretches below. On its far side is a wide sidewalk, lined with a rococo balustrade, then the river, its opaque waters shimmering in the morning heat. Directly opposite our windows, an island blocks its broad expanse. Due to its being the dry season, exposed sandbanks are visible for hundreds of feet. To our right and left are sharp curves in the river, so we cannot see far on either side.

Our hotel is large, heavily built, old-fashioned, and comfortable. As the Captain warned us, in spite of the grandeur, things don't work very well. There's no hot water in the bathroom, and only a trickle of cold. The air-conditioning went off after an hour or so. Now we're expecting that the electricity also will soon go off!

In the lobby, two gorgeous live toucans display themselves in the window on one side of the front door, while on the other brilliantly-coloured macaws sit on perches. Small boys stand by the door, selling miniature monkeys. One man brought an alligator on a leach into the lobby. I did not like that. The

A heavy load, particularly when the river is low.

alligator, out of his own element, looked very unhappy. Boys sell seed-pod necklaces and straw hats – the hats are 140 soles, or nearly $6.00! Overpriced, by far. The lobby swarms with tourists, American, English, Peruvian.

All around the hotel outside are travel agents advertising Jungle Tours. "Visit the Indians, with a cooling drink in one hand, a camera in the other!" $100. for a motor launch to take you up a tributary; or $100. an hour for a plane to the Headhunter country. What the tourists won't realize is that the headhunters are 3 hours away by plane. And, if they land there, they may lose their heads!

Shops sell masks, necklaces, and imitation shrunken heads. One Beatnik couple from Los Angeles are selling costume jewelry, made of nuts, barks, feathers, and beattle wings, at New York prices. In other words, after travelling 2,300 miles up the Amazon to escape civilization, what does one find? The same old commercial trap as everywhere else! Only much later can the special warm-hearted quality of the town reveal itself.

At first sight, Iquitos appears rather bleak and stiff. It lacks the trees and gardens of Belém and Manaus. Yet one soon discovers many old tile-covered Spanish buildings, with their traditional charm.

The waterfront esplanade, with its pompous balustrade, has caved in during high water. Part of the street is blocked off for cars. Looking a mile or so upriver, over the vast stretches of exposed sand, one sees palm-thatched houses of the very poor. I thought at first that here was the abode of Indians, but find out that it is Chinatown! Most of the residents of Iquitos are of Spanish descent, or Mestizos (half-Indian, half-white). The pure-blooded Indians, as usual, have been pushed out altogether.

All over town, men in Army uniforms wander. Later, we discover that this is the 5th biggest military district in Peru. Who are they on guard against? A governmental change? Attack from Ecuador? Colombia? Or are they still subduing forest Indians? [1]

George accuses me of having come here with preconceived ideas about championing Indians. I admit that I do have preconceived ideas, after reading a lot about their struggles. What I now see merely confirms that these ideas are correct. The only pure-blooded primitive Indians I've seen in this town are ragged, under-nourished men carrying huge burdens at the docks; or enormous packages of fish ("paiche") wrapped in palm leaves, up the steep ramp from the river to the market. They correspond to slaves! An ordinary workman's salary here is about $1.00 a day, we were told.

Sitting in the bar of the "Tourista" before lunch, waiting for Ogonowski, we slowly absorb the torrid atmosphere. The bar is the kind of place where any kind of plot or dirty business could be hatched. Decorated with bamboo walls, palm-thatched ceiling, and mahogany parquet floor, stuffed monkeys and grotesque Indians masks peer down at the customers. Hemingway or Somerset Maugham would have revelled in its entourage, and in the possibility it offers to overhear local gossip.

Its an interesting place to sit, talk, and drink. Commerce is discussed here, expeditions arranged, friendships made or broken, and love affairs blossom, while, perhaps, a secret agent – or, a writer! – sits quietly in a corner observing everything. In the evening, one can watch the sun setting blood-red on the river, and the Southern Cross arising to shine on iguanas, which crawl up every night to eat garbage dumped on the banks. Or else, Somerset Maugham's "Rain" floods the streets and the upstairs bedrooms, which have no glass protecting the windows. The water goes off, and the air-conditioning – but that's part of the fun!

Everyone who is anyone here drifts in sometime during the day, mingling with the newcomers. What else is there to do? I would say the bar attracts habitués, people who know each other, rather than the casual tourists. We were at an advantage, as we were not alone. (If you're alone, its harder to meet people, or find out what's going on.) Ogonowski, when he arrived, immediately saw the agents from the Booth Line, one a Peruvian, the other, Pat Nicholls (the Resident Manager) British. We were looking for Maryla.

The agents had already seen her in town, looking for Ogonowski. So it goes, in a small town!

At lunch, Pat Nicholls brought Maryla to our table, with her adopted daughter, Yvette, a sophisticated 17-year old (who only speaks Spanish). Maryla is Belgian, but lived in Poland and speaks fluent Polish, so its a pleasure for George to meet her. Her "fiancé", and her husband were both Polish. She fought in the war as a Captain in the Women's Air Corps Auxiliary. After the war, she came to Peru, and taught English, first at the University near Cuzco, but did not like it. "I don't like cold places. I love heat."

Her husband left her to live with an Indian woman in Lima, and she had to educate her 5 children alone. "You don't know how difficult it was for a woman alone, in a Latin country."

She now teaches English and French at the Naval School here in the morning, and works for a travel agent in the afternoon, taking people on guided tours of the jungle. She knows the jungle well, and has even been to the Headhunter country. She says she adores Iquitos, and has never loved a place more. "Here I have found a spiritual life."

Before our arrival, she had organized Harry Payne Whitney's expedition. He came here to catch some rare Amazon pink dolphins for the St. Augustine (Florida) Zoo. On his safari, she had run his camp for 12 days.

Iquitos has fast revealed itself as a friendly, spontaneous town, its people eager for new contacts. Within hours we already had many acquaintances. We were invited to dinner our first evening by a former officer of the Polish Army, who had settled here 35 years ago, and married a native Indian girl, whom he had educated. She is an elegant, distinguished hostess. He is a former Mayor of Iquitos, and one of its most respected citizens. His daughter, a graduate of the Lima Medical School, now working at the Iquitos Children's Hospital, is the most beautiful doctor I have ever seen! Iquitos is known as the "city of beautiful women", and she must be one of the loveliest. In her company, we saw our first "Morpho" butterfly, in a field near an orchid garden. Its size and brilliant iridescent blue is indescribable – a real bit of heaven.

Sunday, August 28

This evening we held the "party" with the 3 ship's officers. Not in our room, but downstairs in the bar, as no "blue laws" exist here on Sunday.

It turned out to be an unfortunate affair. George had told Eva and Jerzy that they must stay upstairs, as a bar was no place for them. However, as soon as we were all settled with our drinks, the children came downstairs anyway. They said they did not want to be left out, and wanted to join us. George became angry, saying they were disobedient. They should go right back to their room, and do as they were told. I quietly agreed.

They did not budge. Richard said calmly: "Well, they don't like being left alone, and, as they're already here they might as well stay."

George then blew his top. "Get out of my sight!" he yelled at them. He pointed to the door. "Go out on the street! Take a walk!"

Richard, as he told me afterwards, thought that this was a terrible thing to make them do. He knew the streets of South American towns, and they were no place for children at night, especially American children. He would never forgive George for treating his own children in such a way. George himself was not concerned. They would come to no harm, he grumbled. With George in this mood, I was afraid to open my mouth, and our guests were obviously embarrassed.

To my relief, the children did not stay outside long, and I soon saw them going upstairs. Our party broke up early. Before leaving, Richard took me aside, and said he would meet me here again tomorrow evening without the others.

Monday, August 29

This morning we investigated the shopping centre, which does a thriving business, due to the fact that the State of Loreto has been declared tax-free for 10 years, to encourage development. As an example, I bought a good American bathing suit for about the same price I would pay at home. Besides the river boats, many planes (a daily flight from Lima alone) bring shoppers to the town.

This evening, George accompanied me into the bar for an after dinner drink. The children had gone up to their room. When George had finished his "night-cap", he said he was tired, and going to bed. Richard appeared in the doorway, then casually walked past our table. I told George that I was not sleepy, and would stay down for a while.

"You do what you like," he muttered, glancing ominously over his shoulder. "I'm sick and tired of sitting around here seeing the same faces from the ship. We're on shore now, and the voyage has finished!"

As soon as George had left, Richard came over to where I was sitting. He said it was not a good place for a private meeting. He suggested a walk along the river.

It was hot and steamy outside, but there was no rain tonight. The sweet perfume of tropical vegetation drifted up from the river banks. We found a footpath going down to the water, where we sat under some thick bushes, well hidden from a distant light on the road. No one was down here, and, except for starlight, it was quite dark. We had our arms around each other, and were soon kissing, and making passionate love. Time stood still.

Only recently, I have found out that Iquitos has been called "the most perverted town on the Amazon." It turns women into volcanoes!

That is why, when our affair became known, people laughed, and said: "Ha! Ha! A typical example of Jungle Fever!" Isn't this what the Amazon is famous for – the stripping away of all inhibitions?

In our case, no! The river, for both of us, represented reality. We loved the river for its beauty, its wildness, and the mysterious challenge of the jungle; and, especially, because it had brought us together. But, when we left the Amazon, we knew our love for each other would still remain. From the very beginning, we knew our feelings towards each other would be true and lasting.

Richard afterwards often laughed: "If this was `Jungle Fever', it must have been a fatal case!"

Tuesday, August 30

I had not stayed away last night long enough for it to be noticeable. When I slipped quietly into the room, George did not wake up, and there was no sound from the children.

Today, we continued our sightseeing. First, I must mention breakfast in the hotel, which is notable for a specialty, ripe papaya whipped up in a blender with sugar and lime juice. Delicious!

Then, we started out with Maryla on a jungle tour. I can easily say that this was an enchanted experience. In three dugout canoes, we paddled all day

Eva Podbereski, the author's daughter, on canoe trip near Iquitos.

on a series of lakes, which were connected by narrow channels. Sometimes, we had to get out and push the boats over fallen logs, in spite of the danger of piranhas and electric eels.

Here, in the dark waters under towering trees looped with Tarzan vines, tiny iridescent fish abound, brighter than in any aquarium. Around our boats darted dozens of the illusive, shimmering Morpho butterflies. Alas, they are too swift to catch in a photograph!

At noon, we stopped for a picnic lunch. Afterwards, Maryla, machete in hand, led the way along a jungle trail. Here, we could study the exotic tropical vegetation at close range. We could feel the sticky sap of the rubber tree, or watch the leaf-cutter ants at work. A coral orchid high up caught my fancy. One of the boys who paddled the canoes climbed up and cut it for me. Maryla and I walked barefoot through the underbrush, over fallen logs, and mouldering humus, ankle-deep. It makes one feel closer to the earth. I must admit, the rest of the family looked alarmed, on account of the danger of snakes. However, I thought if Maryla did this, it was safe. No jungle boots for her! She only wore flip-flops on the expedition, so the rest of us did the same. She said snakes are rarely seen on the trails, and stay clear of people, if one makes a lot of noise. But at times we stood very quietly, listening for the Bell Bird, which we finally heard from distant forest depths.

Another day, my children and I swam with Yvette, a vivaciously lovely teenager, in Ixtacocha, a lake by the fish hatchery. A local legend says that this lake is inhabited by a giant anaconda, who guards it against intruders.

"But he won't harm us," Yvette promised. "I swim here all the time."

Entertainment is limited in Iquitos, a French girl lamented. Every Sunday the main excitement is the cock-fights. This bloody, cruel sport is at least fairer than bull-fights, as the birds are evenly matched. They do not always become seriously maimed. Some cocks live to become the champions of many battles.

I thought watching the spectators' faces was more interesting than the actual fights. Besides myself, only two other women were present. This form of entertainment appeals largely to men of the roughest variety.

While we attended the fights, Pat Nicholls, a helpful, cheery chap, took Eva and Jerzy to see his large house, a local showplace owned by the Booth Line, dating from Rubber Boom days – it even has an indoor swimming pool! Pat, who Richard told us is half British, half Brazilian, is also the British Consul (and was destined to be the last in Iquitos). He keeps a lot of local animals in the garden. It is half park, half zoo, the children told us.

A story his friends tell about Pat goes like this: One day an adventurous type of English traveller appeared in town. This man was very inquisitive, looking Pat up especially to question him about the Headhunters. Just where were they located? Was the area accessible? What were they like? Had outsiders ever visited them? Later, he came back to tell Pat that he had decided to go to see them for himself. Pat strongly advised against this. There was no point in taking such fool-hearty chances.

"Don't worry!" the man laughed. "I would enjoy roughing it in the jungle. And what a chance to see an authentic primitive tribe with my own eyes! What a story I could tell when I get home! I'll go well equipped, taking plenty of provisions and presents with me. These people will know I'm friendly."

He went on his way, and Pat heard no more about him. Some time elapsed. One day, Pat received a package from a distant outpost. Inside was a shrunken head! Pat believed that this was the head of the same man. Although shrunken, Pat believed that it resembled him! He was extremely upset, as he had been the person who had told the man where this special tribe of Headhunters could be found, although he had certainly tried to discourage him from actually going there.

Pat kept the head, and has it on display in his house, as a warning, perhaps, to other such adventurers.

Before we left Iquitos, Pat presented Jerzy not with a human head, but with a strange, large-headed furry insect, carefully preserved on cotton in a box. Although not uncommon, to us it was a new and curious species. Its head lights up at night, like a glow-worm. He also showed us one evening the largest variety of moth, whose black wings have a span of over a foot. They were congregated around a street-light near our hotel. Fortunately, the light was high up, so they did not fly down near me!

While here, we have also attended a boxing match, held in a large arena filled by practically the town's whole population. Davila, Peruvian heavy-weight champion, fought and beat an American from North Carolina, Waban Thomas. Later, in a café, we were introduced to Thomas. who complained to us that against his will the referee had forced him to stop fighting. However, there was good reason for this, as, rather past his prime, he had been taking an awful beating from Davila.

The prize-fight had the atmosphere of a college football game, with a cheer leader working the crowd up into a frenzy for Davila. The poor American had very few supporters in the audience.

Monday, September 5

Our last day in Iquitos! Richard and I had arranged to meet in town. When George, and even the children, had flopped down after lunch for the traditional "siesta" (which lasts until the worst heat of the day is over), I told them that, in spite of the overpowering heat, I did not want to waste our last afternoon sleeping, and was going to take a walk on my own to look in some of the shops.

I walked to the main plaza, where I sat down nervously in an open-air café, and ordered a coca-cola. Would Richard appear? Or would George follow me, and perhaps make a public scene?

Within minutes, Richard did appear, with a big grin on his face. He was so glad to see me, he had no worries. In spite of having taken the hot, crowded bus into town, he looked cool in light-weight trousers and a short-sleeved drip-dry shirt, here the universal fashion for men around town.

We ambled slowly around the sizzling plaza, where there was very little life, most people being flat out in cool, shuttered rooms at this time of day. The town would not come to life again until about 5. Down a side street, we saw a small hotel, called the "Lima".

"Lets get a room there for a few hours, and cool off." Richard daringly suggested. With a straight face, he went up to a bored, sweating clerk. who drooped, half-asleep, on a chair in the doorway. He explained that we were from a ship, and that "la Señora" (me!) was overcome by the heat, and needed to rest. Could we have a room for a siesta?

Richard has such a reliable look that, without any questions, or demands for passports or other identification, we were immediately taken to a clean, fan-cooled room, complete with a shower, fresh towels, and a pitcher of ice-water.

We got right under the cool shower!

A lot of love-making took place in that room. We knew we could only stay for a few hours without being missed, and there was not much time to talk, but Richard's optimistic nature would not accept any obstacles in our future together. He repeated that I was the person he had been waiting for all his life. He was certain about this, even though we knew little about each other. He knew it was right for us to be together, and that was that! I felt the same way. To me, he seemed as stable as the Rock of Gibraltar, and I trusted him absolutely. And, of course, I found him to be a most attractive man, and irresistible as a lover. We were living in the moment, intuitively, when we should have been planning when and where we would meet again. Hard-headed thinking would come later. We had so little time. We needed to be together, but that was impossible.

Richard had to take the ship back to New York. Then, he was due home for leave until his next trip on the river, but did not yet know the date of that, or which ship he would have. As for me, I could not stay with him, abandon my family, and return on the *Veloz* to New York. I had to get the children safely up over the Andes, and back into school in Monterey, before I could think of how to meet Richard again. I promised him I would somehow sort things out when I got home. In the meantime, we would write to each other.

I did not think this was the proper time to tell George, although I believed he suspected something. He would blow his top, and make the trip back unbearable for all of us, so it was better to keep quiet.

Time rushed quickly by. Too soon we were walking back to the plaza, where we had to separate, happy with the knowledge of our love, but faced with almost insurmountable difficulties.

Walking back alone to "La Tourista", my emotions in a turmoil, I met Maryla. We sat down on a bench to have a chat. Each of us was worried about her own problems.

"Oh, Maryla, I am in a terrible mess!" I confided. Not only was it not very sensible to confide in someone I scarcely knew (something I hardly ever did), but with her strong Polish associations, wouldn't she defend George, and think that I was acting outrageously? But she was there, when I needed someone to talk to, seemingly part of the environment which had brought Richard and myself together. Maybe fuzzy thinking? She had faced family difficulties herself, so she might be sympathetic, but was she unconventional? That remained to be seen. I poured out a stream of words about how I was in an incredible situation and did not want to leave, but had to rejoin George, and get the children safely home.

She appeared quite world-weary and unmoved by my story, expressing no opinion, nor making any comment at all upon the affair. Presumably, she was embarrassed by what I had confided. No doubt she had seen too many love affairs born on the river fizzle out later to be convinced that this was a great love. Then, after all, her only relationship with me was as a tour operator. All this flashed through my mind when I had stopped speaking, then suddenly I realized she was telling me her own troubles, which were financial. She poured out how she was flat broke, and needed $100. to make a payment on a house, a home for herself and Yvette.

"If I can't find $100. somewhere, I'll have to sell my daughter for a hundred!" she cried. She seemed as wrought up about this as I was about Richard. Perhaps she hoped I was a wealthy American with plenty of extra cash.

"Oh! don't sell Yvette!" I cried, alarmed. I had never heard of anything like this, and was horrified. Did she want $100. for one night, or was she selling Yvette forever? And would Yvette agree to this?

Here I was, a complete romanticist, living in a romance, suddenly confronted by a complete materialist. It would make a good scene in a melodrama! Yet, I rather admired Maryla, who was fighting for the survival of herself and her family in very dangerous conditions. Would I do as well? She, too, must have her own strong convictions.

We had no extra money with us. We needed all we had to get back to California. And $100. in the 60's still had some value. I promised Maryla that as soon as I got home I would send her the money. I told George about this later, and he thought I was crazy to do it.

"You've been taken", he remarked, scornfully. "You are too naïve." Adding nastily, "But go ahead! Its your money."

19. THE ANDES AND BEYOND

Tuesday, September 6

We have flown to Pucallpa, as the river boat looked primitive and unreliable. Unless we had our own hammocks, mosquito nettings, and supplies of food, it would have been pretty grim. Besides, the river being so low, we might be stuck on a sandbar for days. I hate to think what the sanitary conditions would be like.

It was worth flying to look down on endless jungle, cut only by the contorted curves of the yellow Solimões, which soon ended in a fork. To the right, it becomes the Marañón, to the left, the Ucayali. We followed the Ucayali.

Near Pucallpa, the forest seems to recede. The town, at this season, is in a dust bowl, where constant traffic of trucks and buses stir up the wide, unpaved streets. This is the starting place of the road over the Andes (fancily named the "Trans-Andean Highway"), the connecting commercial link with Lima. All the wind-blown sand from the bleak Andean heights seems to tumble down the slopes, swirling through the small flat town, which becomes. without a doubt, in the wet season, a mire. Pigs wander at will in and out of doorways and along the streets, followed by chickens, urubus, iguanas – and rats!

Boarding a small local bus, we travelled several miles upriver to Dr. Binder's hospital. We found it to be a modern, low-lying building, with a series of connecting verandas serving as wards. A guard at the gate regarded us suspiciously.

The Binders were away, he said. When we divulged that they had invited us to see the hospital, he called the Matron, an unsmiling, unbending Swiss, obviously displeased by our visit. Scarcely revealing any information about the place, she marched us with Germanic efficiency quickly through the wards, pointing out some modern equipment in the operating room. A personal tour by the Binders, who would have amiably talked to us about their work, would have been more interesting. As it was, an atmosphere of mistrust prevailed, perhaps due to Dr. Binder's difficulties with the Government.

We then moved on to a nearby Shipibo village, which was under Dr. Binder's protection. This looked like a prepared stage-set. A group of huts on stilts stood on hard, well-swept ground, interspersed by a few shade-giving cassia trees. Open at the sides, with palm-leaf roofs, hammocks were slung in the shelters, while outside, cooking pots simmered over charcoal fires. Dogs, pigs, chickens and naked children ran scurrying away when we appeared. The adults were clean, well nourished, and conventionally dressed in skirts and trousers. No nose-rings, beads, paint or feathers for them! They did not appear surprised by our visit. When we produced our cameras, and photographed the village, they immediately demanded money. To us, it was a flat and disappointing experience.

Wednesday, September 7

Today, we climbed into a bulging "Caminonetta" (bus), where local people were tightly squeezed. Market produce, boxes, and suitcases were heaved onto the roof. We bumped and twisted 5,000 feet up arid Andean foothills, leaving the river and distant forest behind. Jungle vegetation was now replaced with low-lying bushes and scrub. of a dull yellowish green or brown, reminding one of the Mojave Desert. However, as we approached Tingo Maria, the market town for the long, lush valley of the Rio Hullaga, the character of the surroundings again changed. Now we drove through verdant groves of citrus fruit trees, mangoes, avocados, papayas, and bananas. In spite of the altitude, a hot climate exists in this protected valley, where the soil is extremely rich.

George Podbereski with son Jerzy at bus stop
on the Trans-Andean Highway.

It was dark by the time we were deposited with our now very dusty suitcases onto a deserted, badly lit street. Fortunately, a man materialized out of the gloom, and picking up our cases, said he would guide us to the best hotel. This proved to be simple, but clean.

Thursday, September 8

I sat on the balcony outside our room this morning drying my hair, from which I had washed the travel dust. In blazing sunlight I wrote a long letter to Richard. This seemed most important. I knew that he would worry that the farther away from him I went the more hopeless our affair might seem. He might fear that I would be overcome by the difficulties that lay ahead, and that he might never see me again. I had to try to reinstate my love for him in writing. I wanted him to get my letter when the *Veloz* got down to Belém, but I did not know how long an airmail letter would take from here. It might take weeks!

I did not want anyone to see to whom the letter was addressed. Faced with this difficulty, I told my family I was going to the post office to buy some stamps, but insisted that no one come with me. With my poor Mexican variety of Spanish (beautiful Castellano is spoken in Peru) it was a challenge to find the post office. This proved to be just a tiny counter opening onto the street. My unsociable behaviour had caused bad feeling, particularly with the children, who always liked to tag along on such expeditions. However, tempers were soothed, before it was again time to take the bus, by drinking freshly squeezed orange juice from local oranges. Stalls with fruit juices squeezed on demand were on every corner. The oranges were large, with green skins, and pale yellow juice, but they were the juiciest and sweetest I have ever tasted.

The Huallago Valley stretches north to where its river joins the Marañón. A thriving agricultural centre of small farms when we visited it, besides fruits and vegetables, it was planted with coca, whose leaves, in their natural state, were traditionally chewed by Indians, to boost their energy when working at high altitudes, whether farming in rough terrain, or transporting heavy loads of produce on their backs over the mountains. When they climbed to altitudes of over 10,000 feet, such a stimulant became a necessity. For hundreds of years the Indians had been taking this with no ill effect. Sadly, with the increasing value of cocaine, the small farmers have now (1995) been squeezed off the land, and a large part of the valley converted into vast coca plantations. The coca is then taken to hidden jungle locations, where it is processed into the drug. The cocaine is then smuggled out through Tingo Maria, Iquitos, Leticia, and other off-beat localities. The once-peaceful valley is now controlled by anarchists and terrorists, such as Peru's "Shining Path", in league with international drug mafias. Farmers cannot resist the enormous sums of money offered for this crop. In Uchiza, a small town near Tingo Maria, an airport has been built, and a military base established, to fight the drug dealers. The jungle has been levelled, and desecrated with pre-fab housing built with American aid and money, to house the Peruvian Army. New specially made American river vessels are used by the Peruvian and Colombian Navies to patrol the headwaters of the Amazon and their tributaries. With soldiers and terrorists fighting each other, not only here but in Colombia and Equador, traditional ways of life are gravely endangered, and so is the environment.

But this peaceful afternoon in September, 1966, we were again in a bus being driven upwards, the road making endless zigzags. From the "puna" (sierra), to the "Altiplano", it is open, uninhabited, uniformly brown desert, disappointingly without views of snow-capped mountains or plunging gorges. Although seemingly adventurous, in actuality it was a dusty, tiring, and monotonous trip. One had no real sense of climbing, nor of change of altitude, except in the motion of the bus as it bumped and joggled continuously up increasingly steeper grades. As the afternoon progressed, we did feel noticeably colder, and more tired, having made too quick a change from the tropical valley. I gradually felt a headache coming on, and a disconnected feeling (as when seasick), but all the same was surprised to find, when finally heaving myself out of the bus, that I wobbled rather than walked into the hotel in Huanuco, where we were to spend the night.

"She needs oxygen," the hotel manager exclaimed, after one look at my white face. A row of oxygen tanks were lined up by the door, for just such emergencies. Breathing some in, I immediately felt better. We were up at nearly 10,000 feet, and I had not adjusted to this. The rest of the family were luckier, and felt OK. Perhaps a mermaid should remain at sea level.

Friday, September 9

After a good night's sleep, I could, after lots of strong coffee, pull myself together enough to visit the market. It is worth the effort of going to Huanuco to see here the real Indian inhabitants, seemingly untouched by the outside world. All wear hand-knit or woven shawls or heavy ponchos, made from the brilliantly dyed wool of llama, guanaco, alpaca, or vicuña. The men wear equally bright clothes as the women, with multicoloured knitted caps with ear-flaps, the women wearing the characteristic high-crowned brown felt bowler hats that are worn, with slight variations in shape, throughout the Altiplano. I like to imagine some jovial Victorian English salesman of Derby hats introducing them to this style!

The high plateau is well settled, with many small cultivated holdings on its rocky, poor-looking soil. Farther up along steep mountain sides we observed the stepped gardens traditionally carved out of bare rock, their soil laboriously transported up in baskets. These have been in continuous use since prehistoric times. Potatoes and maize are the main crops.

Everyone from outlaying districts comes in to the enormous open-air market. One finds not only food and household goods, but wonderful hand-woven and embroidered clothes and rugs for sale. These are for their own daily use, not just for tourists. It is one of the most naturally artistic and tempting markets to be found anywhere. The people here are entirely different from the poor, exploited jungle Indians we have seen. Although in repose their faces are as inflexible as the ancient stone Inca masks unearthed by archaeologists, yet when spoken to, although rarely smiling, they respond in a friendly and cheerful manner. Needless to say, we bought as much as we could carry, and at reasonable prices.

From here, we continued onwards, again by bus, to Cerro de Pasco, over 13,000 feet up, where we took, as advertised, "the world's highest train". This climbs over the high Andes to 16,409 feet, then descends to sea-level at Lima. Oxygen tanks were conspicuous in the carriages, but this time, none of us required them.

According to "The Times Atlas of the World", "the source of the Amazon" bubbles up from a small lake between Huanuco and Cerro de Pasco. This is in reality the start of the Rio Marañón. We can now boast that we have actually travelled over 3,000 miles from the mouth of the Amazon to its very headwaters!

So here ends my Amazon Journal.

EPILOGUE

The true "Source of the Amazon" is controversial. In the "National Geographic" of April, 1987, Loren McIntyre claims he discovered this, on October 15, 1971, coming from a lake 16,700 ft. up called in Quechua "Amazonasmaya Puquiococha" ("Source Lake of the Amazon River"). This lake feeds the Apurimac River (here in its upper regions called the Rio Hornillos), which many miles further down again changes its name and becomes the Ucayali. This is the Amazon's longest tributary.

On the other hand, Piotr Chmielinski, in the same issue of the"Geographic", says he discovered the real headwaters of the river, not far from McIntyre's lake, but coming from the melting snow field 18,000 ft. up the "Volcan Misti". The volcano Misti is due West from Lake Titicaca, near the Bolivian border.

The mighty Amazon as we know it is fed by many rivers, so perhaps it is wrong to pinpoint one single source.

Richard sighting the little island, Sombrero, from the *Venimos*

Into the Maelstrom

20. LOVE LETTERS

For Richard and myself the next few months were a period of waiting, the long-drawn out calm before a storm. On the surface, our lives continued on an even keel; but within ourselves was intense turbulence. Writing and receiving each other's letters assumed major importance. With each letter an electrical charge was building up between us which would soon strengthen to hurricane force.

Each day I vigilantly watched for the postman's truck. When I saw it approaching, I would hurry out to get the mail before it was put into our box. If I saw a letter from Richard, I would hide it in my pocket. George, who often wandered out to get the mail himself, became suspicious of my unusual behaviour, although he never succeeded in confiscating my letters.

A lively letter arrived from Maryla, thanking me for the $100. which I had sent her. George received letters, written in Polish, from Ogonowski. He translated very few extracts for me. I believe he felt the less said about life on the *Veloz* the better, and that if I received little or no news about the ship I would soon recover from what he believed to be my case of "Jungle Fever".

As soon as the children were settled back in school we ourselves became very busy seeing friends, who all seemed keen to hear about our impressions of the Amazon. We described the river and the jungle in vivid detail, although making no special mention of the ship, nor of Richard. But as the days progressed, and the trip no longer seemed a novelty, there began to be some lifted eyebrows when I did not return to my musical work, and indeed, showed no desire to do so.

"Did not the Amazon inspire some new ideas for composition?" people asked.

I could not explain that my mind was occupied elsewhere. Nor could I face the newspaper editor, who had so recently bitterly complained: "My Music Critic has gone up the Amazon – and just before the Bach Festival!"

Richard's letters to me revealed his romantic soul, and the depth of his feelings for me. Although extremely intimate and personal, I now feel called upon to share part of them with others. So many people say that the word "Love" has no meaning, and that they do not know what it is. It is important for people who have experienced it to show that it does exist, and how it has changed their lives. This mystic union of two souls (as well as bodies) is really possible.

Richard's first letter was from Iquitos, dated Sept. 8th:
"Dale, my dearest,

"Thank you Dale darling for the most wonderful letter of my life. I love you Dale like I've never loved before, this all consuming fire between us darling is as you say met only once in a lifetime. . . We were meant for each other darling and nothing but complete union would ease the agony.

". . . You've lit a tremendous fire in me I never thought capable of – one which will never die. I love you dearest one and whatever happens we will have this oneness if that's the word, there will be part of each of us inside each other for life – it can't be otherwise. Oh! Dale, we must meet again – must- must. Love like ours will find a way somehow.

". . . I do feel you near me darling however far apart we may be. . . I can say I have lived if only briefly on Ambrosia- the food of the Gods. I have never in my life written like this before Dale but the understanding and love which flowed between us like a flame made all understanding possible without words. We may have known each other in some pre dawn era which once we realised our love we know all.

"I don't have to pretend you are right here beside me, I know you are. . . We must must meet again because this is NOT Jungle Fever this is forever."

Other letters followed:

Sept. 24, At Sea

"My dearest darling Dale,
"At last we are away from the River and its jungle fever but oh my Dale I love you so much the fire is more intense than ever. . . I feel we are near and still together. Love such as ours my darling must have that oneness, we are part of each other for ever. . . Every little wave that laps the dear old *Veloz* whispers your name and your love to me. I don't have to pretend you are here my love I know you are.

"At the moment we are on our way from Belém to Georgetown, Guyana, to load shrimps for N. York. Ginger the cat is a little seasick and sitting on my lap looking pathetically at me. . ."

30th Sept. Trinidad

"Arrived here today and received your Pucallpa letter, it was forwarded on to N. York and then back here. I'm sorry you had such a tough time on your way darling but I'm with you all the time close beside as one person my darling Dale. I so love you my darling that its agony and to think it will be months before we can meet again. Even so we will always be together.

"We are only here for fresh oil and stores so will be away in a few hours arriving Charleston, S.C. on the 7th October. Write to N. York darling and tell me you love me again. I can never hear it often enough, hurry that day when we can really say it to each other my dearest one."

M.V. *Veloz*
At Sea
Sunday, 2nd Oct. '66

"My dearest darling.

"As you see we are at sea following up in the wake of Hurricane `Inez'. We are nearly up to Santo Domingo and ready to go through the Mona passage. The sky is overcast and a fairly high sea running and the dear old *Veloz* is rolling and pitching more than usual. Its now 10 PM but Oh! Dale all day I've been feeling much closer than usual to you – from dawn to now I've had that oneness as if we've been talking and touching each other. Its amazing darling how all the time we have been separated time, distance doesn't mean a thing we are so much united in our deep love that we are just one. I love you Dale so much so that I couldn't believe possible. Day and night I feel you close beside me there is a definite psychic connection between us darling. . . Its difficult trying to put it into words but Dale darling heavenly music is nearer. I feel between us words are nothing- we know.

"Well, Dale its midnight so I'm drinking a toast to us' love everlasting and now my darling I'm going to bed and dream of you. You are always with me but Oh! Dale I'm longing and aching for the reality – together united as one. Tell me why! oh! why! this should happen to me of all people an old sea dog unused to sentiment and a 100% realist but Dale it just happened and its forever."

4th Oct.

"This will be my last chance to write because I have so much accounting and letters to the office to type as I go home after handing the ship over in N. York. I am not flying home I'll go via one of the Queens. Before I go I shall write to you. . . As I said we are following up in the wake of hurricane Inez who has now turned around and is directly in my path. However she is not a great threat as the winds are now only 80 mph and the dear old *Veloz* maybe can withstand the buffeting. I hope to arrive Charleston on the 7th Oct. where I shall mail this. At present I should arrive at Brooklyn 13/14 Oct.

"Oh! Dale, I dread going home I love you so, all I think about is you. . . my dearest one why do I love you so utterly and completely, my reason is because it's mutual otherwise it couldn't be possible."

Oct. 6

"I still believe Dale we were meant for each other and our love will overcome all that's in the way of our meeting again. The dear old *Veloz* is really bouncing up and down and trying to write this on my lap and then hang on to the chair takes some doing.

"Tomorrow I shall arrive at Charleston and be there the weekend. The weather due to hurricane `Inez' has held us back a bit so I'll be very busy over the weekend bringing my voyage accounts to date. . . even alone trying to calculate this and the other I feel your nearness and darling I then go into a daydream and re-live our hours together."

7th

"I'm just two hours away from the Charleston pilot arriving there at 2 PM this afternoon. Its over three weeks since we parted and it feels like three years but I feel you are near me and our love is stronger than ever."

Off N. Carolina Coast
Oct. 8th

"We arrived at Charleston at 4 PM yesterday afternoon and sailed at 6 AM today, and us thinking we would have a nice quiet weekend to catch up on our work. Now I hope to arrive in N.Y. on Monday afternoon, the 10th.

"I mailed a long letter to you on arrival yesterday and received two wonderful letters from you my darling. Oh! Dale I love you so more than ever if that is possible and its 4 PM and I feel so close to you. We are just one darling that's what love such as ours means. A fusion mentally and physically naked and unashamed and without fear. We just know each other and no words needed. . . Please let it not be too long before we meet again. The glory and joy of that meeting will be something not often given to mortals it will be from Paradise and Venus herself.

"I'm writing this now because I know I'll hardly have a chance in N. York. When I write to you my Dale I really want to be alone and feel your nearness then I can write what I feel right out from the heart and that's just where your are and come what may my darling nothing absolutely nothing can take from us that love we have for each other. When I wrote those last letters with the outpouring of my love I was a little afraid in a sense but Oh! Dale since receiving your letters and knowing we both feel the same the joy of really knowing that it was not a `Jungle Fever' infatuation on your part if it had that would have killed me. I still can't realise the miracle and wonder of it, why such a beautiful woman and those stars for eyes would return my love and yet right from the beginning I knew we were meant for each other from the beginning of time. We had to meet, one look into each others eyes and I saw Paradise with such love and understanding that from that moment darling we were completely one and will remain so even beyond our mortal lives. . ."

"I've read your letters four to date dozens of times until I know them off by heart and when I go to bed at night I will read each one at least three or four times to extract every bit of your love from them. Then dream of our next meeting. Oh! Dale how I'm longing for that to have my arms around you – I'll never let you go again, I couldn't. In my wildest dreams I never thought

I would ever be writing letters like this but dearest Dale its so natural to write of our love and need of each other.

"I shall write again from N. York before I go home and again on the *Queen*. . . I shall also write to you from dear old Wales and you will still be with me. I'll show you the mountains, the sea and the hills because I shall be a wanderer dreaming of Monterey and you and thinking of that wonderful day to come when we are united really as one again.

"All my love sweetheart mine."

I now knew that I must meet Richard in New York when he went there to pick up his next ship. I realized that if I did that we would surely never part again.

How was I to break the shock of this to my family? I also wondered about Richard's very difficult problem with his ultra-conservative family in Wales. How would he cope with this? Did he want the disagreeable upheaval of breaking up his life at home? Or did he want a double life, as some men do? (He would have been very angry if he had known I ever had such a thought.) But he, himself, I later discovered, had had similar worries about me. I had a much younger family to care for, so for me the situation was even more difficult. We both knew we would eventually be together, but had not discussed when or how. We had been living in our own intangible world, but now the time had arrived to come down to earth. In every letter Richard had written he emphasized that he must see me soon. He could not come to Monterey, so it was up to me to make the first move.

I did not want to frighten him by demanding too much! So I wrote saying I would meet him when he came to New York "if only for one night". What I meant was that if he was only in New York for one night, and I was unable to get on his ship, still one night with him would make the trip from Monterey worthwhile. I knew subconsciously that it could never be just for one night, it would be forever. Unfortunately, I did not explain this in my letter. Mistakenly, I believed he would realize what I meant.

The days went by, then weeks crept by, but no answer came from Richard. It was well into November. What had happened? Was he ill? Or had he become so engulfed by his family life in Wales that he felt he should not communicate with me? After everything he had written to me, I knew this could not be true. He is a sincere and straight-forward person, and would never have written as he did if he had not deeply meant it. I still felt the same psychic communication between us as strongly as ever. Therefore, nothing was changed. I must ignore his silence, little though I understood it, and make plans how I could get to New York.

This upsetting period of silence was the only major misunderstanding that Richard and I ever had, and it was due to my use of words. Much later, he explained that when I had written that I would meet him "if only for one night" he was horrified. He thought that I was treating our love like a "one night stand". He took my letter to Harlech beach and tearing it into fragments, threw it into the sea. If it had not been for the strong psychic communication between us - I knew he still loved me – we might never have met again.

The use of a wrong word can wreck lives. Many times during the first year of our life together minor disagreements arose through my use of words. The American meaning of a word might be entirely different from the British, which I did not at first realize. I could be saying something insulting, and not know it. Add to that the fact that Richard often translated what was said to him into Welsh in his mind, and you have a fine muddle! But when we were together I could quickly explain my meaning of a word. As time went on, he became used to my Americanisms.

My way seemed to open up when I had the idea of saying that I was writing a book on the Amazon. This would make a logical reason to take another trip of the river, would stop unpleasant gossip, and would give Richard and myself the time we needed to reorganize our lives. Had I not kept a daily journal on our trip, excerpts from which had been published in the "Monterey Herald"?

I slowly dropped hints to George about this plan. Explaining that as we had only been on the river during the dry season, I now would need to see it during high water to give a complete picture of the environment. As the wet season started in February, I would have to go during the school year, but I was sure that George would be able to cope with the children for the period in which I'd be away. He was a good cook, handy around the house, and not involved with a steady job. In fact, I thought (although I did not say this) that it would give him a focus to his life which might be beneficial. What I had decided to do was nothing extraordinary, if one did not know the real reason behind it. Lots of wives today have work that take them away from home for periods of time. Lots of husbands of working wives look after the children!

George seemed to go along with this plan, "if it's really what you want to do". However, I had the feeling that he saw through it, and did not like it.

Next, I wrote to the New York office of the Booth line, saying that I had recently had a trip on the *Veloz*, and as I was writing a book on the Amazon, needed to make another trip. I wanted to sail again under Captain Humphreys, as he had been so helpful and knowledgeable about the area. Would they please inform me what ship he would have next, and make a reservation on it for me? I enclosed a deposit.

Fortunately, one could, in those days, live as a passenger on board a Booth Line ship cheaper than living on shore. I easily had enough in my own personal banking account to make the trip without disturbing my family's finances.

A prompt reply informed me that Capt. Humphreys was still on vacation. They did not yet know which ship he would have next, but it would not be until after the New Year. Details would be given to me later.

The dye was cast.

In January the Company wrote that Capt. Humphreys would have the *Venimos* (sister-ship to the *Veloz*), sailing from New York about the end of the month.

I departed for New York early, in case the sailing date was changed. And I sent Richard a brief letter, care the Liverpool office, saying that I loved him as much as ever, I would be in New York when he arrived, and that I had booked a round-trip passage on his ship.

Leaving home was not easy. There was an hysterical scene, with George and Eva trying to physically detain me as I went out the door. That evening, a neighbour was sent down to the motel near the airport where I had to spend the night, to try to persuade me to return home. To complicate matters, I had a terrible cold, and generally felt awful. But my conviction that I was doing the right thing did not change.

Arriving to New York the following evening after dark, when freezing winter cold had set in, I took a taxi to the hotel where I had made a booking. It turned out to be in a claustrophobic side street, my room thoroughly gloomy, with windows facing a stone wall. I was looking hopelessly around, when my step-son (whom George had telephoned) appeared at my door. Jan Tereszczenko,[1] known to the family as "Janek", was an architect then living and working in the city. He insisted that I spend the night with him and his wife in their apartment, where a tense evening followed. They did not take my love affair seriously, thinking that George and I must just be having a "lovers' quarrel", and that it would be best for me to go back to California.

Much later that night, Janek took me downstairs, where there was a bar, and over drinks exclaimed "I do not care who you sleep with!" But, he said, I owed his mother (George's ex-wife, who lived in Poland) thousands of dollars in back alimony, on which George, he claimed, had defaulted.

It was my moral duty, he continued, to pay this, rather than take a ship to South America.

George paid her a small monthly sum, which, if he had not paid for sometime would, of course, mount up. But, I thought, if George had been unable to pay, he would have told me before it added up, so I could help him out, as that had been our previous understanding. It was therefore George's responsibility to tell me, and he had never mentioned it. For all I knew, he could have cooked this up to keep me from getting on the ship.

My step-son shouted across the drinks: "You go to work in the New York Public Library until you have paid my mother this money!"

Little did he know that the New York Public Library, for which I had once worked, at that time paid so little that even if I worked there the rest of my life I would never be able to save even a few thousand dollars.

Jan then went on to describe his miserable childhood in Warsaw under the Nazi and then Russian occupation. I was sorry that any child had to grow up under these horrible conditions, but that was all in the past, and I could do nothing to remove his bitter memories.

The following morning, thoroughly depressed and exhausted, I took the train for Philadelphia, where I took refuge with my old friend Hebe Bulley and her family, whose welcoming kindness and lack of criticism was heartwarming. The, to me, sordid emotionalism of the previous night had made me feel that I had really hit rock bottom. It was an extreme test of my love for Richard not to go under. In this case, good friends were a salvation. Although they did not know Richard, and the whole situation came as a surprise to them, they were willing to accept that we loved each other, and they wished us both well.

Here, at last, a letter from Richard arrived, dated Harlech, Jan. 18, '67.

"Darling:

Thank the Lord for your letter and address. Am in a terrific hurry but will I hope see you next week.

I'm flying via Air Lingus to N. York on Monday 23rd so I hope this arrives on Saturday,

Send me your phone number. All my love my darling."

What a relief to have this confirmation of his continuing love! I only received this letter on the 23rd, but immediately sent Richard a "Special Delivery" care his New York office. I wrote:

"I'll come right over to New York today, and I shall be at the Hotel Lexington, 45th & Lexington, until I hear from you. Darling, call me right away, or better still, just come right over to see me. I won't budge from the hotel until you come!"

The next morning, the miracle happened. The phone rang in my hotel room, and it was Richard. He had been to the office and received my letter. He had no special work to do for the next few days. He had, in fact, arrived in New York a week before needed, just to be with me.

Within the hour, he was knocking at my door. There he stood, looking great in a stylish Harris tweed jacket and a jaunty Welsh tweed hat, adorned with a feather. (I had only seen him before in tropical clothes, but he looked equally good to me in winter ones.) A huge smile was on his face. He looked so assuring and comforting that any doubts I might have had disappeared forever. We fell into each other's arms. Nothing had changed between us. We still deeply loved each other, but now even more so. We knew this without speaking, but it was nice to tell each other, too. Our long separation and misunderstanding was forgotten in our happiness at being together.

21. HONEYMOON SHIP

After a day spent making love, talking, eating sandwiches, and toasting each other with drinks supplied by Room Service, by evening we ventured out for some fresh air and dinner. Richard, who knew the neighborhood well, guided me to a top-notch Eastside restaurant, where we ate crab cocktails and huge steaks washed down by the best vintage "Nuit St. George".

Richard joked that "the only trouble with American steaks is that they taste delicious at the beginning, but as one works one's way through one eats slower and slower until its like chewing cardboard. They are far too big! A complete waste of good food."

Later, he confided that being served too much always took his appetite away.

Manhattan, often a cruel and heartless city, now became enchanted by love, its towering buildings transformed, a fantastic stage-set just for us. The next day we explored its streets in a daze, looking only at each other. Richard even forgot his tender feet, the sun shone for us, and the wintry air was invigorating. Richard remarked that our happiness must be contagious, as many rushing passersby looked at us, then slowed down, relaxing their mask-like city faces, and smiled. When tired, we found refuge in a quiet alcove of a small neighborhood bar, where we sat for hours, still endlessly talking. Then, we moved on to the "Towers Hotel" in Brooklyn Heights, within walking distance of Pier One, where the Booth Line ships berthed.

The days just before sailing were busy times for Richard, supervising the loading of cargo, and getting everything in order for the long voyage ahead. He had a new crew to work with, so it was important to see them settled into a smoothly running routine. Some evenings he had to stay late on the ship, but always took time out to eat dinner with me.

We had discovered a small Italian family-style restaurant nearby, with the prosaic name of the "Plymouth Steak Pub". This served tastier steaks at half the price of those we had eaten in Manhattan, and the house-wine was good. I think the staff enjoyed having obvious lovers as customers, and gave us extra special service, particularly as we ate there every night for a week. Richard told the Manager and the waiters, all very chatty, that we had been married for 20 years and had 5 children! I'm sure no one believed him. When we checked out of the Towers Hotel, he also said I was his wife when he paid our bill. No comment from the clerk, but Richard took a chance. Booth Line officers often stayed there, and someone he knew might have overheard him. Extracts follow from my Notes:

Thursday, Feb. 2, 1967

Sailing day! Richard went down to the ship early this morning. I followed at 1 PM by taxi for the short trip to Pier 1.

The same pier, the same spectacular view of Manhattan as when we sailed on the *Veloz*. Its a sunny day, with an almost spring-like atmosphere. Everything seems familiar. The *Venimos*, being a sister-ship, looks exactly like the *Veloz*. Even her floor plan is similar. So it was like a homecoming as I walked towards her through the warehouse. Only a few stevedores were at work on the pier, and the ship's deck was quite deserted.

Although overcome with the joy of knowing that Richard was on board, and that now we should be together, I somehow managed to keep calm and talk in a reasonable way when the Chief Steward (personally sent by Richard) appeared to help me up the gangplank with my suitcases.

My cabin on this voyage is right across the hall from Richard's. The Steward took me in to formally "meet the Captain", who greeted me as an old friend.

"She sailed on the *Veloz* with me last voyage," he explained. He invited me to join him and some shipping officials for drinks and sandwiches.

There are four other passengers: Ellen and her husband, Rus. with their friend Emil, all from North Dakota; and a Roman Catholic missionary from Louisiana, who calls himself a "Lay Brother".

This person is actually a Franciscan monk, although he conceals it by wearing civilian clothes. He is youngish, with cold blue roving eyes, and does not appear at all spiritual. He has been stationed for 3 years in Santarém on the Amazon, and is now returning after a leave in the U.S., together with a lot of "equipment", whatever that might mean. Probably, when home, he has collected money and necessities for the mission, which is run by a group called "The New Tribes".

The North Dakotans are out-giving, fun-loving people. Down-to-earth country folk, they (like the "Beverly Hill-Billies"!) had discovered oil on their property, and are now using some of the proceeds to see the world. Naïve and wide- eyed about travel, they chose the Amazon purely by chance, when a friend told them about this trip.

Returning to my cabin, the Steward brought in a box containing a dozen red roses, sent by Hebe to me and Richard – a touching symbol that for us this will be a real honeymoon.

We shall not sail at 5 PM today after all, but at 11 AM tomorrow. The *Crispin*, another Booth Line ship docked near us, will go out late this afternoon. Ronny Low, Richard's friend, and Supervisor of Electricity for the Booth Line ships here, comes on board, and tells us that he is going for a farewell drink on the *Crispin*. He invites both of us, but Richard decides not to go. He tells me later it will be a formal occasion, with some of the

Supervisors there, and he thinks it best for us to keep a low profile.

Around 6, Richard invites me formally, as "Mrs. Podbereski", to have a drink with him in his sitting room. It is good to be there alone with him for a few minutes, although he does not let me sit beside him. I have to sit on the opposite side of the table! The 2nd Officer comes in and asks for passes to bring two girls on board. I had not realized that passes were necessary, but Richard explains that on account of the danger of smuggling dope, the Port Authorities have to keep track of everyone who comes and goes.

Later that evening, we have a mad escapade ashore. Everything is quiet as we leave the ship. I suppose the other passengers have also gone off. We sneak away, walking around the warehouse and down the long road to the gate. Richard tells the watchman that we are passengers from the *Venimos*. Guess the watchman is not very efficient, if he did not recognize the Master of the ship!

We spend the evening at our old hang-out, the "Plymouth". where the "Maitre D" gives us a big welcome. We are, undoubtedly, the craziest lovers they have ever seen! After dinner, we phone Philadelphia and talk to Hebe. All I remember about that call is that we were both trying to convince her how much we love each other. (I think she is convinced!)

It is very cold walking back to the ship, the lights of New York and Brooklyn Bridge flashing and sparkling like icicles. Brooklyn truly seems the most beautiful place in the world when I am with Richard and he with me! We stop crazily on the street and hug and kiss each other. Do the same back of the warehouse while wading through pools (it must have rained, but we had not noticed). Richard's hat blows off and spins madly through mud and water. Rounding the corner, there is our dream ship, floating still and mysterious in the night. Not a soul around as we climb on board. Together we go to Richard's cabin, but I cannot stay the night. I have been spoilt by our being together at the Lexington and Towers hotels! Richard has to put on his stern Sea-Captain's look, and I go meekly to my cabin, where Richard has insisted that I shut and lock the door, on account of thieves when in port. But a closed door does not separate us. For us, there will never be another real separation. In Richard's words, we are now in truth one, not two people, so when I write about myself, I am also writing about him.

Friday, Feb 3

Sailed at 11 AM promptly. It has turned bitterly cold, with a penetrating wind. Snow is in the air. Patches of ice have formed overnight on deck, particularly up on the wings of the bridge, where there's enough underfoot to skate on. One has to be careful walking around.

Ellen remarks: "The pumpkins have frozen!" The hold looks rather empty, and nothing is stacked on deck this time. We're carrying 1,000 tons. but will pick up more in the islands. Similarly to the *Veloz* , we are carrying a miscellaneous cargo: cars, machinery, frozen and fresh fruits and vegetables, including the pumpkins, much loved by Caribbeans; and even some items from Japan, such as cotton and silk materials.

There is a terrible mess of trash (boards, papers, etc.) dumped on the forward deck; and the boat-deck looks dirty and disorganized. This ship isn't "well-founded". Richard says she has been called "an unhappy ship", due to different clashes of personalities amongst crew members. It will take him a while to straighten things out. He has to be a psychologist, among plenty of other things. The A,B.'s and the dining-room and cabin stewards on this ship are from Barbados. Confusing at the start, 3 of these crew members look just alike!

We left the pier with a little difficulty, due to a tug-boat strike. Richard had to pay the Pilot $50. extra for the tricky job of backing her out, then ended by taking over himself. I braved the wintry blast on deck to watch him as he skilfully manoeuvred the ship away from the dock. In midnight blue military-style duffle coat with its traditional horn fastenings, his head protected by his Merchant Navy Master's cap, he made a properly nautical figure.

The West Indian sailors are slower taking commands than the Brazilians, which made his job harder. There was a lot of traffic on the Hudson, which had to be carefully watched before backing out. I never realized before that a ship doesn't have brakes, so if she backs out too fast into a swift current, she may go too far, and crash into something, therefore the help of a tug is important. But Richard went out quite safely. He knew what he was doing.

It was a fine sight sailing out of New York harbour, past the skyscrapers, the Statue of Liberty, and plenty of freighters and tankers at anchor. I took photos until my hands became so cold that I was forced inside. Outside the harbour the sea was much calmer than in July, almost no motion at all. However, in the evening when we were far offshore making way fast, the ship started to pitch and roll.

It is very cold in my cabin. The heater does not work properly. But there will not be much use for it, if we are heading for the Tropics!

From the start, I conspicuously got out my notebook, loudly proclaiming that I am writing a book. What no one yet knew, but would soon guess as my frantic scribbling diminished, was that Richard interested me more than my book.

The North Dakotans were ready to enjoy everything on the trip, beginning with New York, where they had never been. They also had never been on a ship. Richard, who excelled at games, spent many evenings on this voyage playing "Crib" with Rus. A game popular in Victorian times, I myself had never played it, so sat and watched, completely baffled, I'm ashamed to say, by the scoring. Later on, they taught me Poker, an easier, although dangerous, game enjoyed by all!

We did not fraternize much with the "Lay Brother", nicknamed "The

Padre" by the crew. Talking to him occasionally in the lounge after dinner, I got the impression of a slick, worldly man, a definite opportunist. He had once worked as a seaman, and on this trip associated mainly with some of the younger crew members. After he left the ship in Belém, the rumour circulated that he had told many risqué stories, so later the words "Lay Brother" would always provoke raucous laughter.

As we neared Sombrero, our first glimpse of land before approaching Puerto Rico, Richard called me up to the Bridge. He had previously on the *Veloz* pointed out this landmark. Now he challenged me to be the first to see it when it appeared over the horizon. Several other officers were also searching for it through binoculars. Quite naturally, Richard, with his hawk-like eyesight, beat me, and everyone else, in spotting it. He often teased me afterwards about "Sombrero, your favourite little island", as I got so excited when I did spot it from afar. It is actually a fine landmark, as well as being entertaining. From a distance, it does resemble a huge sombrero.

Now I was being exposed to some (to me) new nautical terms, such as watching for the "loom" of a lighthouse at night, or observing Richard taking "sights". Even basic mechanics of the engine-room baffled me, as when an engineer would appear with a part clutched in greasy hands, dramatically exclaiming: "That there impala has gone!"

Early in the voyage, Richard had started asking me frequently up to the Bridge. Soon it became obvious to everyone that I was getting V.I.P. treatment. By the time we were nearing the Amazon, a high stool was even found for me, so that I could keep Richard company comfortably. I remember one night on our return voyage particularly. We were sailing off New Jersey, heading for the entrance to the Hudson River. Richard and I had been sitting outside on the Starboard "wing" of the Bridge in a chill breeze from 3 AM until early dawn, when the coast was sighted. There had been a turn-over of crew before leaving Belém, and we again had Brazilian sailors. One, an elderly man whom Richard knew well, had cooking talents. He made big mugs of strong, bitter hot chocolate, which he carried up to us. Nothing had ever tasted so good!

Perhaps it will not surprise the reader to learn that I only occupied the lonely bunk in my cabin for the first few nights of the voyage. When the ship settled into a routine, I slept with Richard in his comfortable double bunk. Probably this was asking for trouble! But lovers are never noted for being sensible. Richard asked Ivan, a reliable, cheery person from Barbados whom he had had as his personal steward on many voyages, to bring my early morning tea on the same tray as Richard's, and leave it on the sitting-room table. Richard would then carry the cups into his cabin. When I returned to my own cabin to dress, it seemed like a bright idea to rumple up the the sheets of my bunk. However, I soon gave up doing this, as Richard said Ivan (and, presumably, pretty soon everyone else) knew where I was sleeping anyway. After that, my cabin was only used to keep my clothes, or to disappear into when in port Richard had business conferences with shipping agents.

At sea, when he was busy, I would sit quietly on the sofa in his sitting room and read a book, or do some writing. In the tropics, we spent most of the time on deck. Before dinner (which, as on the *Veloz*, was in the middle of the day), we usually had a drink in Richard's quarters with one or two of the officers. Most evenings, when not in the "Smoking Room" playing games, we sat in Richard's sitting room and talked. Usually the Chief Officer and the Chief Engineer would join us, if not on duty. Many interesting tales were told. In these sessions, I was a passive listener, learning a lot this way about life at sea. I also learnt about professional "football"(soccer), for which they all had a passion.

Richard made it a point to stay up very late. He did not want to turn in until he was sure everything was well under control for the night. On the wall next to his bunk he had a "blower", which was connected to the Bridge, which was immediately above his cabin. In case of emergency, he could be immediately called through this.

Richard's old crony, Arthur Resson, was not on the *Venimos*, nor was Ogonowski. The Chief Officer on this ship was Eamon McGee, a lively, humorous Irishman. One knew right away he was Irish by the number of "spuds" he could eat, yet remain thin! He had a quick Celtic temperament, and easily flared up; nevertheless, one could not help liking him.

Richard, as the voyage progressed, did not conceal how he felt about me. He was proud of our love, and wished everyone could be equally lucky. Eamon understood this, and accepted our relationship. Happily married himself, he wished us well. After Richard had been dismissed from the Company, he continued showing his friendship, inviting us to his home in Dublin, where his delightful family gave us a warm welcome.

The Chief Engineer, Alan, was a different type altogether, with a cynical (or some might prefer to say, "realistic") approach to life. He appeared unconvinced that there was such a thing as "true love", so seemed sceptical about ours. Richard spent hours talking about what love meant to him, and trying to explain how he and I had found it. I don't believe Alan, a fairly young man, was serious in an emotional way about anyone, and Richard thought this was sad. Alan always listened patiently to Richard, and was polite to me, but said very little, knowing, I suppose, that it would not be expedient to argue with his superior officer. It may be that he was secretly envious of us, but if he did not believe in the seriousness of our relationship, might also have felt that we should not be so openly unconventional, if others on board could not do the same. Richard did not worry about this. As he felt our love was right, he believed (too optimistically, as it turned out) that everyone would accept our relationship and be inspired by it.

The crew eagerly looked forward to their shore leaves, when most of the British contingent headed for the local dance halls. This was not so noticeable amongst the A.B.'s, the majority of whom were West Indian or Brazilian, so were not long separated from family and friends. But it remains true that most seafarers have "girls in every port". Their nights ashore often ended, as I could see for myself, in their returning to the ship with hangovers and in fighting moods, bad if the ship was due to sail, or if any hard work had to be done. The 2nd Mate, a fellow with fiery red hair to match his temper, always seemed to be in trouble and ready for a fight. The 2nd had a wife at home whom he said he loved, yet he and others from the ship associated with the lowest type of street girls ashore. Richard often had a job calming things down after their binges so that work could return to normal.

Richard told a story about himself that always went over big with a crew. When a young cadet, he had gone with some others from his ship to a nightclub in Barcelona. When they were there, fighting broke out amongst the locals, who started punching each other, and smashing tables and chairs. Richard, used to boxing, joined in, and enjoyed it! The police were called and Richard, along with some of the Spanish instigators of the disturbance, were carted off to jail (his pals having wisely escaped). Richard was held prisoner for several days, before he could get help from the British Consul. The food in a Spanish jail at that time was notoriously bad, but as he luckily had some money with him, he was allowed to order meals to be brought in from an outside restaurant. His main worry was that his ship might sail without him, and that his family at home would learn what had happened to him. It might even get into a British newspaper, and they would be horrified. Fortunately, the Consul arranged for his release, and he got back safely on his ship before she left the port. We can imagine that he got a very stern lecture from the Captain.

Richard pursued no hobby when at sea. He spent his spare time being sociable, talking, and getting to know his men. If all was quiet, he did some reading. Many of the Captains had hobbies, such as painting, or working on stamp collections. One Master brought an expensive Hi-Fi system on board, which he installed in his cabin, along with a big collection of records. Such Masters desired to remain alone and undisturbed during their free time, but in doing so, they lost some important rapport with their men. I believe Richard thought it unwise to shut himself away to concentrate on outside interests, when in charge of a ship. He felt that an officer, particularly a Master, had to be alert at all times. Even a slight change in the sound of the engine might mean trouble. The responsibilities of a Master could not be regulated by Union rules of so many hours on, so many off. The *Veloz* had had a happy, cooperative crew. But when Richard took over the *Venimos*, she was considered to be a problem ship, with a rebellious crew (rebellious against their former Captain). Richard would be faced with plenty of problems: liquor disappearing from the stores, unbalanced books, plus too much drinking leading to clashes of personalities, all adding up to situations difficult to handle. Richard thought that perhaps this was why he had been given command of this particular ship. He was known to be good at getting along with all sorts of people, and was fair in his judgements, so he might be able to straighten out these disturbances. Richard later told me he had turned down an offer of a better ship, with her home port Liverpool, because this would have made it too difficult to meet me.

When the *Venimos* was mentioned, some unfriendly people would sneer: "M.V. *Venomos*". Such a blatant pun was bound to be made. However, they must have forgotten their Latin, or had never learnt it. The word "venom" bears no relationship to *Venimos*, (translation: "We came".} Who remembers "Veni, Vedi, Vici"?

A disturbed crew meant, of course, loss of money for the Company. Richard worked hard to clear this up. Unusual situations, however, did continue to occur on board, including (what the Company could not foresee) our own relationship.

For us, personally, the *Venimos* was always remembered as our "Honeymoon Ship", and a happy one.

Just 10 days after leaving New York, I celebrated my birthday on board. I was greeted with heart-warming cards, Richard's, of course, coming first, then ones from Ellen, Rus and Emil, and many of the crew.

From B.E. McGee came these sentiments:
"To wish you birthday pleasures,
The brightest and the best,
In fact a day that really proves
Your very happiest."

From the *Venimos* Engineering Department:
"Birthday greetings come your way,
May you have a happy day
Best of future, good luck too,
Be with you in all you do."

From the Catering Department:
"Just like every Birthday
Here's hoping you will find
That this one brings adventures
Of a really tip-top kind."
"We one and all wish you a very happy Birthday."
Signed by the Chief Steward, 2 Assistant Stewards, the Chief Cook, and the 2nd Cook.

"This shows," Richard happily commented, "that people already are on our side."

George, the Chief Steward, immediately created a major problem for his new Captain. Older than the other officers, he had actually retired, but when his wife died had returned to sea. He had access to the large "Duty Free" liquor supply, and could easily drown his sorrows. A main problem here was that he enjoyed company, and became overly generous in his entertaining. No wonder he was universally liked. His cabin came to be known as "George's Bar".

All very well, but endless drinks were being handed out at Company expense. According to rank, the men were allowed a strictly limited amount of free liquor, any additional drinks being put on their expense accounts. It was the Chief Steward's job to keep track of these. I do not think George wanted to cheat the Company, but in a warm-hearted glow of hospitality he became a sloppy book-keeper. This added up to a big head-ache for Richard. Half-way in the voyage, he wrote in a report from Iquitos, dated 19 March:

"He drinks only beer but he cannot drink a lot without getting quite stupid. . . He was also a victim of last voyage so much so that I had to deduct 70 pounds from his wages for this voyage to square the Bar Accounts in New York. It appears that Captain Ellston tore up all the free and his private chits leaving him to pay up. . . he is proving very expensive despite frequent warnings I just cannot get him to cut down on his stores. . . So far I have collected all Bar Sales cash in each port so that he cannot spend it."

All the same, at the end of the voyage, when the accounts were handed in George's were still in a mess. Richard had to spend hours checking the stores, and questioning people as to what they remembered drinking, an almost impossible task, but the books had to be balanced somehow, or Richard himself would be blamed.

Stress from the previous voyage had also affected McGee. "A couple of beers, and he talks his head off!" wrote Richard. "Complaints about his insobriety were not unfounded . . . conditions last voyage were mainly to blame. . . but now he has behaved very well and given me full co-operation."

We were fond of Eamon, and Richard felt badly when the Company let him go at the end of the next voyage, although Richard had given him a clean discharge. He soon joined another company, where he became Master of a ship.

The 3rd Engineer, Ronald Poole, we already knew, as he had served on the *Veloz*. He was a pleasant young Englishman, who had played football when still in school for Manchester United's trainee team- a big point in his favour with Richard! But even he had problems, marital ones. Richard tried to give him fatherly advice. Ronald certainly admired Richard, and was, from the start, on our side. Several years later, when we had our own ship, the

Yacht *Jacaré*, in the Caribbean, he became our Engineer.

We had only been at sea a few days before Richard put his arms around me, and said he wanted me to be his "Mrs. H." "Then, nothing can separate us."

Of course, this is what I wanted, too. '

This moment was a major turning point in our lives. Once decided on, we knew we would have to be particularly strong and brave to face the upheavals in both our families which lay ahead before we could marry. Neither divorce would be easy. Richard was willing to treat my children as his own, but I knew George would fight against that. Richard's children, already grown up and living their own lives, did not present the same problem.

Richard told me that his divorce would come as a special shock to his sisters, for he had not talked to them much about feeling uncongenial with Chrissie. Even worse, Chrissie herself did not seem to be aware that anything was wrong with their marriage.

Divorce in the U.S. was no longer frowned upon, except by the strictest church groups, but in Wales there were very few divorces. Divorce still carried a stigma with it. There had never been a divorce in Richard's family, so he knew it would take them a long time to get used to it.

"But they will, and they will love you!" Richard cheerily told me. An optimist at heart, he knew that we would surmount all difficulties.

In the meantime, he was faced with the emotional task of writing to his wife saying that he wanted a divorce; and also to his three sisters, of whom he was so fond, trying to explain the situation. I do not believe he wrote to Clar and Meurig, as he wanted to tell them about it personally, and take me to meet them. He felt sure of understanding there.

On this trip, our first port of call was Barbados, and here some fun began. Richard could not go ashore when cargo was being unloaded, but I went with Ellen, Rus and Emil. We wandered around the picturesque inner harbour, which still had "island schooners" in use. These were locally made wooden-hulled sailing vessels used for inter-island cargo throughout the Caribbean. We took lots of photos, bought souvenirs, and drank the famous "Planter's Punch". Returning to the ship, we found that our departure had been delayed until late that night, so Rus disappeared on shore again to do some exploring on his own. It was our first taste of sub-tropical heat, so the rest of us flopped down for heavy siestas.

When the sun had set (promptly at 6, as all over the Caribbean), Rus still had not returned. Ellen started to worry. Richard sent a crew member on shore to look for him.

"If he's not back by sailing time, I'll have to sail anyway," Richard said firmly, which worried Ellen even more.

Later on, the sailor returned, and taking Richard aside, told him that he had quite easily found Rus, who obviously had been curious to sample the pleasures ashore as described to him by our sailors. He was in a local brothel, where he had been drinking, and refused to leave. Richard, always kind-hearted, and not wanting to further upset Ellen, said he would go and bring Rus back himself. I said I would go with Richard, as I had never been in a brothel. This remark caused much laughter among some crew members who happened to overhear it!

We set off in a taxi, whose driver took us straight to the house, which was well-known. Richard marched in, with me at his heels. Inside was a lobby, with a wide flight of stairs, up which we went. Half-way up, we were met by a plump, middle-aged West Indian woman, evidently the "Madam", who came hurrying down, a worried look on her face. From rooms on the upper landing, alarmed, chattering young girls peered out. They wore simple cotton dresses, and used no make up – not at all the Mae West types I had expected.

Richard explained to the Madam who he was, and why we had come.

"Yes, he is here." she replied, pointing to a large, airy sitting-room, with an open balcony overlooking the street. There, sprawled out on a chaise-longue, was Rus, evidently quite plastered.

"Come on, Rus!" said Richard, giving him a shake. "We have to get you up, and in some kind of condition to return to the ship. We don't want Ellen to see you like this." Pulling Rus up, and half-supporting him, he managed, now closely watched by the curious girls, to guide him down the stairs and out to the waiting taxi. Richard slipped some money into the Madam's hand, and told her not to worry, there would be no trouble.

Richard asked the driver to take us to the Paradise Beach Club, where we would get a good dinner. This should fix Rus up. We must have caused some comment going into the formal dining-room, where waiters in tuxedos ushered us to a table. The room was full of dressy tourists, and we were obviously not dressed for the occasion. Besides, Rus looked very dishevelled, and was still unsteady on his feet. "Now Rus," Richard said firmly as we sat down, taking over as a commanding officer should, "you can have one drink and that will fix you up. Then, we'll have a good meal." Which we did. As Rus ate, he began to look a lot better, and by the time we returned to the ship he appeared, although subdued, to be quite rational. He quietly went with a relieved Ellen into their cabin, and shortly after that we sailed.

Arriving in Trinidad, I was to meet for the first time Arthur Winter, the Harbour Master in Port of Spain, who was an old friend of Richard's. We would see a lot of him in years to come, when we had our yacht there. He was always helpful, besides being good company.

"Just mention that you are a friend of Arthur's and you will have no trouble with the Harbour Authorities," Richard would advise other sailing friends.

Arthur held the position of Harbour Master for years, and was highly respected all over the large island. Upon retirement, he became owner of a coaster himself.

He had a lovely wife and daughter, Marge and Charmain. It was a privilege to know them, too, and we had many happy times together. We often met Arthur at the "China Clipper", a small restaurant which had become the lunch-time meeting place of ship-owners, officers, and agents. Just two blocks from the docks, and around the corner from the Booth Line office, here one could immediately find out what friends were in port and what ships they were on. Richard always met someone he knew, and would get caught up with the latest shipping news. Additionally, one could make a whole meal there of delicious Chinese deep-fried "Wong Tong" shrimps, washed down by the tough seafarers with Trinidad's dark rum.

On this visit, we were moored at the dock in Port of Spain for several days. From there, Richard sent me as his agent to escort a passenger, from another Booth Line ship berthed next to us, on the scenic drive to Maracas Beach. This suited me fine, as it was a good chance for a swim. The passenger turned out to be a lady from Rio, speaking in Portuguese – but no English! I guess this was why Richard was asked to escort her, but he was busy with cargo and did not have time to do it. However, we managed nicely with sign language, a little French, and some poor Spanish on my part.

Soon the *Venimos* was again at sea. Richard enjoyed amusing the passengers, and had promised something extra special for this passage. It was making clouds disappear! This special magic, no doubt bequeathed by Merlin, was only good, it seems, between Trinidad and the Amazon. The Magic, which was limited, only worked on clouds to be seen here, and sometimes on the River itself. Not just any old cloud would do – it had to be a special kind of cloud. When he spotted one, a small puffy variety (no huge thunder clouds!) he would tell everybody to watch it very carefully. Rus was particularly fascinated by this "trick", if so it was.

"Now Rus," Richard would say, "don't take your eyes off that cloud for one minute! Pretty soon it is going to disappear." And it would slowly get smaller and smaller until it was no longer visible. Very strong magic, indeed.

As we neared the Equator, there was special excitement, as Rus, Ellen and Emil had never crossed "The Line".

"How shall we know when we are crossing it?" Rus inquired.

"Oh, you can't miss it!" laughed Richard. "There will be a big bump, and you'll fall off your chair."

That evening we were all lined up on deck, sitting anxiously in deck chairs, awaiting the "big bump". Richard, having gone up to the bridge to check our position, returned with a twinkle in his eyes.

"Prepare yourselves," he joked. "We are now crossing the Line." As he

Although the Captain had warned that there would be a big bump when crossing the Equator, Rus, a passenger, was startled when his deck-chair collapsed.

said these words, Rus's chair collapsed, and Rus found himself folded up inside it, flat on the deck boards. I happened to have my camera at hand, and quickly snapped a really candid shot.

Three pairs of startled North Dakotan eyes stared unbelievingly at Richard. Rus, pulling himself up, looked as though he had been struck by some magical force. But when he recovered from the shock and thought about it logically, he could not be convinced that Richard had not rigged the chair, although Richard hotly denied it. A great laugh was had by everyone on board. It was surely a memorable crossing of the Line!

In Belém, Richard took me ashore to eat at a very popular restaurant which specialized in a local delicacy, "churrasco cabrito"- barbecued kid. This was roasted in special wall ovens, after being marinated in a piquant sauce. These ovens, surrounded by colourfully decorated Portuguese tiles, were in the dining-room, so we could watch the cooking procedure. The meat was served on spits. One might imagine that the flavour of young goat would

Left: Good service on board from a Steward on the *Venimos*.

Below: Richard and Dale relax on the deck of the *Venimos*.

Richard standing under bow of his ship at Belém dock.

be strong and unappetizing, and the meat tough, but when its cooked like this, its a tasty treat.

It was not only fun to travel on the River with Richard, but educational. His knowledge of the area and his many personal contacts along the way opened up for me an understanding of the whole region that would be impossible for the casual tourist. In Belém, his very special friend was Captain Aled Parry, whom Ogonowski had talked about on the *Veloz*. He was an unusual Welshman, having had a career in the Brazilian Navy. Now retired, and living in Belém with his Brazilian wife and family, he retained a deeply emotional love for the land of his birth. He enjoyed telling about how he had once sailed into a Welsh port on a Brazilian naval vessel. Stepping ashore from the ship in a full Brazilian Captain's uniform decorated with plenty of gold braid and medals, he startled the port authorities by addressing them in perfect Welsh!

Richard always went to see Aled and his family whenever he was in Belém. On our return voyage downstream, they invited us both for dinner. They gave me an especially warm welcome, as Richard had already told them all about me. They were a big family. Several generations were seated around an enormous dining-room table; Mrs. Parry's mother, the Parry's own grown children with their wives and husbands, and even grandchildren, were present. After the meal, which was a feast in best Brazilian style, Welsh music was played on their prized imported "Hi-Fi" record player. This was the first time I had heard the famous Welsh choral singing. Listening to it, tears came to the eyes of the two Welshmen, overcome by "hiraeth"(nostalgia), and, I must admit, in mine also, as the music was extremely moving.

As we left Belém on our trip upriver, and approached the western end of Marajó, Richard pointed out a small, heavily wooded island, privately owned by an enterprising Brazilian woman, a widow who ran her own lumber business. Richard had often stopped there, and was always welcomed. She would insist that he come to her house for dinner. There, one of her many daughters would stand back of each guest's chair, to see that they lacked nothing. It impressed Richard that here in the wilds, formalities were strictly observed. The meal was served on beautiful china, the menu well-planned, the food especially good, as they grew all their own produce. Richard was also amazed that they invariably remembered that he loved "creme caramelo" for desert. Booth Line ships were a life-line here, so he was, indeed, for them, a V.I.P. Additionally, he loved the Brazilians. People sensed this and responded to it.

On this trip, we turned to starboard into a narrow channel leading to the northern branch of the river. Here the trees almost touched each side of the ship, forming an archway overhead. Another ship could not have passed us. The water was black, opaque and still, except for the splash of an occasional heron. We spent the time leaning over the railing looking for alligators, but they were almost impossible to spot unless one could go quietly by canoe.

We stopped at a rickety wooden pier half the length of our ship to deliver provisions to a small settlement at the water's edge. This was a logging camp, a collection point for logs felled deeper in the jungle and floated down the waters of smaller branches of the river. Richard knew the people here. As he wanted to examine the wood, we stepped ashore, cautiously treading on wobbly planks stretched over flooded paths. The village remained dark, under thick canopies of intertwining foliage, dripping and steaming from the constant "rainy season" downpours. In such settlements, there was no steady electrical current. People were dependent on unreliable private generators, or else used oil lamps. Those lucky enough to own fridges ran them on butane gas – when available!

Then we sailed out into the brightness of the main river, and headed east to Macapá, outlet for one of the world's largest aluminium mines. Arriving there, we heard much alarming talk of the infamous "tidal bore", which can be extremely dangerous, without warning flooding the area for miles,

Rickety pier to which we tied up at logging camp near the Narrows.

endangering small craft and lives alike in its powerful surge. I was again reminded of the strength of ocean tides here, which are felt for 200 miles upriver. The Northern Delta is a huge labyrinth of small islands and channels. As far as I know, the southernmost channel of this branch of the river is not navigable; the central one is marked "Perigoso" ("dangerous") in the "Times Atlas"; the Northern Channel is navigable, but at that period hardly ever used. It was considered to be risky due to the build-up of conflicting currents. Richard, however, had successfully taken a ship through it, and after that others followed suit.

In Manaus, I met more of Richard's friends, among them Joy Bomer and her daughter, with whom we spent an enjoyable evening at their apartment. Joy was the widow of a Brazilian Booth Line agent whom Richard had especially liked.

It was obvious that Richard was much loved and admired by many people along the River. I was happy to discover that his friends were real friends, uncritical and willing to accept us as a couple, although our legal difficulties were still unsolved. The warmth of the natural environment radiated into these inhabitants, perhaps opening their hearts like flowers. It was left to lawyers to worry about legalities.

As we approached Manaus, the crew talked excitedly about what they would do in their time ashore. The consensus of opinion was meeting girls, drinking, dancing – and more girls! Rus's escapade had been nothing unusual. The younger British officers were not in Richard's lucky position of having old friends along the river, whose houses they could visit for relaxation. Most of them had signed on for only one or two voyages, and then were eager to be transferred elsewhere.

I heard one favourite dance-hall much discussed. Even Alan and Eamon were talking about the place.

"Right in the middle of the jungle! You can't imagine anything like it!"

I said to Richard that I'd like to see such a place. How about us going dancing? It would be fun, and a relaxation for him to leave the ship for a few hours. He agreed, if all was going smoothly on board. He was not keen on dancing at home, he told me, but he loved the rhythms of Brazilian dance music, so could forget his feet and let himself be carried along by the music. Besides the fast dances, the sad Portuguese songs called "Fado" were very popular. Richard had grown to like these in Portugal.

The Manaus dance-hall was on the outskirts of town, away from the river. First glimpsed through a screen of flowering bushes, it appeared attractive, a big raised dance floor mysteriously lit with "fairy lights". It was protected by a roof against heavy showers, but was otherwise open to the warmth and perfume of the night.

The girls, mostly teenagers, were lined up on the side-lines waiting to be asked to dance, reminding me of country-club dances I had attended as a school-girl. They were dressed accordingly, in sleeveless evening dresses of buffante voile, tulle and taffeta, which would have been just right for unsophisticated girls in the '30's. But here no proper dance manager acted as chaperon. Instead, each girl had her "protector", to whom she had to give her dance money. If a man wanted more than just to dance, he had to pay more before disappearing with her into one of the shacks discretely hidden behind the trees.

When we sat down at a table for drinks, we spotted Alan dancing with one of the girls. Richard beckoned them over to join us. The girl had an inflamed, badly bruised face, and looked miserable. She was on the verge of tears. Her "protector", she said, had beaten her up. We felt very sorry for her, and for all the others. Like tropical butterflies, how many of them would survive for long?

I did enjoy dancing with Richard to the rhythmic music. But whether in a jungle dance-hall or in a first-class city hotel, the South American girls, and even the older women. all dance with a wiggle to their hips, which comes naturally. I must have been very inhibited, as it took me a long time to catch on. On other occasions, when we went dancing somewhere with a group of friends, Richard would often leave me sitting, and pick out dance partners who could do it better. Then, I became very jealous!

Sailing past Leticia to Pifuelle, we contacted the real natives of this land, a tribe of Indians who lived near an immense tree that Richard had pointed out to us from the *Veloz*. I had then thought it was an amazing feat to be able

At Pifuelle on the Solimões – an immense tree to which we tied up.

to single out one tree in an area containing billions! But surprisingly, I now found myself recognizing it from afar, its trunk a huge pillar towering high above all other forest giants, with an umbrella burst of foliage at the top. This time we stopped and tied up to it, the water level being high enough to facilitate this.

These Indians, a cheerful lot, were short, fine-looking people, all with sharply filed teeth – to them, an important sign of beauty, but, additionally, I was told that when they ate tough game, it made chewing easier.

They were the same group who had brought us gifts to the *Veloz*. Now they appeared in their canoes as soon as they saw the *Venimos* approaching. They knew that Richard had their welfare at heart, as indeed he did. He had the freezers full of ice-cream for the children, brightly coloured ribbons for their mothers, cigarettes for the men, plus "boiled sweets" (hard candy) and chocolate bars for all. He waved to them to come on board, and the whole crowd, several dozen of them, climbed up the accommodation ladder. They swarmed over the decks, peering into the Bridge, dining and smoking rooms, and even some cabins. They were orderly and polite, appearing to be honest.

I did not want to take their photographs without asking, as some tribes

Pifuelle - an Indian woman with baby comes aboard.

consider it to be unlucky. But when Richard asked in their own dialect, they seemed pleased to have me do so. A smiling young woman carrying a baby made a good picture. When I admired the necklace of seed-pods she was wearing, she gave it to me in return for some ribbon.

When we arrived in Iquitos, Richard continued introducing me to acquaintances, amongst them the Chief of Customs, an entertaining person whom Richard had known for years. His position was a political one. He would come and go, as the local government changed. As he had good friends in the capital, Lima, he was not long without his job, so he and his family had bought a nice house in Iquitos, where Richard had been their guest. He was quite a character. While waiting for other ships to come into port to be cleared, he would often come on board the *Venimos* for a chat. Sometimes he appeared early in the morning, and would wander around the decks, soon gravitating towards Richard's private cocktail cabinet, hoping to be offered a "Duty Free" drink. But Richard kept the cupboard locked, even to the Chief of Customs.

"No, no, Alberto!" Richard would say, playfully wagging a finger. "Nothing but orange juice until the sun is over the yard-arm." Richard always waited until well after 11.30 AM before serving alcoholic drinks to anyone – even important officials!

Alberto would often invite himself for lunch, ending up napping, with his nose in his plate, due to the intense heat combined with the unaccustomed heavy British fare, unsuitably served at the hottest time of day. No air-conditioning on board in those days, either.

He had a teenage son, who admired the Beetles, then at the height of their fame. When we returned to New York, I bought their latest recording, and took it back to him on our next voyage. He was delighted, and gave me a set of Indian bow, arrow and spear to take back for Jerzy.

Pat Nicholls, the Booth Line agent, remembered me from the *Veloz*, and would, I fear, be remembering me only too well after our next trip upriver. Richard liked Pat, but felt it better to leave well-enough alone, and not mention our relationship at that point. However, we did not need to be so circumspect, as we later discovered that Maryla had told Pat the whole story, which I, of course, had told her in confidence. But such gossip, in a place like Iquitos, was too juicy to be kept under cover. And people's first reaction, of course, unless they knew us well, was "Jungle Fever"!

We did not see Maryla this trip, as she was visiting family in Lima; but her daughter had not been "sold". We found her working as cashier in a good Iquitos restaurant. She looked well and happy and greeted us enthusiastically. Perhaps my sending her mother the money had really helped.

Here we said farewell to our North Dakotans. We would miss them. Rus, before leaving the ship, had one more escapade. As we neared Iquitos, Richard and I were sitting on the little open deck above the Bridge, enjoying watching the river life (which here is lively). Looking up, we saw Rus climbing to the top of the mast! I again had my camera handy, and quickly snapped a picture.

Richard feared that Rus might fall, and shouted in his sternest Captain's voice: "Rus! come down immediately!"

We received a nice note from all of them when we returned to Belém. They wrote that they had had a great trip on the *Venimos*, and they wished us both continuing happiness. They had mailed a present to New York for Richard – a handsome ashtray made from North Dakota agates.

A letter I wrote to a friend in California from Iquitos, dated March 19,

"Mrs Captain" helps Richard keep a watch.

transmits a little of the feeling of our surroundings:

"Right now we are tied up several miles down river, on a tributary, the Nanaye, at a saw-mill of the American-backed Astoria Importing & Manufacturing Company. We've loaded a lot of plywood veneer. This morning 3 barges with a tug arrived from Pucallpa (700 miles up the Ucayali) loaded with heavy mahogany boards. It will take us all day to load these, and by tomorrow we should be starting back down river. The saw-mill is fascinating – on the banks of the river, surrounded by thick jungle. We walked around it yesterday, and saw some gorgeous butterflies, bright green lizards, etc. About a mile upstream is a fishing village. We started to walk there on a muddy path up a hill, but the mud was so thick we could hardly

The Sawmill of the Astoria Importing & Manufacturing Company, on the Nanaye River.

The *Venimos* docked at the Sawmill

The Sawmill's Manager and Richard consult ashore.

Tugs and barges delivering mahogany from Pucallpa.

Loading the hold with plywood

The ship loading plywood

Deck cargo on the *Venimos* for New York

stand up, much too slippery to walk over! So we'll have to wait for the "Dry Season" to take that expedition.

"High water on the Amazon (average 85 ft.) is May 15th, but this year its already up 80.5 feet. Actually, the water comes more from the melting snow in the Andes than from rain – but there are showers every day, and the sky is grey most of the time. Its still hot and muggy though! Plenty of mosquitos!

. . . Richard called me out on deck to see a snake, a thin bright emerald green water snake about 2 ft. long, slithering up the gangway, with its jaws open. He said it was a deadly variety, and if it bit you you'd be dead in 2 minutes! All the seamen came running with boards and killed it by smashing it over the head. Imagine, just yesterday 2 of our Junior officers went swimming right off the dock, just at the same place the snake came from! One becomes fool-hearty here, as actually one sees very few snakes (they're not hanging from trees as you see in the movies!) but they are hidden somewhere nearby, all the same. . . we have already seen 2 more, right on the dock."

An interesting note that I made at the time was that my friend to whom I had written, Janet Turpin, had a brother who was in the American Merchant Marine. He received a salary then of $1,000. a month as Master with the United Fruit Company.

"This is big money!" Richard had exclaimed.

Richard had turned down the offer of a job with them some years back, and now is sorry! His British company pays starvation wages, only equalling about $300. U.S. a month, but this is considered to be good in Britain. He probably could not switch to an American company now, due to much tighter Union rules. Also, they always want to sign up much younger men.

My thought, however, is that he really loves the Amazon run, and as he knows it inside out it would be a pity to change. Booth still has a monopoly on the River, so he will have to stick with them.

Before leaving the saw-mill I became fascinated by huge rounds of wood, sawed across the complete width of gigantic trees, dozens of which were floating unused in the water.

"These would make sensational patio tables," I suggested.

"Well, then lets take some!" Richard agreed.

It was a poor idea. After the effort of getting several heaved up on deck, where they were lashed down, and transported to New York, the U.S. Agricultural Authorities would not let us unload them.

"They are full of worms!" was their verdict. They had to be taken back to the Amazon, and dumped exactly where they had come from, in worm-infested water,

We had better luck further down river, where we had a large dinging-room table made from the beautiful Brazilian hardwood, "Macapá Uba", also some smaller tables and chairs, all well-made by a local carpenter. These were successfully transhipped to Britain for us via a helpful Booth Line, and we received them in Liverpool without any problems.

On our return voyage down river, there occurred a drama not to be equalled in any "soap opera".

We had stopped at Santarém, close to where the blue Rio Tapajós joins the Amazon. Shortly after we had docked, George, the Chief Steward, appeared in Richard's quarters with a young woman who had come on board to see him. He told Richard that he wanted to marry her, and asked if Richard would perform the ceremony?

George had forgotten that Ships' Captains no longer do this. If, under special circumstances, such a marriage is performed, it is not really legal, and another civil marriage must take place.

The woman was slim and attractive, with dark hair well-styled, and was fashionably dressed. She was, however, as Richard knew, a kind of superior courtesan, going on board many of the ships. Most of our crew knew her as such. Her story was that she had been abandoned by her husband (or lover?) and had to support her child, a boy of 7. George felt very sorry for her, and wanted to rescue her.

Richard did not want to encourage him to hastily do something he might later regret.

"If you insist upon being married, you will have to be married on shore," he told them.

Even if George found someone who could legally marry them at short notice, Richard did not want the ceremony to take place on his ship, which was flying a U.K. flag (Burmudan), and was operated by a British company. This would probably encourage the woman to believe that she had a right to get British citizenship, and that the Company would be obliged to give her financial support as s crew-member's wife.

All very fine under normal circumstances, but Richard strongly suspected that the marriage might be taking place under false pretences. How could he check whether it would be legal? There was no time to find out, as the *Venimos* was only staying in Santarém for one day and night. The woman might be already legally married, and not divorced. She did not have any written proof of her status.

"I've only just arrived here, and have left my papers in the South," she prevaricated.

"I'll find a priest then, who would be willing to marry us," George soothingly told her.

To complicate matters, it was a Sunday, and the town's Registry office was shut. How could the marriage be legalized without a licence?

George. however, was determined to go through with it, and he went ashore to see what he could do. Much later in the day, he returned with a Catholic priest, dredged up from God knows what jungle mission, who seemed to be willing (at a price, no doubt) to marry them then and there.

Intense excitement possessed our crew. Without asking permission, there was a general exodus from the ship. They all assembled on the dock for the ceremony. It was almost a mutiny! Everyone gave us accusing looks as they went ashore. Weren't we the couple who talked so much about "love"? Yet now we refused to help another couple in love! We could see that they thought we were double-faced.

I must admit that we felt rather strange, sitting isolated on the deck, like judges, while the ceremony took place on the shore beneath us.

"I do think there's something fishy about this," Richard confided. "I feel badly, as I know what people are thinking about us, but I cannot take the chance of getting the Company in trouble. As Master, I would be the person responsible," he added, with a worried look.

Early the next morning, we sailed away, leaving the "bride" and her son waving disconsolately from the pier. There was a gloomy atmosphere on board. The men were quiet and subdued.

When we arrived in New York, Richard was told by the Superintendent at the office that the "bride" had indeed immediately gone to the Booth Line office in Santarém, and had demanded money, a wife's share of George's pay.

This the the Company refused to give her without full proof that their marriage was legal. No such proof was ever given. How right Richard had been! However, George had promised this náive woman that when he returned to Britain he would send her money so she could join him.

She waited and waited, but the money never came. A year or so later, we heard that George had married an English woman at home, the other "marriage" forgotten, except on the River, where it became known as the sad story of an Amazon "Madame Butterfly"!

At the end of the voyage, Richard recommended that the Company should not renew George's contract. He was not a bad person, but in too mixed up an emotional state to be a reliable Chief Steward.

Our "honeymoon" voyage had drawn to a close. This had, for us, been a perfect trip. In Iquitos, we had bought each other wedding rings of the rich, warm coloured Peruvian gold, the purest gold that is ever made into jewelry, which we immediately wore. Richard said that when we had discovered our love for each other on our first trip to Iquitos, that to him was our real wedding. Now the uncritical acceptance of our situation by Richard's friends along the River was a good omen. Even the workers around the docks, some of whom Richard had known for years, were calling me "Mrs. Captain".

Richard laughed: "I know you get a kick out of that!" We made a pact never to separate again, no matter what. I would go to Wales with Richard when he was arranging for his divorce, and he would come with me to the United States when I went to get mine.

Richard sent a radiogram to the New York Booth Line office to reserve my cabin again for our next, and final, voyage on the *Venimos*.

22. MERLIN'S HERITAGE

If the banner of Merlin contained a fighting red dragon, breathing fire across the skies (now presumed by astronomers to symbolize a fiery comet or group of earth-threatening asteroids), Merlin's modern country-men must inherit his strength, to survive not only geographical upheavals but emotional ones. Richard was truly "Merlin's Man" in the valour he showed under stress. He was never afraid to stand up for his beliefs, no matter if they went against conventions, and the "powers that be".

If I was "Merlin's Woman", I must follow suit. Richard was risking his career by his open and uncompromising approach to our relationship. He had my complete support, and we stood firmly together. If critics called us headstrong, rash, naïve, unworldly, selfish, or morally wrong that was their opinion, not ours.

The honeymoon was over. Now we must face the stern side of the business world, as well as that of family. Richard had already received cruelly critical letters from two of his sisters, which upset him very much.

On arriving to New York, I went cheerfully to the Booth Line office to collect my ticket for the next trip. When I gave my name, I was told by a clerk that the cabins were all engaged, and that there was no room for me. I knew this was untrue, as Richard, to whom all listings were sent, had told me no bookings had yet been made. When I told Richard what had been said, he hurried back to the office with me to complain.

We were ushered into a private room where the Office Manager, the Marine Superintendent, and several other officials were assembled. The atmosphere was grim, and made us feel like naughty school-children called up to the Head Master's office.

They told us that complaints had been made about our behaviour. Due to this, they had received orders from Ronald Vestey himself not to let me back on the ship as a passenger.

We defended ourselves by telling them that this was no light affair, we were seriously in love, and intended to marry as soon as possible. Richard told them of our pledge never again to be separated. I would be paying for my cabin, and was not asking for free transportation. Richard reminded them that he had asked for "compassionate leave" at the end of the coming voyage, so he could go home and arrange for his divorce. How could Ronald Vestey judge us if he had not talked to us personally? I added, hotly, that Richard was one of their best Captains, and that the Company should stand behind him.

Our emotional pleas did not move them. What we did not know until later was that Chrissie had sent her son to the Liverpool office to complain about me; and in Manhattan, George had sent Janek to complain about Richard. Additionally, the company had received a letter from "an officer" on the *Veloz* complaining about us. I knew that George had threatened that he would ask a crew member to write such a letter.

In Britain, Chrissie had asked the Company to send Richard right home, thinking she could patch things up. She did not take what she thought was an "affair" seriously, and saw no reason for divorce.

On the other side of the Atlantic, George (unknown to me) arrived in New York. He had gone to see his new grandson (Janek and Iza's baby), and in doing so, had left our own children completely unattended in California. He and Janek went on board the *Veloz*, which was in port, to stir up more trouble for Richard. Rumours were spread as far as California that it was a dirty old tramp, and that the Captain of such a ship was beneath me socially!

"I could have understood it better if at least you had fallen for the Captain of the "QE 2'", wrote George, snobbishly. "Anyway, he's a hopeless drunkard, and he'll never get another ship!" he gloated.

Such nasty pressures from both sides of the ocean were too much for an old, conservative British company. Scandal would mean loss of prestige and of money. Most of the crew, and certainly Richard's friends along the River, seemed to be on our side. If there had been no complaints, I think we could have quietly taken the next voyage together, and afterwards been given time to settle our affairs. But at it was, Company policy had to come before sentiment.

However, looking at our distressed faces, some human sympathy was shown by these straight-laced businessmen. After all, they did admit that Richard was one of their finest officers (to me, THE finest!) They had worked with him for years, and liked him personally. Therefore, they agreed on a compromise. I could fly to meet the ship, at whatever ports I wanted, and go on board in the daytime, but I must not spend the night! Richard and I could also meet on shore during his time off. What he did then was not the Company's business.

The *Venimos* was not sailing for a few days, so I took Richard to Villanova, Pennsylvania, to see my family property, "Woodstock". My cousins, Jack and Louisa Brooke, were renting one of my houses there, and invited us for dinner, in spite of our unconventional situation. Richard was very nervous, as these were the first relatives of mine he had met. The Brookes took to Richard immediately – Louisa afterwards called him "a charmer"– and they even thought we were doing the right thing living together. To find such broad-mindedness in staid old Philadelphia was nothing short of a miracle. We always loved the Brookes for it.

Sailing time came only too soon. This time I was left standing on Pier 1, with tears rolling down my cheeks. It was good that Bill Hobday, the

Purchasing Manager, and Richard's special friend in the Company, was there to give me moral support, as I stood on the edge of the dock waving good-bye.

"Don't throw yourself into the water!" he half-jokingly cautioned.

Richard managed to get a brief note delivered to me via the Pilot. "I'm crying, Dale, which I've never done before sailing. . . Darling, be brave for my sake. It just broke my heart to see you on the quay so please God keep you until we meet again at Iquitos. . . the time will soon pass and we will be together again. My Dale, our love will survive anything, so be brave. . . Please Dale believe that eventually we will be legally married because I have faith that love such as ours cannot be denied."

Excerpts from a letter (dated May 3) that I wrote to Richard describes this departure:

"Wasn't our farewell on the ship dramatic? I thought I'd never make it down the accommodation ladder and along the deck, I was crying so hard, but I couldn't help it. I think some of the others were crying, too. . . anyway, I felt they were all for us, didn't you? Eamon looked as though he were going to cry and that's what made me kiss him spontaneously (I hope you did not mind!) because at that moment I loved everyone on the ship because they were there with you. Afterwards, I told Bill I must have been out of my mind to kiss Eamon, and he thoroughly agreed with me!!

". . . We stayed on the dock until the ship got so far away we couldn't make out your figure on the bridge. . . When she was in the middle of the river with New York in the background she looked so beautiful with all her fresh paint – but Bill laughed bitterly and said she couldn't be beautiful, being a Booth Line ship!

"Darling, your friends were wonderful to me, and it did help. Bill and Ronny took me to the office, and even" (Capt.) " St. Rose tagged along. . . they brought out a bottle of rum and ice from somewhere, and we sat there for about an hour until I stopped crying. I felt I had to stop, for their sakes. They were all teasing me and saying it was only for a month's separation, and it'd be much worse if you were going to Vietnam. . . Of course, the conversation was mostly about love, and Ronny cynically said one thinks one's in love, but after one's married for a year or so it fades away. . . By the way, Captain Lenham (the Marine Super.) passed me on his way out, and gave me a pleasant smile and a V-for Victory sign, so maybe you're right, that he's not against us personally.

"Bill took me to the `Plymouth' for dinner, and bought me a steak, but you can imagine, I wasn't very hungry. . . I do feel that he is very friendly."

I spent a lonely night at the Towers Hotel, and the next day was back with my long-suffering friends, the Bulleys.

Hebe had met Richard when I took him to Philadelphia. She liked him very much, but felt she did not know him very well yet. She would not admit that we have what she calls "real love". She wishes us both well, but keeps harping on the fact that we've both made mistakes before. She thinks it may just be a strong physical attraction (that will wear off), and takes the point of view that if it is real love we should obey the so-called "moral code", and not make love until we are legally married. She said if we had been content to do that, I could still be a passenger on the ship, and everything would be alright. But this I doubt. I don't think either Chrissie or George would put up with us being together on the same ship, even in a platonic way, since they know we love each other.

The answer to all this, I wrote to Richard, is "that you and I know we have the most wonderful, complete love its possible to have on earth; and that's the main thing, that we really know it, no matter what other people may think."

Richard wrote:

M.V. *Venimos,*
At Sea,
Sunday, May 7

"This afternoon we passed Sombrero and how I longed for you to be with me. All the officers came up and said "This is your island and Dale's", and I could have cried. I went close in and took a special photograph just for you. . . Everyone on board has been so kind and understanding and their one wish is to see you with me again. Even the priest who has talked a lot to me says live your own lives, love such as ours isn't given to many. The lady passenger has even said when you leave Iquitos to come and visit her at Bogotá for as long as you like. . . To me Dale, this is something wonderful, there are people in this world who can see the wonderful love we have for each other and want us just for the love and happiness we might possibly spread. . . how many have this? to me the only ones I know are Clar and Meurig. Maybe there are others who possibly hide it. . . I have maybe a mystic sense helped possibly by Merlin that our love will go beyond this life, as I so strongly believe that we have loved before, because otherwise no two like us could reach this perfect understanding, have so complete a trust and love right from the time we touched and looked into each other's eyes. It was there and we both realized it and we were both scared because it was beyond normal understanding, yet the wonder and the beauty and glory of it was that we both knew yet then could not understand it."

Time crawled sluggishly by. I waited dreary weeks until Richard could cable me when and where to meet him. He had told me he would stay such a short time in Caribbean ports that it would not be worthwhile my going there. The longest time he would have in port would be in Iquitos, hopefully, 10 days, so we had better plan to meet there. He would try to speed up by loading cargo "on the double".

The Bulleys did their best to cheer me up. Being with dear old friends (who seemed almost like family), helped a lot. On May 13, I wrote to Richard that "Hebe is now slowly becoming convinced" that we have the real thing. She suddenly started to change after she saw all my Amazon slides, with pictures of Richard and me together, looking very happy.

Although not a church-goer by nature, I accompanied Hebe, an enthusiastic Orthodox, to some of her services. The spiritual quality of the ceremony, along with the beautiful singing, was very sustaining in this time of crisis in my life, as was the uncritical welcome given me by the priest, Father Vladimir Borichevsky, and his wife, "Matushka", who invited us to dinner at their home.

Perhaps those closest to God are more open to human love. Father Michael, a Roman Catholic monk stationed in Grenada, (the priest Richard had written to me about who was a passenger on this voyage of the *Venimos*), said to Richard:

"Captain, never let anything come between your love of each other. This is a love that God gave you and God is love, and God bless you."

"I felt like crying," Richard wrote me, "because he said that in front of the Island Bishop, and both said visit us anytime you come to Grenada, and bring Dale with you and stay as long as you like with us."

Richard's birthday was on May 11, and he then wrote:

"I had lots of birthday cards – all from the officers and crew, plus one from the lady passenger, who came on the bridge and put her arms around me and said: `Happy Birthday!' I thought she was going to kiss but thank God she didn't!"

He went on to say that my birthday cable was a day late in arriving, as "Sparks told me yesterday there was a message from Chatham" (the cable office) "for me but because we were loading cargo the antennae were down and he just couldn't receive it. I knew you were going to tell me you love me because all day I felt you so close. . ."

"Your cable was the most wonderful message I've ever received and I just `bubbled', though I had tears in my eyes because we were separated. I was on the boat-deck for the first time, sitting in a deck-chair when Sparks brought the message. I walked to the cabin, on my way meeting the lady passenger. She took one look at my joyous face and said: `You got it at last. . . how wonderful you both must feel.' I told her it is Heaven right down here on earth. She talks quite a lot about you and she believes our love is so wonderful. Its obvious to everyone, my darling, that's why everyone is all for us, except the bitter jealous ones who realize what they have missed in life when they see us radiating our love to all because we can't hide it or even try and conceal it in any way, because we love each other so completely and are proud of our love – for the simple reason we are truly in love, with the understanding, trust and honesty between us as one person that to hide it would be the greatest lie of all time for the pair of us. I'm proud of my love for you, my darling. Oh! Dale, I can't even say how much I love you or even express it in words. All I know that without you to me it would be a world of darkness, lifeless and hopeless and a prayer for quick death. I shouldn't write like this but, my darling Dale, I know we understand each other so beyond the understanding of others that we can tell the innermost thoughts, doubts, trouble, everything, because of our love and trust in each other. I never thought it possible to write like this to a living person, but as you know from my first letter I've written from the heart with a love I never knew a mortal could have. . . it is for ever and ever. The only trouble is people cannot understand it but let us my darling say this is ours, and ours alone to the end of time."

At long last, on June 1 a cable arrived from Richard from Manaus, asking me to meet him in Leticia. The "lady passenger" had told him to advise me to fly Bogotá-Leticia. It was faster and cheaper than flying to Lima, then over the Andes.

After getting my ticket, which read "Philadelphia, New York, Bogotá, Leticia, Iquitos", I wrote to Richard:

"I told Mr. MacArthur, my travel agent, all about you, and I never saw anyone so startled! He was the person who told George and myself about Booth in the beginning, so I said in a way he's responsible for my meeting you, and he really ought to be at our wedding, when we get married! He said this proves one should never go up the Amazon unless one is prepared for something extraordinary to happen! It has long been his dream to go himself."

We could not foresee it, but, with our decision to meet in Leticia, Fate took over our future. A series of small events, seemingly unimportant in themselves, would now change the course of our lives.

To start with, this trip was a major adventure for me. For a still fairly young unescorted woman to travel alone to Bogotá, which already had a bad reputation for drugs and crime, was not particularly safe. And not being fluent in Spanish put me at a disadvantage. I had reserved a hotel room ahead at the "Hotel Tequendama", but did not know the city, nor in which area the hotel was located. No knowledge about that in Philadelphia! The airport was far out of town, so I would have to trust an unknown taxi driver to get me safely to the hotel.

In the plane, I was seated next to a talkative American businessman, who said he knew the city well. He was also going to a hotel in Bogotá, so it might help me if we shared a taxi. I was glad I had agreed, as we drove dismal miles past miserable shanties, smothered in perpetual dust. No trees nor visible green on this arid mountain plateau. My hotel turned out to be on the outskirts of town, still in bleak surroundings; however it, itself, appeared to be quite luxurious. When we arrived, my companion, although heading for a different hotel, got out of the cab and followed me into the lobby. He lingered on while I registered, and I guessed that he was hoping I was an easy "pick-up. Fortunately, there was a bell-boy handy, so I did not have to find my room alone. I curtly said good-bye to the man, and quickly stepped into the elevator. When I told Richard this tale, he said he'd never let me out of his sight again. Worry No. 1 for Richard!

Added to my nervousness, the altitude combined with a tiring flight had given me a bad migraine. Going down later to find an orange-juice or 7-Up , as I was afraid to drink the water, I was ushered into a huge empty dining-room (no sign of a coffee shop or bar), where a swarm of eager waiters looked disgusted at my meagre order!   Worry No. 2 for Richard was my description of the flight next morning, to Leticia. I bumped over rocky mountains, then dense jungle in an ancient wartime "Dakota", which sounded and behaved as though it was tied together with string. The door to the cockpit was kept permanently open, while two stewardesses rushed back and forth balancing endless trays of alcoholic drinks for the officers at the controls! Spanish voices became louder and louder, laughter became raucous, flirtations hotly in progress. Most of the passengers, equally inebriated, noisily joined in the fun. I was relieved when we made a rough landing on Leticia's tiny airfield, in a tropical deluge. Fortunately, there was Mike the animal catcher in his jeep, who offered me a lift to the hotel.

Marcy and her friend, Johnny, gave me a great welcome at the "Victoria Regia", and listened with interest when, over drinks, I told them the story of why I had come. The ship had not yet arrived. I told them I would probably be spending 4 nights at the hotel.

The first thing Marcy did was to take me for a walk on a path through the jungle. After a quarter of a mile or so, she stopped and said:

"This is the Brazilian border, if you need to leave Colombia fast!"

It seems almost everyone who came to Leticia was smuggling something, and it was her policy to helpfully show where the best escape route was!

The first person I saw later, when wandering down to the river, was Maryla, wearing brief white shorts, with a large pistol at her belt. She was climbing out of a motor launch full of drums of petrol, which, no doubt, had to be protected. But, as I soon learnt, here a pistol was no sure protection against thieves.

"Why, Maryla!," I cheerfully greeted her, "how nice to see you again!"

"Oh! Oh! I can't speak now'" she cried, distractedly. "Someone has stolen my purse! See you later!" She rushed away, and it was the last I ever saw of her.

Another interesting encounter was with Ada, a young German "back-packer" from the Black Forest, who had hitch-hiked on small local boats up

Marcy Elden, Proprietor of the Hotel Victoria Regia, Leticia, with her friend Johnny.

the river, sleeping out in a hammock, and taking pot-luck as to food. She seemed to be self-assured and fearless, qualities I greatly admired, and which I felt I lacked in myself. She was sturdily built, wore a shapeless and colourless "tent dress", and used no make-up. Perhaps these features protected her. Her companion was a tiny "spider monkey", which, alas, did not survive the flight back to Germany, she wrote me later. I asked Marcy for permission to let her swing her hammock in the hotel garden.

Marcy's hotel was now full of people. When I asked who they all were, she said they were tourists who had been stranded since Monday – it was now Thursday (June 8th). They had reservations to fly to Iquitos, but there was an air-strike on. My reservation was for June 12th – "Cruzeiro Airlines, between Manaus, Leticia, and Iquitos, one flight a week on a Monday", read the brochure! Would the plane be flying then? If not, what would we all do? Everyone was worried.

"Maybe the strike will be over!" Marcy said, soothingly at dinner.

To amuse us the following evening, she organized a "bug- hunting" safari.

One of the men, an American, was an amateur entomologist, who wanted to catch night-flying moths. We all put on jungle boots, lent by Marcy, and wore heavy jackets against biting insects. The entomologist gave us boxes, with cords attached to hang around our necks, containing cotton saturated with chloroform.

"I'll just kill the moth by squeezing its thorax," he gloated, staring at me with marble-like eyes, as he pointed to my box, "then I'll put it in here."

When I lifted the lid, perhaps I, also, would be overcome by the fumes! And I did not dare admit that I was terrified of moths. The Amazon "Captain Jacaré's" fiancée should present to the world the appearance of an intrepid jungle explorer!

Our large group marched conspicuously through town, whose residents, sitting in their doorways in the cool of evening, eyed us curiously. But we did not go far. I had expected a trek by flash-light through the forest. But there, on the outskirts of town, was the big generator of the electric company, brilliantly lighted, with hundreds of huge moths flapping senselessly around. Plenty were put into my box.

Worry No. 3 for Richard! When he heard this tale he said the bug hunter must have hypnotized me with his unblinking eyes. "I shouldn't let you out of my sight," he again groaned.

I would have a surprise for Richard when he came up river. By now, I was feeling sorry for these stranded tourists, and had told them brightly:

"The man I'm going to marry is Captain of the *Venimos*, due in tomorrow. I'll do my best to have him take you up to Iquitos."

The hotel was very low in supplies, as no ships or planes had been in for a while. Beans, rice, and a little salt fish for dinner; heavy bread and an "essence" of syrupy coffee with condensed milk for breakfast. The guests were already grumbling about this diet. But every evening, Venus, enormously magnified in the humid air, hung low and glowing over the river, a good omen for the future.

In honour of Richard's arrival, I decided to wash my hair. When I had colour shampoo all over my head, and was ready to rinse it out, the water in my wash-basin stopped running. I sneaked out into the patio, where I found the water tank. It was empty! Wrapping my gooey hair in a towel, I spent a worried night. I could not go on board the *Venimos* like this! And would keeping the colour shampoo on all night make my hair fall out? Fortunately, early the next morning, someone had filled the tank, and I could rescue my hair, just in the nick of time, as at breakfast, Alfonso Galindo, the Booth Line agent (who was also a local merchant), came to inform me that the *Venimos* had been sighted. When I hurried down to the pier, the ship's launch appeared with the papers for clearance. Then it took me out to the middle of the river, where the ship was anchored.

There was Richard, waiting on top of the ladder, with the whole crew lined up to give me a tremendous welcome. Strung up over the door inside Richard's quarters was a huge banner, decorated with shafts of palm leaves and flowers, on which in big letters was written "WELCOME HOME, DALE!" It was really heart-warming.

I spent a gloriously happy day on board, then returned to the hotel in the late afternoon, taking with me a big leg of New Zealand lamb from the ship's freezer, a present for Marcy from Richard for looking after me. When she saw it, her eyes were like saucers! She barbecued it that evening, while we all sat around in the garden watching. Richard was fully occupied with cargo, so could not join us, but he was sorry he had missed the party.

I was very popular that night, as more important than the lamb, I had brought back the news that if the air-strike was still on the next day when Richard was due to sail, he would take them all up to Iquitos. It had been an unusual request, as picking up casual passengers along the way was not encouraged by the Company. They used to take "hitch-hikers" from one river port to another, letting them sleep on deck, if necessary; but had had many bad experiences with people who did not have proper visas, or, who might even be trying to smuggle drugs. Additionally, if they used the ship's facilities, and wanted food, they were expected to pay, but very often, too late, it was discovered that they had no money. However, as the people from the hotel were really stranded, were bona-fida tourists possessing money, and with papers all in order, Richard was willing to bend the rules. It was an overnight journey, but with some doubling up among willing crew-members, he managed to find bunks for everybody.

"And what about me?" I glumly asked. I'm not allowed to spend a night on board!"

"You are coming with me," he answered, firmly. "I'm not leaving you stranded in the jungle!"

We arrived uneventfully to Iquitos on Monday, the 12th, as scheduled, and saw the grateful group safely ashore. The river trip had been an unexpected bonus to their vacations, showing them a section of the heart of the Amazon they would otherwise never have seen. The "bug-hunter" later mailed me from the U.S. an agate he had polished himself and set in silver as a locket. People really do appreciate help in the wilds. On his ships, Richard always had enthusiastic passengers who afterwards wrote him appreciative letters, and sent him presents. He was very popular, and some returned for second trips with him, as his willingness to share his love and knowledge of the river made all the difference in their enjoyment of the trip.

Arnold W. Monks, from Devon, was one such passenger. In 1965 he had made a trip upriver with Richard on the *Dunstan*, and wrote, for publication, an interesting detailed account of this, mentioning "Commandanté Jacaré":

Richard with enthusiastic British passenger, Arnold W. Monks

"The Master of the ship who had been in these waters for many years almost looks upon this giant waterway as his pet, and one gets the feeling that the Master and the River are `sympaticos'. They understand each other and know each other."

On our first trip on the *Venimos*, he had also been Richard's passenger, boarding at Belém, then getting off at Itacotiara to explore the Rio Madeira on a local boat.

Another passenger, whom I knew briefly on board, was a lady, Dr. Tamara Brunnschweiler, from East Lansing, Michigan. She had been travelling in Northern Brazil, and showed us a collection of the famous local amethysts she had bought. When she learnt about our romance, she was so moved that she gave me a square cut stone, perfect to set in a ring, flawless and crystal-clear. Amethyst is my birth-stone, and this was the most beautiful I had ever seen. Such a spontaneous gift was unusual, and Richard and I both felt very touched by it. In truth, I do believe that our mutual love did transmit warmth and inspiration to many others.

The evening of our arrival in Iquitos, Richard and I went ashore, and booked into the "Hotel Imperial Amazonas", which was just behind the "Tourista", where I had previously stayed, and cheaper – a double room was only $10. per night, for "Capt. R. Humphreys y Señora", I noted in my diary.

We enjoyed our stay. We took the bus to the docks every day, but still had plenty of free time, so could attend a Peru-Brazil soccer match in the local stadium. Richard had seen Pelé play here before, but for me this was the first professional match I had ever seen, so was a red letter day. It was a lively game, with excitable rival teams, but everyone was obviously having a great time. There was no fighting amongst team members nor spectators.

Unfortunately, this trip there was no long wait for cargo. We had only four nights ashore before the ship was ready to start her journey back. We had been briefly living in an unnaturally carefree state, perhaps because so far there had been no repercussions about my trip up from Leticia, and Pat Nicholls had seemed sympathetic about it.

On sailing day, the air strike was still on. No one knew when it would end. Richard said I might be stuck there for weeks, and he did not want that. I would have to again come with him. As he was the agent, Pat Nicholls had to be told, as it was his job to check the number of passengers on board, and collect their fares. Pat seemed to understand our difficulties, and would not prevent my going, but all the same, he said he would have to send in his report, which had my name on it. Richard, always an optimist, hoped it would be alright. My passage was not premeditated.

We were living in a fool's paradise.

Not stopping in Leticia this time, we went very fast downriver, pushed along by the rushing water, and reached Manaus early Sunday morning.

I felt very nervous, and was anxious to leave the ship as soon as possible. After all, we had taken a chance, and should not press our luck too far. There was a new agent in Manaus, George Clark, who was due to come out to the ship. I could return to shore with him, Richard said, and he would see that I got a room in a decent hotel. It was better for me to have an escort in this city!

We were anchored out in the river, as no work was going on. The docks were deserted. As it was Sunday, I guess George Clark decided to take it easy, and he did not appear until late afternoon. It was dark by the time we went ashore.

Before we left, George had given Richard the information that he was not to take the ship to New York, but was to leave her in Trinidad, and fly home from there, thus saving time and money for the Company, we guessed. Or was this a forewarning of worse trouble to come? It certainly was! The reason for this change of plan we learnt much later was because Chrissie had been telephoning the Company every day insisting that Richard be sent home immediately. No doubt they found this pressure disturbing, and wanted to put an end to it.

George very kindly took me to the (then) best hotel, another "Amazonas", where I had to spend the night, before catching the daily Manaus-Belém flight on Varig Airlines. No air strike here!

At the time of writing, George Clark is still in Manaus, and is now "Honorary British Consul". When asked by Nicholas Shakespeare whether he planned to stay on after he retired, he replied: "No, absolutely not. Absolutely not." [1]

The hotel had a strange atmosphere. When I walked up a broad flight of stairs to the 2nd floor, I found elderly women dressed in black, looking like house-keepers, sitting behind tables along the landing. They looked me over severely. I was reminded of old thrillers with the scene set in Stalin's Moscow! Knowing no Portuguese, it was impossible to talk to them. Holding up my key, which I had been given downstairs, one of them nodded, and pointed towards the bedrooms. In the labyrinthine halls suspicious-looking men, also dressed in black, who may only have been innocent night porters, gossiped around corners, but openly stared as I walked towards my room. Were they guards or jailors? I quickly went inside and locked the door.

In Belém, everything crashed around our heads. Fate, in the guise of the air strike, had added strength to the storm. There was no escape.

Innocently not guessing the worst, I checked into the "Hotel Excelsior y Gran Para", and set about the business of getting transportation to Trinidad, so that Richard and I could fly to Britain together. I immediately discovered that there were no flights from Belém to Trinidad, nor were there any from neighbouring countries, such as Venezuela. Flights from Guyana to Trinidad? Yes. But Belém to Guyana? No! No ships were sailing there, either, except the Booth Line ones. This was hard to believe, but if some small independent tramp freighters went, I did not find them.

Not to be daunted, I hastened to the Booth Line, hoping to persuade them to reconsider, and let me go as a passenger on the *Venimos*. The situation had now changed, as Richard was not returning to New York, so perhaps they would also change their attitude towards me. After all, we would both be leaving for Britain in Trinidad to start settling our affairs, so really what difference would it make if I took a Booth Line ship out of necessity?

"No, you cannot go. Definitely not!" Willie Purcell, the stern, unbending Office Manager curtly snapped.

"Why?" I dared ask. "It would harm no one. I merely need to get to Trinidad."

"Because we do not want people like you on our ships," he hissed.

I slunk out the door, feeling insulted and humiliated. He was, however, only doing what he had been told. Moreover, he was ill (he died of cancer the following year.) How little does one guess the emotional and health problems of people whom we casually contact in offices, which surely influence their attitude and their actions.

I did not give up. I next contacted the British Consul. If I was going to marry a British Master Mariner, surely he could use his influence to get me accepted on my fiancé's ship! Could he not get me on a British ship to Port of Spain?

He listened courteously, but answered no, as I was not a British National, he could do nothing for me.

"But I'm very sorry," he added, gloomily.

In a desperate final attempt, I went to the American Consul. I certainly was an American citizen in distress! Was it not his duty to help such a person? I secretly thought that in a city like London, a person like me would probably not succeed in seeing the Consul himself, and would not even get past the first clerk spoken to, as I was not really "distressed", of course, in their meaning of the word. I was not a political refugee, nor penniless.

However, this particular Consul was extremely decent. Although a busy businessman, I'm sure, he not only saw me, but listened patiently to my rather long-winded tale of woe, which was really a lament for forcibly separated lovers.

Well, he said, he could not get me upon a British ship sailing to Trinidad, but he could get me on an American ship sailing to New Orleans. Alas, this would do me no good! But I thanked him kindly for listening to me.

I had to wait over a week before the *Venimos* arrived from Manaus. I wandered around taking photographs, particularly of the market, and the boats bringing in fish; and I did a lot of reading, and writing letters. A single woman in the hotel restaurant in the evening was still conspicuous, as I could tell from the curious looks people gave me. There were few tourists who stayed in Belém, so I seemed to be an oddity! I decided it was best to eat a large lunch in one of the popular cafés, then buy fruit, crackers and cheese, and bottles of soft drinks to have in my room in the evening.

As the days ticked by, I began to wonder how I would know when the ship was expected here? I hated to go back to the office to ask, but screwed up my courage. This time I found a pleasant person there who was willing to telephone me at the hotel when the ship's E.T.A. was known. He kept his promise, and I was waiting on the dock when she arrived.

Richard was looking out for me, and waved from the Bridge to come aboard right away. He greeted me ecstatically, but the day turned out to be one of the most unhappy of his life.

As soon as the Booth Line agents came on board, he was told that he would not be going to Trinidad with the ship. He was to fly to Britain from Belém. Another Company Master was being flown out to take over. Not only that, but he was told to hand in his resignation with the Booth Line. They would pay for his ticket home, and give him any back pay owed, but that was all. No "Golden Handshake" for his years of service with the Company. It was a bitter ending to their long association, and the end of his distinguished career in the Merchant Navy.

When it came right down to it, Richard, with his cheery, easy-going nature, had never really believed that they would treat him so badly – a long leave, yes, but not to be fired! There was no necessity for them to do this. All they needed to do was to let him quietly go home to arrange for his divorce. The fact that he had had me on board for several nights, breaking our agreement, was, no doubt, what brought things to a head. Even so, did Ronald Vestey himself ever know that the reason for this was that Richard felt he could not abandon me in the jungle? He deserved a medal, rather than being fired! But perhaps all the big-wigs in London and Liverpool knew about it was that I was on board, and not the reason why. We felt too cowed by what had happened to inquire. The Company was afraid of more complaints about us, when they should have valued their veteran Master more, and stood behind him. I wonder if Timothy Vestey, Ronald Vestey's grandson, who now heads the Vestey concerns, would today be more liberal?

Even now, when thinking about it, I feel angry. If this situation had occurred in the present less conservative era, I believe the Officer's Union might have stood behind Richard. In the 60's Richard believed there was no point in even asking. More important people than Richard have often been cast aside like trash, if they did not tow the conventional line. Look at what happened to King Edward VIII.

Richard's flight out of Belém was for Tuesday, July 4th, which gave him a long week-end to leave everything in order. I, myself, again went to the travel bureau and managed to get a reservation for the same Varig flight to Rio as Richard, where we would change to BOAC for London. It was a long and expensive flight, which I had not foreseen, and I did not have that much money with me. A nerve-wracking hitch occurred when the travel bureau would not accept my personal cheque in dollars on the Fidelity Bank, Philadelphia. (This was, of course, before Credit Cards were in universal use.) I phoned the Fidelity to see whether they could verbally confirm my account, or if not, whether they could cable the money. This idea was no good. I had forgotten that it was the long 4th of July holiday in the U.S. and not only my Trust Officer was away on vacation, but anyone else in the bank who could have helped me.

I would have to try a local bank, suggested the travel agent. Perhaps if I showed my passport, they might cash my cheque. But, in typical South American style, I found that all the banks in Belém had shut up tight at noon. This was a Thursday, and when I asked at a nearby store what time they reopened, I was told they always shut up at noon on a Thursday, and did not reopen until the following Monday!

Again, Richard came to my rescue. He immediately telephoned to Aled

Parry, who said that cashing my cheque would be no problem for him. His son held a position of importance in a local bank, and even had the key. "Just give me the cheque," said Capt. Parry, amiably, "and my son will get you the money!"

I shall always be grateful to this family for their unwaveringly friendship, and their firm faith in Richard.

The final days were hectic for Richard. He did not have time to get emotional, as he had to sit continuously at his desk, working to bring all the ship's accounts up to date, and correctly balanced, then typing them up neatly – not only cargo manifests, but crew's salaries, with deductions such as wives' benefits and pension deposits. Such calculations were usually done at the end of a voyage, so it was an unexpected and difficult chore to be done in haste. Unluckily for him, it was before personal calculators and computers were used to help. It was fortunate that he was very good with figures.

I helped by packing his trunk, a job he hated. Not only his uniform went into it, and most of his clothes, but treasured books, and much prized gifts and souvenirs acquired on his voyages. Alas, my care in packing was in vain. This is the trunk that disappeared in Trinidad, where it was to be transhipped onto another Booth Line ship for Liverpool. Richard never traced it, and in low moments almost believed that someone on the *Venimos* had allowed it to be stolen out of spite.

On July 4th, Richard was due to pick me up at the hotel on his way to the airport. The designated time came and went. I stood by the door, surrounded by my bags, while it got later and later. I became more and more nervous, as I was afraid we would miss the plane. Then, in my imagination, I saw nasty shipping officials forcing him to drive directly to the airport, so it would be too late for me to join him on the plane, and I would be left here without any money. This kind of thinking shows the state I was in.

But Richard finally did arrive, jumping out of a taxi and grabbing my suitcases. "Hurry! Hurry!" he told the driver, who drove like mad out of town.

Arriving at the airport, we by-passed the main terminal entrance, and went on to the service entrance to the field. When the driver explained that we were late and might miss our flight, the guard opened the gate and the cab went careering right up to the plane.

"Get in immediately!" shouted the Stewardess, who had been about to shut the door. Our bags were hauled up after us. No security checks in those days! This was the first and only time such V.I.P treatment was ever given to us in an airport.

At last, relaxing in our seats after drinks, sandwiches and coffee, Richard told me a little about his last hours on the *Venimos* that morning. When it was time for him to leave, he found that his heavy bags had been dumped on the

After the long flight home from Brazil, Richard smiles happily as he reaches the border of Merionnydd.

dock. There was no taxi waiting there to meet him, no one around to help him carry the bags down the long pier to the entrance, where he might find a cab. The decks of the ship were deserted. It could have been a ghost ship. No one appeared to say a few pleasant words of farewell, no crew members came up to say he would be missed. Were they all so afraid of the Company?

Going down the gangway, Richard looked up, and saw Alan on an upper deck, leaning over the railing. He looked as though turned to stone, and did not turn his head in Richard's direction. Had he right along been jealous and resentful?

But Richard's momentary bitterness soon passed. In truth, "Commandanté Jacaré" was not forgotten on the River, nor elsewhere amongst his friends. We discovered this when later we had our own ship, named the *Jacaré*. She was greeted enthusiastically by sea-faring friends in almost every port, as was

Richard, himself. And, surprisingly, we were both always invited on board Booth Line ships and warmly received by the many Masters and officers whom Richard knew.

So we left Brazil, flying over our beloved and familiar river, over the encompassing jungle, over the sparkling crescent of Rio's bay, then onwards towards Wales, the United States, and a new life together.

Richard and I, after untold difficulties, finally got our divorces. We were married in Nevada in 1968, with my son Jerzy and Richard's daughter Janet as witnesses. Shortly afterwards, we set sail in the charter yacht *Carlotta*, which we had bought in San Diego, renaming her the *Jacaré*. She was a topsail schooner (or Brigantine), strongly reminding Richard of his father's old ship, the *Venedocian*. We sailed happily in her for the next 7 years, taking

Richard's younger daughter, Janet, with whom we celebrated with an evening at a Tremadog hotel.

Jerzy in Reno, Nevada, where his mother and Richard were married.

passengers around the Caribbean, with Richard, of course, as Master.

If Richard had stayed with Booth until retirement age, we probably never would have bought this ship, and would have missed out on some wonderful experiences. It goes to show that you can't keep a good man down!

EPILOGUE

Shortly after Booth had cavalierly let its best Captain go, Fate (or was it Merlin?) seemingly took a hand in retribution. With the fast proliferation of container ships, along with growing competition from South American companies, small cargo ships were no longer profitable. Booth commenced to sell theirs off. By 1973, the company had given up trading from New York (at the same time, inexplicably destroying their American records.) By 1986, they no longer owned any ships, but had chartered, from a Netherlands company, two container ships, which sailed from England, going up the Amazon only as far as Manaus. Booth relinquished their Liverpool dock, using instead the small Cumbrian port of Heysham. This, a frustratingly inconvenient location forced upon passengers travelling the Irish Sea by ferry, was now also being used by some cargo ship owners for the same reasons: lower fees and less chance of union troubles than in the decayed port of Liverpool.

The February, 1992 issue of "Shipping" magazine [2] contains the following, which reads like a sad obituary for the famous old river run:

"End of an era up the Amazon"

The ending of the Booth Steamship Co.'s scheduled service between Liverpool and the Amazon and North Brazil severs a link that began in February, 1866."

Richard and Dale before their wedding.

NOTES

With grateful thanks from the author to the copyright owners, who have kindly given me permission to use the listed quotations.

Chapter 1
1   "Porthmadog Ships", Emrys Hughes and Aled Eames, p.77
2   In the old Welsh fashion, when there were two brothers, only one would use his father's surname, the other adopting his mother's maiden name. This confusing custom seems to have been dropped at the beginning of the 20th Century
3   "Welcome to Deudraeth, the Official Guide", pp.31-2
4   "Harlech Castle", Alan Phillips (M.A., Oxon.), p.11 Courtesy of CADW (Welsh Historical Monuments)

Chapter 2
1   From programs reproduced in "Hen Draf Harlech a Pentre Llanfair", Dr. Lewis Lloyd and Martin Eckley, pp.15 & 20
2   "History of the Church of the Cymry", Rev. William Hughes, as quoted by A.G. Bradley in "Highways and Byways in North Wales", p.349
3   "Merlin", Norma Lorre Goodrich, p. 347; also see Ch.12, pp.297-328; and Appendix C, pp.344-7

Chapter 3
1   "MERCHANT FLEETS; Ellerman Lines", Duncan Haws, p.18

Chapter 5
1   "The Set of the Sails", Alan Villiers, p.215. Thanks to the Estate of Alan Villiers

Chapter 6
1   "The Twentieth Century, An Almanac", General Editor, Robert H. Ferrell, p.188, 190
2   "Welsh Blockade Runners in the Spanish Civil War": P.M. Heaton, p.30
3   "The World at War", Mark Arnold-Forster, pp. 32, 79
4   "Welsh Blockade Runners", pp.17, 18, 29
5   "The Twentieth Century, An Almanac", p.197: "28 Nov. 1937"
6   "A Walk With a White Bushman", Laurens Van Der Post, pp.301-2
7   "Welsh Blockade Runners" gives their story.

Chapter 7,
1. Letter to author, 18 June 1993
2. The Admiralty files give this as 37 (ADM 199/26- 2130)
3. "The World at War", p.85
4. "The Merchant Navy", Ronald Hope, p.25
5. "The World at War", p.100
6. "   "   "   "   p.85
7. A brief account of this clandestine operation can be found on p.42 of "Operation Autonomous", by Ivor Porter.
8. "Special Operations Executive", established and financed by the Ministry of Economic Warfare.
9. From BBC Summaries of World Broadcasts, Copyright by the British Broadcasting Corporation, London, (Records from BBC Written Archives Centre, Reading), File No. 1A(v):
"DEUTSCHLANDERSENDER" (Germany) Long Wave: in German for Germany
11.30 BST   8.6.40
Item 14 DANUBE PLOT"
(Contains 4 paragraphs concerning this)
10. "The Red Duster at War", John Slader, pp.110, & 66
11. "The Chronology of the War at Sea- 1940", J.Rohwer and G.Hummel, p.51
12. "The World at War", p.89
13. Ebid, p.92
14. "MERCHANT FLEETS: Ellerman Lines", p.51
15. Monthly Anti-Submarine Report, September- October, 1940 Anti-Submarine Warfare Division of the Naval Staff, C.B.04050/40 (9 & 10)
16. Ebid
17. "MERCHANT FLEETS; Ellerman Lines", p.52
18. ADM 199/1179- 13/25
19. "Convoy", John Winton
20. "Periscope Depth", Kenneth Poolman, p.115
21. ADM 199/1179- 13/25

Chapter 8,
1. Historical background to the chapter has been largely supplied by Sir Alexander Glen.
2. Either in the RNR or the RNVR
3. "Guilt Edged": Merlin Minshall. p.83
4. "Operation Autonomous", pp.41, 31
5. "Baker Street Irregular", Bickham Sweet-Escott, p.52
6. "German Military Intelligence", Paul Leverkuehn, as in "SOE Recollections and Reflections, 1940-45" by J.G. Beevor. p.21

7   Letter to author
8   "The Special Operations Executive. 1940-46", M.R.D. Foot, p.15
9   "Baker Street Irregular", p.22
10 "Operation Autonomous", p.43
11 "Disinformation"- a term invented by the Earl of Selbourne, Wartime Head of British Intelligence in New York, to denote falsified or exaggerated information given out to confuse the enemy.
12 Ivor Porter left Romania with the Legation Staff, in February, 1941, but was parachuted back in '43 as a member of the SOE, in a plot to overthrow the pro-Nazi regime.
13 Later Sir Denis Wright, HM Ambassador to Teheran.
14 Letter to author, 25 April, 1990
15 "   "   "   4 July,   "
16 Thanks for locating and mimeographing this file in the Public Record Office at Kew is due to Research-Consultant Robert C. de Bruin.
17 "Baker Street Irregular", pp.27-8
18 "Against the Wind": Geoffrey Household, p.100
19 "Baker Street Irregular", p.23
20 "FO Report on 1940 Operation" (Copyright Foreign and Commonwealth Office, London), Appendix A, written by W. Harris Burland of Anglo-Danube Shipping Co., p.1
21 Ebid, Appendix C, (author unknown), p.1
22 Ebid, Attachment to Appendix C
23 See Acknowledgements, p.vi.
24 "   Appendix B, by G.B. Marshall of the Naval Attache's Staff, p.1
25 Ebid   "
26 "Danube Expedition 1940" Copyright by the Public Record Office, Ref. ADM. 1/21717 171472
    "Letter of Proceedings", addressed to the Admiralty by Cmdr. A.P. Gibson, R.N., dated 20th August, 1940. Marked: "MOST SECRET MEDITERRANEAN PART 1; ROMANIA". Paragraph 8
27 Ebid, Paragraph 5
28 "Against the Wind", p.100
29 "Operation Autonomous", from Diary of Denis Wright, as quoted p.42
30 "Danube Expedition 1940", report on Proceedings sent to the Secretary of the Admiralty by Admiral A.B. Cunningham, R.N. Signed by him on "H.M.S. Warspite", 20 Aug. 1940. Paragraph 9
31 FO Report, Appendix B, Paragraph 6
32 "Against the Wind", p.100
33 FO report, Appendix B, Paragraph 7
34 See Acknowledgements, p.viii
35 FO report, as above, Paragraph 18

36	BBC Summaries of World Broadcasts: "DEUTSCHLANDSENDER" (Germany) Long Wave: 1A(v) Item 14 Ebid, Item 1, Paragraphs 1 & 2 Ebid, 3B (ii) "In Danubian and Balkan Countries" p.78
37	"Danube Expedition 1940", "Letter of Proceedings", Part 1, Paragraphs 15, 16 & 17
38	BBC Summaries: 1A(v) Item 14, Paragraph 3, "Germany"; 3B(ii) "In Danubian and Balkan Countries", Paragraph 1
39	"Danube Expedition 1940": "Letter of Proceedings", Paragraph 26
40	BBC Summaries: 1A(v) Item 1, Paragraphs 1 & 2 1A(vi) Item 1 1A(xi) " " 1A(xx) " 15
41	"Danube Expedition 1940", Paragraph 27
42	Ebid, Paragraphs 28 & 29
43	"Operation Autonomous", pp.42-3
44	"Danube Expedition 1940", Paragraph 30
45	Diary of Denis Wright, "Operation Autonomous", p.42
46	Ebid, p.44
47	FO Report, Appendix B, Paragraph 18
48	"Danube Expedition 1940", Paragraph 51
49	As quoted by Lord Birkenhead in his biography "Walter Monckton, the Life of Viscount Monckton of Benchley", p.200
50	Yugoslavian anti-communist para-military organisation of the Second World War.
51	"Danube Expedition 1940", Admiral Cunningham's letter, Paragraphs 2 & 3

Chapter 9

1	"The Twentieth Century, An Almanac", pp.258, 260,
2	In 1988, the first Bomber Command commemorative medal was finally struck.

Chapter 10

1	See "The World at War", p.143, for full account.
2	"The Daily Telegraph", London, Monday, May 20, 1989
3	"The Chronology of the War at Sea", by J.Rohwer and G.Hummel
4	"Nortraships Flate", Vol.2, p.330 Translated from Norwegian for me by C.N. Rimmer

5 From "The Ghost of the Alkimos", by Ian Stewart, "Sea Breezes", February, 1992, p.97
6 From "The Ghost of the Alkimos"
7 "History of U.S. Naval Operations in World War II", Vol. X. by Samuel Eliot Morrison
8 "The War at Sea", Vol. VI, January- December, 1944, compiled by the Historical Section, Tactical & Staff Duties Division, Naval Staff, Admiralty, 1946
9 "The Ghost of the Alkimos". Much of Mr. Stewart's research material came from "Nortraships Flate".
10 Dictionary of American Fighting Ships", Vol.IV., 1969. Navy Department, Naval History Division, Washington, D.C.

Chapter 13
1 This, and other statistics about Booth Line ships, have been researched and verified in "Booth Line", by P.M. Heaton, 1987.
2 Letter to author, May 23, 1990

Chapter 14
1 Letter to author, May 16, 1990
2 "Sea Breezes", Spring, 1973, p.242
3 See "The Holy Blood and the Holy Grail", and "The Messianic Legacy", both by Michael Baignent, Richard Leigh, and Henry Lincoln.

Chapter 15
1 Swansea. H.M. Tomlinson, "The Sea and the Jungle". pp.10-18 contain an interesting account of waiting for his ship to sail.
2 I later learnt that a Chief Steward not only is responsible for provisions (and typing menus!) but, on a small ship, has the duties of a Purser, keeping track of accounts.
3 "Behold the West Indies": Amy Oakley.

Chapter 17
1 "In the Kingdom of the Amazons", feature article by Nicholas Shakespeare, "The Sunday Telegraph Review", March 25, 1990
2 Ebid
3 SPECIAL NOTE: The Opera House has now been restored, a project lasting 3 years, and costing $14 million. Nicholas Shakespeare's headline, for his article of March 25, reads:
". . . the Teatro Amazonas this Saturday welcomes Placido Domingo in its first opera for over 80 years."
The opera was "Carmen", which was preceded by an evening of

classical Brazilian music and ballet. The seats for Domingo, costing $400. each, were occupied by the wealthy in flashy evening clothes, most of whom had flown in for only a few hours.

The festivities were somewhat marred by a noisy demonstration outside by Labour Party members protesting against the poor pay of school teachers, the cost of the restoration, the exorbitant price of the tickets, and the presumption that the Teatro would only stage "safe art".

All politics aside, it is to be hoped that with the growth of Manaus as a tourist and commercial centre, this original, historical building may finally come into its own, providing a happy setting in which to enjoy the best in music and drama, at reasonable prices.

My critics may now well ask: "What does all this have to do with Richard?"

It may be tendentious, but describing a region where Richard worked for many years may bring a better understanding of this little known part of the world, and of the man who loved it. One must also remember that, as Nicholas Shakespeare has noted, "practically everything in Manaus including the Teatro, was shipped there on Booth Line steamers."

4 Little did he suspect that by 1991 this, to a surprising extent, would have happened, to the great consternation of those who already could see the dire effects on world climate by the devastation of the rain forest.

Chapter 18

1 Much later I learnt that the frontier war in 1941 between Ecuador and Peru had left their borders still unsettled, causing much military activity on each side, even in the 60's, when Iquitos was headquarters for the Jungle Division of the Peruvian army, often numbering 5,000 men.

Chapter 20

1 He kept the Russian name the family had forcibly been given after taking part in an unsuccessful uprising against Russia in the 19th Century. George, however, when becoming an American citizen, had legally changed his name back to the original Polish one, Podbereski.

Chapter 22

1 Nicholas Shakespeare, "In the Kingdom of the Amazons"
2 "Shipping Today and Yesterday", monthly magazine published Bournemouth, Dorset. February, 1992, pp.4, 30

BIBLIOGRAPHY

Arnold-Forster, Mark: "The World at War". London, 1973, William Collins Sons & Co. Ltd; 1976, Fontana Books; and Copyright Thames Television Limited, 1973

Baignet, Michael; Leigh, Richard; and Lincoln, Henry: "The Holy Blood and the Holy Grail", London, 1983, Corgi Books
"The Messianic Legacy:, 1987, Corgi Books

Bates, Henry Walter: "The Naturalist on the River Amazon" 1969, London & New York, J.M. Dent & Sons, Ltd. (first included in "Everyman's Library", 1910)

Beevor, J.G.: "SOE Reflections and Reflections, 1940-45", London, Sydney, Toronto, 1981, The Bodley Head

Birkenhead, Lord: "Walter Monckton, The Life of Viscount Monckton of Benchley", London, 1969, Weidenfeld & Nicholson

Bradley, A.G.: "Highways and Byways in North Wales", London, 1898, MacMillan & Co., Ltd.

Deudraeth Rural District Council: "Welcome to Deudraeth, The Official Guide", Penrhyndeudraeth, Merioneth, 1965

Ferrell, Robert H. (General Editor): "The Twentieth Century, An Almanac", London, 1986, Harrap Ltd., (c)1985, Bison Books Corp.

Foot, M.R.D." "The Special Operations Executive, 1940- 46", London, 1984, a BBC Book

Goodrich, Norma Lorre: "Merlin", New York, Toronto, 1987, Franklin Watts

Haws, Duncan: "MERCHANT FLEETS; Ellerman Lines", Hereford, 1989, Travel Contours Ltd. (TCL Publications)

Heaton, P.M.: "Booth Line", Pontypool, Gwent, 1987
"Welsh Blockade Runners in the Spanish Civil War", Ebid, 1985

Hope, Ronald: "The Merchant Navy", London, 1980, Copyright The Marine Society, Stanford Maritime Ltd. (now taken over by A.& C. Black)

Hough, Richard: "Mountbatten, Hero of Our Time", London, 1980, Weidenfeld & Nicholson

Household, Geoffrey: "Against the Wind", London, 1958, Michael Joseph

Hughes, Emrys, and Eames, Aled: "Porthmadog Ships", Caernarfon, 1975, Gwynedd Archives Service

Linke, Lilo: "People of the Amazon". London, 1963 Robert Hale, Ltd.

Lloyd, Dr. Lewis, and Eckley, Martin; "Hen Draf Harlech a Pentre Llanfair", Harlech, 1978, Gwasg Harlech

Manning, Olivia: "The Balkan Trilogy", London, 1987, Heineman

Matthiessen, Peter: "At Play in the Fields of the Lord", New York, 1965,

Random House, Inc., & Signet Books, 1967
"The Cloud Forest", New York, 1961, Viking Press, Inc., & Pyramid Books, 1966

Maxwell, Nicole: "The Jungle Search for Nature's Cures", New York, 1961, Ace Books Inc.

Minshall, Merlin: "Guilt Edged", London, 1975, Bachman & Turner (This publisher now defunct.)

Morrison, Samuel Eliot: "History of U.S. Naval Oeprations in World War II.", Vol. X. Boston, 1956, Little, Brown & Co.

Oakley, Amy: "Behold the West Indies". New York, London, 1943, D. Appleton-Century Company; New York, London, Toronto, 1951, Longmans, Green, and Co.

Pelling, Henry: "Winston Churchill". London, 1974, MacMillan

Poolman, Kenneth: "Periscope Depth- Submarines at War". London, 1981, William Kimber & Co., Ltd.

Porter, Ivor: "Operation Autonomous", London, 1989, Chatto & Windus Ltd.

Rowher, J. and Hummel, G.: "The Chronology of the War at Sea- 1940". London, 1972, 1992, Ian Allan

Slader, John: "The Red Duster at War". London, 1988, William Kimber & Co., Ltd.

Sweet-Escott, Bickham: "Baker Street Irregular", London, 1965, Methuen and Co., Ltd. (now under Routledge)

Tomlinson, H.M.: "The Sea and the Jungle", New York, Random House "Modern Library Paperbacks"

Van Der Post, Laurens: "A Walk With a White Bushman", London, 1988, Penguin Books

Villiers, Alan: "The Set of the Sails", London, 1949, Hodder & Stoughton Ltd.; Pan Books Ltd. 1955

West, Nigel: "MI6- British Secret Intelligence Service Operations, 1909-45", London, 1983, Weidenfeld & Nicholson

Winton, John: "Convoy- The Defence of Sea Trade, 1890-1990", London, 1983, Michael Joseph Ltd. (now Penguin Books, Ltd.)

Ziegler, Philip: "Mountbatten- The Official Biography", London, 1985, Collins